COBOL

THE LANGUAGE OF BUSINESS

To a person who has touched my life
in a very special way:
My father-in-law

Eliot A. Tanner

A man whom I love and respect

I would like to thank IBM, Micro Focus Ltd. and Digital Research for the use of their superbly designed COBOL compilers. I would also like to thank Dr. J.D. Robertson of Bentley College, Greg Gagne of Bentley College, and my wife Kim for their assistance and inspiration.

COBOL

THE LANGUAGE OF BUSINESS

ERIC P. BLOOM

TAB BOOKS Inc.
Blue Ridge Summit, PA 17214

TAB BOOKS Inc. offers software for
sale. For information and a catalog,
please contact TAB Software
Department, Blue Ridge Summit,
PA 17294-0850.

FIRST EDITION
FIRST PRINTING

Library of Congress Cataloging in Publication Data

Bloom, Eric P.
COBOL : the language of business.

Includes index.
1. COBOL (Computer program language)   I. Title.
QA76.73.C25B56   1986   005.13'3   85-27835
ISBN 0-8306-0590-8
ISBN 0-8306-2690-5 (pbk.)

Contents

Preface

To become a programmer, you must understand two things about computers: first, computers are very fast; second, they are very unintelligent. Programs written in COBOL, PASCAL and other computer languages provide the rules and algorithms that allow these electronic marvels to perform meaningful tasks. Without these instructions the computer would sit idle and collect dust. It is the software that acts as the driving force causing the computer to function.

As a business tool COBOL has provided companies of all sizes with processes to collect raw data, transform the data into intelligible information, and present the information to business people in a manner that facilitates productivity and sound business planning and control.

For many years COBOL has been the backbone of the business data processing industry. Since its inception in the early sixties, it has been the language of choice of computer professionals automating accounting, financial, manufacturing and other corporate functions. COBOL is chosen because of its flexibility, self-documenting nature, and func-

tional capabilities. Because of its widespread use over a period of years, COBOL has become an integral part of the automated capabilities of thousands of corporations across the globe. COBOL is functionally an ideal language for processing large volumes of data and wading through the complex logic characteristic of business applications.

This book is designed for use by beginners and seasoned COBOL programmers. To reach this end, it is divided into five sections. Chapter 2 describes some common techniques used to define a program's function. Chapter 7 discusses the structured programming ideologies used to facilitate the development of quality software. Chapters 1, 3, 4, 5 and 6 provide detailed information on the construction of COBOL statements and how these statements interrelate. Chapters 8, 9, 10, 11 and 12 illustrate how the language can be used to meet the needs of its users. Finally, the appendix provides various ready-made techniques called *program shells,* which may be used to speed the software development process.

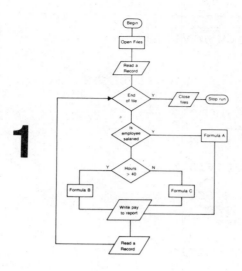

1

The COBOL Language

The COBOL programming language was designed as a development tool for business-related application software. Even its name shows its business orientation: The word COBOL is an acronym for "COmmon Business Oriented Language." COBOL is rich with the special capabilities needed to successfully build business software.

Most applications dealing with the day to day operations of a company, regardless of their specific function, are similar in three main respects: they require large volumes of data, countless numbers of reports and complex conditional logic. The creators of COBOL included many niceties that facilitate effective data handling, flexibility in report formatting, and a very powerful IF/THEN/ELSE process to define and interpret various situations.

LANGUAGE STRUCTURE

All COBOL programs are divided into four main sections, called divisions. The divisions perform special and unique functions, and are named IDENTIFICATION DIVISION, ENVIRONMENT DIVISION, DATA DIVISION and PROCEDURE DIVISION. The divisions can be seen in the sample COBOL program shown in Fig. 1-1.

The IDENTIFICATION DIVISION is placed at the top of all COBOL programs. As the name suggests, this division documents the program's name, author, function and similar items. In fact, its purpose is totally documentational; it contains no executable statements.

The ENVIRONMENT DIVISION deals with factors external to the program. It establishes the lines of communication between the executing program and the data files being processed. This link is made by way of a SELECT statement. This statement connects the DATA DIVISION's file description to the disk or tape drive on which the file physically resides.

The DATA DIVISION defines the names and formats of the files and variables used in the program. This division is divided into two sections: the FILE SECTION and the WORKING-STORAGE SECTION. The FILE SECTION describes the specific characteristics of a data file in terms of the way it is stored on disk or tape, and the field lay

```
IDENTIFICATION DIVISION.

PROGRAM-ID.
AUTHOR.            ERIC P. BLOOM.
INSTALLATION.      BOSTON.
DATE-WRITTEN.      SEP. 1, 1985.
DATE-COMPILED.     SEP, 1, 1985.
SECURITY.          NONE.

ENVIRONMENT DIVISION.

CONFIGURATION SECTION.
SOURCE-COMPUTER.      IBM.
OBJECT-COMPUTER.      IBM.

INPUT-OUTPUT SECTION.
FILE-CONTROL.

      SELECT IN-FILE ASSIGN TO 'EMPLOYEE.MST'.
      SELECT REP-REC ASSIGN TO 'REPORT.OUT'

DATA DIVISION.

FILE SECTION.
FD IN-FILE
   RECORD CONTAINS 80 CHARACTERS
   LABEL RECORDS ARE OMITTED
   DATA RECORD IS IN-REC.

01 IN-REC.
   05 IN-EMP-NO        PIC X(5).
   05 IN-EMP-NAME      PIC X(25).
   05 IN-DEPT          PIC X(10).
   05 IN-SALARY        PIC 999V99.

FD REP-FILE
   RECORD CONTAINS 80 CHARACTERS
   LABEL RECORDS ARE OMITTED
   DATA RECORD IS REP-REC.

01 REP-REC             PIC X(71).

WORKING-STORAGE.

01 DETAIL-REC.
   05 DET-DEPT         PIC X(10).
   05 FILLER           PIC X(5).
   05 DET-EMP-NAME     PIC X(25).
```

Fig. 1-1. Program example.

```
        05  FILLER              PIC X(5).
        05  DET-EMP-NO          PIC X(5).
        05  FILLER              PIC X(5).
        05  DET-SALARY          PIC ZZ9.99.

    01  TITLE-1.
        05  FILLER PIC X(25) VALUE IS 'PROGRAM: REP001'.
        05  FILLER PIC X(25) VALUE IS 'EMPLOYEE MASTER LISTING'.
        05  FILLER PIC X(21).

    01  HEADINGS-1.
        05  FILLER PIC X(10) VALUE IS 'DEPARTMENT'.
        05  FILLER PIC X(5).
        05  FILLER PIC X(25) VALUE IS 'EMPLOYEE NAME'.
        05  FILLER PIC X(5).
        05  FILLER PIC X(5) VALUE IS 'EMP NO.'.
        05  FILLER PIC X(5).
        05  FILLER PIC X(5) VALUE IS ' WAGE'.

    01  HEADINGS-2.
        05  FILLER PIC X(10) VALUE IS '----------'.
        05  FILLER PIC X(5).
        05  FILLER PIC X(25) VALUE IS '-------------'.
        05  FILLER PIC X(5).
        05  FILLER PIC X(5) VALUE IS '-------'.
        05  FILLER PIC X(5).
        05  FILLER PIC X(5) VALUE IS '------'.


    01  OUT-OF-RECS             PIC X.

    PROCEDURE DIVISION.
    START-PAR.
        MOVE 'N' TO OUT-OF-RECS.
        OPEN INPUT  IN-FILE, OUTPUT REP-FILE.
        READ IN-FILE AT END MOVE 'N' TO OUT-OF-RECS.
        PERFORM HEADINGS-PAR THRU HEADINGS-PAR-END.
        IF OUT-OF-RECS = 'N'
           PERFORM LOOP-PAR THRU LOOP-PAR-END UNTIL OUT-OF-RECS
           = 'Y'.
        CLOSE IN-FILE, OUT-FILE.
        STOP RUN.

    LOOP-PAR.
        MOVE IN-EMP-NO       TO DET-EMP-NO.
        MOVE IN-EMP-NAME     TO DET-EMP-NAME.
        MOVE IN-DEPT         TO DET-DEPT.
        MOVE IN-SALARY       TO DET-SALARY.
        WRITE REP-REC FROM DETAIL-REC.
        READ IN-FILE AT END MOVE 'Y' TO OUT-OF-RECS.
```

```
LOOP-PAR-END.

HEADINGS-PAR.
    WRITE REP-REC FROM TITLE-1 AFTER ADVANCING TOP-OF-FORM.
    WRITE REP-REC FROM HEADINGS-1 AFTER ADVANCING 2 LINES.
    WRITE REP-REC FROM HEADINGS-2 AFTER ADVANCING 1 LINES.
HEADINGS-PAR-END.
```

outs of the records contained within it. The WORKING-STORAGE SECTION describes the names and sizes of variables used only internally by the program (for example, counters and totalers). This section is also commonly used to format titles, column headings and alternate report print lines.

The PROCEDURE DIVISION defines the specific rules and step-by-step procedures used to update files, display menus and generate reports. These procedures are defined by action statements and paragraph names. *Action statements* are special COBOL words that perform specific functions. For example, the word DISPLAY can be used to print information on the user's screen, and the word READ retrieves a record from a previously opened data file. Paragraph names are used to package action statements in small, definable groups that can be referenced and executed as one complete procedure.

The program listed in Fig. 1-1 reads a file from disk, reformats the retrieved data fields, and writes a simple report. Look at the program's format: first note that all program statements and titles begin in one of two vertical locations. These locations are called *areas*. Area-A is from column eight to column 11 and Area-B is from column 12 forward. COBOL requires that specific statements begin in specific areas. All division names, section names, FD statements, 01 record definitions and paragraph names must begin in Area-A. All field definitions and PROCEDURE DIVISION action statements must begin in Area-B.

All titles and statements end with a period. This requirement was incorporated into the language as part of the attempt to make COBOL as English-like as possible. In most cases the period is nothing more than a required inconvenience; however, in

the case of multi-line statements like IF and SEARCH, it is an ideal way to specify the statement end.

When this program is executed, the computer will first analyze the ENVIRONMENT DIVISION and DATA DIVISION. From this analysis the computer will allocate the amount of storage space in memory needed to accommodate the defined records and variables. Buffers will be established in preparation for the processing of the defined data files. When the PROCEDURE DIVISION is reached, START-PAR is processed. Within this paragraph, OUT-OF-RECS will be set to the value N by a move statement, and IN-FILE will be opened for input. REP-FILE will be opened for output, a record will be retrieved, headings will be printed, and LOOP-PAR will be performed.

LOOP-PAR moves the data, field by field, from the input record to the output record, writes the output record to the report file, and reads another record from IN-FILE. This looping process will continue until IN-FILE is out of records and OUT-OF-RECS is set to Y. Then control is passed from LOOP-PAR back to START-PAR, where the files are closed and program execution ends.

The statements used to define this logic are MOVE, OPEN, READ, IF, PERFORM, WRITE, CLOSE and STOP. The MOVE statement is used to copy a value from one variable to another variable. For example, if IN-EMP-NO originally had a value of 00238, and DET-EMP-NO originally had a value of 54123, the execution of the statement "MOVE IN-EMP-NO TO DET-EMP-NO" would result in both variables containing the value 00238.

The OPEN statement prepares a file for processing and specifies the way that file will be used. In the case of Fig. 1-1, IN-FILE was opened for input and OUT-FILE was opened for output. Both these files were previously selected in the EN-VIRONMENT DIVISION and defined in the DATA DIVISION.

The READ statement is used to retrieve data from a specified input file. Each time this statement is executed one record is read from the file and placed in a special input area. In Fig. 1-1 this area is IN-REC, defined in the DATA DIVISION as part of IN-FILE's file definition.

The IF statement is used to define and interpret procedural logic. For example, in START-PAR LOOP-PAR will be performed if OUT-OF-RECS has a value of N. IF is a multi-line statement; it is important to place a period at the end of the entire IF statement only, and not at the end of every line.

The PERFORM statement names a particular paragraph or group of paragraphs to be called and executed in a fashion resembling a subroutine. After the execution of this is complete, control is passed back to the PERFORM statement, and processing at the original location continues. For example, the fourth line of START-PAR is "PER-FORM HEADINGS-PAR THRU HEADINGS-PAR-END." This statement instructs the computer to go to paragraph HEADINGS-PAR and process all the statements between HEADINGS-PAR and HEADINGS-PAR-END. When HEADINGS-PAR-END is reached control is returned to START-PAR and processing continues.

The WRITE statement takes information contained in the program and places it in a data file. Fig. 1-1 contains four WRITE statements. The three WRITE statements in HEADINGS-PAR print the report title and report column headings to the output report file. The WRITE statement in LOOP-PAR prints the data retrieved from IN-FILE to the report file. Figure 1-2, lists the input data file retrieved by Fig. 1-1.

Figure 1-3 displays the report generated by executing Fig. 1-2.

There are two additional considerations about Fig. 1-1 that should be discussed; the overall appearance of the program and the conventions used to name the variables. The appearance of a program can significantly increase its readability. Throughout the program statements are lined up vertically. For example, the PICTURE clauses in the DATA DIVISION all start in the same column, and the MOVE statements within LOOP-PAR are lined up at the TO clause. This alignment is not required by the language, but since is makes programs easier to read it is generally considered good programming practice.

Variable names also contribute to a program's readability. These names should clearly define the variable's function and content. For example, the input record name in Fig. 1-1 is called IN-REC and the report title definition is named TITLE-1. COBOL lets the programmer use up to 30 characters for each variable name.

```
00283Bloom, Eric P.          Accounting00475
03932Smith, Jonathan S.      Accounting00650
20003Tompson, William A.     Accounting00350
31212Conley, Steve J.        Computer  00626
65432Davis, John R.          Computer  00450
00421Olson, Kenny L.         Sales     00850
00534Patterson Sally D.      Sales     00750
04329Stone Samual T.         Sales     00325
05713Zide, Neal M.           Sales     00775
33321Jones, Allen F.         Training  00425
00094Wells Erwin T.          Training  00375
```

Fig. 1-2. Sample report input data file.

```
PROGRAM: REP001          EMPLOYEE MASTER LISTING

DEPARTMENT         EMPLOYEE NAME              EMP NO      WAGE
----------         -------------              ------      -----

Accounting         Bloom, Eric P.             00283       4.75
Accounting         Smith, Jonathan S.         03932       6.50
Accounting         Tompson, William A.        20003       3.50
Computer           Conley, Steve J.           31212       6.25
Computer           Davis, John R.             65432       4.50
Sales              Olson, Kenny L.            00421       8.50
Sales              Patterson Sally D.         00534       7.50
Sales              Stone Samual T.            04329       3.25
Sales              Zide, Neal M.              05721       7.75
Training           Jones, Allen F.            33321       4.25
Training           Wells Erwin T.             00094       3.75
```

Fig. 1-3. Report program output.

QUESTIONS

1. What is the meaning of the word COBOL?

2. Name and briefly explain the four COBOL divisions.

3. What is the significance of columns 1-6, 7, 8-12 and 13-72 when coding in COBOL?

4. What function does a period play in COBOL programming?

5. What is the purpose of the FILE-SECTION?

6. What is the purpose of the WORKING-STORAGE SECTION?

7. What are action statements?

8. What is the function of the PERFORM statement?

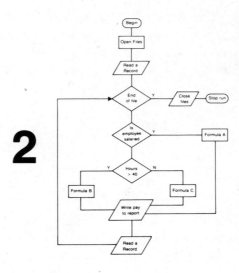

2

Program Design

Developing a program requires more than just sitting down and typing in code. It requires preparation: analyzing what the program should do, how it should be structured, and how it should be implemented. This chapter discusses the program development process that should be followed to ensure the successful implementation of stand-alone programs and entire applications.

The program development process is divided into many steps: conceptualization, functional design, technical design, programming, implementation and maintenance.

PROGRAM CONCEPTUALIZATION

All programs begin as an idea. In this stage the originator of the idea plays mental "what if" games in an effort to consolidate and refine the program's size and function. If the program still seems worthwhile, "back of the envelope" analysis begins. In this step, the originator places his thoughts on paper, scratching out notes, report formats, input screens or lines and arrows showing the flow of data. Once these notes are reasonably complete and the program is conceptually clear in the mind of the author, it is time to employ a more formal, structured design approach. This step is the functional design phase.

FUNCTIONAL DESIGN

The functional design phase is the process of formalizing the user's requirements and developing functional documentation. All programs, regardless of application—financial, scientific or process control—can be described in terms of its input, processes and output. Input are the bits of information entered into a program. Output are the reports, files, screens and so forth sent from the program to the users. Processes are the step-by-step instructions used to transform input into output. When defining functional segments, the analyst should first define the program output, then decide what input is needed to create the output, and finally, develop the process needed to transform the input into the output. Many techniques have been developed to assist in the design process. The techniques I shall briefly introduce in this chapter are program logic flowcharts, data dictionaries, decision trees, and decision tables.

Program Logic Flowcharts

Flowcharts are a series of lines, boxes and circles that graphically represent the logical process contained in a program. This technique helps the

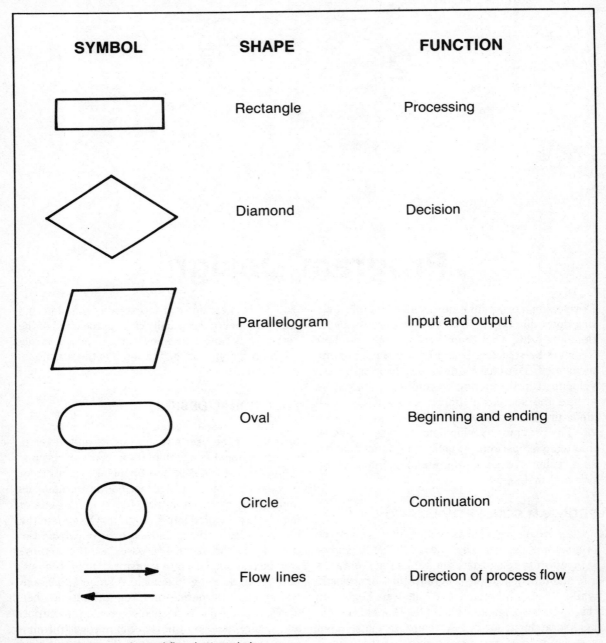

SYMBOL	SHAPE	FUNCTION
	Rectangle	Processing
	Diamond	Decision
	Parallelogram	Input and output
	Oval	Beginning and ending
	Circle	Continuation
	Flow lines	Direction of process flow

Fig. 2-1. Most commonly used flowchart symbols.

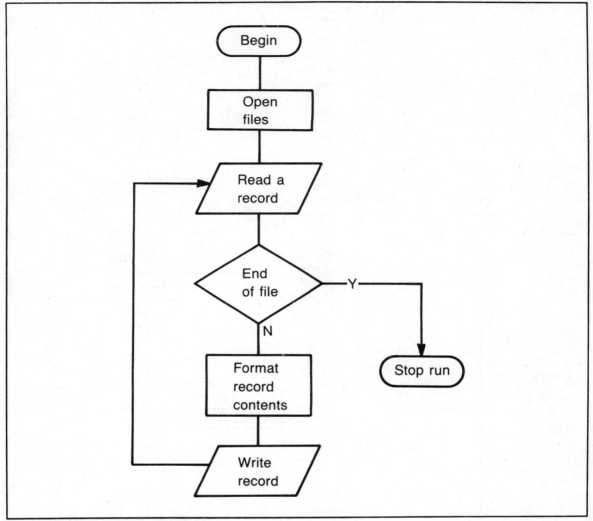

Fig. 2-2. Report logic flowchart examples.

analyst describe the program in a way easily understood and simple to create and modify. The symbols employed in the flowcharting process are shown in Fig. 2-1.

The flowchart in Fig. 2-2 is the representation of a report program similar to the one discussed in Chapter 1. In the report program logic flowchart the files are opened and a record is read from the file. If a record is retrieved it is formatted, written to the file, and another record is read. This process continues until an end of file condition is reached.

At that time the files are closed and the program ends.

As shown in Fig. 2-3, this technique can be used to illustrate complex logic in a very simple way. This figure describes the process needed to calculate an employee's gross pay. Two pay-related questions are asked. The first assesses whether an employee is paid on an hourly or salaried basis. If the employee is salaried, the gross pay is calculated as the hourly wage times 40, regardless of the number of hours actually worked. If the employee is not

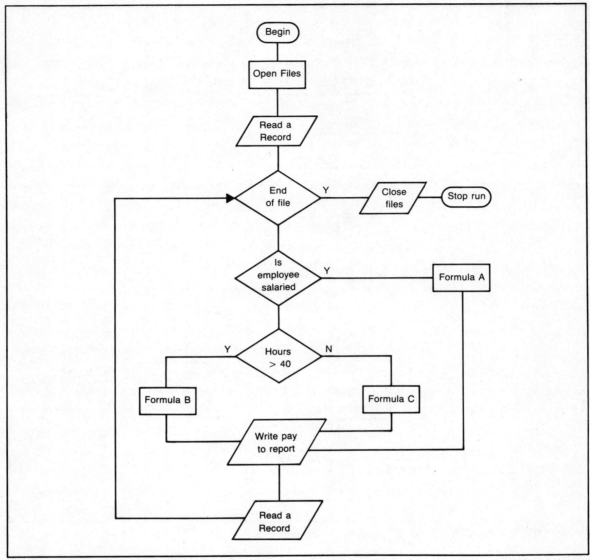

Fig. 2-3. Gross pay calculation flowchart.

salaried, a second question is asked regarding the number of hours worked. If the answer is 40 or less, the gross pay is calculated as the hourly wage times the hours worked. Otherwise the employee is paid for 40 hours at the regular wage and time and a half for all hours over 40.

Data Dictionary

Data dictionaries are used to define the infor-

mation contained in a data file. This tool is divided into two parts. The first part provides a description of the file, including a list of its elements. The second part contains detailed information about each field. Figure 2-4 is an example of a fact sheet used to describe each data file. The File Name line states the name of the file being described. The File ID is filled in after the program's technical design is completed, and the file is given the name that

```
                     File Description Sheet
FILE NAME      : Payroll Master File
FILE ID        : PAYMAST.DAT
DESCRIPTION    : This is the main payroll system master file and contains all needed employee payroll in-
                 formation.
FILE LOCATION  : The file is stored on tape and is kept in the computer room safe.
SECURITY       : The data is considered confidential and company proprietary. It may only be removed
                 from the safe for scheduled payroll runs or by the signature of the payroll manager.
DATA FIELDS    : EMP-NO, EMP-NAME, EMP-ADDRESS, HOURLY-WAGE, NO-OF-DEDUCTIONS,
                 GROSS-PAY-YTD
MISC           : This file is also used as the main input to the personnel system.
```

Fig. 2-4. Data dictionary file description example.

will identify it on disk or tape. The Description field provides a textual description of the file's function within the application being defined. The File Location line refers to the file's physical location on the disk drive or tape library where the data resides. The Security entry is used to describe any security issues surrounding the file information. For example, if a payroll master file is being described, it may state the people or departments permitted access to it. The Data Fields area is used to list the elements included in the data file. This list should

be carefully entered, because it is used as a cross reference to the data element information that shall shortly be described. The MISC area is used to note other information of interest that does not fit neatly into any of the other categories.

Figure 2-5 is the data element description for the EMP-NO field. The data element field comprises seven categories. The Element Name is the connection to the file description sheets and is also the name that should be used to describe the data field in the program's DATA DIVISION. The Ele-

```
E L E M E N T     D E S C R I P T I O N     S H E E T


ELEMENT NAME     : EMP-NO
ELEMENT TITLE    : Employee Number
SIZE AND FORMAT  : PIC X(5)

DESCRIPTION      : This is the employee identification number
                   used by the payroll system to uniquely identify
                   each employee

SOURCE           : A number is assigned by personnel to each
                   employee at the time of hire.

UPDATE RULES     : This number should never be changed during the
                   employee's employment with the company and
                   should not be re-used after the employee's
                   termination.

ALIASES          : Badge Number, Payroll Check ID Number
```

Fig. 2-5. Data element description example.

ment Title is a two or three word description of the data field. The words used in this title usually coincide with the abbreviations used in the element name. For example, EMP-NO has a title of "Employee Name." The Size and Format line describes the element's length and type in COBOL PICTURE clause format. This format will be described in detail in the DATA DIVISION discussion in Chapter 5. The Description is used to explain the element's function or use in the application. Source is used to describe the location or process from which the data was originally created. This may be a vendor's invoice, the accounting department's control handbook, automatically generated by the computer, or other similar beginning. The Update Rules category specifies the rules and procedures that involve the modification and deletion of the element once it is entered into the system. The Aliases section lists other names for the same element. For example, an employee number is often referred to as a badge number because it is displayed on the employee identification badges.

When applications require many data files, there are usually some data elements contained in more than one file. When this is the case, it is good to maintain two separate alphabetic lists. One list should contain the file description sheets and the other the element description sheets. This saves the step of rewriting the element information over and over when it pops up in many files. A cross reference from the element description sheets to the data file description can be easily maintained by adding one more category to the former element sheets. This category would list the data files in which the element was used.

Decision Trees

A decision tree is a technique used to define and document the possible options associated with a given situation. One nice thing about this definition process is that it is very easy to conceptualize, and can therefore be instantly understood by nontechnical users. Figure 2-6 shows how a decision tree can be used to illustrate the gross pay calculation previously defined during the flowcharting discussion.

The decision tree begins with a block, stating the problem or question being addressed. Stemming out from the block are two branches designating the two possible options of the question being asked: "Is the employee compensated on a salaried or hourly basis?" If salaried, the tree ends and the appropriate gross pay calculation is displayed. If the employee is paid hourly, a circle is reached, which divides the branch into two new lines. This circle and its newly formed branches are called an *event fork*, showing that one question has been answered but another has yet to be addressed. As with the original branches, each option is marked with its specific criteria and corresponding gross pay calculation.

Decision Tables

Decision tables are yet another way to describe the alternatives associated with a given decision. In this technique two lists are developed; the first is called a *condition list*, and contains the criteria to be evaluated. These questions must be answerable with a yes or no. The second list contains the possible actions that could be taken. The process

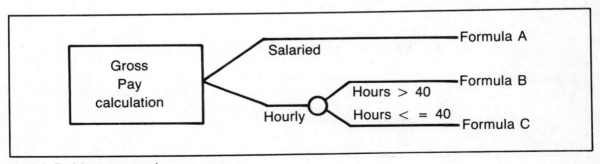

Fig. 2-6. Decision tree example.

Table 2-1. Decision Table Example.

Condition List:		Y	N	N
Is the employee paid by salary		Y	N	N
Is hours worked greater than 40			Y	N
Is hours worked less than or equal to 40			N	Y
Action List:				
Formula A		X		
Formula B			X	
Formula C				X

used to connect the questions to the actions can most easily be explained through illustration. Table 2-1 is a decision table outlining the gross pay calculation example.

In this example each question places answers on one or more of three vertical columns. Each of these columns is associated with the action specified by an X in the action's row. The first gross pay calculation has an X in the first vertical column; if the answers in column one match the answers for a given employee, the first formula should be used. For example, if the employee is not salaried, and worked 35 hours, the first question is answered N, the second is answered Y, and the third is answered N. These three responses match the second column of the decision table, so the calculation "GROSS-PAY = HOURLY-WAGE * HOURS-WORKED" would be used.

In the second and third questions the first column was left blank, because if the first answer was affirmative, the employee is salaried. In that case the number of hours worked has no bearing on the action taken.

TECHNICAL DESIGN

Technical design is the process of defining a program's structure and detailed logic. To effec-

tively describe this logic, the program being discussed should be divided into bite-size sections called *modules*. Modules are distinct program segments, each performing a specific function. The program structure is the way in which these modules interrelate. Detailed logic outlines the steps and algorithms that must be performed in each module to complete its logical function.

Like the design step, this process also contains formalized techniques that assist in the process. The techniques I shall discuss here are HIPO, pseudocode, and program flowcharts.

HIPO Charts

The word HIPO stands for Hierarchical Input Process Output technique. This method is composed of two parts. The first is the development of a hierarchical structure chart that arranges the program modules in a top-down fashion. The structure chart for a payroll check-writing report is shown in Fig. 2-7.

The structure chart illustrates the modules contained in a check generation program. The top module is Generate Checks, used to control the five subordinate level modules—Program Initialization, Read Data, Calculate Check Amounts, Print Checks, and End Program. When the program is executed, Generate Checks calls the Program Initialization module. When complete, the program reads a record from the data file, calculates the amount to be paid, prints the check, and goes back to module three to retrieve another record. The looping process will continue until the input file is out of records and the sixth module is called to close the files and end the program.

There are times when a single level of module detail will not adequately describe the program's breakdown. In these cases subordinate modules can be further divided, as shown in Fig. 2-8. An additional level of detail was added to modules 1.3 and 1.5. These new levels were designed to provide a finer level of program detail. Remember, these specifications will be used by the programmer as the blueprint of a program's structure. The better the design specifications, the easier it is for the programmer.

Note the numbering sequence used to identify the modules. This sequence lets each module be traced back to its owner. When viewing these modules in a structure chart format the numbering may seem rather unimportant. However, these numbers will also be placed in the individual module descriptions. There the numbers will not only serve as a cross reference between the structure chart and module descriptions, but it will also assist in assessment of relationship between modules when the

structure chart is not easily accessable. Another service the numbering scheme provides is an easy method of locating a module on a complex structure chart. Even if a chart has hundreds of modules, any module can be quickly found by following its numbering sequence from level to level.

The second part of HIPO is the IPO charts. This stands for Input/Process/Output, used to provide detailed information about each module identified in the structure chart. Figure 2-9 is the IPO chart associated with module 1.3 in the second structure chart example. This IPO chart is divided into many parts. The System Name is used to place the name of the application being designed. In this case the program is part of the payroll system. Program Name is used to record the name of the program being written. The Module Name and Module Number are the cross-reference to the structure chart. These fields should be filled to exactly match that in the structure chart. The Prepared By area specifies the person who completed the IPO form. The Date field may contain either the date the chart was originally prepared or the date it was approved; the date used will depend on the custom of the data processing department doing the work. In some places both dates are required, and another date field is added to the form.

The next section of the IPO chart describes how the module relates to other modules. The

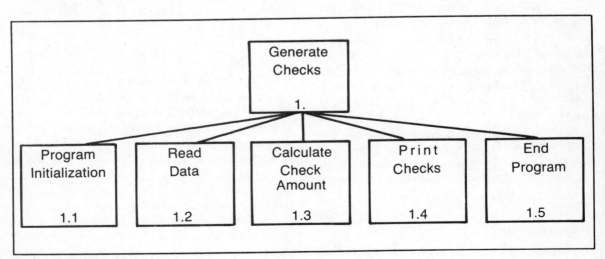

Fig. 2-7. Sample structure chart.

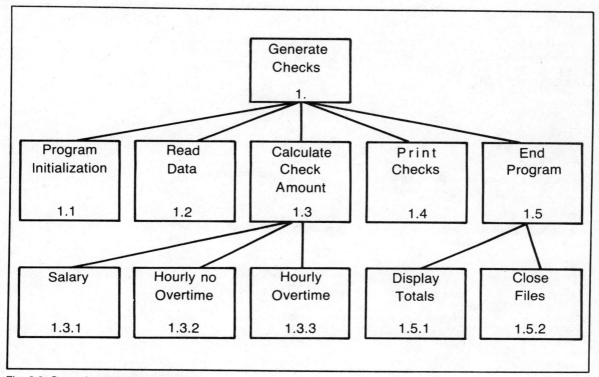

Fig. 2-8. Second sample structure chart.

Called By area lists the names and numbers of the modules that call the module being defined. The section It Calls states its subordinate modules. The Input and Output blocks list the variables passed to and from the module during processing.

The last section explains the processes that will be performed in the module. The Desc area provides a textual description of the modules process. The Process area describes the module logic in a COBOL-like format. This near-COBOL description is called *Structured English,* and can later be easily transformed into code, assisting the programmer writing the internal program logic. The Local Data Elements field lists those variables only referenced in the module and not passed from place to place. The Misc section is used for pertinent information that does not fit into any other category.

PSEUDOCODE

Pseudocode is a tool used to design and later document the processes in a module, using English words in a COBOL-like format. The difference between this process and structured English is that pseudocode includes all programming steps needed to execute the module, not just selected pieces of logic. The format of the pseudocode used to design an application is dictated by the language in which the application will be programmed. Because pseudocode is so close to the actual program code most programmers dislike it. The general feeling is that the text being written is almost the actual program; why not, therefore, just write the actual code? Figure 2-10 is an example of the pseudocode for a small report program.

In this example there are three types of commands being used: functional, conditional logic, and repetition. The functional commands are executed in sequence and perform specific functions, like opening and closing files, moving values from variable to variable, and mathematics. The IF commands facilitate conditional logic, and PERFORM allows subroutining and looping. As shall be seen

IPO CHART

SYSTEM NAME : Payroll	PREPARED BY : E. Bloom
PROGRAM NAME : PRL009.CBL	DATE : 8/30/85
MODULE NAME : Get Check Amount	APPROVED BY : E. Wells
MODULE NUMBER : 1.3	

CALLED BY : 1. Create Checks

IT CALLS : 1.3.1 Salaried
              1.3.2 Hourly No Overtime
              1.3.3 Hourly With Overtime

INPUTS : Hourly-wage, Salary-type,
             Gross-Pay, Hours-worked

OUTPUTS : Gross-pay

DESCRIPTION : This Module decides which gross pay calculation should be used and calls the appropriate
                module.

PROCESS   : If Salary-type = 'salaried'
             Then do module 1.3.1
         Else
            If Hours-worked < = 40
               Then do module 1.3.2
         Else
            Do module 1.3.3

LOCAL DATA ELEMENTS: None

MISC : Gross pay is actually calculated
       in the submodules and the value
       is passed back to this module
       and up to module 1.

Fig. 2-9. IPO chart example.

in Chapter 7, these three functions are closely tied to structured programming ideologies.

PROGRAMMING

The programming phase consists of three steps: writing the source code, compilation, and preliminary testing.

Writing The Source Code

There are two ways programs are written and entered into the computer. The first method is to write the program out by hand on lined paper or on some type of special COBOL coding form, then keying in the entire program. As programmers be-

come more experienced they try to type the program directly into the computer without first writing on paper. The success of this second method depends on the talent of the programmer and the complexity of the application. There is a trick that can be used to speed up the process and help ensure a quality product: program the PROCEDURE DIVISION first, and on a nearby piece of paper write down all the variable names, file names and paragraph names created as the code is entered. After the PROCEDURE DIVISION is complete, type in the first three divisions. All variables and files used in the fourth division must be defined in the DATA DIVISION, and in the ENVIRONMENT DIVISION in the case of file names.

```
Start:    Open Master File for input
          Open Report File for output
          Set record flag to NO
          Read report master file, at end set record flag to Yes
          If record Flag is equal to No
             Perform Loop until record flag is NO
          Close master file and report file
          Stop run

Loop :    Move master file data to report record
          Write report record to report file
          Read master file, at end move NO to record flag
```

Fig. 2-10. Pseudocode example.

The Compilation Process

Once the source code is written and typed into the computer it must be translated from a human-readable format into computer-readable form. This translation process is known as *compilation,* illustrated in Fig. 2-11.

To compile a program the programmer must execute the COBOL compiler and specify the name of the program to be transformed. This process leaves the input source code unchanged and creates two outputs: a program listing and a file containing the program object code. The program listing is different from the source code listing because it contains information about the compilation, including the number of errors, the error locations, a variable cross-reference list, and other similar information that can be used in the program debugging process. The object code is the source code in a computer readable format (binary).

After the compilation process is complete, there is one more step that must be performed before the program can be executed. This step is called *program linkage.* The linkage process is illustrated in Fig. 2-12.

The linkage process connects all processes needed to successfully execute the program and places them together in one file. In the linkage example there are three files being consolidated. The first file is the program's object code. The second file contains the object code from a subroutine pro-

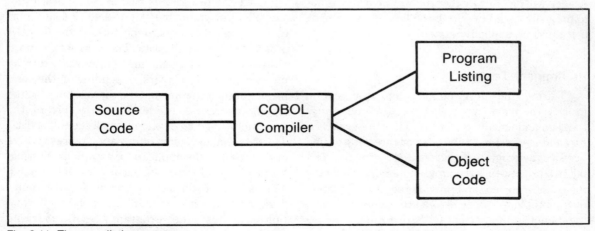

Fig. 2-11. The compilation process.

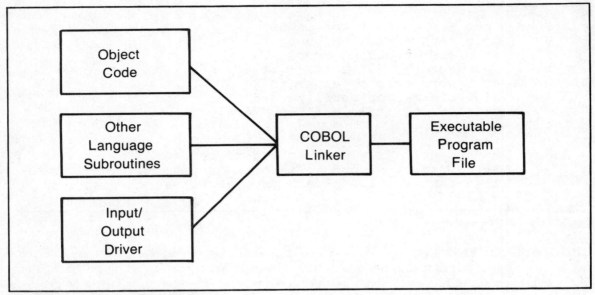

Fig. 2-12. The program linking process.

gram written in another language, such as BASIC or PASCAL. Routines written in other programming languages can be called into a COBOL program during program execution through the ENTER statement. The input/output driver is required by all executing programs, regardless of the language in which it was written. This routine connects the program's logic to the terminals, disk drives and other input or output devices. The hardware and operating system on which the program resides will dictate whether this device driver is automatically called in during the linkage process or if it must be explicitly stated.

Preliminary Testing

During the programming and compilation process there are two types of programming bugs that can and usually do, occur. They are *syntax errors* and *logic errors*. Syntax errors are easy to find because the program listing created during the compilation process tells the programmer exactly where the error occurred, and provides some explanation of the problem. These errors are caused by statements not in the correct COBOL format. For example, the statement "MOVEE X TO Y" will cause

an error because MOVEE is not a valid statement and cannot be understood by the compiler. A second example is the statement "IF A = B." This IF statement is incomplete; like the MOVE example it cannot be interpreted by the computer. This IF error may be caused in one of two ways: the statement was never finished, as shown in Fig. 2-13 and must be completed, or the period after the "B" was accidently placed at the end of the line, also shown in Fig. 2-13, and must be removed.

Once the program is free of syntactical problems, logical errors must be identified and corrected. Logical errors are mistakes in the way the program processes the data. These errors are much more difficult to find and may periodically turn up for months, or even years, depending on the complexity of the program and the thoroughness of the testing process. To identify these errors the programmer should develop a small set of test data. The data should contain information representative of that used in the application, as well as information with out of range values and invalid formats. The valid data will assist in the testing of the program's processing logic, and the invalid information will test the program's error-checking capabilities.

PROGRAM IMPLEMENTATION

The implementation of a program or system is the final step in the software development process. This step comprises final testing, implementation and program maintenence.

The Final Testing and Implementation Process

Once the program is completed and seems ready for production, it should go through one more round of testing. When possible these tests should not be performed by the program's author. The person who wrote the program tests it to see if it works; others test a program to find the errors. It is this difference in mental attitude that helps provide a more thorough and complete test.

A very common practice in testing new programs is to develop a testing team. The team usually consists of the program's author, a fellow programmer, and a user of the program once it is implemented. The program's author is present only to provide technical background about the program's development. The testing is performed by the second programmer and the user.

The team approach seems to work well because the second programmer can evaluate the program's technical aspects without being hindered by pride of authorship, and the user has the application knowledge to analyze the program's functional merit. Also, the user has a strong vested interest: he or she will have to rely on the ability and correctness of this program.

There are many techniques that can be used to test programs. Three of the most common are parallel testing, prior testing, and simulation testing. Parallel testing is the process of running two systems simultaneously. Using this technique requires one to continue the old methods and also take on the task in the new way. This may mean simply running another report over the weekend, or it may mean manually inputting data into two systems. Once complete, the output of the two systems are compared. If the results are the same, or at least reconcilable, the new system continues and the old mode of operation is discontinued. If the test results are unsatisfactory, the programmer goes back to work, to make appropriate changes.

Parallel testing sounds good in theory, but in actuality, it can be impractical or even impossible to perform, due to lack of resources needed to do twice the work, or the inability to capture the data in two places at once. Two alternate approaches were developed that can be performed by the testing team. The first technique is called *prior testing*. This process uses the same principles as parallel testing, except it uses data from past months. For example, if a new payroll system is being installed in November, establish the test files as of a few months before, for instance, March. Then enter April's data and compare the test reports to the actual April numbers. Continue this process through October, and if all looks good, go with only the new system in November.

The third testing process is similar to the second, except the test data is strictly simulated. This alternative will not produce as thorough a test, but if the test data is selected carefully it should suffice. To implement a system using this test method, the files used by the new programs should be copied and converted to the new format, and on an appropriate day the old method is turned off and the new method is turned on.

Program Maintenance

Regardless of the implementation method used to put into operation the new program or system,

```
PART A :    MOVE X TO Y
            IF A = B.

PART B :    MOVE A TO C.
            IF A = B.
                MOVE X TO Y.
```

Fig. 2-13. Example IF statement errors.

there is usually a need for maintenance programming. Maintenance programming becomes necessary for many reasons. Errors may be found in the code that must be corrected. Company policies or procedures may change. Growing firms may outgrow current systems, or enhancements may be needed to meet new business challenges. Whatever the reason, this task can be made easier if the software being written is well-documented, written in a clear, concise, structured format, and carefully modified so as not to violate structured principles or outdate the documentation.

QUESTIONS

1. List and briefly explain the steps contained in the programming development process.

2. What are logic flowcharts, and what is their purpose?

3. Explain the function of a data dictionary, and describe its two main components.

4. What are decision trees, and what role do they play in the program development process?

5. What are decision tables?

6. Explain the purpose of HIPO and describe its two components.

7. Why is the numbering sequence on HIPO structure charts important?

8. What is pseudocode?

9. What is program compilation?

10. Why must COBOL programs be linked, and what must they be linked to?

11. What is the difference between syntax errors and logic errors?

12. What is a testing team, and who should be part of it?

13. Why shouldn't a program's author perform all program testing?

14. How does the team testing approach work?

15. What are the advantages and disadvantages of parallel testing?

16. Why is maintenence programming almost always needed?

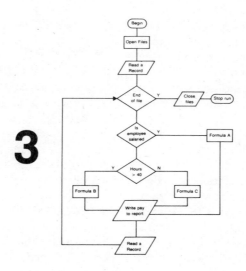

3

The IDENTIFICATION DIVISION

This chapter will discuss the first of the four COBOL divisions, the IDENTIFICATION DIVISION. The discussion will include the format of appropriate language statements and the use of this first division as an internal program documentation tool.

THE IDENTIFICATION DIVISION

All COBOL programs must begin with an IDENTIFICATION DIVISION. As the name suggests, this area is used to identify the program's name, author, and function. Its only function is to require a minimum level of internal program documentation. The statements used in this division are PROGRAM-ID, AUTHOR, INSTALLATION, DATE-WRITTEN, DATE-COMPILED, and SECURITY. Older versions of COBOL also have a REMARKS statement, phased out in modern day compilers.

The PROGRAM-ID Statement

The PROGRAM-ID statement has two func-

tions. First, it identifies the program name. Industry standards generally demand that the name placed in the PROGRAM-ID is the same as the disk file name in which the program is stored. Some versions of COBOL have a second use for this statement. When a program is passed through the compilation process, a compiled version of the program is placed in a file on disk. The default name for this file is the name specified in PROGRAM-ID. The line shown below illustrates the format of this statement.

PROGRAM-ID. Program-name.

PROGRAM-ID is divided into two sections. The first section is the statement name followed by a period. The second section is the name of the program being identified followed by another period. The program name should not include any extension. The line below is an example of the PROGRAM-ID statement.

PROGRAM-ID. PAYLIST.

The AUTHOR Statement

The AUTHOR statement identifies the person who originally wrote the program. Programmers like this requirement, because it places their name in the documentation for many years after the work is completed. The line below illustrates the format of this statement.

AUTHOR. Freeform Text of Authors Name.

Unlike PROGRAM-ID, this statement allows much flexibility on how the author's name appears. The only rules are that it must begin with the word AUTHOR, followed by a period, and the author's name must also end with a period. Shown in Fig. 3-1 are examples of the AUTHOR statement.

The INSTALLATION Statement

The INSTALLATION statement documents the computer facility where the program was written. This statement is used by companies that have many computer centers, so as to identify the program's original facility, and by large multi-computer data centers to identify the CPU on which the program resides. The line below shows this statement's format.

INSTALLATION. Freeform Text of Installation Name.

The format of the INSTALLATION statement is the word INSTALLATION, followed by a period, and a freeform name followed by a second period. Figure 3-2 provides some examples.

The DATE-WRITTEN Statement

The DATE-WRITTEN statement documents on appropriate date during the program development process. This date may be when the program was started, finished, tested or even entered into production. The date that should be used is usually specified by the management of the data center in which the program was developed. The line below illustrates the statement's format.

DATE-WRITTEN. Freeform date.

The format is the words DATE-WRITTEN and a period, followed by the date, in any format the user desires. Examples are shown in Fig. 3-3.

The DATE-COMPILED Statement

The DATE-COMPILED statement shows the date the program was last compiled. In some versions of COBOL the compiler provides the option to automatically change the date as part of the compilation process. In other versions it must be manually updated. The format of this statement is shown below.

DATE-COMPILED. Freeform date.

Figure 3-4 provides various examples.

The SECURITY Statement

The SECURITY statement provides informa-

```
AUTHOR. EPB.

AUTHOR. Eric P. Bloom.

AUTHOR.
        Eric P. Bloom.

AUTHOR. E. Bloom and G. Gagne

AUTHOR. KIER Associates International, Inc.
```

Fig. 3-1. AUTHOR statement examples.

Fig. 3-2. INSTALLATION statement examples.

```
INSTALLATION. Corporate Data center.

INSTALLATION. Data Center - A, CPU 4x.

INSTALLATION.  IBM 4300.
```

```
DATE-WRITTEN. 8-30-85.

DATE-WRITTEN. Aug 30, 1985.

DATE-WRITTEN. Aug-30-85.
```

Fig. 3-3. DATE-WRITTEN statement examples.

Fig. 3-4. DATE-COMPILED statement examples.

```
DATE-COMPILED. August 30, 1095.

DATE-COMPILED. 8/30/85.

DATE-COMPILED. AUG-30-85.
```

tion regarding the sensitivity of the data being compiled or extracted by the program. If security is an issue, the appropriate rules and regulations describing the proper use of the data should be written in the program as part of this statement.

Security information should not be confined to comments at the beginning of the source code. The source code is only accessed when the program is modified. Security notices should also be displayed on the terminal or in the job stream during program execution. Security policies and regulations should be discussed with the appropriate people to ensure that sensitive information is handled correctly.

The SECURITY statement format is shown below.

SECURITY. Freeform Security information.

The format is primarily the same as that of the statements previously explained. However, because security issues may be rather complex and long-winded the text may use many lines as needed. When all the text is entered, the statement may be ended by a period, the presence of another state-

```
SECURITY. None.

SECURITY. The report generated by this program contains
          company planning data and should be considered
          very confidential.

SECURITY. Handle using rule set 1 in the security handbook.
```

Fig. 3-5. SECURITY statement examples.

```
REMARKS. This program runs after the weekly payroll update.

REMARKS. Compiling instructions are:
               1) COBOL PAYLIST/nocref/map/debug
               2) LINK PAYLIST, COBLIB, SCRFORMAT /debug.
```

Fig. 3-6. REMARKS statement examples.

ment, or the ENVIRONMENT DIVISION header line. Shown in Fig. 3-5 are some SECURITY statement examples.

The REMARKS Statement

The REMARKS statement has been phased out as a valid COBOL statement. However, because many systems written in the mid- and late-1970's are still being run under the old COBOL compilers, we will discuss the statement.

REMARK was used to document general information about the program. The information could be a textual description of the program's function, rules for compilation, linkage and execution, or other pertinent data. Its format is very similar to the SECURITY statement, and is shown below.

REMARKS. Freeform text.

Shown in Fig. 3-6 are various REMARKS examples.

```
SECURITY. None.
*
******************************************
*
* This is a comment line which means it is ignored by
* the compliler during compilation and is here just
* to assist the programmer in understanding the program's
* function and usage.
*
******************************************
* Program Function:
*    To generate payroll checks and a payroll check register
*    report.
******************************************
* Compilation Instructions:
*    1. COBOL PAYLIST/debug/map/nocref
*    2. LINK PAYLIST, DEVDRIVE, COBLIB, MENUS/debug
******************************************
* Change Log:
*    E. Wells - 9-15-85 - Bug found in check formatting routine
*                         modified CHECK-FORMAT-PAR.
*
*    E. Bloom - 9-16-85 - Fixed title on the check register
*                         report, modified TITLES-PAR.
******************************************
```

Fig. 3-7. Example comment lines.

As the REMARKS statement began to phase out, its function was continued by the use of comment lines, discussed below.

Comment Lines

Comment lines can appear anywhere, in any of the COBOL divisions, and are used to place documentation in the program. Comments are identified by an asterisk placed in the seventh column of a line. Many compilers are less rigid, and only require that the asterisk be the first character of the line. Comments are not used or required by the COBOL compiler, but because they contain information about the program's functions and processes they are a good programming practice. Figure 3-7 shows an example of the comment line format.

Many data processing departments require that comments be used in the IDENTIFICATION DIVISION to document program compilation instructions, the business function of the program, and a change log. The compilation instructions document the process that must be followed to correctly compile and link the program in preparation for execution. The business function describes the overall purpose of the program, and if applicable, its role within a larger system. Finally, the change log displays a list of all the modifications made to the program since it was first completed, tested and placed in production. This audit trail of programming updates may provide insight into the correction procedure of future problems, or the development of future enhancements.

```
IDENTIFICATION DIVISION.
PROGRAM-ID.        PAYLIST.
AUTHOR.            ERIC P. BLOOM.
INSTALLATION       CORPORATE DATA CENTER - CPU 4X.
DATE-WRITTEN.      AUG 30, 1985.
DATE-COMPILED.     SEP 3, 1985.
*
SECURITY.          THIS REPORT GENERATES PAYCHECKS AND SHOULD BE
                   RUN FOLLOWING RULE SET 1 IN THE SECURITY
                   HANDBOOK.
*
*******************************************
* Program Function:
*    To generate payroll checks and a payroll check register
*    report.
*******************************************
* Compilation Instructions:
*    1. COBOL PAYLIST/debug/map/nocref
*    2. LINK PAYLIST, DEVDRIVE, COBLIB, MENUS/debug
*******************************************
* Change Log:
*    E. Wells - 9-15-85 - Bug found in check formatting routine
*                         modified CHECK-FORMAT-PAR.
*
*    E. Bloom - 9-16-85 - Fixed title on the check register
*                         report, modified TITLES-PAR.
*******************************************
```

Fig. 3-8. Complete IDENTIFICATION DIVISION example.

THE COMPLETE DIVISION

When the statements previously discussed are combined they create a documentation package that is a sound beginning to any COBOL program. This package is known as the IDENTIFICATION DIVISION. This division is displayed in its entirety in Fig. 3-8.

QUESTIONS

1. What is the function of the IDENTIFICATION DIVISION?

2. Explain the two uses of the PROGRAM-ID statement.

3. What is the function of the AUTHOR statement?

4. Under what circumstances is the INSTALLATION statement most useful?

5. What are the two ways by which the DATE-COMPILED statement can be updated?

6. What function does the SECURITY statement perform?

7. What method of documentation has been used to replace the REMARKS statement?

8. Why is it advantageous to use the comment statement throughout a program?

9. What is a change log?

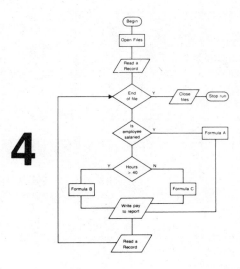

4

The ENVIRONMENT DIVISION

This chapter explains the second of the four COBOL divisions, the ENVIRONMENT DIVISION, including a discussion of the division's format and the way it establishes communication links between the program being executed and the data files being processed.

The ENVIRONMENT DIVISION deals with factors external to the COBOL program. Its main functions are to document the program's surrounding environment and, most importantly, open the lines of communication between the program and its data files. Some software manufacturers add special options to their products, like screen handlers and networking services. Very often these special features are first introduced to the application in this division and are later called for use within the DATA DIVISION and PROCEDURE DIVISION. Special features aside, however, the ENVIRONMENT DIVISION is divided into two main sections: the CONFIGURATION SECTION and the INPUT-OUTPUT SECTION.

THE CONFIGURATION SECTION

The CONFIGURATION SECTION documents on which computer the program's source and object codes reside. In most cases they are both on the same machine. However, there are data processing centers where software development is not performed on the production computer, in an effort to separate the production and development activities. In these environments a smaller, compatible computer is set aside specifically for programmers. Here the COBOL source code is written, tested, and debugged. When the program is complete it is moved to the production computer for final compilation and execution.

The SOURCE-COMPUTER Statement

The SOURCE-COMPUTER statement is used to define the computer on which the source code resides. Source code is the program in its original state as input by the user: in a human-readable

```
SOURCE-COMPUTER.  IBM S-34 ROOM 341.

SOURCE-COMPUTER.  BOSTON.

SOURCE-COMPUTER.  IBM PC/XT.
```

Fig. 4-1. SOURCE-COMPUTER statement examples.

form. The line below contains the format of this statement.

SOURCE-COMPUTER. Freeform Computer name.

The statement begins with the words SOURCE-COMPUTER, separated by a comma, and ending with a period. This is followed by the appropriate computer identification in whatever format best meets the programmer's needs, and is also followed by a period. Figure 4-1 provides some examples of this statement.

The OBJECT-COMPUTER Statement

The OBJECT-COMPUTER statement documents the computer on which the program's object code is stored. Object code is the primary output of the compilation process, and is a copy of the source program in machine-readable format. The line below illustrates the proper syntax of this statement.

OBJECT-COMPUTER. Freeform Computer Name.

The format of this statement is the statement name and a period, followed by the name of the appropriate computer in a user defined format, followed by a period. Examples of this statement are shown in Fig. 4-2.

Fig. 4-2. OBJECT-COMPUTER statement examples.

THE INPUT-OUTPUT SECTION

The INPUT-OUTPUT SECTION contains the FILE-CONTROL paragraph, which provides a communications gateway between the files on disk or tape and the internal program file names, as defined in the DATA DIVISION of the program. This file linkage is performed by use of the SELECT statement.

The SELECT Statement

The SELECT statement is the only non-documentational element of the ENVIRONMENT DIVISION. Its function is to list the files described in the DATA DIVISION and connect each description to a data file on disk, tape, or other storage media. The format of this statement is shown below.

SELECT file-name ASSIGN TO file-name.

The SELECT Statement is composed of two clauses: the SELECT clause and the ASSIGN clause. The SELECT clause begins with the word SELECT, followed by a file name described in the DATA DIVISION. The second clause begins with the words ASSIGN TO and states the device and file name in which the data is stored. Many versions of COBOL provide additional optional clauses to describe the special characteristics associated with files stored in an index sequential, random access,

```
OBJECT-COMPUTER.  IBM S-34 ROOM 341.

OBJECT-COMPUTER.  BOSTON.

OBJECT-COMPUTER.  IBM PC/XT.
```

```
ENVIRONMENT DIVISION.
*
CONFIGURATION SECTION.
SOURCE-COMPUTER.    IBM  4043 - PRODUCTION.
OBJECT-COMPUTER.    IBM  4043 - DEVELOPMENT.
*
INPUT-OUTPUT SECTION.
FILE-CONTROL.
*
       SELECT  IN-PAY-FILE      ASSIGN TO "PAYMAST.DAT".
       SELECT OUT-REPORT-FILE ASSIGN TO "PAYRPT.LIS".
*
```

Fig. 4-3. Complete ENVIRONMENT DIVISION example.

or database format. An example of this statement is shown below.

SELECT IN-PAY-FILE ASSIGN TO ''PAY-MAST.DAT.

The example in Fig. 4-6 is selecting file IN-PAY-FILE, which is presumably defined in the DATA DIVISION, and is stating that it will reside on disk in file "PAYMAST.DAT''.

THE COMPLETE DIVISION

When all the statements described in this chapter are placed together, they form a complete ENVIRONMENT DIVISION. An example of this division is shown in Fig. 4-3.

QUESTIONS

1. What function does the ENVIRONMENT DIVISION perform?

2. List and describe the two sections contained in the ENVIRONMENT DIVISION.

3. Describe the difference between source code and object code.

4. Under what circumstances are the SOURCE-COMPUTER statement and OBJECT-COMPUTER statement most helpful?

5. What is the function of the INPUT-OUTPUT SECTION?

6. Where is the FILE-CONTROL SECTION located?

7. What is the purpose of the SELECT statement?

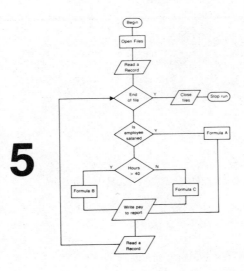

5

The DATA DIVISION

This chapter explains the third of the four COBOL divisions, the DATA DIVISION, and will include the procedures needed to define data files, internal variables and report layouts.

All files that are processed, and are variables that are referenced in a program must be defined in the DATA DIVISION. When a COBOL program is executed the computer reads through this division and establishes memory locations in primary memory for each defined variable. Once defined variables can be accessed and updated by commands in the PROCEDURE DIVISION. The DATA DIVISION is divided into two main sections: the FILE SECTION and the WORKING-STORAGE section. The FILE SECTION defines the program's data files, and the WORKING-STORAGE SECTION defines the non-file variables needed to execute the program.

THE FILE SECTION

The FILE SECTION is used to define the size and format of the data files being processed by the program. Even though this section is not required, it is almost always present because of the need for file access.

Each file used in the program must be defined with FD and 01 definition statements. FD stands for *File Description*, and addresses the file in terms of its size and physical storage characteristics. The 01 statement describes the format of the information contained in the file.

The FD Statement

The FD statement is used to define the file's name and storage characteristics, and is divided into four parts—the internal file name, RECORD CONTAINS clause, LABEL RECORDS clause, and DATA RECORD clause. The format of this statement and its four components are shown in Fig. 5-1.

The FD statement begins with the letters FD and the file name that will be used in the PROCE-DURE DIVISION to reference the file. This name must also have been identified by a SELECT state-

```
FD      filename
        RECORD CONTAINS [ integer-1 TO ] integer-2 CHARACTERS

        LABEL {RECORD IS  } {STANDARD}
              {RECORDS ARE} {OMMITTED}

        DATA  {RECORD IS  } record-name-1 [ record-name-2 ... ]
              {RECORDS ARE}
```

Fig. 5-1. FD statement format.

ment in the ENVIRONMENT DIVISION. It is the SELECT statement that connects the FD and 01 descriptions to the actual file on disk or tape. Figure 5-2 is an example of the first FD line.

The RECORD CONTAINS clause defines the minimum and maximum character size of the data records contained in the file. When a COBOL program is executed the computer uses these record lengths to set up buffers. Buffers are special locations in memory that serve as passage ways and holding areas through which data is passed on the route between the program and disk or tape drive. The record size stated in this clause must match the record size described in the 01 record definition. Figure 5-3 provides an example of the RECORD CONTAINS clause. The clause states that the record length will be between 50 and 80 characters. Generally, all records contained in a data file are the same length. This is true even for those files with many record formats. Therefore, the "TO integer-2" clause is seldomly used.

The third FD clause is the LABEL RECORD clause, which provides information about the physical attributes of the data file. When writing data onto a magnetic tape, the programmer has the option of beginning that tape with a header label. The

header label contains the tape number, which should be consistent with the number written on the outside of the tape reel. This number is used by the computer as a safeguard that the computer operator placed the correct tape on the drive. If the label exists the computer automatically compares the number on the tape label to the tape number requested by the application program. Processing will only continue if a match is made. The header label feature is generally not used for files residing on disk. Disk files are rarely taken off-line, so there is no operator intervention and no chance of operator error. The clause is shown in Fig. 5-4.

The DATA RECORD clause connects the data file to the data record descriptions. Figure 5-5 is an example of this final FD clause. Note that in the DATA RECORD clause example IN-PAYROLL-REC has been defined as the data record name. This name must tie into the 01 record description, below.

The 01 Record Definition Statement

Once a file's FD is complete the data records associated with that file must be described. This description is performed by an 01 statement. Figure 5-6 lists the record description of IN-

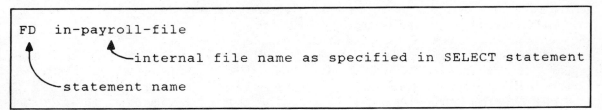

Fig. 5-2. First FD statement clause example.

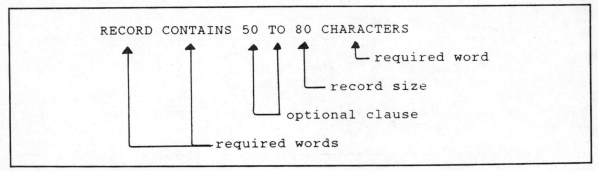

Fig. 5-3. RECORD CONTAINS clause example.

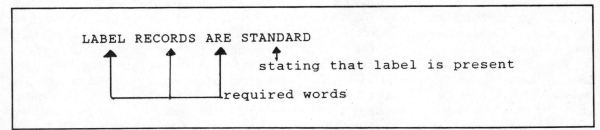

Fig. 5-4. LABEL RECORDS clause example.

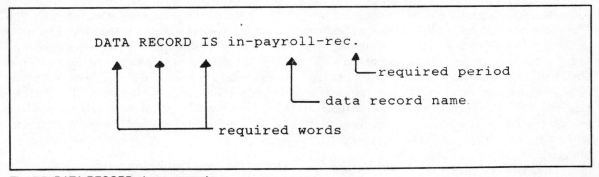

Fig. 5-5. DATA RECORD clause example.

PAYROLL-REC. In this example each line begins with a number, followed by a file name and optionally followed by a PIC clause. The format is described in Fig. 5-7.

Level numbers are used to define the relationship between the various field description lines. Level 01 has the special function of specifying the beginning of a logical record. Note that the data name in the 01 is the record name specified in the DATA RECORD clause of the FD statement. Level numbers from 2 to 99 are used to establish a hier-

archy among the other field definitions in the 01. There are therefore two types of field definitions: detail and rollups. Detail definitions describe one logical field of data. Rollups encompass more then one field, and are used to process groups of related data fields at one time.

When viewing or constructing a data record format it is easy to differentiate between detail and rollup definitions. Detail statements have PICTURE clauses and rollups do not. The size of a rollup is automatically calculated as the sum size of

```
01   in-payroll-rec.
     05 in-pay-emp-no                     PIC 9(5).
     05 in-pay-employee-name.
        10 in-pay-first name              PIC X(10).
        10 in-pay-middle-initial          PIC X.
        10 in-pay-last-name               PIC X(15).
     05 in-pay-address.
        10 in-pay-street                  PIC X(10).
        10 in-pay-city                    PIC X(10).
        10 in-pay-state                   PIC XX.
        10 in-pay-zip                     PIC X(9).
     05 in-pay-job-title                  PIC X(10).
     05 in-pay-hourly-wage                PIC 9999V99.
     05 in-pay-pay-type                   PIC X.
     05 in-pay-status                     PIC X.
     05 in-pay-pay-info.
        10 in-pay-gross-ytd               PIC 9(5)V99.
        10 in-pay-fed-wld                 PIC 9(5)V99.
        10 in-pay-state-wld               PIC 9(5)V99.
        10 in-pay-no-of-exemps            PIC 99.
        10 in-pay-other-wlds              PIC 9(5)V99.
```

Fig. 5-6. Payroll record definition.

the subordinate detail fields. As a result all rollups must have subordinate statements. Figure 5-8 pictorally illustrates the hierarchical structure described in the IN-PAYROLL-REC definition in Fig. 5-6.

As an example of this structure, IN-FIRST-NAME is considered a detail statement because it only includes one logical unit, the employee's first name. IN-EMPLOYEE-NAME is a rollup because it includes information relating to three fields: IN-FIRST-NAME, IN- MIDDLE-INITIAL, and IN-LAST-NAME.

The PICTURE clause describes the size and format of a data field and is required in all detail definition statements. This clause is one of the few reserved words in COBOL that may be abbreviated. The standard industry abbreviation is PIC; however, some compilers require an additional letter, making the word PICT. Figure 5-9 illustrates the format of the PICTURE clause.

The PICTURE clause is composed of two main sections: the work PICTURE (or PIC) and the field format. This format is divided into two parts, a format type and an optional format repeater. Figure 5-10 shows the PICTURE clause being used to define the employee number field. It contains an "X" as the PICTURE format type. The format type defines the category of data contained in the field. There are three possible data types: alpha, numeric, and alphanumeric. Alpha variables are specified by

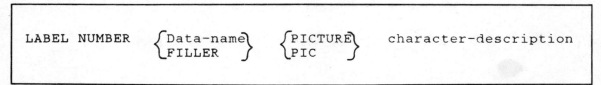

```
LABEL NUMBER   ⎰Data-name⎱   ⎰PICTURE⎱   character-description
               ⎱FILLER   ⎭   ⎱PIC    ⎭
```

Fig. 5-7. Field description format.

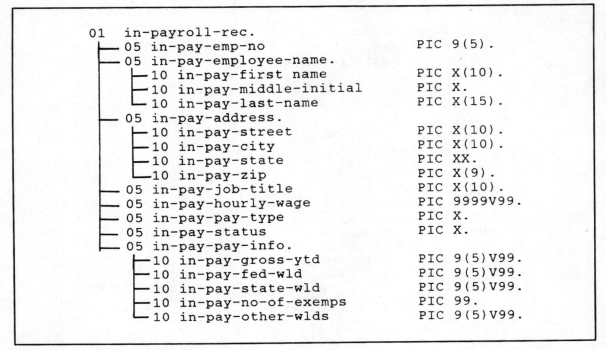

```
    01   in-payroll-rec.
       ─ 05 in-pay-emp-no                PIC 9(5).
       ─ 05 in-pay-employee-name.
          ─10 in-pay-first name          PIC X(10).
          ─10 in-pay-middle-initial      PIC X.
          └─10 in-pay-last-name          PIC X(15).
       ─ 05 in-pay-address.
          ─10 in-pay-street              PIC X(10).
          ─10 in-pay-city                PIC X(10).
          ─10 in-pay-state               PIC XX.
          └─10 in-pay-zip                PIC X(9).
       ─ 05 in-pay-job-title             PIC X(10).
       ─ 05 in-pay-hourly-wage           PIC 9999V99.
       ─ 05 in-pay-pay-type              PIC X.
       ─ 05 in-pay-status                PIC X.
       ─ 05 in-pay-pay-info.
          ─10 in-pay-gross-ytd           PIC 9(5)V99.
          ─10 in-pay-fed-wld             PIC 9(5)V99.
          ─10 in-pay-state-wld           PIC 9(5)V99.
          ─10 in-pay-no-of-exemps        PIC 99.
          └─10 in-pay-other-wlds         PIC 9(5)V99.
```

Fig. 5-8. Payroll record structure chart.

an A, and may only include the letters A through Z. Numeric variables are specified by the number 9 and may contain only numbers. Alphanumeric variables are specified by the letter X and may contain letters, numbers, and special characters.

The format repeater specifies the length of the variable being defined. This length may be stated in two ways. The first, by placing a number in parentheses, is shown in Fig. 5-10, and denotes a length of five characters. The second way is to specify the variable length by repeating the format descriptor. PIC XXXXX would also denote an alphanumeric string of length five. Industry standard, however, generally requires that variables of three characters or less use a repeated data type,

and variables of four of more characters use a number in parentheses.

When defining numeric variables there is an additional consideration—the decimal point. The decimal point can be defined logically and physically; the definition used will depend on the format of the data file being processed. If the data file physically contains a period, the programmer must specify the column in which the period resides. PIC 999.99 specifies that the field is a numeric variable with three places before the decimal point, a period, and two places after the decimal point. In many cases, however, the period is not physically placed in the data file; the programmer must know where the decimal point would logically be placed. This is a

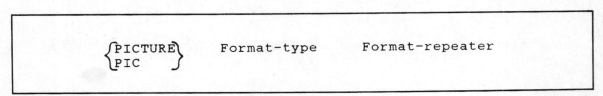

Fig. 5-9. PICTURE clause format.

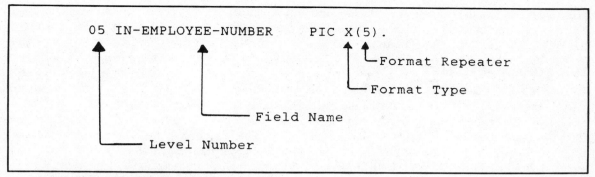

Fig. 5-10. PICTURE clause format in correct context.

very common technique used to save space in the data file. The letter V is used to show the logical placement of the decimal point. PIC 999V99 specifies a numeric variable of length five with three whole numbers, a logical decimal point and two places after the decimal point. Figure 5-11 illustrates various field formats.

The PICTURE clause also contains special for-

As Contained Data File	PICTURE Clause	Seen By COBOL	Explanation
ABC	PIC XXX	ABC	Alphanumeric of length three
ABC	PIC X(3)	ABC	Alphanumeric of length three
B25	PIC X(3)	B25	Alphanumeric of length three
350	PIC 999	350	Numeric variable of length three
350	PIC 9(3)	350	Numeric variable of length three
123.45	PIC 999.99	123.45	Numeric of length three with a decimal point physically placed in the data file
12345	PIC 9(3)V99	123.45	Numeric variable of length three and two decimal places without a decimal actually placed in the file.

Fig. 5-11. Numeric PICTURE clause examples.

mats that allow data to be neatly printed on reports. These output formats will be discussed as part of the WORKING-STORAGE section.

THE WORKING-STORAGE SECTION

The WORKING-STORAGE SECTION is located in the DATA DIVISION, following the FILE SECTION. It defines all the internal non-file variables needed to execute the program. These variables are defined in a manner similar to the data record definitions in the FILE SECTION. Figure 5-12 is an example of the WORKING-STORAGE SECTION.

Lines 332-343 of Fig. 5-12 are the internal program variables needed for the PROCEDURE DIVISION to perform the required programming tasks. These lines are specifically arranged for documentation purposes. Lines 332 and 333 are the program flags. Lines 335-340 are counters and totalers. Common variable types should be grouped together and documented appropriately; the grouping of these catagories, however, varies from data center to data center.

Program flags assist in the control of program logic. These flags are regular variables used to help manage end of-file conditions, error-trapping and other programming scenarios. For example, Line 333 defines the flag used to assist in transferring program control when all payroll master file records have been read and processed. The VALUE IS clause included in this line is used to give a variable an initial value. In this case, the variable ANY-MORE-RECORDS is initially loaded with the value "YES." The VALUE clause must be placed after the PICTURE clause, and is outlined in Fig. 5-13.

Lines 335-340 are the totalers used to sum gross pay, federal taxes, state taxes, other deductions, and net pay. These fields are defined as numeric variables with five numbers to the left and two numbers to right of the decimal point. These fields could have been defined individually as a 01 and the result would have been the same. The 01-05 format is used to improve the readability of the WORKING-STORAGE SECTION.

The payroll report titles and report column headings are defined in lines 344-359. The varia-

ble name used to describe these titles and headings is the word *filler*. FILLER is a COBOL reserved word, which acts as a placeholder by filling space between variables. In the report title definition FILLER is used to format the print line. The words specified in the VALUE IS clause are the words actually used in the report titles.

Lines 361-373 define the detail print line format. The PICTURE clauses in these lines are used to format the numeric variables being printed. This formatting feature is available to provide the flexibility needed to maximize report readability. Figure 5-14 outlines the possible editing options.

The Z is used to suppress the printing of leading zeros. Leading zeros are the zeros printed to the left of a number. For example, if a numeric field is defined as 9(5), then regardless of the variable value the computer stores the value in a five digit field. As a result, the number 455 would be stored in the computer and printed on the report as 00455. This full number format provides the correct value, but is hard to read and is not visually pleasing. Figure 5-15 gives some examples of zero suppression.

The comma specifies that, if appropriate, a comma will be printed in the numeric field. If zero suppression is used and there are no non-zero values to the left of the comma, the comma will not be printed. Figure 5-16 illustrates the use of the comma as an editing option.

A single dollar sign instructs COBOL to place a dollar sign at the specified print location. This figure will be printed regardless of the variable's value or size. Figure 5-17 shows examples to the single $ function.

The multi-dollar sign editing option combines zero suppression with a floating dollar sign. Like the Z, leading zeroes are not printed, but a dollar sign is placed next to the left-most non-zero number. Unlike the option Z, however, there must be room to print the dollar sign. Therefore, a format of six dollar signs can print only a five digit number. The sixth space is reserved for the $. Figure 5-18 outlines the usage of this option.

Single plus and minus signs may be used as a number prefix or suffix. The minus sign format will only print when the number is negative. The plus

```
330    WORKING-STORAGE SECTION.
331
332    01 PROGRAM-FLAGS-AND-COUNTERS.
333       05 ANY-MORE-RECORDS          PIC XXX VALUE IS 'YES'.
334       05 NEY-PAY                    PIC 9(5)V99.
335       05 PAGE-NO                    PIC 999.
336
337    01 PROGRAM-TOTALERS.
338       05 TOT-GROSS-PAY                 PIC 9(5)V99.
339       05 TOT-FED-TAX                   PIC 9(5)V99.
340       05 TOT-STATE-TAX                 PIC 9(5)V99.
341       05 TOT-OTHER-TAX                 PIC 9(5)V99.
342       05 TOT-NEY-PAY                   PIC 9(5)V99.
343
344    01 REPORT-TITLE.
345       05 FILLER    PIC X(10) VALUE IS 'PAYLIST".
346       05 FILLER    PIC X(20).
347       05 FILLER    PIC X(20) VALUE IS 'PAYROLL LISTING'.
348       05 FILLER    PIC X(20).
349       05 FILLER    PIC X(5) VALUE IS 'PAGE:'.
350       05 PAGE-NUM PIC ZZ9.
351
352    01 REPORT-HEADINGS.
353       05 FILLER     PIC X(25) VALUE IS 'NAME'.
354       05 FILLER     PIC XX.
355       05 FILLER     PIC X(10) VALUE IS 'GROSS PAY'.
356       05 FILLER     PIC X(10) VALUE IS 'FED TAX'.
357       05 FILLER     PIC X(10) VALUE IS `STATE TAX'.
368       05 FILLER     PIC X(10) VALUE IS 'OTHER TAX'.
368       05 FILLER     PIC X(10) VALUE IS 'NET PAY'.
360
361    01 REPORT-DETAIL.
362       05 OUT-LAST-NAME          PIC X(15).
363       05 FILLER                 PIC X.
364       05 OUT-FIRST-NAME         PIC X(9).
365       05 FILLER                 PIC X.
366       05 OUT-GROSS-PAY          PIC ZZ,ZZ9.99.
367       05 FILLER                 PIC X.
368       05 OUT-FED-TAX            PIC ZZ,ZZ9.99.
369       05 FILLER                 PIC X.
370       05 OUT-STATE-TAX          PIC ZZ,ZZ9.99.
371       05 FILLER                 PIC X.
372       05 OUT-OTHER-TAX          PIC ZZ,ZZ9.99.
373       05 FILLER                 PIC X.
374       05 OUT-NET-PAY            PIC ZZ,ZZ9.99.
```

Fig. 5-12. WORKING-STORAGE SECTION example.

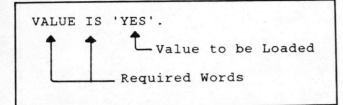

```
VALUE IS 'YES'.
```

Value to be Loaded

Required Words

Fig. 5-13. The VALUE IS clause.

sign will print + if the number is positive and − if the number is negative. If a single plus or dash is specified in the PICTURE clause the appropriate character will print in the defined position. Figure 5-19 illustrates the use of these two options.

The multiple plus and minus signs may be used

OPTION	EXPLANATION
Z	To suppress the printing of the left most zeros
,	To print a comma where specified, such as between the hundreds and thousands column
$	To place a dollar sign in a specified column
$$$$	To zero suppress the printing of left most zeros and place a dollar sign next to the highest printed digit
-	To print a minus sign in a specified position if the number being printed is negative
------	To zero suppress left most zeros and place a minus sign next to the highest printed digit if the number is negative
+	To place a plus or minus sign at a specified location. If the number printed is positive, a plus sign will appear. If the number is negative, a minus sign will print.
+++++	To suppress the printing of leading zeros and place a plus or minus sign next to the highest printed digit.
Key Stoke	Letters and other characters can be inserted and thus printed within a numeric field
B	To place a blank space in a specified column

Fig. 5-14. Valid PICTURE Editing options.

Value	PICTURE Clause	Output
12345	PIC 9(5)	12345
12345	PIC Z(4)9	12345
1234	PIC 9(5)	01234
1234	PIC ZZZZ9	1234
123	PIC 9(5)	00123
123	PIC ZZZZ9	123
0	PIC 9(5)	00000
0	PIC ZZZZ9	0
0	Z(5)	Nothing will print

Fig. 5-15. Zero suppression examples.

Value	PICTURE Clause	Output
1280	PIC Z,ZZ9	1,280
280	PIC Z,ZZ9	280
1234567	PIC Z,ZZZ,ZZ9	1,234,567
123456	PIC Z,ZZZ,ZZ9	123,456

Fig. 5-16. Comma as a formatting option.

Value	PICTURE Clause	Output
123	PIC $Z,ZZZ,ZZ9	$ 123
12345	PIC $Z,ZZZ,ZZ9	$ 12,345
1234567	PIC Z$,ZZZ,ZZ9	$1,234,567

Fig. 5-17. Single dollar sign formatting.

Value	PICTURE Clause	Output
123	PIC $$,$$$,$$9	$123
12345	PIC $$,$$$,$$9	$12,345
123456	PIC $$,$$$,$$9	$123,456
1234567	PIC $$,$$$,$$9	$1,234,567

Fig. 5-18. Multi-dollar-sign formatting.

```
       Value              PICTURE Clause            Output
  --------------      --------------------      ------------

        12             PIC  -Z,ZZ9                     12
       -12             PIC  -Z,ZZ9               -     12
        123            PIC  -Z,ZZ9                    123
       -123            PIC  -Z,ZZ9               -    123
       1234            PIC  -Z,ZZ9                  1,234
      -1234            PIC  -Z,ZZ9                 -1,234
       -12             PIC  Z9-                       12-
        12             PIC  +Z,ZZ9               +     12
        12             PIC  99+                       12+
       -12             PIC  99+                       12-
       -12             PIC  +Z,ZZ9               -     12
```

Fig. 5-19. Single minus and plus sign examples.

```
       Value              PICTURE Clause            Output
  --------------      --------------------      ------------

        12             PIC   --,--9                   12
       -12             PIC   --,--9                  -12
       -123            PIC   --,--9                 -123
      -1234            PIC   --,--9               -1,234
        12             PIC   ++,++9                 +12
       -12             PIC   ++,++9                 -12
       1234            PIC   ++,++9               +1,234
      -1234            PIC   ++,++9               -1,234
```

Fig. 5-20. Floating plus and minus sign examples.

```
       Value              PICTURE Clause            Output
  --------------      --------------------      ------------

       123             PIC 999B9                     12 3
       1234            PIC 999B9                    132 4
       122383          PIC 99/99/99              12/23/83
```

Fig. 5-21. Blanks and special characters insert example.

to combine the functions of zero suppression and a floating sign character. As with the single plus sign and minus sign, the + and − symbols will print under the same circumstances. The difference is where the symbol is placed. In this case the sign symbol prints in the space directly to the left of the variable's value. Figure 5-20 illustrates this feature.

Spaces and other characters can be printed in the middle of numeric and alphanumeric fields.

Spaces are inserted into the field by placing a B in the PICTURE CLAUSE. Other characters may be inserted by placing that character in the PICTURE clause. Figure 5-21 illustrates these features.

THE COMPLETE DIVISION

Figure 5-22 is an example of a complete DATA DIVISION.

```
DATA DIVISION.

FILE SECTION.

FD  in-payroll-file
    RECORD CONTAINS 80 CHARACTERS
    LABEL RECORDS ARE STANDARD
    DATA RECORD IS in-payroll-rec.

01  in-payroll-rec.
    05 in-pay-emp-no                    PIC 9(5).
    05 in-pay-employee-name.
       10 in-pay-first name             PIC X(10).
       10 in-pay-middle-initial         PIC X.
       10 in-pay-last-name              PIC X(15).
    05 in-pay-address.
       10 in-pay-street                 PIC X(10).
       10 in-pay-city                   PIC X(10).
       10 in-pay-state                  PIC XX.
       10 in-pay-zip                    PIC X(9).
    05 in-pay-job-title                 PIC X(10).
    05 in-pay-hourly-wage               PIC 9999V99.
    05 in-pay-pay-type                  PIC X.
    05 in-pay-status                    PIC X.
    05 in-pay-pay-info.
       10 in-pay-gross-ytd              PIC 9(5)V99.
       10 in-pay-fed-wld                PIC 9(5)V99.
       10 in-pay-state-wld              PIC 9(5)V99.
       10 in-pay-no-of-exemps           PIC 99.
       10 in-pay-other-wlds             PIC 9(5)V99.

FD  out-report-file
    RECORD CONTAINS 132 CHARACTERS
    LABEL RECORDS ARE STANDARD
    DATA RECORD IS out-rep-rec.
```

Fig. 5-22. Complete DATA DIVISION example.

```
01  out-rep-rec                           PIC X(132).

WORKING-STORAGE SECTION.

01 PROGRAM-FLAGS-AND-COUNTERS.
   05 ANY-MORE-RECORDS              PIC XXX VALUE IS 'YES'.
   05 NEY-PAY                       PIC 9(5)V99.
   05 PAGE-NO                       PIC 999.

01 PROGRAM-TOTALERS.
   05 TOT-GROSS-PAY                    PIC 9(5)V99.
   05 TOT-FED-TAX                      PIC 9(5)V99.
   05 TOT-STATE-TAX                    PIC 9(5)V99.
   05 TOT-OTHER-TAX                    PIC 9(5)V99.
   05 TOT-NEY-PAY                      PIC 9(5)V99.


01 REPORT-TITLE.
   05 FILLER   PIC X(10) VALUE IS 'PAYLIST".
   05 FILLER   PIC X(20).
   05 FILLER   PIC X(20) VALUE IS 'PAYROLL LISTING'.
   05 FILLER   PIC X(20).
   05 FILLER   PIC X(5) VALUE IS 'PAGE:'.
   05 PAGE-NUM PIC ZZ9.

01 REPORT-HEADINGS.
   05 FILLER    PIC X(25) VALUE IS 'NAME'.
   05 FILLER    PIC XX.
   05 FILLER    PIC X(10) VALUE IS 'GROSS PAY'.
   05 FILLER    PIC X(10) VALUE IS 'FED TAX'.
   05 FILLER    PIC X(10) VALUE IS `STATE TAX'.
   05 FILLER    PIC X(10) VALUE IS 'OTHER TAX'.
   05 FILLER    PIC X(10) VALUE IS 'NET PAY'.

01 REPORT-DETAIL.
   05 OUT-LAST-NAME          PIC X(15).
   05 FILLER                 PIC X.
   05 OUT-FIRST-NAME         PIC X(9).
   05 FILLER                 PIC X.
   05 OUT-GROSS-PAY          PIC ZZ,ZZ9.99.
   05 FILLER                 PIC X.
   05 OUT-FED-TAX            PIC ZZ,ZZ9.99.
   05 FILLER                 PIC X.
   05 OUT-STATE-TAX          PIC ZZ,ZZ9.99.
   05 FILLER                 PIC X.
   05 OUT-OTHER-TAX          PIC ZZ,ZZ9.99.
   05 FILLER                 PIC X.
   05 OUT-NET-PAY            PIC ZZ,ZZ9.99.
```

QUESTIONS

1. What function does the DATA DIVISION perform?

2. List and describe the two DATA DIVISION sections.

3. What is the function of the FD statement, and where is it located?

4. List and describe the four FD statement clauses.

5. How does a field definition statement establish a field hierarchy in the record?

6. What is the difference between detail fields and roll-up fields?

7. What is a PICTURE clause and how is it used?

8. How are numeric, alpha, and alphanumeric data types portrayed within a PICTURE clause?

9. What is the difference between PIC 99V9 and PIC 99.9?

10. What is the function of the WORKING-STORAGE SECTION?

11. What are program flags?

12. How are counters and totalers defined?

13. How are report titles and headings defined?

14. What is zero suppression and why is it used?

15. What function does a comma play in numeric report formatting?

16. In what ways can a dollar sign be placed at the beginning of a numeric field?

17. What is the difference between a plus sign and a minus sign with regard to numeric formatting?

18. How are blank spaces placed in numeric fields during report printing?

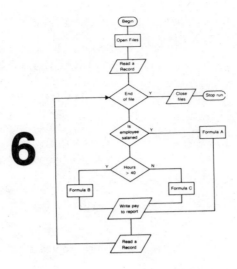

6

The PROCEDURE DIVISION

This chapter explains the final COBOL division, the PROCEDURE DIVISION. This will finish your introduction and leave you with a working knowledge of almost all the COBOL statements and commands. You will then go on to learn the procedures and techniques that maximize COBOL's power and expand its flexibility.

The first three divisions provided documentation, a look at the program's external environment, and information about the logical and physical attributes of files and variables. The PROCEDURE DIVISION combines this information with procedural logic. The *procedures* are the rules and algorithms needed to update files, display menus, generate reports, and perform countless other functions. The statements used to perform these functions are called "action verbs." The verbs tell the computer what files to access, how and what to process, and where to place the information when processing is complete.

This division's statements can be divided into ten subjects: mathematics, completion, location definition, terminal interface, data movement, string manipulation, conditional logic, branching, file processing, and table handling.

The mathematical capabilities of COBOL are designed to meet the needs of business data processing. As a result, COBOL is able to solve complex financial-oriented equations through addition, subtraction, multiplication, division, exponential notation and other mathematical procedures. However, it does not include geometric and scientific functions such as tangent and cosine.

The completion category contains one verb, the STOP statement. COBOL programs stop executing for two reasons: first, the bottom of the program has been reached and there are no more statements to process, or second, by reaching a STOP statement somewhere in the program.

Location definition statements are better known as *paragraph names*. The names serve as reference points used by the branching statements when moving from point to point in the program. They are also used to divide the PROCEDURE DIVISION into bit-size single function segments.

Terminal interface statements let information pass between executing programs and video display terminals. This feature is essential when programming on-line applications. For example, when executing a program menu the menu options are displayed on the screen, then the user selects and enters a value. This value is accepted and interpreted by the program.

Data movement commands provide the ability to move information from place to place. This function can perform the simple task of moving a value from variable to variable or perform complex data movement by simultaneously moving many data values at one time.

String manipulation statements concatenate, divide, analyze and modify alphanumeric values. These functions are primarily used to format information before it is displayed to the user (for example, placing dashes in a social security number), to analyze data input for validation purposes, and to perform other field manipulation functions.

Conditional logic is the ability to appropriately respond to circumstances. The IF statement provides this function by interpreting various conditions and performing the needed action. Applications like payroll are very demanding on the decision-making capabilities of a language, which must understand simple questions like "Did the employee work more than forty hours?" Additionally, it must be able to wade through the complex algorithms needed to calculate federal, state and local tax withholdings.

Procedural branching is the process of transferring program control from one statement to another. It is this ability that facilitates looping and automatically maintains the counters and pointers needed to program in a structured format. This category includes two types of statements: transfer of control and subroutining. Transfer of control statements permanently pass control from one place in the program to another. Subroutine statements temporarily allow execution of other sections of the code, with the expectation that control will return to the original location.

The file processing statements manage the input and output of data files. These statements prepare the files for use, facilitate data reading and writing, and handle all the housekeeping associated with data file manipulation.

Table handling is the process of loading, manipulating, and processing data contained in a program. Data tables are groups of related data elements defined in the DATA DIVISION as arrays, by use of an OCCURS clause. Arrays are stored in primary computer memory and can be accessed very quickly by the program. This feature can in some cases improve program performance and increase functionality.

COBOL MATHEMATICS

COBOL contains five arithmetic statements: ADD, SUBTRACT, MULTIPLY, DIVIDE, and COMPUTE. The first four statements perform the indicated actions. The COMPUTE statement performs the complex mathematics required to solve special business and financially-oriented calculations.

The ADD Statement

The ADD statement adds two or more numbers together. It can also be used to automatically perform rounding and error control functions. Figures 6-1 and 6-2 describe the ADD statement formats. Both formats begin with the verb name "ADD." They then list the variables being added. The variables may be constants, literals, or just other variables. They must all be defined in the DATA DIVISION as a numeric format.

The next clause is where the two formats differ. Format 1 uses the word GIVING. This required word states that the variable that follows (identifier-n) will be given the sum of the numbers previously specified. Format 2 requires the word "TO," followed by a variable. In this format the variables previously mentioned are added to identifier-n. The difference between GIVING and TO is that GIVING replaces the value in identifier-n and TO adds to the value in identifier-n.

The rounding option is not required. Its function is to appropriately round the value placed in the output variable identifier-n. This function may

```
         ADD  ⎧identifier-1⎫   ⎧identifier-2⎫   GIVING identifier-3
              ⎩literal-1   ⎭   ⎩literal-2   ⎭

         [ ROUNDED ] [ ON ERROR imperative statement ]
```

Fig. 6-1. ADD statement format.

be used when identifier-n has fewer decimal points than any of the numbers being added. For example, if 5.5 and 1.17 are added the total is 6.67. If this value is placed in a variable with a format of "PIC 99V9," the right-most digits must either be rounded or truncated. The rounding function rounds the number to the nearest tenth, 6.7. The absence of the rounding function causes the value to be truncated and stored as 6.6.

The ON SIZE ERROR option is also optional. It performs the specified error statements if the numbers being added are too large to fit in the output variable. For example, the sum of 50 and 60 is 110. If the addition output field was formatted as "PIC 99" the ON SIZE ERROR condition would be met and the imperative statements following the error clause would be executed.

The line below is an example of the GIVING format of the ADD statement.

ADD federal-tax, state-tax GIVING total-tax.

FEDERAL-TAX and STATE-TAX are added together and the sum is placed in TOTAL-TAX. For example, if FEDERAL-TAX had a value of 50 and STATE-TAX had a value of 25, TOTAL-TAX would be given a value of 75.

Figure 6-2 is an example of the TO format of the ADD statement.

ADD federal-tax TO total-tax

FEDERAL-TAX is being added to the value currently stored in TOTAL-TAX. For example, if prior to the above addition FEDERAL-TAX had a value of 20 and TOTAL-TAX had a value of 50, the new value in TOTAL_TAX would be 70.

Table 6-1 provides additional ADD statement examples.

The SUBTRACT Statement

The SUBTRACT statement is used to subtract one number from another. Like the ADD statement, SUBTRACT has two options; one that places the answer in the variable being subtracted from, and a format that places the answer in a third variable. Figure 6-3 outlines the SUBTRACT statement formats.

The line below is an example of the first subtract format. In this example TOTAL-TAX is being subtracted from PAY-AMOUNT, and the resulting value is being placed in PAY-AMOUNT. If PAY-AMOUNT was 10 and TOTAL-TAX was three, the resulting value in PAY-AMOUNT would be seven.

SUBTRACT TOTAL-TAX FROM PAY-AMOUNT ROUNDED ON SIZE ERROR GOTO ERROR-PARAGRAPH.

```
         ADD  ⎧identifier-1⎫   ⎧identifier-2⎫    to identifier-3
              ⎩literal-1   ⎭   ⎩literal-2   ⎭

              [ ROUNDED ] [ON ERROR imperative statement ]
```

Fig. 6-2. A second ADD statement format.

Table 6-1. Additional ADD Statement Examples.

Statement	Before				After			
	A	B	C	D	A	B	C	D
ADD A TO B	1	2			1	3		
ADD A, B TO C	1	2	3		1	2	6	
ADD A, B GIVING C	1	2	3		1	2	3	
ADD A, B TO C ROUNDED	1	2	3		1	2	3	
ADD A, B, C TO D	1	2	3	4	1	2	3	10

The line below is an example of the second SUBTRACT format. In this example TOTAL-TAX is subtracted from GROSS-PAY and the resulting answer is placed in NET-PAY. When using this format the GROSS-PAY field does not change. If GROSS-PAY had a value of 10 and TOTAL-TAX had a value of three, the values would be GROSS-PAY equals 10, TOTAL-TAX equals three, and NET-PAY equals seven.

SUBTRACT TOTAL-TAX FROM GROSS-PAY GIVING NET-PAY.

Table 6-2 contains additional examples of the SUBTRACT statement.

The MULTIPLY Statement

The MULTIPLY statement is used to multiply two numbers. This statement also comes in two formats, one with the word "GIVING" and one without. Figure 6-4, presents the multiply statement formats. The lines below illustrate the two formats.

The line below shows an example of the first

```
SUBTRACT {identifier-1} {identifier-2} FROM identifier-3 [ ROUNDED ]
         {literal-1   } {literal-2   }

    [ ON SIZE ERROR ]  imperative statement


SUBTRACT   {identifier-1} {identifier-2}  FROM    identifier-n
           {literal-1   } {literal-2   }

    GIVING identifier-m [ ROUNDED ]

    [ ON SIZE ERROR imperative statement ]
```

Fig. 6-3. SUBTRACT formats.

```
MULTIPLY   {identifier-1} BY identifier-2   [ ROUNDED ]
           {literal-1   }

   [ ON SIZE ERROR imperative statement ]


MULTIPLY   identifier-1   BY identifier-2   GIVING identifier-3

   [ ROUNDED ] [ ON SIZE ERROR imperative statement ]
```

Fig. 6-4. MULTIPLY statement formats.

MULTIPLY format. In this example some lucky employee is receiving an increase in salary. GROSS-PAY is multiplied by PERCENT-RAISE and the product is in GROSS-PAY, replacing the old GROSS-PAY value. Also, the rounding option is used to round off the right-most digits so the generated answer can fit in the GROSS-PAY field definition, specified in the DATA DIVISION. Given this scenario, if the employee's old gross pay was $10,000 and he received a 10 percent increase (PERCENT-RAISE field would be 1.10), the new value placed in GROSS-PAY would be $11,000.

MULTIPLY GROSS-PAY BY PERCENT-RAISE ROUNDED

The line below illustrates the use of the second

MULTIPLY format. In this example an employee's bonus is being calculated and the product placed in EMP-BONUS. The employee's bonus will be equal to 10 percent of GROSS-PAY. Note that the literal ".10" is used in the bonus calculation. Placing actual values that have the potential to change in the code is not considered a good programming practice; to change these values the program must be edited and recompiled. However, it is valid from a syntactical viewpoint.

MULTIPLY GROSS-PAY BY .10 GIVING EMP-BONUS

Table 6-3 provides additional examples of the MULTIPLY statement.

Table 6-2. Additional SUBTRACT Statement Formats.

Statement	Before				After			
	A	B	C	D	A	B	C	D
SUBTRACT A FROM B	1	2			1	1		
SUBTRACT A, B FROM C	1	2	5		1	2	2	
SUBTRACT A FROM B GIVING C	1	2	3		1	2	1	
SUBTRACT A, B FROM C GIVING D	1	2	5	7	1	2	5	2

Table 6-3. Additional MULTIPLY Statement Formats.

Statement	Before				After			
	A	B	C	D	A	B	C	D
MULTIPLY A BY B	2	4			8	4		
MULTIPLY A BY B ROUNDED	2	4			8	4		
MULTIPLY A BY B GIVING C	2	4	6		2	4	8	

The DIVIDE Statement

The function of the DIVIDE statement is to perform division. Unlike the other mathematical statements, DIVIDE has three formats: one without the word GIVING and two with it. All three divide formats have one feature in common—the ability to save the divided remainder. The remainder is the value left over after the division process has been completed. Figure 6-5 outlines the three DIVIDE formats.

The first DIVIDE format does not include the GIVING clause. In this case identifier-1 is divided into identifier-2 and the answer is placed in identifier-2. For example, in the line below GROSS-PAY will be converted from a yearly to monthly basis by dividing GROSS-PAY by 12. If before execution GROSS-PAY has a value of $12,000 it would contain the value of $1,000 after the division was performed.

DIVIDE 12 INTO GROSS-PAY

The second DIVIDE format also divides identifier-1 into identifier-2. In this case identifier-2

```
DIVIDE  {identifier-1}   INTO identifier-2   [ ROUNDED ]
        {literal-1    }

   [ ON SIZE ERROR imperative statement ]


DIVIDE  {identifier-1}   INTO  {identifier-2}   GIVING identifier-3
        {literal-1    }        {literal-2    }

   [ ROUNDED ] [ ON SIZE ERROR imperative statement ]


DIVIDE   identifier-1   BY   identifier-2   GIVING   identifier-3

   [ ROUNDED ] [ ON ERROR SIZE imperative statement ]
```

Fig. 6-5. Three DIVIDE formats.

is left unchanged and the answer is placed in identifier-3. Using the scenario of changing GROSS-PAY from a yearly to monthly basis, when dividing the annual GROSS-PAY by 12 the answer of $1,000 is placed in MONTH-PAY. This example is shown below.

DIVIDE 12 INTO GROSS-PAY GIVING MONTH-PAY

The third DIVIDE format replaces the "INTO" clause with the word "BY." Here identifier-2 is divided into identifier-1. The line below produces the same results as the line above. Note that the 12 and GROSS-PAY fields have been reversed and the INTO clause has been replaced by the word "BY."

DIVIDE GROSS-PAY BY 12 GIVING MONTH-PAY

Table 6-4 provides additional examples of the DIVIDE statement.

The COMPUTE Statement

The COMPUTE statement lets mathematical equations be expressed in a standard algebraic format. The lines below outline the syntax of this statement.

COMPUTE identifier-1 = arithmetic expression [ROUNDED] [ON SIZE ERROR imperative statement]

The format for the COMPUTE statement is the word COMPUTE followed by the variable into which the answer will be placed. This is followed by an equals sign and the mathematical expression being performed. For example, the line shown below divides GROSS-PAY by 12 and places the answer in MONTH-PAY.

COMPUTE MONTH-PAY = GROSS-PAY / 12

This statement can be used to solve complex expressions through the use of multiple operations. The line below illustrates the use of the COMPUTE statement to calculate gross pay for a door-to-door salesman.

GROSS-PAY = (HOURS-WORKED * HOURS-PAY-RATE) + ((SALES-VOLUME – SALES-RETURNS) * COMMISSION-RATE)

Table 6-5 outlines the mathematical operations that may be used with the COMPUTE statement. The square root is not included as a valid operation; a square root can, however, be performed

Table 6-4. Additional DIVIDE Statement Examples.

Statement	Before				After			
	A	B	C	D	A	B	C	D
DIVIDE 5 INTO A	10				2			
DIVIDE A INTO B	5	10			5	2		
DIVIDE A INTO B GIVING C	2	6	9		2	6	3	
DIVIDE 2 INTO A GIVING B	4	7			4	2		
DIVIDE A BY 2 GIVING B	4	7			4	2		

Table 6-5. Valid COMPUTE Arithmetic Operators.

COBOL Format	Arithmetic Operation
+	ADDITION
–	SUBTRACTION
*	MULTIPLICATION
/	DIVISION
**	RAISING TO A POWER

through exponentiation (raising to a power). This is done by raising a number to the .5 power. Remember, powers and square roots are reverse operations, similar to the relationship between multiplication and division. As an example, the COMPUTE statement "COMPUTE PAY = 9 ** .5" calculates the square root of nine. The answer three is placed in the field PAY.

COBOL interprets equations in a way consistent with standard mathematical practices. These practices dictate the way equations should be solved, in three passes from left to right. The first pass calculates exponentiation. The second pass calculates multiplication and division, and the last pass performs addition and subtraction. In many cases, however, this order of operation will not correctly calculate the equation. Therefore, parentheses are used to tailor the operational order. Parentheses are given the highest priority and are always calculated first. In the example equation (A + B)*C, A and B are added together and then the sum is multiplied by C. Without the parentheses B would first be multiplied by C and then the product would be added to A. Table 6-6 provides additional examples of the COMPUTE statement.

PROGRAM COMPLETION

There is one program completion statement:

Table 6-6. Additional COMPUTE Statement Examples.

Statement	Before				After			
	A	B	C	D	A	B	C	D
COMPUTE A = B + C	1	2	3		5	2	3	
COMPUTE A = B – C	1	7	4		3	7	4	
COMPUTE A = (B + C) * D	6	1	3	2	8	1	3	2
COMPUTE A = B / C	4	6	2		3	6	2	
COMPUTE A = B ** C	2	3	2		9	3	2	

STOP RUN. The execution of this statement will terminate the running of a program, close any files left open, cancel any pending subroutine calls, and release any allocated computer memory so it may be used for other purposes.

Unlike in any other programming language, the STOP command does not have to be the last statement in the program. However, because of its function it will always be the last to be executed.

As a general rule of programming style, the STOP statement should not be used to close open data files. The CLOSE statement is the correct way to terminate a program's relationship with a data file. The STOP statement should be used strictly to end program execution and not for general program housekeeping. Some versions of COBOL do not properly perform these functions; as a result, files are not correctly closed and cannot be accessed by other programs.

LOCATION DEFINITIONS

The location definition statements are also known as paragraph names. Paragraph names serve two functions; first, they are are used as a program reference point when performing subroutines, conditional branching, and unconditional transfer of control. Second, they assist in the program's self-documentation by segmenting the PROCEDURE DIVISION processes into bite-size single function units.

When typing in a paragraph name the first character must be placed in the area-A column region and must meet the appropriate naming rules of the COBOL compiler being used. Generally, paragraph names may be from one to thirty charac-ters and may contain letters, numbers and dashes. Also, they must always end with a period. Figure 6-6 shows examples of valid paragraph names.

Each data processing department has its own paragraph naming practices. Industry standards suggest that each paragraph should have a beginning and ending name that explains the function being performed in the paragraph. This works very well in conjunction with the PERFORM statement. Also, many organizations require that all paragraph names be prefixed with a paragraph number. This number is usually added after the program is completed. Its function is to help programmers locate specific paragraphs in the PROCEDURE DIVISION by documenting the paragraph's location in the program. This is done by sequentially numbering the paragraphs in the order in which they physically reside. For example, if paragraph 100-CALCULATE-TOTALS transfers control to paragraph 300-PRINT-TOTALS, the programmer can easily locate the new paragraph name by referencing the name prefix. Following this scenario, paragraph 300-PRINT-TOTALS would be physically closer to the bottom of the program than 100-CALCULATE-TOTALS.

Paragraph names are a very important part of the structured programming methodologies. Programs should be segmented into distinct, logical units. Each of these units is identified by a paragraph name, and is only called and executed when its function is needed. Figure 6-7 illustrates the use of paragraph names.

TERMINAL INTERFACE STATEMENTS

Terminal interface statements are used to in-

```
100-VALIDATE-INPUT.

CALCULATE-TOTALS.

READ-DATA-INPUT-PARAGRAPH.

WRITE-TOTALS-PAR.

DATA-OUTPUT-OF-FORM-1040.
```

Fig. 6-6. Valid paragraph name examples.

```
PROCEDURE DIVISION

START-PAR.
     PERFORM 100-PROCESS-DATA-PAR THRU 100-PROCESS-DATA-PAR-END.
     STOP RUN.

100-PROCESS-DATA-PAR.
                .
                .
                .
                .
100-PROCESS-DATA-PAR-END.
```

Fig. 6-7. Paragraph name use example.

teractively accept and display information to and from the user. With the exception of data files, information can be entered into an executing program from job streams or files. A job stream is a list of predefined commands resembling a program that tells the computer what tasks to perform, and is usually associated with batch processing.

These command procedures, among other things, can automatically execute COBOL programs. For COBOL programs to execute correctly, they may require the input of special information, which may include the current accounting period, passwords, or special instructions that relate to decisions made in the program. These fields, passed from the job stream to the program, are called parameters. If the parameters change from day to day, such as a date or an accounting period, they are entered into the job stream at the time it is run. Otherwise the parameters can be permanently placed in the job stream as part of its logic. In either case the job stream will contain the pre-defined dialogue needed to execute the COBOL program being called.

Unlike programs executed by job streams, online systems do not require predefined answers. These programs interact directly with a user via the terminal. The design and development of these on-line systems will be discussed in depth in Chapter 10.

The two commands that facilitate COBOL's input and output processes are the ACCEPT and DISPLAY statements.

The ACCEPT Statement

The ACCEPT statement lets information be entered into a program. This input can be supplied from an on-line terminal, job stream, or other input device like a card reader or optical scanner. The format of the accept statement is shown below.

ACCEPT identifier-1.

When an ACCEPT statement is reached, the program stops executing and waits for the user, job stream, or other device to input a value. Once a value is entered, the variable specified in the ACCEPT statement is set to the value entered and processing continues. The lines below are examples of the accept statement.

ACCEPT GROSS-PAY.
ACCEPT NET-PAY.

The DISPLAY Statement

The DISPLAY statement is used to output information from a program into a job stream log or onto a user's terminal. When a job stream is run, a file is created to log all the processes and activities performed throughout its execution. In this mode the information displayed by the program will be entered as part of the log. When running in a job stream environment, the messages displayed by the COBOL program are generally short and relate to the success or failure of the program's execution. For example, if a program updates a sequential payroll master file, it reads the old master file and a transaction file. These files are then compared and a new master file is created. At the completion of this process the program should display a message stating the number of old master file records, the number of transaction records, the number of records on the new master file, and also that the program ran successfully. The line below shows the format of the DISPLAY statement, and Fig. 6-8 illustrates the master file update example.

$$\text{DISPLAY} \left\{ \begin{array}{l} \text{identifier-1} \\ \text{literal-1} \end{array} \right\} \left[\left\{ \begin{array}{l} \text{identifier-2} \\ \text{literal-2} \end{array} \right\} \right].$$

The DISPLAY statement can print both literals and variables. Literals are characters placed in either single or double quotation marks, depending on the compiler being used. These characters are displayed to the user in the exact way they have been represented in the program. Variables specified for display are not placed in quotation marks and must be defined as variables in the DATA DIVISION. When variables are specified for display, the data contained in the variable, and not the name of the variable, is printed. Figure 6-8 illustrates the display of both literals and variables.

DATA MOVEMENT STATEMENTS

One of COBOL's greatest assets is its ability to efficiently process large volumes of data. This processing efficiency is in large part realized by the use of the MOVE and MOVE CORRESPONDING statements. They are used to copy either a literal or a value contained in a variable to another variable. These statements, if used wisely, have the ability to move groups of fields by a single statement, separate large fields into subfields, and concatenate small fields into one large field. These seemingly diverse functions are performed simply by moving data in and out of various WORKING-STORAGE variables.

```
        Statements
        ---------------

    DISPLAY "OLD MASTER FILE RECORD COUNT: ",OLD-MAS-COUNT.
    DISPLAY "NUMBER OF TRANSACTIONS       : ",TRANS-COUNT.
    DISPLAY "NEW MASTER FILE RECORD COUNT: ",NEW-MAS-COUNT.
    DISPLAY " ".
    DISPLAY "NUMBER OF RECORDS MODIFIED   : ",MOD-COUNT.
    DISPLAY "NUMBER OF RECORDS ADDED      : ",ADD-COUNT.
    DISPLAY "NUMBER OF RECORDS DELETED    : ",DELETE-COUNT.

        output
        ----------


    OLD MASTER FILE RECORD COUNT:   1000
    NUMBER OF TRANSACTIONS     :    325
    NEW MASTER FILE RECORD COUNT:   1050

    NUMBER OF RECORDS MODIFIED :    225
    NUMBER OF RECORDS ADDED    :     75
    NUMBER OF RECORDS DELETED  :     25
```

Fig. 6-8. DISPLAY statement example.

```
        WORKING-STORAGE SECTION.
  01    INPUT-PAYROLL-REC.
        05 IN-EMPLOYEE-NAME.
           10 IN-LAST-NAME              PIC X(20).
           10 IN-FIRST-NAME             PIC X(15).
           10 IN-MIDDLE-INITIAL         PIC X.

  01    OUT-NEW-PAYROLL-REC.
        05 OUT-EMPLOYEE-NAME.
           10 OUT-LAST-NAME             PIC X(20).
           10 OUT-FIRST-NAME            PIC X(15).
           10 OUT-MIDDLE-INITIAL        PIC X.
```

Fig. 6-9. DATA DIVISION set-up example.

The MOVE Statement

The MOVE statement is used to copy data from one variable to another. The line below shows the statement format.

MOVE $\begin{Bmatrix} \text{identifier-1} \\ \text{literal-1} \end{Bmatrix}$ TO identifier-2

[, identifier-3]

Identifier-1 is the field containing the value to be moved. Identifier-2, and optionally identifier-3, and so on, are the recipients of identifier-1's information.

The line below is an example of the MOVE statement.

MOVE NET-PAY TO PAYMENT-AMOUNT.

The value of NET-PAY is being moved to the variable PAYMENT-AMOUNT. If NET-PAY had a value of $50 and PAY-AMOUNT had the value of $40 prior to the statement execution, after the completion of the statement both variables would have a value of $50.

The MOVE statement can also move many fields at one time. This is done by moving roll-up fields instead of individual variables. Figure 6-9 shows the partial record description of two data files. One file is being read as input, the other is being used for output.

By executing the statement "MOVE in-employee-name TO out-employee-name," all subordinate fields will also be moved. These fields are IN-LAST-NAME, IN-FIRST-NAME, and IN-MIDDLE-NAME. However, one note of caution: the data contained in the roll-up fields will be moved character for character, including leading zeros and spaces. Therefore, the fields in the roll-up being updated should appropriately line up with the fields being moved.

There are some cases where an application requires a field be shortened. For example, the job title field is fifty characters long, but there is only room on the report to print the first thirty. Figure 6-10 displays the statements needed to illustrate two possible alternatives.

The first MOVE option in Fig. 6-10 moves JOB-TITLE, which is 50 characters, into JOB-TITLE-SHORT, which is 30 characters. When this move occurs the right-most 20 characters will be truncated, leaving JOB-TITLE-SHORT with the first 30 characters. When the COBOL program is compiled, a message will be printed stating that the move statement will cause the truncation of characters. This message is just a warning and will not affect the compilation, linkage or execution process.

The second MOVE option in Fig. 6-10 moves JOB-TITLE to JOB-TITLE-SPLIT. Unlike option one, both these fields contain 50 characters. Note, however, that JOB-TITLE-SPLIT is a roll-up field containing two detail fields: JOB-TITLE-SHORT,

```
         WORKING-STORAGE SECTION.
         01 JOB-TITLE                  PIC X(50).
         01 JOB-TITLE-SHORT            PIC X(30).

         01 JOB-TITLE-SPLIT.
            05 JOB-TITLE-SHORT         PIC X(30).
            05 FILLER                  PIC X(20).

         PROCEDURE DIVISION.

      A: MOVE JOB-TITLE TO JOB-TITLE-SHORT.

      B: MOVE JOB-TITLE TO JOB-TITLE-SPLIT.
```

Fig. 6-10. MOVE field shortening example.

which is 30 characters, and FILLER, which is 20 characters. Remember, FILLER is a reserved WORKING-STORAGE name and is used to reserve space. This option will also place the first 30 characters of the job title into JOB-TITLE-SHORT, but it will not produce a warning message during compilation and will provide cleaner internal program documentation. The documentation is improved because the code will unmistakingly show that a decision was made to make JOB-TITLE-SHORT 30 characters.

The third and most efficient way to give JOB-TITLE-SHORT its appropriate value is by defining the JOB-TITLE field as a roll-up within the file input data record. Then when JOB-TITLE is assigned a value, JOB-TITLE-SHORT is automatically loaded and no additional move is needed.

In a process similar to that used to shorten JOB-TITLE, small fields can be concatenated into large fields. If your application requires employee name and employee number to be referenced as one field, a working storage roll-up can be designed to include two detail fields into which employee name and number could be moved. At that time the new roll-up can be used to reference both fields. Figure 6-11 outlines the process. Table 6-7 provides additional MOVE statement examples.

The MOVE CORRESPONDING Statement

There are times when two or more data records contain the same field names. For example, a data item may be defined using the same name in a master file and a WORKING-STORAGE area. In this case there is a short cut that can move all identi-

Table 6-7. Additional MOVE Statement Examples.

Statement	Before				After			
	A	B	C	D	A	B	C	D
MOVE A TO B	5	3			5	5		
MOVE A TO B, C	5	3	1		5	5	5	
MOVE A TO B, C, D	5	6	7	3	5	5	5	5

```
            WORKING-STORAGE SECTION.
            01  EMP-NAME                    PIC  X(25).
            01  EMP-NUMBER                  PIC  X(5).
            01  EMP-NO-AND-NAME.
                05  EMP-NO-CONCAT           PIC  X(5).
                05  EMP-NAME-CONCAT         PIC  X(25).

            PROCEDURE DIVISION.

            START-PAR.
                MOVE EMP-NAME TO EMP-NAME-CONCAT.
                MOVE EMP-NUMBER TO EMP-NO-CONCAT.
                DISPLAY EMP-NO-AND-NAME.
```

Fig. 6-11. MOVE concatenation example.

cally named fields from one defined record to another. This short cut is the MOVE CORRESPONDING statement. The line below shows its format.

MOVE CORRESPONDING RECORD-1 TO RECORD-2

Field names that are identically defined in record-1 and record-2 will be moved from record-1 to record-2. Figure 6-12 is an example of the MOVE CORRESPONDING statement; it shows the two record definitions being affected by the execution.

The two data records defined in the figure have five field names in common. These field names are:

```
            WORKING-STORAGE SECTION.
            01  IN-EMP-REC.
                05  EMP-NO                  PIC  X(5).
                05  EMP-NAME                PIC  X(25).
                05  EMP-ADDRESS             PIC  X(25).
                05  EMP-GROSS-PAY           PIC  9(6)V99.
                05  EMP-SSN                 PIC  X(9).
                05  EMP-DATE-OF-BIRTH       PIC  X(7).

            01  OUT-REPORT-REC.
                05  EMP-NO                  PIC  X(5).
                05  FILLER                  PIC  XXX.
                05  EMP-NAME                PIC  X(25).
                05  FILLER                  PIC  XXX.
                05  EMP-ADDRESS             PIC  X(25).
                05  FILLER                  PIC  XXX.
                05  EMP-SSN                 PIC  X(9).
                05  FILLER                  PIC  XXX.
                05  EMP-DATE-OF-BIRTH       PIC  X(7).

            PROCEDURE DIVISION.
                MOVE CORRESPONDING IN-EMP-REC TO OUT-EMP-REC.
```

Fig. 6-12. MOVE CORRESONDING statement example.

EMP-NO, EMP-NAME, EMP-ADDRESS, EMP-SSN, and EMP-DATE-OF-BIRTH. When the MOVE CORRESPONDING statement at the bottom of the example is executed, these five fields are moved from IN-EMP-REC to OUT-REPORT-REC. Also note that the EMP-GROSS-PAY field in the first record is not in the second. Because there is no match in the record, this field will not be affected. If OUT-REPORT-REC contains fields that did not have counterparts in the first record, they would also be unaffected by the move.

Moving Numeric Fields

When two numeric variables are defined to a similar data size and format, moving a value from one to the other is easy and clean-cut. However, applications often require values to be moved between differently defined variables. Depending on the formats of the variables being processed this may or may not cause truncations on the value being moved. There are two kinds of truncations—most significant digits and least significant digits. Most significant digits are the numbers left-most to the decimal point. Say that HOURLY-PAY was defined as 999V999 and had a value of 123.456. If moved to a field defined as 99V999, the hundreds place would be lost and the value 23.456 would remain. The loss of the hundreds column in this case is considered the loss of the most significant digit.

The least significant digits are the decimal places right-most to the decimal point. Using the above scenario of HOURLY-PAY having a value of 123.456, move HOURLY-PAY to a field defined as 999V99. The resulting value would be 123.45. The loss of the .006 is considered the loss of the least significant digit.

Depending on the circumstances, the loss of least and most significant digits may be acceptable. In any case the programmer should be made aware of the potential problem. Each time the program is compiled warning messages are printed stating the line containing the move statement, and that least or most significant digits are being truncated.

FILE PROCESSING STATEMENTS

File processing statements are used to communicate with data files. These statements fall into three categories: file status, file input, and file update. There are two file status statements: OPEN and CLOSE. OPEN is used to prepare the field for processing. The CLOSE statement informs the computer that no more processing will be performed on the stated file.

The file input statement is used to get information from a file and move it into the record definition stated in the FILE SECTION of the DATA DIVISION. There is only one file input statement, the READ verb, which will be discussed later in this chapter. The third and last file processing category is file update. These statements are used to write, replace and delete file information. They consist of the WRITE, DELETE, and REWRITE verbs.

The OPEN Statement

The OPEN statement is used to open the channels of communication between the data file being accessed and the program being executed. It also defines the way in which the file will be used. Figure 6-13 illustrates the format of the OPEN statement.

The OPEN statement always begins with the word OPEN followed by the file use clause that must be worded in one of three ways: INPUT, OUTPUT, or I-O. INPUT and OUTPUT are used in conjunction with sequential processing. The INPUT option states that the file being opened will

```
OPEN    INPUT     filename-1     [, filename-2 ... ]
        OUTPUT    filename-3     [, filename-4 ... ]
        I-O       filename-5     [, filename-6 ... ]
```

Fig. 6-13. OPEN statement format.

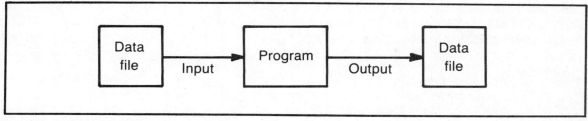

Fig. 6-14. Defining file modes.

be used to provide information to the program. When a file is opened in this format the READ statement is used to access the data file. The OUT-PUT clause states that data will be passed from the program to the data file. When a file is opened in this mode the WRITE statement should be used to record the information in the file. A note of caution—when a file is opened for output, the information currently residing in the file is deleted and the file is rebuilt with only the new information provided by the current execution of the program. The I-O (Input-Output) refers to random access and index-sequential file structures. The action verbs associated with this mode are; READ, READ NEXT, READ PRIOR, WRITE, RE-WRITE, and DELETE. Using these verbs, a selected record can be added, modified or deleted.

A common question often asked with regard to defining the mode of a file, is "Do I input to the file, or do I input to the program?" The answer is that the program is always the center of attention. This means use the INPUT option to input information from the file to the program. OUTPUT is used when outputting information from the pro-gram to the file. Figure 6-14 illustrates the input-output process.

Following the file mode clause comes the name of the file being opened. The file names specified in the OPEN statement must first be selected in the ENVIRONMENT DIVISION by a SELECT statement and logically and physically defined in the FILE-CONTROL section of the DATA DIVISION. As Fig. 6-13 illustrates, more than one file may be opened by a single OPEN statement. Figure 6-15 provides examples of the various file opening options.

The READ Statement

The READ statement is used to access data contained in a file. Each time a READ statement is executed one logical record is retrieved and is placed in the program. The line below shows the format of the READ statement.

READ filename [INTO identifier] [AT END imperative-statement]

A READ statement has four parts, of which two

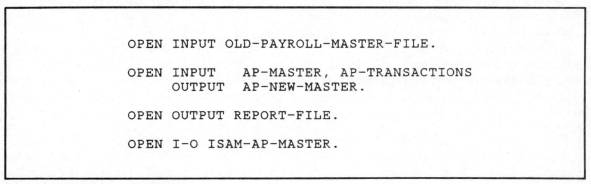

```
OPEN INPUT OLD-PAYROLL-MASTER-FILE.

OPEN INPUT    AP-MASTER, AP-TRANSACTIONS
     OUTPUT   AP-NEW-MASTER.

OPEN OUTPUT REPORT-FILE.

OPEN I-O ISAM-AP-MASTER.
```

Fig. 6-15. OPEN statement examples.

```
        DATA DIVISION.
        INPUT-OUTPUT SECTION.

        FD IN-PAY-REC
           RECORD CONTAINS 80 CHARACTERS
           LABEL RECORDS ARE STANDARD
           DATA RECORD IS IN-PAY-REC.

        01 INPAY-REC              PIC X(80).

        WORKING-STORAGE SECTION.

    01 MORE-RECORDS           PIC X.
    01 WS-PAY-INFO.
        05 EMP-NAME           PIC X(30).
        05 EMP-GROSS-PAY      PIC 9(6)V99.
        05 EMP-TAXES-PAYED    PIC 9(6)V99.

    PROCEDURE DIVISION.

        READ IN-PAY-FILE AT END MOVE 'N' TO MORE-RECORDS.

        READ IN-PAY-FILE INTO WS-PAY-INFO
             AT END MOVE `N` TO MORE-RECORDS.
```

Fig. 6-16. READ statement example.

parts are required and the remaining two parts are optional. The required parts are the word READ and a valid field name, as defined in the DATA DIVISION. The first optional phrase is the INTO clause. Within the FILE-CONTROL section of the DATA DIVISION files are defined in two ways: first, general file information is specified in the FD section, and second, the file's record layout is defined in the 01 area. By default, if the INTO clause is not present when the READ statement is executed, the information retrieved from the file will be placed in the defined 01 data record. The INTO clause allows the option of redirecting the retrieved information to another place. This alternate place would be a field or group of fields defined with the WORKING-STORAGE section. In the first READ statement of Fig. 6-16 the retrieved data is placed in IN-PAY-REC. In the second READ it is placed in WS-PAY-INFO. The WS prefix is a convention used by some data processing shops to denote variables defined in WORKING-STORAGE.

Note that in the figure both READ statements contain an AT END clause. This clause is not required, but it is highly recommended. This clause tells the program what to do if there are no more records to read. If the end of file is reached and the AT END option is not present the program will not know what to do and it will abort.

The WRITE Statement

The WRITE statement is used to output information from the program to a data file or other output device, such as a line printer. This statement is employed for both building reports and the creation and update of data files. Figure 6-17 describes the WRITE statement format, which must begin with the word WRITE followed by the name of the record to be written. This record name must be defined in the FILE-CONTROL section of the DATA DIVISION as an 01 related to a file description

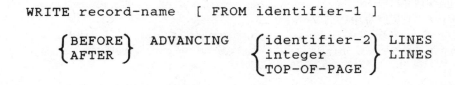

```
WRITE record-name   [ FROM identifier-1 ]

⎧BEFORE⎫  ADVANCING  ⎧identifier-2⎫ LINES
⎩AFTER ⎭             ⎨integer     ⎬ LINES
                     ⎩TOP-OF-PAGE ⎭
```

Fig. 6-17. WRITE statement format.

(FD). Before the WRITE statement can be executed the file must be opened for OUTPUT or I-O by an OPEN verb.

The first optional phrase is the FROM clause. Normally for information to be written to a file or report the data must be moved to the appropriate 01/FD data record. Then when the WRITE is executed the data residing in that data area is output to the assigned location. The FROM option allows information residing in WORKING-STORAGE fields to be written directly to the file without first being moved to the output record. Figure 6-18 illustrates the use of this clause.

The first WRITE statement will write the information currently contained in OUT-PAY-REC. The second WRITE statement will write the information residing in WS-PAY-INFO as specified in the FROM clause. Use caution with this technique—the number of characters specified in the RECORD CONTAINS clause of the FD will

Fig. 6-18. WRITE statement example.

```
DATA DIVISION.

INPUT-OUTPUT SECTION.
FILE CONTROL.

FD OUT-PAY-FILE
   RECORD CONTAINS 132 CHARACTERS
   LABEL RECORDS ARE STANDARD
   DATA RECORD IS OUT-PAY-REC.

01 OUT-PAY-REC          PIC X(80).

WORKING-STORAGE SECTION.
01 WS-PAY-REC
   05 EMP-NAME          PIC X(30).
   05 EMP-ADDRESS       PIC X(50).


PROCEDURE DIVISION.

   OPEN OUTPUT OUT-PAY-FILE.

   MOVE WS-PAY-REC TO OUT-PAY-REC.
   WRITE OUT-PAY-REC.

   WRITE OUTPUT-REC FROM WS-PAY-INFO.
```

control the width of the record being written. Therefore, if the FD specifies 80 characters and the WORKING-STORAGE record is 100 characters, the last 20 characters of the 100 character record will be truncated. Conversely, if the FD calls for 100 characters and the WORKING-STORAGE record is only 80 characters, 20 spaces will automatically be added to the end of the data being written to fill the requirement.

The next WRITE statement clause is the ADVANCING option. This option allows the programmer to control vertical spacing. Vertical spacing allows the program to skip lines between the report headings and the report detail and go to the top of a page, as specified by some logical criteria. The ADVANCING option has two basic formats: BEFORE ADVANCING and AFTER ADVANCING. BEFORE ADVANCING states that the information should be written before advancing the specified number of lines. AFTER ADVANCING states that information should not be written until the specified number of lines have been skipped. Both advancing options specify the number of lines to be skipped in one of three ways—variables, literal, and special mnemonics. Figure 6-19 illustrates these three options.

The first WRITE uses a literal to specify the number of lines to be skipped. Upon execution of this statement two lines will be skipped and then OUT-REC will be printed. The second WRITE will print OUT-REC and then skip the number of lines specified by the variable LINE-SKIP. For this option to work correctly LINE-SKIP must be defined as a numeric field. The third WRITE uses a mnemonic. Some versions of COBOL contain a reserved word allowing advancing to the top of a page. This reserved word, however, is not standard with all manufacturers and may be defined as PAGE, TOP-OF-PAGE, TOP-OF-FORM, or some similar designation. Other software manufacturers allow the programmer to specify the top-of-page phrase in a special section of the ENVIRONMENT DIVISION called SPECIAL-NAMES. The manufacturers using this page-feed option use their own syntax. The best way to discover the correct format is to look in previously written programs or to consult the COBOL programmer's reference manual accompanying the COBOL compiler.

The CLOSE Statement

The CLOSE statement is used to close the channels of communication between the COBOL program and an open data file. When a data file is initialized and opened for processing via an OPEN statement, space in memory called *buffers* are reserved to store incoming and outgoing file information. When a CLOSE statement is executed the buffers are deleted and all other logical and physical connections between the program and file are cancelled, thus closing the file. The line below shows the CLOSE statement format.

CLOSE filename-1 [, filename-2 . . .]

The CLOSE statement must begin with the word CLOSE, followed by the name of the file or files to be closed. For this statement to execute properly two conditions must be met: first, the files specified for closing must be defined by an FD in the FILE-CONTROL area of the DATA DIVISION. Second, the file must be open at the time the CLOSE is executed.

```
WRITE OUT-REC AFTER ADVANCING 2 LINES.

WRITE OUT-REC BEFORE ADVANCING LINE-SKIP LINES.

WRITE OUT-REC AFTER ADVANCING TOP-OF-PAGE.
```

Fig. 6-19. WRITE statement examples.

PROCEDURAL BRANCHING

Procedural branching is the process of transferring program control from one section of the program to another. This transfer can be executed in one of three ways: GOTO statements, PERFORM statements, or CALL statements. GOTO and PERFORM statements provide the capability to jump from the line being executed to a statement elsewhere in the same program. The program location receiving control is specified by a paragraph name (previously discussed as location definition statements) included as part of the GOTO and PERFORM statement format. The difference between these two statements is that the PERFORM statement temporarily transfers control in a subroutine-like fashion, whereas the GOTO statement permanently transfers control.

The CALL statement lets one COBOL program call another COBOL program as a subroutine. This means that like the PERFORM statement, the transfer of control is temporary. However, in this case a second COBOL program is called rather than a selected section of the same program.

The GOTO Statement

The GOTO statement is used to permanently transfer control from the statement being executed to a specified paragraph name somewhere else in the program.

Since the concept of structured programming was introduced as a method of standardized programming techniques the GOTO statement has somewhat fallen from grace. Structured programming relies heavily on subroutines and the PERFORM statement as the preferred branching process. However, GOTO is still a commonly used programming option. The line below shows the format of the GOTO statement.

GOTO paragraph-name

The GOTO statement consists of two parts: the word GOTO and a paragraph name. For the statement to function correctly, the specified paragraph name must exist in a valid format somewhere in the program. Figure 6-20 illustrates the use of the GOTO statement.

Two GOTO statements are used. The first is in the imperative section of an IF statement, and the other is as a stand-allow function. The GOTO's are used to process a loop. When PARAGRAPH-1 is executed the user is asked to enter a Y or N. If an N is entered the IF condition in line 433 is satisfied and the program transfers control to PARAGRAPH-2. If the user does not enter an N the IF condition is not met and the GOTO in line 434 sends control back to PARAGRAPH-1. This GOTO looping process is not ideal structured programming, but it will work, and it effectively illustrates the functions of the GOTO statement.

```
400 PROCEDURE DIVISION
      .
      .
      .
430 PARAGRAPH-1.
431     DISPLAY 'DO YOU WISH TO CONTINUE ( Y OR N ): '.
432     ACCEPT ANSWER.
433     IF ANSWER = 'N' GOTO PARAGRAPH-1-END.
434     GOTO PARAGRAPH-1.
435 PARAGRAPH-1-END.
436
437 PARAGRAPH-2.
```

Fig. 6-20. GOTO statement example.

The PERFORM Statement

The PERFORM statement is used to temporarily transfer control in a subroutine-like fashion. This statement allows the programmer to specify where control should be passed and under what conditions control should return to the PERFORM statement. Figure 6-21 outlines the five PERFORM formats. Format-1 is the simplest of the PERFORM formats. It consists of two parts: the word PERFORM and the name of the paragraph to be performéd. Figure 6-22 shows an example of this format.

When the partial program is executed the perform statement in line 402 passes control to paragraph-B in line 405. From there the DISPLAY statement in line 406 is processed. When the paragraph name in line 407 is reached the old paragraph is considered completed and control is passed back to PERFORM in line 402, and passes to STOP RUN in line 403.

The second PERFORM format is similar to the first, with the exception that an ending paragraph name is specified. The ending paragraph name defines the range of statements that should be processed. Figure 6-23 illustrates the use of this second format. The partial program executes exactly the same as the program in Fig. 6-20. There are, however, two important differences. PARAGRAPH-B has an ending paragraph name in line 407 called PARAGRAPH-B-END. The similarity between the beginning and ending paragraph names is not required but is strongly suggested, and is considered standard. The second difference is that format-2 of the PERFORM statement is used. There are two major advantages of using the second and not the first PERFORM format; it improves the internal program documentation by dramatically defining each paragraph, and allows for more flexibility in regard to the programming techniques used in the paragraph being called. Figure 6-24 illustrates an example of a program looping process that could not be used without an ending paragraph name.

Paragraph-B is a working routine that could be

```
Format-1 : PERFORM    paragraph-name.

Format-2 : PERFORM    paragraph-name-1  [ THRU paragraph-name-2 ].

Format-3 : PERFORM    paragraph-name-1  [ THRU paragraph-name-2 ]
                      ⎧integer-1   ⎫    TIMES.
                      ⎨identifier-1⎬
                      ⎩            ⎭

Format-4 : PERFORM    paragraph-name-1 [ THRU paragraph-name-2 ]
                      UNTIL condition-1.

Format-5 : PERFORM    paragraph-name-1 [ thru paragraph-name-2 ]
                      VARYING identifier-1 FROM ⎧identifier-2⎫
                                               ⎨literal-1   ⎬
                                               ⎩            ⎭
                      BY  ⎧identifier-3⎫    UNTIL  condition-1.
                          ⎨literal-2   ⎬
                          ⎩            ⎭
```

Fig. 6-21. Five PERFORM formats.

64

```
400 PROCEDURE DIVISION.
401 PARAGRAPH-A.
402     PERFORM PARAGRAPH-B.
403     STOP RUN.
404
405 PARAGRAPH-B.
406     DISPLAY 'HAVE A NICE DAY'.
407 PARAGRAPH-B-END.
```

Fig. 6-22. PERFORM format-1 example.

```
400 PROCEDURE DIVISION.
401 PARAGRAPH-A.
402     PERFORM PARAGRAPH-B THRU PARAGRAPH-B-END.
403     STOP RUN.
404
405 PARAGRAPH-B.
406     DISPLAY 'HAVE A NICE DAY'.
407 PARAGRAPH-B-END.
408
409 PARAGRAPH-C.
```

Fig. 6-23. PERFORM format-2 example.

```
400 PROCEDURE DIVISION.
401
402 PARAGRAPH-A.
403     PERFORM PARAGRAPH-B THRU PARAGRAPH-B-END.
404     STOP RUN.
405
406 PARAGRAPH-B.
407     DISPLAY 'DO YOU WISH TO CONTINUE (Y or N): '.
408     ACCEPT ANSWER.
409     IF ANSWER = 'Y' GOTO PARAGRAPH-B-END.
410     IF ANSWER = 'N' GOTO PARAGRAPH-B-END.
411     DISPLAY 'ERROR: ANSWER MUST BE Y or N, PLEASE REENTER'.
412     GOTO PARAGRAPH-B.
413 PARAGRAPH-B-END.
```

Fig. 6-24. Second PERFORM format-2 example.

called from many places in a program. This routine asks a question, waits for a response, validates the response, and performs the appropriate action based on the results of the validation. This particular user input technique could not have been written as easily without the presence of the ending paragraph name and the PERFORM verb. The PERFORM verb automatically saves the location of the PERFORM that called PARAGRAPH-B. PARAGRAPH-B, therefore, needs no logic to

```
PROCEDURE DIVISION.
     PERFORM PARAGRAPH-A THRU PARAGRAPH-A-END 5 TIMES.
     STOP RUN.

PARAGRAPH-A.
     DISPLAY 'I LOVE TO PROGRAM IN COBOL'.
PARAGRAPH-A-END.
```

Fig. 6-25. PERFORM format-3 example.

transfer control back to the correct location. Without the ending paragraph name the IF statements would have to have been written in a more complex manner because there would be no way to branch to the end of the paragraph.

The third PERFORM format automatically creates a loop by allowing the programmer to specify the number of times a paragraph should be executed. Figure 6-25 illustrates the use of this third PERFORM format.

The partial program will display the words "I love to program in COBOL" five times. After the fifth reiteration program control passes back to the PERFORM statement that called the paragraph. Next, control will fall through the previously executed PERFORM to the STOP RUN and the program will end.

The fourth PERFORM format states that the paragraph being called will continue to loop until some condition is met. This condition is defined in the UNTIL clause. Figure 6-26 provides an example of this format. The variable LOOP-COUNT is being used as a counter. To perform this function LOOP-COUNTER must have been previously defined as a numeric field, such as PIC 999. When this example is executed LOOP-COUNTER is set to zero. The PERFORM in line 401 will specify that paragraph-A should be executed until LOOP-COUNTER is equal to 10. From there control is passed to paragraph-A in line 405. Then a value of one will be added to LOOP-COUNTER, and LOOP-COUNTER will be displayed on the terminal. This process will reiterate 9 times more or until the PERFORM UNTIL clause is satisfied when LOOP-COUNTER = 10.

This format example could have been written using the TIMES clause in format three, but unlike TIMES, the UNTIL option can be used to test for an end-of-file condition or a specific user response. Figure 6-27 is another example of the UN-

```
PROCEDURE DIVISION.

START-PAR.
    MOVE 0 TO LOOP-COUNT.
    PERFORM  PARAGRAPH-A THRU PARAGRAPH-A-END
        UNTIL LOOP-COUNTER  = 10.
    STOP RUN.

PARAGRAPH-A.
    ADD 1 TO LOOP-COUNT.
    DISPLAY LOOP-COUNT.
PARAGRAPH-A-END.
```

Fig. 6-26. PERFORM format-4 example.

```
400 PROCEDURE DIVISION.
401     DISPLAY 'ENTER YOUR NAME ( END TO END ): '.
402     ACCEPT ANSWER.
403     IF ANSWER = 'END' STOP RUN.
404     PERFORM PARAGRAPH-A THRU PARAGRAPH-A-END
405        UNTIL ANSWER = 'END'.
406     STOP RUN.
407
408 PARAGRAPH-A.
409     DISPLAY 'HI, YOUR NAME IS ', ANSWER.
410     DISPLAY ENTER YOUR NAME ( END TO END ): '.
411     ACCEPT ANSWER.
412 PARAGRAPH-A-END.
```

Fig. 6-27. Another PERFORM format-4 example.

TIL option, but now the exit condition depends on user response.

This figure is an example of how to use the PERFORM statement in a truly structured format. Lines 401-403 begin the process by getting the first answer. PERFORM is reached and control is passed to PARAGRAPH-A. Line 409 displays the text "Hi, your name is" and the answer is accepted in line 402. From there, in line 410, the program once again asks for a name. The answer is input in line 411 and control loops back to line 408 until the user enters the word "end." Once "end" is entered the UNTIL clause is satisfied and control returns to PERFORM in line 404.

The fifth and final PERFORM format combines a counter with a specified variable name of the condition expression. As in format-4, the para-graph being performed continues to loop until the condition in the UNTIL clause is satisfied. The additional nicety of this format is the ability to automatically increment a counter each time the performing paragraph loops. This is done with the VARYING clause. This clause has three parts: VARYING, FROM, and BY. VARYING specifies the variable name of the counter. FROM states the initial value at which the counter will be set. BY specifies by what amount the counter will be incremented each time the performing paragraph loops. Figure 6-28 provides an example of this PERFORM format.

PARAGRAPH-A will loop ten times. During each of these reiterations the variable LOOP-COUNTER, originally set to zero by the FROM clause, will be increased by one, specified in the BY

```
PROCEDURE DIVISION.
    PERFORM PARAGRAPH-A THRU PARAGRAPH-A-END
        VARYING LOOP-COUNTER FROM 0 BY 1
        UNTIL LOOP-COUNTER = 10.
    STOP RUN.

PARAGRAPH-A.
    DISPLAY LOOP-COUNTER.
PARAGRAPH-A-END.
```

Fig. 6-28. PERFORM format-5 example.

clause. Similar to format-4, the UNTIL clause does not have to be a numeric condition and may bear no relationship to the VARYING option. The UNTIL feature may refer to user input, file conditions, or other requirements. Figure 6-29 provides additional PERFORM statement examples.

The CALL Statement

The CALL statement works like the PERFORM statement with the exception that CALL passes temporary control to another program and not to a paragraph in the same program. Also, CALL cannot specify any conditions regarding the return of program control. The subprogram being called must specifically relinquish control by executing an EXIT statement. The line below shows the format of the CALL statement.

CALL $\begin{Bmatrix} \text{identifier-1} \\ \text{literal-1} \end{Bmatrix}$ [USING dataname-1

[, dataname-2 . . .]

The format is the word CALL followed by the name of the program that will receive control. This program name may be specified with a literal in quotation marks or by way of an alphanumeric or alphabetic variable during program execution.

The USING clause is optional. Its function is to specify the variables and data records that must be passed to the program being called. The format of this clause is the word USING followed by the names of the variables containing the data to be passed. The variable names may be data records, roll-ups in data records, or stand-alone data fields. In any case, they must be defined in the DATA DIVISION of the main program. The line below is an example of the CALL statement.

CALL PROG2 USING PAY-INFO, GENERALS, ERROR-FLAG.

When the CALL statement is executed program control is temporarily transferred to PROG2. With it is passed the data contained in PAY-INFO, GENERALS, and ERROR-FLAG. Once PROG2 starts execution, program control is only passed to the main program when an EXIT statement is reached in the subprogram, PROG2. If STOP RUN is reached in PROG2, total program execution will stop and control will not be returned to the main program. Chapter 12 will explain how this state-

```
PERFORM PARAGRAPH-A.

PERFORM PARAGRAPH-A THRU PARAGRAPH-A-END.

PERFORM OPEN-FILES-PAR THROUGH OPEN-FILES-END.

PERFORM MATH-PAR THRU MATH-PAR-END 5 TIMES.

PERFORM TOTALING-PAR 5 TIMES.

PERFORM INPUT-PAR THRU INPUT-PAR-END
    UNTIL EMPLOYEE-NAME = SPACES.

PERFORM GET-PAR THRU GET-PAR-END UNTIL DATA-FLAG = 'OFF'.

PERFORM LOOPING-PAR THRU LOOPING-PAY-END
    VARYING X FROM 1 BY 1 UNTIL OUT-OF-RECORDS-FLAG = 'Y'.
```

Fig. 6-29. Additional PERFORM statement examples.

Table 6-8. IF Conditional Operators.

Symbolic	Textual	Meaning
=	IS EQUAL TO	Equal to
>	IS GREATER THAN	Greater than
<	IS LESS THAN	Less than
not =	IS NOT EQUAL TO	Not equal to
not >	IS NOT GREATER THAN	Not greater than
not <	IS NOT LESS THAN	Not less than

ment and other linkage statements work together to successfully pass control from program to program.

The EXIT Statement

The EXIT statement is used in conjunction with the CALL statement. The CALL statement executes a COBOL program from another COBOL program. The EXIT statement is used in the sub-program to pass control back to the main process. The line below shows the format of the EXIT statement.

EXIT [PROGRAM]

As with the CALL statement, the use of EXIT and its relationship to other program linkage functions will be discussed in Chapter 12.

CONDITIONAL LOGIC STATEMENTS

Conditional logic is the ability to appropriately respond to specific circumstances. In a business programming context this means the program being executed can determine what tasks to perform by assessing what needs to be done. This assessment is performed by the IF statement. The IF statement can be used to perform simple as well as extremely complex decision logic.

The IF Statement

The IF statement is divided into three sections: conditional logic, positive statements, and else statements. The word IF begins the conditional logic section and is followed by the conditions to be examined. Next are the positive statements, the commands that should be executed if the IF conditions are met. The optional ELSE statements begin with the word ELSE and are only executed when the IF conditions are not met. The line below shows the IF statement format and Table 6-8 lists the conditional symbols that may be used in the IF section as conditional operators.

$$\text{IF condition} \left\{ \begin{array}{l} \text{statement-1} \\ \text{NEXT SENTENCE} \end{array} \right\}$$
$$\text{ELSE} \left\{ \begin{array}{l} \text{statement-2} \\ \text{NEXT SENTENCE} \end{array} \right\}$$

In the table there are two sets of valid conditional operators: symbolic and textual. The symbolic operators, shown on the left, are similar to those used in mathematics. The textual operators in the center column were incorporated into the language in an effort to make programming more English-like. Generally speaking, unless otherwise required by management programmers tend to prefer the symbolic operators because they are easier to read and shorter to type. Figure 6-30 shows some IF statement examples.

```
Ex. 1   IF HOURS-WORKED > 40 PERFORM OVERTIME-PAR.

Ex. 2   IF HOURS-WORKED > 40 PERFORM OVERTIME-PAR ELSE PERFORM
        REG-PAR.

Ex. 3   IF EMPLOYEE-STATUS = 'ACTIVE' NEXT SENTENCE
        ELSE MOVE 'Y' TO ERROR-FLAG.

Ex. 4   IF      EMPLOYEE-STATUS = 'ACTIVE'
                PERFORM ACTIVE-PAR
                MOVE 'A' TO STATUS-INDICATOR
                ADD 1 TO EMPLOYEE-COUNT
        ELSE    MOVE 'Y' TO ERROR-COUNT
                PERFORM ERROR-PAR.
```

Fig. 6-30. IF statement examples.

The first IF statement checks to see if HOURS-WORKED is greater then 40. If it is the condition is satisfied and OVERTIME-PAR is performed. If HOURS-WORKED is less than 40 the IF condition is not met, the PERFORM statement is not executed, and program control is passed to the next sequential statement.

The second IF statement example is very similar to the first. The difference is that an ELSE clause has been added. The ELSE clause tells the computer that if the condition (HOURS-WORKED > 40) is not true it should perform REG-TIME-PAR.

The third IF statement tests for active employees. This line states that if an employee is active then continue to NEXT SENTENCE. The phrase NEXT SENTENCE is a reserved word. Its function is to logically end the IF statement. In the context of this third statement, the underlying logic is to do nothing if the employee is active but to set an error flag to Y if the employee is not active. In this simple example, the NEXT SENTENCE option is marginally useful, but when IF statement nesting is discussed, the real need for this option will become more apparent.

The fourth and final example contains two new aspects of the IF statement. First is the option of executing many statements after the conditional logic and ELSE clause. When exercising this option, each statement must be separated by a comma. Many compilers allow the programmer to exclude the comma if the statements are placed on separate lines. The second new aspect of the fourth example is the format that should be followed when using multi-line IF statements. This format is designed to ease readability by vertically lining up the words IF and ELSE and evenly indenting the condition logic and statements being executed. Also, it is important to remember that the period is only placed at the logical end of the IF statement and not at the end of every line.

Multi-IF Conditions

There are many occasions where a single IF condition cannot completely decide a course of action. To fill this void, AND and OR operators allow for more advanced logic. Figure 6-31 provides examples of the AND and OR conditions. The first statement uses the ADD clause to connect two conditions. The AND clause states that both conditions must be met for the condition to be true. The second IF example uses the OR option. The OR connector specifies that only one of the conditions must be met for the IF to be true.

The third IF statement example contains both AND's and OR's. In this case, as in mathematical expressions, there is an order of operation. The order dictates that conditions in parentheses are

```
IF HOURS-WORKED > 40 AND PAY-TYPE = 'HOURLY'
        MOVE 'Y' TO OVERTIME-FLAG.

IF NET-PAY < 0 OR NET-PAY > 10000 PERFORM ERROR-PAR.

IF EMPLOYEE-STATUS = 'ACTIVE' OR ( EMPLOYEE-STATUS = 'LAYOFF'
        AND PAY-INDICATOR = 'Y' )
                PERFORM CUT-CHECK-PAR THROUGH CUT-CHECK-PAR-END.
```

Fig. 6-31. Multi-IF conditional examples.

considered first, then AND's, then OR's. In the statement "IF A = A AND B = B OR C = C," condition A and B are processed first and the outcome of A and B is compared to C. Either A and B must be true or C must be true. The adding of parentheses could change this scenario. In the statement "IF A = A AND (B = B OR C = C)," A must be true and either B or C must also be true. Therefore, in the third IF example the result of (EMPLOYEE-STATUS = 'LAYOFF' AND PAY-INDICATOR = 'Y') is decided first and then the outcome is compared to EMPLOYEE-STATUS = 'ACTIVE'. Because AND's are processed before OR's, this statement would have executed the same way with or without the parentheses. Including the parentheses is a good programming practice because it clearly documents the way the IF statement will be executed.

Nested IF Statements

COBOL has the ability to define and interpret complex logic by placing IF statements within IF statements. This "IF within an IF" is called *nest-ing*. Figure 6-32 shows a nested IF example. There is an IF statement contained in an IF statement. The first IF asks if the employee pay type is hourly. If the pay type is not hourly, the else statement is executed and the paragraph SALARIED-EMP-PAR is performed. If the employee is hourly, then a second question is asked about the number of hours worked. Remember, the inner IF will only be reached when pay type is hourly. This inner IF statement will perform REGULAR-HOURS-PAR if the employee worked 40 hours or less and OVERTIME-PAR if more than 40 hours were worked. Figure 6-33 flowcharts the nested IF logic.

Tandem IF Statements

There are times when it is necessary to ask a group of related questions. An example of this is a program to calculate the number of employees making $5,000-$10,000, $10,001-$15,000, and so on, up to $100,000. There are two programming methods that can be employed to calculate the answer. The first method is to type twenty single-line IF statements, as shown in Part A of Fig. 6-34. The

```
IF PAY-TYPE = 'HOURLY'
    IF HOURS-WORKED > 40
        PERFORM REGULAR-HOURS-PAR THRU REGULAR-HOURS-PAR-END
    ELSE
        PERFORM OVERTIME-HOURS-PAR THRU OVERTIME-HOURS-PAR-END
ELSE
    PERFORM SALARIED-EMP-PAR THRU SALARIED-EMP-PAR-END.
```

Fig. 6-32. Nested IF example.

71

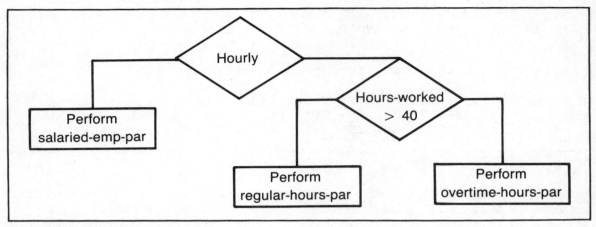

Fig. 6-33. Flowchart of nested IFs.

second is to use tandem IF statements, as shown in Part B of the figure.

The statements in both Part A and Part B will provide the same answer. The important questions are, "How long will it take to process?" and "How self-documenting is the procedure?" In this case, both Part A and Part B are self-documenting. The

difference lies in the processing time needed to run the program. When Part A is executed all twenty individual IF statements are executed. Each IF statement has two conditions that must be examined (a greater than and a less than condition). In Part B, the entire procedure ends when the first conditional statement is met. This means that all

```
Part A:     IF SALARY =>   5000 AND SALARY < 10000 ADD 1 TO LEVEL-5-SALARY.
            IF SALARY => 10000 AND SALARY < 15000 ADD 1 TO LEVEL-10-SALARY.
            IF SALARY => 15000 AND SALARY < 20000 ADD 1 TO LEVEL-15-SALARY.
            IF SALARY => 20000 AND SALARY < 25000 ADD 1 TO LEVEL-20-SALARY.
                          .                .              .
                          .                .              .
                          .                .              .
            IF SALARY => 95000 AND SALARY < 100000 ADD 1 TO LEVEL-95-SALARY.


Part B:     IF SALARY < 10000
                ADD 1 TO LEVEL-5-SALARY
            ELSE IF SALARY < 15000
                ADD 1 TO LEVEL-10-SALARY
            ELSE IF SALARY < 20000
                ADD 1 TO LEVEL-15-SALARY
            ELSE IF SALARY < 25000
                ADD 1 TO LEVEL-20-SALARY
               .          .          .
               .          .          .
               .          .          .
            ELSE IF SALARY < 100000
                ADD 1 TO LEVEL-95-SALARY.
```

Fig. 6-34. Tandem IF example.

```
IF OUT-OF-RECORDS-FLAG = 'N'
     PERFORM GET-A-REC-PAR THRU GET-A-REC-PAR-END.

IF STATUS = 'ACTIVE' ADD 1 TO ACTIVE-COUNT.

IF ERROR-COUNT > 10 DISPLAY 'ERROR COUNT OVER 10, JOB ABORTED'.

IF JOB-CLASS = '1' OR JOB-CLASS = '2'
     ADD 1 TO PROGRAMMING-STAFF
     PERFORM JOB-RECLASS-PAR THRU JOB-RECLASS-PAR-END
ELSE  ADD 1 TO NON-TECHNICAL-STAFF.
```

Fig. 6-35. Additional IF statement examples.

twenty questions are not always asked. Also, each question only contains one condition, again minimizing the required processing time.

Figure 6-35 provides additional IF statement examples.

STRING MANIPULATION STATEMENTS

The next main area of the PROCEDURE DIVISION is string manipulation statements. These statements are used to concatenate, separate, examine and modify alphanumeric data. Three statements comprise this category: STRING, UNSTRING, and EXAMINE. The string statement is used to concatenate, or bring together, two or more fields. The UNSTRING statement separates a field into smaller parts, and the EXAMINE statement analyzes and modifies aphanumeric fields.

The STRING Statement

The function of the STRING statement is to concatenate two or more fields into one large field. Its main use is the formatting of data in preparation for output. Formatting is most commonly seen when printing mailing lists or printing the words on bank checks specifying an amount of money.

Figure 6-36 shows the format of the STRING statement. The statement begins with the word STRING, followed by the first literal or variable to be concatenated. The first concatenated field is followed by the DELIMITED BY clause. This

```
⎰identifier-1⎱  ⎰, identifier-2⎱  ... DELIMITED BY⎰identifier-3⎱
⎱literal-1   ⎰  ⎱, literal-2   ⎰               ⎱literal-3   ⎰
                                                ⎱SIZE        ⎰


⎰identifier-4⎱  , ⎰identifier-5⎱  ... DELIMITED BY⎰identifier-6⎱
⎱literal-4   ⎰  , ⎱identifier-6⎰               ⎱literal-6   ⎰
                                                ⎱SIZE        ⎰

INTO  identifier-7 [ WITH POINTER identifier-8 ]

[ ON OVERFLOW imperative-statement ]
```

Fig. 6-36. STRING statement format.

clause is used to truncate trailing spaces and other superfluous characters that need not be moved to the concatenated area. For example, if the field LAST-NAME was defined in the DATA DIVISION as PIC X(15), the last name of SMITH would be followed by ten trailing spaces. By stating DELIMITED BY " " the program is instructed to move only those characters located before the first space, hence, not move the trailing spaces. The SIZE option in the DELIMITED BY clause instructs the program to transfer all characters in the defined field to the concatenated area regardless of the field's content. This procedure of defining the string variables and their delimiters is repeated for each field to be placed in the concatenated area.

After all the input fields have been defined the output or concatenated area must be specified. This is done by the word INTO followed by the output field name. Next is the optional and seldomly used POINTER clause. POINTER's function is to specify the starting position of the concatenated data in the output variable. This means that if the application requires that the concatenated field be indented 5 spaces, the WITH POINTER is set to 5. The next, and final STRING clause, is ON OVERFLOW followed by an imperative statement.

This clause tells the program some specific action to perform if the concatenated data does not fit in the defined output variable. Figure 6-37 is an example of the STRING statement.

The example reformats the employee name into a format that can be used on mailing labels. These are two display statements, one printing the name fields as is, and the other printing the formatted name FULL-NAME. The difference between the values output is the period after the middle initial and the spacing between first and middle names. These differences are caused by the STRING statement. In this example, the FIRST-NAME is delimited by a space portrayed as ' '. This delimiter truncated the trailing spaces and moved "ERIC" into FULL-NAME. The next line is the literal " " delimited by size. This line places a space after the first name in preparation for the middle initial. MIDDLE INITIAL is then added to FULL-NAME, followed by a period and the space between middle and last name. Finally, the LAST-NAME is added and the statement ends.

The UNSTRING Statement

The UNSTRING statement performs a function opposite to that of the STRING statement. It

```
PROGRAM:

        DISPLAY FIRST-NAME, MIDDLE-INITIAL, LAST-NAME.

        STRING    FIRST-NAME DELIMITED BY ' ',
                  ' ' DELIMITED BY SIZE,
                  MIDDLE-INITIAL DELIMITED BY SIZE,
                  '. ' DELIMITED BY SIZE,
                  LAST-NAME DELIMITED BY ' '
            INTO  FULL-NAME
            ON OVERFLOW MOVE 'WARNING: LAST NAME TRUNCATED' TO
            WARNING-TEXT

        DISPLAY ' '.
        DISPLAY FULL-NAME.

OUTPUT:  ERIC        PBLOOM

         ERIC P. BLOOM
```

Fig. 6-37. STRING statement example.

74

```
UNSTRING    identifier-1

DELIMITED BY [ ALL ] {identifier-2}[, OR [ALL] {identifier-3} ...
                     {literal-1    }          {literal-2    }

INTO identifier-4  [, DELIMITER IN identifier-5 ] [COUNT IN
identifier-6

  [   identifier-7  [, DELIMITER IN identifier-8 ] [COUNT IN
  identifier-9

  [ WITH POINTER identifier-10 ] [ TALLYING IN identifier-11 ]

  [ ON OVERFLOW imperative-statement ]
```

Fig. 6-38. UNSTRING statement format.

is used to separate an alphanumeric data field into smaller fields based on some defined deliminating character. A common use of this statement is to separate and validate data input via a terminal. For example, if a user is required to input a date in the format "mm/dd/yy," UNSTRING can separate the input value into its year, month, and day parts. These parts can then be individually checked and validated. Figure 6-38 shows the UNSTRING statement format.

The statement begins with the word UN-STRING followed by the name of the alphanumeric variable being divided. The DELIMITED BY clause specifies the criteria to be used when separating identifier-1 into its parts. Next is the INTO clause. Its function is to specify the fields that will be receiving the divided information. This clause is broken into three parts: INTO, DELIMITER IN, and COUNT IN. Identifier-4 placed after the word INTO receives the first section of the divided identifier-1. Identifier-5 placed after the optional phrase DELIMITER IN contains the delimiter used to isolate the data placed in the previous field. The COUNT IN phrase counts the number of characters placed in identifier-4 and places that value in the numeric field identifier-6. Additional output fields are defined by repeating the process from identifier-4 through identifier-6. The word INTO should not be repeated. Finally,

after all the output fields have been defined, the WITH POINTER field can be added.

The WITH POINTER option tracks the number of characters in the input field, identifier-1, that have been analyzed by the UNSTRING statement. Given an input field of "ABC-DEF-GHI-JKL," and "–" defined as the delimiter, the first field, "ABC," would be placed in the first INTO defined variable and the pointer variable would be set to 5, the position just to the right of the first dash. This option is very useful when the UNSTRING statement is contained in a loop and the delimited data is extracted one field at a time. This one-field-at-a-time extraction is done by specifying only one output field in the INTO statement. When the second field is reached there is nowhere to place the data and an overflow condition occurs. The overflow ends the UNSTRING statement, leaving the pointer variable set to the end of the first delimited field. When UNSTRING is executed during the second loop reiteration it picks up in the location specified by the pointer variable.

The TALLYING IN clause counts the number of fields that have been extracted by UNSTRING. This clause has two basic uses. First, it assists in date validation by specifying the number of fields extracted from the input value. Assuming that the correct input format is "MM/DD/YY," if input correctly the tallying field would have a value of three.

If not, the program logic should then detect that an input error has occurred. The second use of the tallying function is when the field being divided is placed into consecutive array locations. The procedure is to use the tallying variable as the subscript of the array specified in the INTO clause. As each set of characters is extracted, the subscript is incremented and the extracted value is placed in the next appropriate array location.

The ON OVERFLOW clause is an error-handling feature. If the data being separated can not fit in the fields assigned as output, when this clause is present the system performs the specified error instructions. Figure 6-39 is an example of the UNSTRING statement.

The INSPECT Statement

The INSPECT statement analyzes and modifies alphanumeric fields. It is commonly used to assess the validity of incoming data and to modify the contents of fields in preparation for data display or storage. For example, a particular application may require that a telephone number is input in the format "(555)555-5555." INSPECT can be used to analyze that the parentheses and dash are in the current columns and that the entire field contains 13 characters. INSPECT can also delete the parentheses and dash by replacing these characters with " ", a blank field. Figure 6-40 shows the format of the INSPECT statement.

All three formats begin with the word IN-SPECT followed by the fields being analyzed. From this point forward, however, the three formats differ greatly. The first INSPECT format uses a TALLYING option. This option has the ability to count the number of times a specified character or characters occur in an alphanumeric field. This function is primarily used to assist in assessing the quality of information input on-line by a user, and is commonly used to check for dashes in social secu-

```
PROGRAM:

        WORKING-STORAGE SECTION.
        01  INDATE          PIC X(8).
        01  THE-DATE.
            05  THE-YEAR     PIC XX.
            05  THE-MONTH    PIC XX.
            05  THE-DAY      PIC XX.

        PROCEDURE DIVISION.
        START-PAR.
            DISPLAY 'ENTER A DATE IN THE FORMAT MM-DD-YY:'.
            ACCEPT INDATE.

            UNSTRING INDATE
                DELIMITED BY '-' OR '/'
                INTO THE-MONTH, THE-DAY, THE-YEAR.

        DISPLAY THE-DATE.

WHEN RUN:

        ENTER A DATE IN THE FORMAT MM-DD-YY: 07/25/85
        850725
```

Fig. 6-39. UNSTRING statement example.

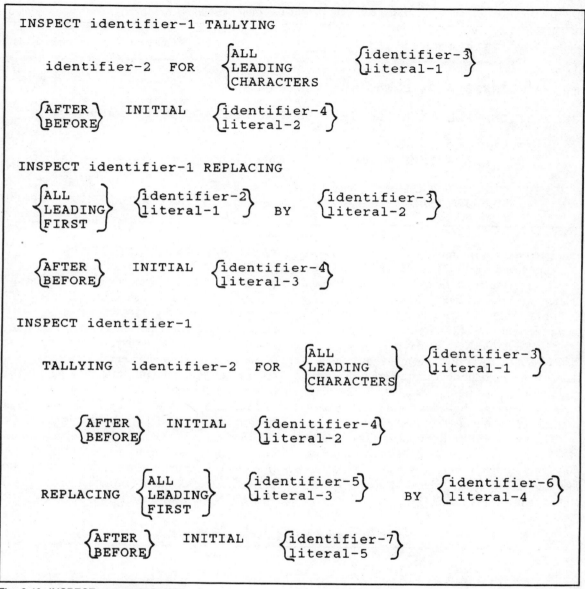

Fig. 6-40. INSPECT statement formats.

rity numbers, dollar signs in money fields, and other similar tests. Table 6-9 provides an example of the first INSPECT format.

IN-FIELD is analyzed for various characters and the answers are placed in THE-NUM. In these examples, various tallying options are used. The ALL option states that all occurrences of the com-paring character should be included in the count. The LEADING option states that only the charac-ters occurring at the beginning of the field, before any other characters are found, should be counted. The BEFORE and AFTER options instruct the pro-gram to only analyze a certain segment of the field being analyzed. It may say to only inspect those

Table 6-9. First INSPECT Format Examples.

Statement	INFIELD	THE-NUM
INSPECT INFIELD TALLYING THE-NUM FOR ALL '-'	555-1212	1
INSPECT INFIELD TALLYING THE-NUM FOR ALL '-'	999-99-9999	2
INSPECT INFIELD TALLYING THE-NUM FOR CHARACTERS BEFORE INITIAL 'X'	12345X222	5
INSPECT INFIELD TALLYING THE-NUM FOR 'X' AFTER INITIAL '-'	XXX-XX-XXXX	6

characters before the initial dash is encountered.

The second INSPECT format replaces characters in alphanumeric fields. The format could change the field ABCDE to XBCDX by replacing A with X. Table 6-10 provides various examples of this second INSPECT format.

The REPLACING clause is very similar to the TALLYING CLAUSE. The major difference is that instead of counting a character occurrence it replaces it with a different character. This replacement character is specified in the BY section of the REPLACING option.

The third INSPECT format is a combination of the first two formats. Here the programmer can tally the information about a string, and then perform the replacement. Table 6-11 provides an example of this third INSPECT format.

TABLE-HANDLING STATEMENTS

The table-handling statements are used to search and retrieve information contained in arrays. An array is a group of associated data memory locations referenced by the combination of a variable name and a subscript. These arrays, also known as tables, may contain the days of the week, months of the year, a list of valid employee codes or any other group of related information. Figure 6-41 illustrates this array concept.

The array's name and characteristics are defined in the DATA DIVISION by use of an OCCURS clause. The OCCURS clause states that a given variable will occur a specified number of times. For example, an array that contains employee status codes would be defined in the DATA DIVISION as "EMP-STATUS-CODES OCCURS

Table 6-10. Second INSPECT Statement Examples.

Statement	Before	After
INSPECT INFIELD REPLACING ALL 'X' BY 'Z'	XXX-XX-XXXX	ZZZ-ZZ-ZZZZ
INSPECT INFIELD REPLACING FIRST 'X' BY 'Z'	XXX-XX-XXXX	ZXX-XX-XXXX
INSPECT INFIELD REPLACING FIRST 'X' BY 'Z' AFTER INITIAL '-'	XXX-XX-XXXX	XXX-ZX-XXXX

Table 6-11. Third INSPECT Format Examples.

Statement	Before	After	THE-NUM
INSPECT INFIELD TALLYING '*' REPLACING '*' BY '+'	* * * * *	+ + + + +	5
INSPECT INFIELD TALLYING 'X' REPLACING '*' BY '+' AFTER INITIAL '-'	* * X - X X	* * X - + +	3

10 TIMES PIC X" and would be referenced in the PROCEDURE DIVISION as EMP-STATUS-CODES(a-subscript-name). The subscript name that specifies the table location being processed must be numeric and have a a value between one and the array size specified in the OCCURS clause. In the case of EMP-STATUS-CODES, the array value must be between one and 10.

The array variables can be used like regular fields within all COBOL statements. It can be moved, used in an IF statement as part of the conditional logic, or in any other meaningful way. The only real requirement is that it must always be accompanied by a subscript enclosed in parentheses.

There are two statements that specifically deal with tables. These statements are SEARCH and SET. The SEARCH verb is used to search a table for a given value. The SET command places an initial value or changes the value of a subscript variable.

The SEARCH Statement

The SEARCH statement searches a table in hopes of locating a specific value. This table search can be done by serial searching or binary searching. A serial search reads the data in sequential order, beginning with the first array location, until a value is found or the end of the table is reached. To perform a binary search the table being searched must be in sorted order. A binary search picks the middle record of the table and compares that record with the search criteria. If by chance there is a match, the search ends. Otherwise, SEARCH automatically assesses if the table value selected is greater or less than the searching value.

If the searching value is greater, the system knows the record is in the second half of the table. The system then chooses a record midway between the previous record and the end of the file. This process continues until the needed record is found. SEARCH has two formats, shown in Fig. 6-42.

The first SEARCH format performs a serial search through a data table. This statement is divided into four parts: SEARCH, VARYING, AT END, and WHEN. The statement begins with the word SEARCH followed by identifier-1. Identifier-1 is the name of the table being searched. Next is the VARYING clause. Its function is to specify the name of the subscript that will be used to specify the location of the data found in the table. The AT

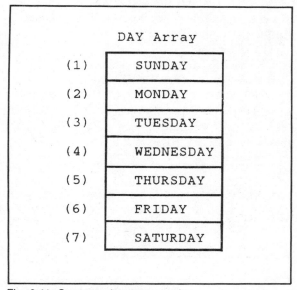

Fig. 6-41. Conceptual array example.

```
SEARCH identifier-1     VARYING      {identifier-2
                                      {index-name-1


           AT END imperative-statement-1

           WHEN condition-1     {imperative-statement-2
                                 {NEXT SENTENCE


SEARCH ALL identifier-1     AT END imperative-statement-1

                           {IS EQUAL TO}  {identifier-2
           WHEN data-name-1 {IS =      }  {literal-1
                                          {arithmetic-expression-1

   {imperative-statement-2}
   {NEXT SENTENCE         }
```

Fig. 6-42. SEARCH statement format.

END clause specifies the statements that should be executed if the search process reaches the end of the table before it finds the data. In effect, the end of the table condition is only realized when the data is not found. The WHEN clause states the conditions to be met and the action and actions that should be taken when the appropriate data is found. Figure 6-43 provides an example of the first SEARCH format.

The SEARCH example is searching STATUS-CODES-TABLE. The WHEN clause states that if the EMPLOYEE-STATUS-CODE in the table is equal to the code input by the user, move the code description associated with the input code to a variable called CODE-DESCRIPTION. If INPUT-CODE does not have a match in the file, then move a Y to ERROR-FLAG.

The second SEARCH statement format performs a binary search. The word ALL is the key that specifies that a binary search is to be performed. This format begins with the words SEARCH ALL followed by the name of the table being searched. Next is the AT END clause, which states what should be done if the data being searched is not found. Last is the WHEN section. This section specifies the conditions that must be met to assure the correct table value is returned.

This SEARCH format is different from the first format in two ways; there is no VARYING clause to specify the subscript index, and only an "equal

```
SEARCH STATUS-CODE-TABLE VARYING STATUS-INDEX
     AT END MOVE 'Y' TO ERROR-FLAG
     WHEN EMPLOYEE-STATUS-CODE = INPUT-CODE
          MOVE STATUS-CODE-DESCRIPTION(STATUS-INDEX) TO CODE-
          DESCRIPTION NEXT SENTENCE.
```

Fig. 6-43. First SEARCH format example.

to" condition can be used. The reason that no VARYING option is present is because binary searching requires the addition of two clauses in the 01 DATA DIVISION statement that defines the table; the first specifies the order in which the table is sorted, and the second states the subscript index variable to be used. The reason for only equal conditions is that binary search logic is designed to search for one value and cannot manage greater or less than conditions.

The SEARCH ALL statement in Fig. 6-44 searches the STATUS-CODE-TABLE trying to match the value entered into the program by the ACCEPT statement in INPUT-STATUS-CODES. Chapter 8 will provide an in-depth discussion of table handling uses and procedures.

The SET Statement

The SET statement is used to maintain the value of the variables used as table subscripts. This statement somewhat combines the features of the MOVE, ADD and SUBTRACT statements. Figure 6-45 shows the two SET statement formats.

The first SET statement format is similar to the MOVE statement. Its function is to set a variable to a given value. The line below is an example of this SET statement option. In this example, CODE-INDEX is being set to a value of one.

SET CODE-INDEX TO 1

The second SET statement format is similar to the ADD and SUBTRACT statements, and is used strictly with numeric variables. The UP BY clause adds the specified amount to identifier-1. The DOWN BY clause subtracts the specified amount from identifier-1. The line below is an example of this second SET format.

SET CODE-INDEX UP BY 1

Figure 6-46 provides additional SET statement examples.

QUESTIONS

1. What is the function of the PROCEDURE DIVISION?

```
WORKING-STORAGE SECTION.
01 STATUS-CODE-TABLE.
    05 FILLER X(10) FILLER VALUE IS 'AACTIVE     '.
    05 FILLER X(10) FILLER VALUE IS 'RRETIRED    '.
    05 FILLER X(10) FILLER VALUE IS 'TTERMINATED'.
    05 FILLER X(10) FILLER VALUE IS 'WON WARNING'.

01 STATUS-CODE-ARRAY REDEFINES STATUS-CODE-TABLE.
    05 STATUS-CODE ACCURS 5 TIMES ASCENDING KEY IS STATUS-CODE-VALUE
                                  INDEXED BY CODE-INDEX.
        10 STATUS-CODE-VALUE      PIC X.
        10 STATUS-CODE-DESC       PIC X(9).

PROCEDURE DIVISION.
ACCEPT INPUT-STATUS-CODE.
SEARCH ALL STATUS-CODES
        AT END DISPLAY 'ERROR: INVALID STATUS CODE MUST BE A,R,T or W'
        WHEN STATUS-CODES-VALUE(CODE-INDEX) = INPUT-STATUS-CODE
            DISPLAY STATUS-CODES-DESC(CODE-INDEX).
```

Fig. 6-44. SEARCH ALL statement example.

```
SET   {identifier-1}   {identifier-2}   TO   {identifier-3}
      {index-name-1}   {index-name-2}        {index-name3}
                                             {integer-1}


SET   index-name-1   index-name-2   {UP BY  }   {identifier-1}
                                    {DOWN BY}   {integer-1}
```

Fig. 6-45. SET statement formats.

```
SET   THE-INDEX DOWN BY 2.

SET   THE-INDEX TO 1.

SET THE-INDEX, ANOTHER-INDEX   TO 1.

SET THE-INDEX, ANOTHER-INDEX UP BY 1.
```

Fig. 6-46. Additional SET statement examples.

2. List and describe the five mathematical statements.

3. What is the purpose of the GIVING clause?

4. Describe the function of the ROUNDING and ON SIZE error clauses.

5. What are the differences between the three DIVIDE statement formats?

6. What is the primary advantage of the COMPUTE statement over the single function mathematical statements?

7. What is the function of the STOP statement?

8. What two functions are performed by paragraph names?

9. What is the purpose of the terminal interface statements?

10. With the exception of data files, from which two places can information be entered into a program?

11. What is the function of the ACCEPT statement?

12. How is the DISPLAY statement used?

13. What is the difference between literals and variables?

14. List and describe the two data movement statements.

15. What two techniques can be used to shorten a variable's length?

16. Describe the function of the MOVE COR-RESPONDING statement.

17. What must be considered when moving numeric data from variable to variable?

18. List and describe the three types of file processing statements.

19. What is the function of the OPEN statement, and what file use modes can it specify?

20. What is the function of a READ statement?

21. What is the use of the INTO clause and AT END clause in a READ statement?

22. What is the purpose of the WRITE statement?

23. What is the connection between a WRITE statement and RECORD CONTAINS clause of the file's DATA DIVISION FD description?

24. Why and when should a CLOSE statement be used?

25. What is procedural branching?

26. Describe the difference between the GOTO and PERFORM statements.

27. How and why is a CALL statement used?

28. List and describe the five PERFORM statement formats.

29. What is the connection between the CALL statement and the EXIT statement?

30. What is the function of the CALL statement's USING clause?

31. What is conditional logic?

32. Describe the format of an IF statement.

33. What are symbolic and textual conditional operators?

34. What role do the AND and OR clauses play in multi-IF conditional expressions?

35. What are nested IF statements?

36. What are tandem IF statements?

37. What is string manipulation?

38. What is the function of the STRING statement?

39. Describe how the UNSTRING statement can assist in date validation.

40. List and describe the three INSPECT formats.

41. What are data tables?

42. What is an OCCURS clause, and where is it used?

43. What is a SEARCH statement, and how is it used?

44. Describe the difference between SEARCH and SEARCH ALL.

45. List and describe the various SET statement formats.

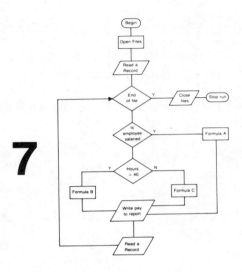

7

Structured Programming

In the early days of computing, computer hardware was the major expenditure in the data processing budget. With the cost of hardware so high and the cost of programming labor relatively so low, it made good business sense to write applications programs that used sophisticated and complex algorithms in an attempt to minimize the need for additional memory and storage. This programming emphasis saved on hardware acquisition expenditures at the cost of extensive labor hours and the development of complex software. In many cases the software was so complex that it could not even be modified by the original author.

As the price of hardware began to decline and the cost per programming hour began to increase, the price of developing and maintaining software became a more significant part of the data processing budget. As a result, a technique was developed to improve programmer productivity, known as structured programming.

When structured programming was implemented improvements were noticeable in many areas. Because of the self-documenting nature of structured programming, programs became easier to read and thereby easier to enhance or modify. Since the program's structure was generally the same from program to program, less time was spent in the program design phase. Also, because of a common formalized structure, many programs could be created just by copying and modifying previously written programs. This was especially true of programs that generated reports. Third, due to the module-like nature of structured programs, they were easier to test and debug. Finally, the software was more reliable and had a longer production life.

A CONCEPTUAL OVERVIEW

Conceptually, the developers of structured programming theorized that all programming procedures can be written using one of three structures. These structures are sequential, If-Then-Else, and Do-While.

Sequential

The flowchart in Fig. 7-1 depicts the sequen-

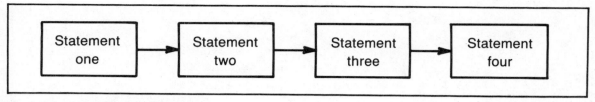

Fig. 7-1. Sequential processing flowchart.

tial processing of statements. The structure is the consecutive execution of statements without the interruption of conditional logic or unconditional branching.

Figure 7-2 is an example of sequentially processed statements. There are very few programs that use just sequentially processed statements. It is very common however, to have a group of statements much like those in the figure incorporated in If-Then-Else logic or in a Do-While looping structure.

If-Then-Else

The If-Then-Else structure is a very powerful and flexible part of the COBOL language, essential to the development of most business application programs. Its function is to define the program's logic and cause the execution of selected statements based on specified criteria. In other words, IF a particular condition is met, THEN perform a function or group of functions, ELSE, if the condition is not met, perform a different set of functions. Figure 7-3 represents the If-Then-Else logic.

In COBOL the If-Then-Else structure is performed by the IF statement. Even though most compilers do not use the word THEN in the IF statement format, they all logically imply its function by the statements placed directly after the conditional expression. Figure 7-4 is an example of an

IF condition. A value of one will be added to SALARY-COUNT if PAY-TYPE is equal to SALARIED. Otherwise one will be added to the hourly employee counter HOURLY-COUNT. Note that both these ADD statements will never be executed for the same employee. Therefore, this Then/Else relationship is always an "either/or" scenario.

Do-While

The last of the structured constructs is the Do-While format. This format is used for looping, and instructs the computer to DO these statements WHILE a particular condition is true. Figure 7-5 represents the Do-While process. Note in the Do-While flowchart that the specified statements are always executed at least once, then the condition is checked to see if the loop should continue. This processing order will have ramifications in regard to how and when the looping process is called. Figure 7-6 displays the loop calling process.

In the partial program shown in the figure, INFILE is opened for input, N is moved to OUT-OF-RECORDS, and the first record is read from the file. If the file is empty no records were retrieved, and LOOP-PAR is not called and the propane ends. However, if a record is returned from the file LOOP-PAR is performed and the retrieved record is processed during the first pass through the loop. At the bottom of the looping paragraph another READ statement is encountered, and then process

Fig. 7-2. Sequentially processed statements.

```
COMPUTE SALARY = HOURLY-WAGE * 40.
MOVE SALARY TO DISPLAY-SALARY.
DISPLAY DISPLAY-SALARY.
```

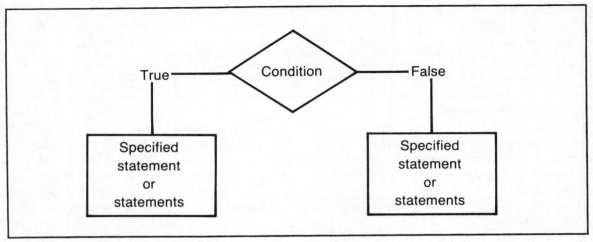

Fig. 7-3. If-Then-Else processing examples.

continues until the file is out of records. At that time, OUT-OF-RECORDS is set to Y and control is passed back to START-PAR.

TOP-DOWN DEVELOPMENT

As research of structured analysis continued, it was discovered that, because of the modular structure caused by the use of only sequential, If-Then-Else, and Do-While processes, programs could be written from the first instruction to the last without having to rework previously entered statements. Therefore, the program could be tested during the coding phase each time logical groups of modules were added. Thus the name *top-down development* was coined. To illustrate this, consider the development process used to create the mailing list update program in Fig. 7-7.

When the program was being designed, the HIPO structure chart shown in Fig. 7-8 was developed. When the mailing list program was developed, START-PAR was developed and then tested

```
IF PAY-TYPE = 'SALARIED'
    ADD 1 TO PAY-TYPE
ELSE
    ADD 1 TO HOURLY-COUNT.
```

Fig. 7-4. If-Then-Else conditional statement.

with the program in the status shown in Fig. 7-9. Once the program was tested, READ-PAR, WRITE-PAR, and MENU-PAR were added and debugged. At that point in time the program was in the state exhibited in Fig. 7-10. The program as seen in the last figure can be compiled, linked, and executed. As a result the paragraphs, or modules, that have been written can be completely tested and

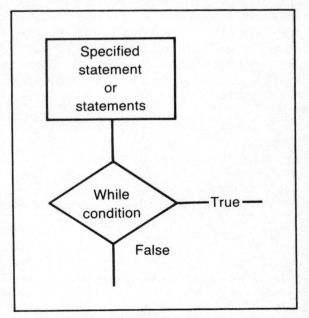

Fig. 7-5. Do-While processing flowchart.

86

```
        PROCEDURE DIVISION.
        START-PAR.
            OPEN INPUT IN-FILE, OUTPUT OUT-FILE.
            MOVE 'N' TO OUT-OF-RECORDS.
            READ IN-FILE AT END MOVE 'N' TO OUT-OF-RECORDS.
            IF OUT-OF-RECORDS = 'N'
                PERFORM LOOP-PAR THROUGH LOOP-PAR-END
                    UNTIL OUT-OF-RECORDS = 'Y'.
            CLOSE IN-FILE.
            STOP RUN.

        LOOP-PAR.
            MOVE IN-REC TO OUT-REC.
            WRITE OUT-REC.
            READ IN-FILE AT END MOVE 'Y' TO OUT-OF-RECORDS.
        LOOP-PAR-END.
```

Fig. 7-6. Do-While processing example.

```
    IDENTIFICATION DIVISION.

    PROGRAM-ID.      MAIL.
    AUTHOR.          ERIC P. BLOOM.
    INSTALLATION.    BOSTON.
    DATE-WRITTEN.    SEP. 1, 1985.
    DATE-COMPILED.   SEP, 1, 1985.
    SECURITY.        NONE.

    ENVIRONMENT DIVISION.

    CONFIGURATION SECTION.
    SOURCE-COMPUTER.      IBM.
    OBJECT-COMPUTER.      IBM.

    INPUT-OUTPUT SECTION.
    FILE-CONTROL.

        SELECT MAIL-FILE ASSIGN TO 'MAIL.MST'.

    DATA DIVISION.
    FILE SECTION.

    FD MAIL-FILE
       RECORD CONTAINS 76 CHARACTERS
       LABEL RECORDS ARE OMITTED
```

Fig. 7-7. Array update program listing.

```
    DATA RECORD IS MAIL-REC.

01 MAIL-REC          PIC X(76).

WORKING-STORAGE SECTION.

01 MAIL-TABLE OCCURS 100 TIMES
    05 NAME                      PIC X(20).
    05 STREET-1                  PIC X(20).
    05 STREET-2                  PIC X(20).
    05 STATE                     PIC XX.
    05 ZIPCODE                   PIC X(9).


01 CONTROL-FIELDS
    05 ANSWER                    PIC X.
    05 ARRAY-SIZE                PIC 999.
    05 ARRAY-INDEX               PIC 999.
    05 OUT-OF-RECS               PIC X.
    05 FOUND-IT                  PIC X.
    05 VALID-OPTION              PIC X


01 WS-FIELDS.
    05 WS-NAME                   PIC X(20).
    05 WS-STREET-1               PIC X(20).
    05 WS-STREET-2               PIC X(20).
    05 WS-STATE                  PIC XX.
    05 WS-ZIPCODE                PIC X(9).


PROCEDURE DIVISION.
START-PAR.
    PERFORM READ-PAR THRU READ-PAR-END.
    PERFORM MENU-PAR THRU MENU-PAR-END.
    PERFORM WRITE-PAR THRU WRITE-PAR-END.
    STOP RUN.


MENU-PAR.
    MOVE 'N' TO VALID-OPTION.
    DISPLAY ' '.
    DISPLAY '                      MAIL LIST SYSTEM'.
    DISPLAY '                        UPDATE MENU'.
    DISPLAY ' '.
    DISPLAY '      1. ADD A NEW LABEL'.
    DISPLAY '      2. CHANGE CURRENT LABEL DATA'.
    DISPLAY '      3. DELETE A LABEL'.
    DISPLAY '      4. DISPLAY A LABEL'.
    DISPLAY '      5. LIST ALL LABELS.
    DISPLAY '      E. EXIT SYSTEM'.
    DISPLAY ' '.
    DISPLAY '                  ENTER OPTION: '.
    ACCEPT ANSWER.
```

```
      IF ANSWER = '1' MOVE 'Y' TO VALID-OPTION
                      PERFORM ADD-PAR THRU ADD-PAR-END.
      IF ANSWER = '2' MOVE 'Y' TO VALID-OPTION
                      PERFORM CHANGE-PAR THRU CHANGE-PAR-END.
      IF ANSWER = '3' MOVE 'Y' TO VALID-OPTION
                      PERFORM DELETE-PAR THRU DELETE-PAR-END.
      IF ANSWER = '4' MOVE 'Y' TO VALID-OPTION
                      PERFORM DISPLAY-PAR THRU DISPLAY-PAR-END.
      IF ANSWER = '5' MOVE 'Y' TO VALID-OPTION
                      PERFORM LIST-PAR THRU LIST-PAR-END
                          VARYING ARRAY-INDEX FROM 1 BY 1
                          UNTIL ARRAY-INDEX = ARRAY-SIZE.
      IF ANSWER = 'E' GOTO MENU-PAR-END.

      IF VALID-OPTION = 'Y' GOTO MENU-PAR.
      DISPLAY ' '.
      DISPLAY 'ERROR: ANSWER MUST BE 1,2,3,4,5 or E, PLEASE
      REENTER'.
      DISPLAY ' '.
      GOTO MENU-PAR.

      MENU-PAR-END.

ADD-PAR.
      ADD 1 TO ARRAY-SIZE.
      MOVE ARRAY-SIZE TO ARRAY-INDEX.
      DISPLAY 'ENTER NAME (LAST, FIRST MI) : '.
      ACCEPT  LAST-NAME(ARRAY-INDEX).
      DISPLAY 'ENTER FIRST STREET ADDRESS :'.
      ACCEPT  STREET-1(ARRAY-INDEX).
      DISPLAY 'ENTER SECOND STREET ADDRESS'.
      ACCEPT  STREET-2(ARRAY-INDEX).
      DISPLAY 'ENTER STATE CODE'.
      ACCEPT  STATE(ARRAY-INDEX).
      DISPLAY 'ENTER ZIPCODE: '.
      ACCEPT ZIPCODE(ARRAP-INDEX).
ADD-PAR-END.

CHANGE-PAR.
    PERFORM FIND-PAR THRU FIND-PAR-END.
    PERFORM LIST-PAR THRU LIST-PAR-END.
    DISPLAY 'ENTER NEW VALUE TO UPDATE OR <CR> TO LEAVE
    VALUE UNCHANGED'.
    DISPLAY ' '.

    DISPLAY 'ENTER NAME ( LAST, FIRST, MI ): '.
    ACCEPT WS-NAME.
    IF WS-NAME NOT = SPACES MOVE WS-NAME TO NAME(ARRAY-INDEX).

    DISPLAY 'ENTER FIRST STREET ADDRESS '.
```

```
         ACCEPT WS-STREET-1.
         IF WS-STREET-1 NOT = SPACES MOVE WS-STREET-1 TO STREET-1
         (ARRAY-INDEX).

         DISPLAY 'ENTER SECOND STREET ADDRESS: '.
         ACCEPT WS-STREET-2.
         IF WS-STREET-2 NOT = SPACES MOVE WS-STREET-2 TO STREET-2
         (ARRAY-INDEX).

         DISPLAY 'ENTER STATE CODE : '.
         ACCEPT WS-STATE.
         IF WS-STATE NOT = SPACES MOVE WS-STATE TO STATE
         (ARRAY-INDEX).

         DISPLAY 'ENTER ZIPCODE '.
         ACCEPT WS-ZIPCODE.
         IF WS-ZIPCODE NOT = SPACES MOVE WS-ZIPCODE TO ZIPCODE
         (ARRAY-INDEX).

CHANGE-PAR-END.

DELETE-PAR.
    PERFORM FIND-PAR THRU FIND-PAR-END.
    IF FOUND-IT = 'Y' MOVE '-----` TO LAST-NAME(ARRAY-INDEX).
DELETE-PAR-END.

DISPLAY-PAR.
      PERFORM FIND-PAR THRU FIND-PAR-END.
      PERFORM LIST-PAR THRU LIST-PAR-END.
DISPLAY-PAR-END.

LIST-PAR.
    DISPLAY 'NAME     : ',NAME(ARRAY-INDEX).
    DISPLAY 'STREET   : ',STREET-1(ARRAY-INDEX).
    DISPLAY 'STREET   : ',STREET-2(ARRAY-INDEX).
    DISPLAY 'STATE    : ',STATE(ARRAY-INDEX).
    DISPLAY 'ZIPCODE : ',ZIPCODE(ARRAY-INDEX).
LIST-PAR-END.

FIND-PAR.
    DISPLAY 'ENTER NAME ( LAST, FIRST, MI ) :'.
    ACCEPT WS-NAME.
    MOVE 'N' TO FOUND-IT.
    PERFORM FIND-1-PAR THRU FIND-1-PAR-END
            VARYING ARRAY-INDEX FROM 1 BY 1
            UNTIL ARRAY-INDEX = ARRAY-SIZE OR FOUND-IT = 'Y'.
    IF FOUND-IT = 'N' DISPLAY 'NOT FOUND'.

FIND-PAR-END.
```

```
FIND-1-PAR.
    IF NAME(ARRAY-INDEX) = WS-NAME
        DISPLAY ' '
        DISPLAY NAME(ARRAY-INDEX), ' ',STREET-1(ARRAY-INDEX)
        DISPLAY ' '
        DISPLAY 'IS THIS IT ( Y or N) : '
        ACCEPT FOUND-IT.
FIND-1-PAR-END.

READ-PAR.
        OPEN INPUT MAIL-FILE AT END MOVE 'Y' TO OUT-OF-RECS.
        MOVE 0 TO ARRAY-SIZE.
        READ MAIL-FILE AT END MOVE 'Y' TO OUT-OF-RECS.
        IF OUT-OF-RECS NOT = 'Y'
            PERFORM READ-2-PAR THRU READ-2-PAR-END UNTIL
            OUT-OF-RECS = 'Y'.
        CLOSE MAIL-FILE.
READ-PAR-END.

READ-1-PAR.
    ADD 1 TO ARRAY-SIZE.
    MOVE MAIL-REC TO MAIL-TABLE(ARRAY-SIZE).
    READ MAIL-FILE AT END MOVE 'Y' TO OUT-OF-RECS.
READ-1-PAR-END.

WRITE-PAR.
  OPER OUTPUT MAIL-FILE.
  PERFORM WRITE-PAR THRU WRITE-PAR-END
            VARYING ARRAY-INDEX FROM 1 BY 1 UNTIL ARRAY-INDEX
            = ARRAY-SIZE.
  CLOSE MAIL-FILE.
WRITE-PAR-END.

WRITE-1-PAR-END.
  IF NAME(ARRAY-INDEX) NOT = '-----'
      WRITE MAIL-REC FROM MAIL-ARRAY(ARRAY-INDEX).
WRITE-1-PAR-END.
```

left alone. As new modules are added only the newly added segments must be reviewed. This divide-and-conquer strategy makes it much easier to identify and correct programming errors.

THE USE OF THE GOTO STATEMENT

Over the years there has been much debate over the use of the GOTO statement in structured programming environment. Many industry specialists believe that this statement has no place in modern COBOL programming and should be avoided under all circumstances. The other school of thought believes that GOTO provides a needed function and may be used if it does not hurt a program's readability and self-documenting nature.

Program Termination

There is one rule on which both sides agree: that a GOTO should never be used to move from one paragraph to another. A GOTO should only be

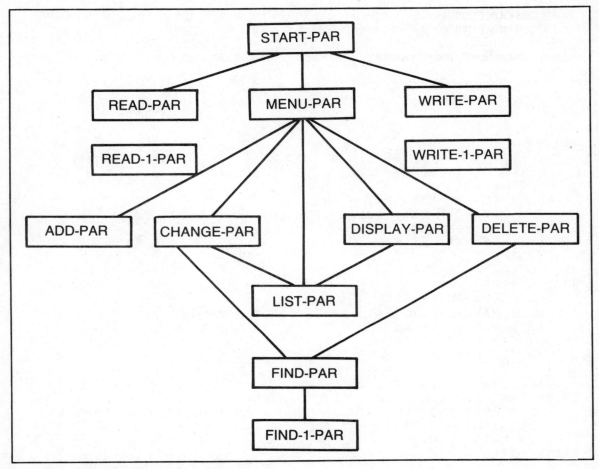

Fig. 7-8. Mailing list program structure chart.

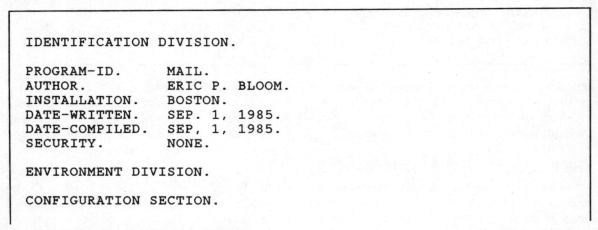

```
IDENTIFICATION DIVISION.

PROGRAM-ID.      MAIL.
AUTHOR.          ERIC P. BLOOM.
INSTALLATION.    BOSTON.
DATE-WRITTEN.    SEP. 1, 1985.
DATE-COMPILED.   SEP, 1, 1985.
SECURITY.        NONE.

ENVIRONMENT DIVISION.

CONFIGURATION SECTION.
```

Fig. 7-9. Mailing list program during development.

```
SOURCE-COMPUTER.        IBM.
OBJECT-COMPUTER.        IBM.

INPUT-OUTPUT SECTION.
FILE-CONTROL.

    SELECT MAIL-FILE ASSIGN TO "MAIL.MST.

DATA DIVISION.
FILE SECTION.

FD MAIL-FILE
   RECORD CONTAINS 76 CHARACTERS
   LABEL RECORDS ARE OMITTED
   DATA RECORD IS MAIL-REC.

01 MAIL-REC          PIC X(76).

WORKING-STORAGE SECTION.

01 MAIL-TABLE OCCURS 100 TIMES
   05 NAME                      PIC X(20).
   05 STREET-1                  PIC X(20).
   05 STREET-2                  PIC X(20).
   05 STATE                     PIC XX.
   05 ZIPCODE                   PIC X(9).

01 CONTROL-FIELDS
   05 ANSWER                    PIC X.
   05 ARRAY-SIZE                PIC 999.
   05 ARRAY-INDEX               PIC 999.
   05 OUT-OF-RECS               PIC X.
   05 FOUND-IT                  PIC X.
   05 VALID-OPTION              PIC X

01 WS-FIELDS.
   05 WS-NAME                   PIC X(20).
   05 WS-STREET-1               PIC X(20).
   05 WS-STREET-2               PIC X(20).
   05 WS-STATE                  PIC XX.
   05 WS-ZIPCODE                PIC X(9).

PROCEDURE DIVISION.
START-PAR.
    PERFORM READ-PAR THRU READ-PAR-END.
    PERFORM MENU-PAR THRU MENU-PAR-END.
    PERFORM WRITE-PAR THRU WRITE-PAR-END.
    STOP RUN.

READ-PAR.
```

```
         DISPLAY 'GOT TO READ-PAR'.
READ-PAR-END.

MENU-PAR.
         DISPLAY 'GOT TO MENU-PAR'.
MENU-PAR-END.

WRITE-PAR.
         DISPLAY 'GOT TO WRITE-PAR'.
WRITE-PAR-END.
```

```
IDENTIFICATION DIVISION.

PROGRAM-ID.       MAIL.
AUTHOR.           ERIC P. BLOOM.
INSTALLATION.     BOSTON.
DATE-WRITTEN.     SEP. 1, 1985.
DATE-COMPILED.    SEP, 1, 1985.
SECURITY.         NONE.

ENVIRONMENT DIVISION.

CONFIGURATION SECTION.
SOURCE-COMPUTER.      IBM.
OBJECT-COMPUTER.      IBM.

INPUT-OUTPUT SECTION.
FILE-CONTROL.

     SELECT MAIL-FILE ASSIGN TO "MAIL.MST".

DATA DIVISION.
FILE SECTION.

FD MAIL-FILE
     RECORD CONTAINS 76 CHARACTERS
     LABEL RECORDS ARE OMITTED
     DATA RECORD IS MAIL-REC.

01 MAIL-REC          PIC X(76).

WORKING-STORAGE SECTION.

01 MAIL-TABLE OCCURS 100 TIMES
     05 NAME                      PIC X(20).
     05 STREET-1                  PIC X(20).
     05 STREET-2                  PIC X(20).
```

Fig. 7-10. Second stage of mailing list program development.

```
      05  STATE                         PIC XX.
      05  ZIPCODE                       PIC X(9).


  01  CONTROL-FIELDS
      05  ANSWER                        PIC X.
      05  ARRAY-SIZE                    PIC 999.
      05  ARRAY-INDEX                   PIC 999.
      05  OUT-OF-RECS                   PIC X.
      05  FOUND-IT                      PIC X.
      05  VALID-OPTION                  PIC X


  01  WS-FIELDS.
      05  WS-NAME                       PIC X(20).
      05  WS-STREET-1                   PIC X(20).
      05  WS-STREET-2                   PIC X(20).
      05  WS-STATE                      PIC XX.
      05  WS-ZIPCODE                    PIC X(9).


  PROCEDURE DIVISION.
  START-PAR.
      PERFORM READ-PAR THRU READ-PAR-END.
      PERFORM MENU-PAR THRU MENU-PAR-END.
      PERFORM WRITE-PAR THRU WRITE-PAR-END.
      STOP RUN.

  MENU-PAR.
      MOVE 'N' TO VALID-OPTION.
      DISPLAY ' '.
      DISPLAY '                          MAIL LIST SYSTEM'.
      DISPLAY '                            UPDATE MENU'.
      DISPLAY ' '.
      DISPLAY '      1. ADD A NEW LABEL'.
      DISPLAY '      2. CHANGE CURRENT LABEL DATA'.
      DISPLAY '      3. DELETE A LABEL'.
      DISPLAY '      4. DISPLAY A LABEL'.
      DISPLAY '      5. LIST ALL LABELS.
      DISPLAY '      E. EXIT SYSTEM'.
      DISPLAY ' '.
      DISPLAY '                    ENTER OPTION: '.
      ACCEPT ANSWER.
      IF ANSWER = '1' MOVE 'Y' TO VALID-OPTION
                      PERFORM ADD-PAR THRU ADD-PAR-END.
      IF ANSWER = '2' MOVE 'Y' TO VALID-OPTION
                      PERFORM CHANGE-PAR THRU CHANGE-PAR-END.
      IF ANSWER = '3' MOVE 'Y' TO VALID-OPTION
                      PERFORM DELETE-PAR THRU DELETE-PAR-END.
      IF ANSWER = '4' MOVE 'Y' TO VALID-OPTION
                      PERFORM DISPLAY-PAR THRU DISPLAY-PAR-END.
      IF ANSWER = '5' MOVE 'Y' TO VALID-OPTION
                      PERFORM LIST-PAR THRU LIST-PAR-END
```

```
                         VARYING ARRAY-INDEX FROM 1 BY 1
                         UNTIL ARRAY-INDEX = ARRAY-SIZE.
     IF ANSWER = 'E' GOTO MENU-PAR-END.

     IF VALID-OPTION = 'Y' GOTO MENU-PAR.
     DISPLAY ' '.
     DISPLAY 'ERROR: ANSWER MUST BE 1,2,3,4,5 or E, PLEASE
     REENTER'.
     DISPLAY ' '.
     GOTO MENU-PAR.

     MENU-PAR-END.

ADD-PAR.
     DISPLAY 'GOT TO THE ADD-PAR'.
ADD-PAR-END.

CHANGE-PAR.
    DISPLAY 'GOT TO THE CHANGE-PAR'.
CHANGE-PAR-END.

DELETE-PAR.
     DISPLAY 'GOT TO THE DELETE-PAR'.
DELETE-PAR-END.

LIST-PAR.
    DISPLAY 'GOT TO THE LIST-PAR'.
LIST-PAR-END.

FIND-PAR.
    DISPLAY 'GOT TO THE FIND-PAR'.
FIND-PAR-END.

DISPLAY-PAR.
    DISPLAY -GOT TO THE DISPLAY-PAR'.
DISPLAY-PAR-END.

READ-PAR.
        OPEN INPUT MAIL-FILE AT END MOVE 'Y' TO OUT-OF-RECS.
        MOVE 0 TO ARRAY-SIZE.
        READ MAIL-FILE AT END MOVE 'Y' TO OUT-OF-RECS.
        IF OUT-OF-RECS NOT = 'Y'
           PERFORM READ-2-PAR THRU READ-2-PAR-END UNTIL
           OUT-OF-RECS = 'Y'.
        CLOSE MAIL-FILE.
READ-PAR-END.

READ-1-PAR.
     ADD 1 TO ARRAY-SIZE.
     MOVE MAIL-REC TO MAIL-TABLE(ARRAY-SIZE).
```

```
        READ MAIL-FILE AT END MOVE 'Y' TO OUT-OF-RECS.
READ-1-PAR-END.

WRITE-PAR.
   OPER OUTPUT MAIL-FILE.
   PERFORM WRITE-PAR THRU WRITE-PAR-END
           VARYING ARRAY-INDEX FROM 1 BY 1 UNTIL ARRAY-INDEX =
           ARRAY-SIZE.
   CLOSE MAIL-FILE.
WRITE-PAR-END.

WRITE-1-PAR-END.
   IF NAME(ARRAY-INDEX) NOT = '-----'
       WRITE MAIL-REC FROM MAIL-ARRAY(ARRAY-INDEX).
WRITE-1-PAR-END.
```

used to pass control to the beginning or ending of the paragraph in which it resides.

GOTO advocates believe there is one situation in which a GOTO statement may transfer control to another paragraph—where the paragraph being called terminates the program's execution. Figure 7-11 contains a partial program showing how GOTO can effectively be used to assist in program termination.

The example does not deserve much merit in

```
        PROCEDURE DIVISION.
        START-PAR.
            DISPLAY 'ENTER TWO NUMBERS: '.
            ACCEPT A,B
            PERFORM ADD-PAR THRU ADD-PAR-END.
            PERFORM SUBTRACT-PAR THRU SUBTRACT-PAR-END.
            PERFORM DIVIDE-PAR THRU DIVIDE-PAR-END.
            STOP RUN.

        ADD-PAR.
            ADD A, B GIVING C ON SIZE ERROR GOTO ERROR-PAR.
        ADD-PAR-END.

        SUBTRACT-PAR.
            SUBTRACT A FROM B ON SIZE ERROR GOTO ERROR-PAR.
        SUBTRACT-PAR-END.

        DIVIDE-PAR.
            DIVIDE A INTO B ON SIZE ERROR GOTO ERROR-PAR.
        DIVIDE-PAR-END.

        ERROR-PAR.
            DISPLAY 'AN OVERFLOW HAS OCCURED'.
            STOP RUN.
```

Fig. 7-11. GOTO program termination example.

```
PROCEDURE DIVISION.
START-PAR.
    PERFORM GET-STATUS-PAR THRU GET-STATUS-PAR-END.
    STOP RUN.

GET-STATUS-PAR.
    DISPLAY 'ENTER EMPLOYEE STATUS CODE ( A or T ): '.
    ACCEPT ANSWER.
    IF ANSWER = 'A' OR ANSWER = 'T' GOTO GET-STATUS-PAR-END.
    DISPLAY ' '.
    DISPLAY 'ERROR:  Status Must be A or T, Please Re-enter'.
    DISPLAY ' '.
    GOTO GET-STATUS-PAR.
GET-STATUS-PAR-END.
```

Fig. 7-12. GOTO example.

regard to its functionality, but it does display a valid use of the GOTO statement. If this termination technique was not present the ERROR-PAR logic could have been placed in each paragraph, or the overflow condition could have set a flag that would be tested when each perform routine passed control back to START-PAR. Either of these alternatives would add to the program's length and complexity.

On-Line Data Validation

The validation of data entered on-line by a user is a classic case where GOTOs can be used to transfer control to the beginning or end of a paragraph. Figure 7-12 is an example of a data validation technique that uses GOTO in this manner. The program performs the needed data validation with relative ease. Figure 7-13 performs the same function using structured "GOTOless" programming. As can

```
PROCEDURE DIVISION.
START-PAR.
    DISPLAY 'ENTER EMPLOYEE STATUS ( A or T ): '.
    ACCEPT ANSWER.
    PERFORM GET-STATUS-PAR THRU GET-STATUS-PAR-END
        UNTIL ANSWER = 'A' OR ANSWER = 'T'.
    STOP RUN.

GET-STATUS-PAR.
    IF ANSWER = 'A' OR ANSWER = 'T'
        NEXT SENTENCE
    ELSE
        DISPLAY ' '
        DISPLAY 'ERROR: Status Must be A or T, Please Re-enter'
        DISPLAY ' '
        DISPLAY 'ENTER EMPLOYEE STATUS ( A or T ): '
        ACCEPT ANSWER.
GET-STATUS-PAR-END.
```

Fig. 7-13. On-line validation alternative.

be seen, the structured technique is a bit more cumbersome, but more consistent with structured principles.

In the final analysis, the rules for using the GOTO statement will differ from company to company. Remember, however, the goal is not to avoid GOTOs, but to write programs that are as clear, reliable, and self-documenting as possible.

QUESTIONS

1. What is structured programming?

2. Why were structured programming techniques developed?

3. What benefits were realized by the implementation of structured programming?

4. List and describe the three structured formats used in structured programming.

5. What COBOL statement is used to execute the Do-While programming structure?

6. What is top-down programming development?

7. Explain the step-by-step process by which structured programs can be coded and tested.

8. What are the pros and cons of using the GOTO statement?

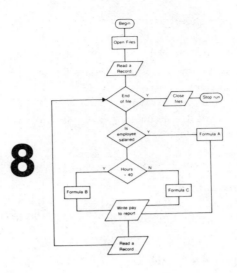

8

Table Handling

A data table is a collection of related data items stored under a common name. These tables, also known as arrays, may contain the days of the week, months of the year, a list of valid employee status codes, or any group of related information. This chapter will discuss the role these tables can play as a programming tool, including: the validation of data entry, date conversion, check writing, the display of text associated with alphabetic and numeric codes, temporary storage in preparation for output to a file, and other techniques and procedures that can be easily incorporated into any business oriented application.

DEFINING TABLES

Tables are defined in the DATA DIVISION by a process similar to the definition of regular single-item variables. The difference is the inclusion of the OCCURS clause and the optional ASCENDING KEY and INDEXED BY clauses. For a complete discussion of this process refer to the table-handling section of Chapter 6.

LOADING INFORMATION INTO A TABLE

Data can be loaded into a table in one of two ways: as part of the table definition or by reading data from a file. The table definition option is by far the most popular. In most cases the information placed in tables does not change from day to day and can therefore be hard-coded into the program. Hardcoding can be done in the DATA DIVISION, shown in Fig. 8-1.

In the first table-loading example the data is placed in the single item variable STATUS-CODE-TAB. From there, it is moved to STATUS-CODE-TABLE by a REDEFINES clause. This clause instructs the computer to copy the contents of STATUS-CODE-TAB to STATUS-CODE-TABLE. Line 357 defines STATUS-CODES as a table by stating that it OCCURS four times. It further states that STATUS-CODES is broken into fields, STATUS-CODE described as one character long and STATUS-CODE-DESCR described as 14 characters long. These size descriptions are consistent with the FILLER/VALUE clauses in

```
350        WORKING-STORAGE SECTION.
351        01 STATUS-CODE-TAB.
352           05 FILLER PIC X(10) VALUE IS 'AACTIVE        '.
353           05 FILLER PIC X(10) VALUE IS 'RRETIRED       '.
354           05 FILLER PIC X(10) VALUE IS 'TTERMINATED    '.
355           05 FILLER PIC X(10) VALUE IS 'WWARNING       '.
356
357        01 STATUS-CODE-TABLE REDEFINES STATUS-CODE-TAB.
358           05 STATUS-CODES OCCURS 4 TIMES.
359              10 STATUS-CODE       PIC X.
360              10 STATUS-CODE-DESC  PIC X(14).
```

Fig. 8-1. First table loading example.

STATUS-CODE-TAB. It is this consistency that loads the correct characters into the correct fields.

The second table-loading option reads the information from a data file. This process is primarily used in applications that should not have information hardwired into the program. For example, a payroll system may contain 30 programs that use employee status information. If all 30 programs had codes explicitly written in the DATA DIVISION the addition of a new code would cause all the programs to be edited and recompiled. However, if the programs read the codes from a small sequential file into memory, then only the small file would require modification. Figure 8-2 shows the table loading process.

TABLES IN DATA VALIDATION

Table look-up techniques are commonly used to validate data input. Validations are performed by comparing the user-entered data with the values contained in the table. If a match is made the entry is valid. If the input value is not found an error has occurred. Chapter 11 outlines many table-driven validation techniques.

DATE CONVERSION

Many applications require the ability to modify a date format from "31-AUG-85" to "80/31/85" or "850831." To perform this conversion the program must be able to connect the name of the month (AUG) with its numeric equivalent (08). A data table is the ideal way to make the connection. Figure 8-3 illustrates the process used to make the first conversion.

The figure asks the user to input a date. Once input, the program converts that date from DD-MMM-YY format to MM/DD/YY format. This conversion is performed by moving the date and year directly from the input variable to the output area. The month is passed through a SEARCH table statement; when a match is made between the entered value and a value in the table, the corresponding month number equivalent is copied from the table to OUT-MONTH.

There is an alternate approach that could have been used to convert the month to its numeric equivalent. This would have been to move the value in MONTH-INDEX to a numerically defined OUT-MONTH. Remember, the months were loaded into the table in chronological order, therefore JAN is in MONTH(1), FEB is in MONTH(2), and so on. Figure 8-4 shows this technique.

There are two approaches that can be employed to convert the month field from a numeric back to a textual format. The first approach uses a SEARCH table statement in a process very similar to Fig. 8-2. The second alternative does not use a table search at all.

Figure 8-5 shows the first numeric-to-text alternative. This program contains two modifications not seen in Fig. 8-3. First, the user is asked to en-

```
DATA DIVISION.
FILE SECTION.

FD  STATUS-CODE-FILE
    RECORD CONTAINS 15 CHARACTERS
    LABEL RECORDS ARE STANDARD
    DATA RECORD IS STATUS-CODE-REC.

01  STATUS-CODE-REC.
    05  IN-STATUS-CODE          PIC X(1).
    05  IN-STATUS-CODE-DESC     PIC X(14).

WORKING-STORAGE SECTION.

01  STATUS-CODES OCCURS 10 TIMES.
    05  STATUS-CODE             PIC X.
    05  STATUS-CODE-DESC        PIC X(14).

01  OUT-OF-RECS                 PIC X.
01  CODE-INDEX                  PIC 9.

PROCEDURE DIVISION.
START-PAR.
    OPEN INPUT STATUS-CODE-FILE.
    MOVE 'N' TO OUT-OF-RECS.
    READ STATUS-CODE-FILE AT END MOVE 'Y' TO OUT-OF-RECS.
    IF OUT-OF-RECS = 'N'
        PERFORM FILL-ARRAY-PAR THRU FILL-ARRAY-PAR-END
            VARYING CODE-INDEX FROM 1 BY 1 UNTIL
            OUT-OF-RECORDS = 'Y'.
    STOP RUN.

FILL-ARRAY-PAR.
    MOVE STATUS-CODE-REC TO STATUS-CODES(CODE-INDEX).
    READ STATUS-CODE-FILE AT END MOVE 'Y' TO OUT-OF-RECS.
FILL-ARRAY-PAR-END.
```

Fig. 8-2. Second table loading example.

ter the date in numeric format; second, the search statement uses MONTH-NO and not MONTH-ALPHA in the table look-up.

The second alternative can be performed because the months were loaded in chronological order: the text corresponding to month 08 (August) can be found in field MONTH(8), so the table does not have to be searched because the array location has already been established. Tables that can be directly accessed in this manner are called *Positional Tables*. Figure 8-6 illustrates this second numeric-to-textual alternative.

TABLES IN CHECK WRITING

When people write personal checks for their bills they write the amount of the check twice once in numeric format ($45) and once in textual format (forty-five). The textual format is used as protec-

```
WORKING-STORAGE SECTION.

01 IN-DATE.
   05 IN-DAY                  PIC XX.
   05 FILLER                  PIC X.
   05 IN-MONTH                PIC XXX.
   05 FILLER                  PIC X.
   05 IN-YEAR                 PIC XX.

01 MONTH-TAB                  PIC X(60)
   VALUE IS '01JAN02FEB03MAR04APR05MAY06JUN07JUL08AUG09SEP10
   OCT11NOV12DEC'.
01 MONTH-TABLE REDEFINES MONTH-TAB.
   05 MONTHS OCCURS 12 TIMES.
      10 MONTH-NO             PIC XX.
      10 MONTH-ALPHA          PIC XXX.

01 MONTH-INDEX               PIC 99.

01 OUT-DATE.
   05 OUT-MONTH               PIC XX.
   05 FILLER                  PIC X VALUE IS '/'.
   05 OUT-DAY                 PIC XX.
   05 FILLER                  PIC X VALUE IS '/'.
   05 OUT-YEAR                PIC XX.

PROCEDURE DIVISION.
START-PAR.
    DISPLAY 'ENTER DATE IN FORMAT DD-MMM-YY: '.
    ACCEPT IN-DATE.
    MOVE IN-DAY       TO OUT-YEAR.
    MOVE IN-YEAR      TO OUT-YEAR.
    SEARCH IN-YEAR VARYING MONTH-INDEX
          AT END DISPLAY 'INVALID MONTH, PLEASE REENTER'
                 GOTO START-PAR
          WHEN MONTH-ALPHA(MONTH-INDEX) = IN-MONTH
               MOVE MONTH-NO(MONTH-INDEX) TO OUT-MONTH.
    DISPLAY OUT-MONTH.
    STOP RUN.

WHEN EXECUTED:
    ENTER DATE IN FORMAT DD-MMM-YY: 31-AUG-85
    08/31/85
```

Fig. 8-3. First date conversion example.

```
WORKING-STORAGE SECTION.

01 IN-DATE.
    05 IN-DAY                   PIC XX.
    05 FILLER                   PIC X.
    05 IN-MONTH                 PIC XXX.
    05 FILLER                   PIC X.
    05 IN-YEAR                  PIC XX.

01 MONTH-TAB                    PIC X(36).
    VALUE IS 'JANFEBMARAPRMAYJUNJULAUGSEPOCTNOVDEC'.
01 MONTH-TABLE REDEFINES MONTH-TAB.
    05 MONTHS OCCURS 12 TIMES.
        10 MONTH-ALPHA          PIC XXX.

01 MONTH-INDEX                  PIC 99.

01 OUT-DATE.
    05 OUT-MONTH                PIC 99.
    05 FILLER                   PIC X VALUE IS '/'.
    05 OUT-DAY                  PIC XX.
    05 FILLER                   PIC X VALUE IS '/'.
    05 OUT-YEAR                 PIC XX.

PROCEDURE DIVISION.
START-PAR.
    DISPLAY 'ENTER DATE IN FORMAT DD-MM-YY: '.
    ACCEPT IN-DATE.
    MOVE IN-DAY      TO OUT-YEAR.
    MOVE IN-YEAR     TO OUT-YEAR.
    SEARCH IN-YEAR VARYING MONTH-INDEX
            AT END DISPLAY 'INVALID MONTH, PLEASE REENTER'
                GOTO START-PAR
            WHEN MONTH-ALPHA(MONTH-INDEX) = IN-MONTH
                MOVE MONTH-INDEX TO OUT-MONTH.
    DISPLAY OUT-DATE.
    STOP RUN.

WHEN EXECUTED:
    ENTER DATE IN FORMAT DD-MM-YY: 31-AUG-85
    08/31/85
```

Fig. 8-4. Second date conversion example.

tion against altering the check value. Accounting systems that automatically generate checks for payroll or other accounting purposes also use this safeguard. Figure 8-7 shows how this process is performed.

The check printing example shown in Fig. 8-7 has been simplified to highlight the numeric to textual conversion process. In this example the user enters a value via a terminal. This value is analyzed and displayed in textual format. If this were an ac-

```
WORKING-STORAGE SECTION.

01  IN-DATE.
    05 IN-MONTH                PIC XX.
    05 FILLER                  PIC X.
    05 IN-DAY                  PIC XX.
    05 FILLER                  PIC X.
    05 IN-YEAR                 PIC XX.

01  MONTH-TAB                  PIC X(60)
    VALUE IS '01JAN02FEB03MAR04APR05MAY06JUN07JUL08AUG09SEP10
    OCT11NOV12DEC'.
01  MONTH-TABLE REDEFINES MONTH-TAB.
    05 MONTHS OCCURS 12 TIMES.
        10 MONTH-NO            PIC XX.
        10 MONTH-ALPHA         PIC XXX.

01  MONTH-INDEX                PIC 99.

01  OUT-DATE.
    05 OUT-DAY                 PIC XX.
    05 FILLER                  PIC X VALUE IS '-'.
    05 OUT-MONTH               PIC XXX.
    05 FILLER                  PIC X VALUE IS '-'.
    05 OUT-YEAR                PIC XX.

PROCEDURE DIVISION.
START-PAR.
    DISPLAY 'ENTER DATE IN FORMAT DD-MMM-YY: '.
    ACCEPT IN-DATE.
    MOVE IN-DAY       TO OUT-YEAR.
    MOVE IN-YEAR      TO OUT-YEAR.
    SEARCH IN-YEAR VARYING MONTH-INDEX
            AT END DISPLAY 'INVALID MONTH, PLEASE REENTER'
                    GOTO START-PAR
            WHEN MONTH-NO(MONTH-INDEX) = IN-MONTH
                 MOVE MONTH-ALPHA(MONTH-INDEX) TO OUT-MONTH.
    DISPLAY OUT-DATE.
    STOP RUN.

WHEN EXECUTED:
    ENTER DATE IN FORMAT DD-MMM-YY: 08/31/85
    31-AUG-85
```

Fig. 8-5. Third date conversion example.

```
       WORKING-STORAGE SECTION.

       01 IN-DATE.
          05 IN-MONTH                   PIC 99.
          05 FILLER                     PIC X.
          05 IN-DAY                     PIC XX.
          05 FILLER                     PIC X.
          05 IN-YEAR                    PIC XX.

       01 MONTH-TAB                     PIC X(36)
          VALUE IS 'JANFEBMARAPRMAYJUNJULAUGSEPOCTNOVDEC'.
       01 MONTH-TABLE REDEFINES MONTH-TAB.
          05 MONTHS OCCURS 12 TIMES.
             10 MONTH-ALPHA             PIC XXX.

       01 MONTH-INDEX                   PIC 99.

       01 OUT-DATE.
          05 OUT-DAY                    PIC XX.
          05 FILLER                     PIC X VALUE IS '-'.
          05 OUT-MONTH                  PIC XXX.
          05 FILLER                     PIC X VALUE IS '-'.
          05 OUT-YEAR                   PIC XX.

       PROCEDURE DIVISION.
       START-PAR.
          DISPLAY 'ENTER DATE IN FORMAT DD-MMM-YY: '.
          ACCEPT IN-DATE.
          MOVE IN-DAY                   TO OUT-YEAR.
          MOVE IN-YEAR                  TO OUT-YEAR.
          MOVE MONTH-ALPHA(IN-MONTH) TO OUT-MONTH.
          DISPLAY OUT-DATE.
          STOP RUN.

       WHEN EXECUTED:
          ENTER DATE IN FORMAT DD-MMM-YY: 08/31/85
          31-AUG-85
```

Fig. 8-6. Fourth date conversion example.

tual check printing application the check amount would not be input from from the screen, it would be read from a file as one of many checks to be processed. The check amount would not be displayed to the user, but formatted with the amount, date and the name and address of the person or organization receiving the check.

When the program is executed the user is asked to enter a check amount. After the amount is entered the program moves the cents to PENNY-AMOUNT and the dollars to AMOUNT-NO-PENNIES. PENNY-AMOUNT will be used later in the program to print the cents on the print line after the textual dollar amount. AMOUNT-NO-PENNIES is then moved to AMOUNT-BREAKUP. This field breaks the dollar amount

```
WORKING-STORAGE SECTION.

01 IN-CHECK-AMOUNT              PIC 9(4).99.
01 AMOUNT-NO-PENNIES           PIC 9(4).
01 PENNY-AMOUNT                PIC .99.
01 OUTPUT-FIELDS.
   05 THOUSAND-1               PIC X(10).
   05 THOUSAND-2               PIC X(10).
   05 HUNDRED-1                PIC X(10).
   05 HUNDRED-2                PIC X(10).
   05 TENS-1                   PIC X(10).
   05 ONES-1                   PIC X(10).
   05 PRINT-TEXT               PIC X(60).
01 AMOUNT-BREAKUP.
   05 THOUSANDS                PIC 9.
   05 HUNDREDS                 PIC 9.
   05 TENS                     PIC 9.
   05 ONES                     PIC 9.

01 ONES-TEXT-TAB.
   05 FILLER PIC X(45)
      VALUE IS 'ONE  TWO  THREEFOUR FIVE SIX  SEVENEIGHTNINE`.
01 ONES-TEXT-TABLE REDEFINES ONES-TEXT-TAB.
   05 ONES-TEXT OCCURS 9 TIMES PIC X(5).

01 TENS-TEXT-TAB.
   05 FILLER PIC X() VALUE IS
      '-------TWENTY THIRTY FORTY FIFTY
             SIXTY  SEVENTYEIGHTYNINETY '.
01 TENS-TEXT-TABLE REDEFINES TENS-TEXT-TAB.
   05 TENS-TEXT OCCURS 9 TIMES PIC X(7).

PROCEDURE DIVISION.
START-PAR.
   DISPLAY 'ENTER CHECK AMOUNT: '.
   ACCEPT IN-CHECK-AMOUNT.
   IF IN-CHECK-AMOUNT = 0 STOP RUN.
   MOVE IN-CHECK-AMOUNT            TO   AMOUNT-NO-PENNIES.
   SUBTRACT AMOUNT-NO-PENNIES   FROM IN-CHECK-AMOUNT GIVING
                                     PENNY-AMOUNT.
   MOVE AMOUNT-NO-PENNIES          TO   AMOUNT-BREAKUP.

   IF THOUSANDS NOT = 0 MOVE ONES-TEXT(THOUSANDS)TO THOUSAND-1
                        MOVE 'THOUSAND'          TO THOUSAND-2.
   IF HUNDREDS  NOT = 0 MOVE ONES-TEXT(HUNDRED)  TO HUNDRED-1
                        MOVE 'HUNDRED'           TO HUNDRED-2.
   IF TENS      NOT = 0 MOVE TENS-TEXT(TENS)     TO TENS-1.
   IF ONES      NOT = 0 MOVE ONES-TEXT(ONES)     TO ONES-1.
```

Fig. 8-7. Check printing example.

```
COMPUTE TEEN-CHECK = ( TENS * 10 ) + ONES.
IF TEEN-CHECK = 11 MOVE SPACES          TO ONES-1
                   MOVE 'ELEVEN'        TO TENS-1.
IF TEEN-CHECK = 12 MOVE SPACES          TO ONES-1
                   MOVE 'TWELVE'        TO TENS-1.
IF TEEN-CHECK = 13 MOVE SPACES          TO ONES-1
                   MOVE 'THIRTEEN'      TO TENS-1.
IF TEEN-CHECK = 14 MOVE SPACES          TO ONES-1
                   MOVE 'FOURTEEN'      TO TENS-1.
IF TEEN-CHECK = 15 MOVE SPACES          TO ONES-1
                   MOVE 'FIFTEEN'       TO TENS-1.
IF TEEN-CHECK = 16 MOVE SPACES          TO ONES-1
                   MOVE 'SIXTEEN'       TO TENS-1.
IF TEEN-CHECK = 17 MOVE SPACES          TO ONES-1
                   MOVE 'SEVENTEEN'     TO TENS-1.
IF TEEN-CHECK = 18 MOVE SPACES          TO ONES-1
                   MOVE 'EIGHTEEN'      TO TENS-1.
IF TEEN-CHECK = 19 MOVE SPACES          TO ONES-1
                   MOVE 'NINETEEN'      TO TENS-1.


STRING THOUSANDS-1 DELINIATED BY ' ',
       ' '         DELINIATED BY SIZE,
       THOUSANDS-2 DELINIATED BY ' ',
       ' '         DELINIATED BY SIZE,
       HUNDREDS-1  DELINIATED BY ' ',
       ' '         DELINIATED BY SIZE,
       TENS-1      DELINIATED BY ' ',
       ' '         DELINEATED BY SIZE,
       ONES-1      DELINIATED BY ' ',
   INTO PRINT-TEXT.

DISPLAY PRINT-TEXT,' ',PENNY-AMOUNT.
STOP RUN.
```

into four single digits. These are then passed through a series of IF statements where they are converted to their textual equals and placed in an intermediate holding area. Then, by use of a STRING statement, the single digits and their denomination labels (thousands or hundreds) are concatenated into one long variable named PRINT-TEXT. Finally, PRINT-TEXT and the value in PENNY-AMOUNT are displayed.

Note the purpose of the IF statements: If values are present the denomination name, where appropriate, and the textual representation of the number are moved to temporary areas. In effect, the IF statements only allow words to be printed if the column has a non-zero value. For example, the word *thousand* will only be printed when there is a value in the thousands column.

DATA DECODING

Virtually all computerized systems use some type of code to represent inventory classifications, employee status, project completion status, or other shorthand representation. Tables serve as an ideal vehicle to track and maintain these codes. For data entry purposes, displaying the clear text associated with a code at the time of input helps the data entry operator validate the entered information. Figure 8-8 shows this process.

```
WORKING-STORAGE SECTION.
01 STATUS-CODE-TAB
    05 FILLER PIC X(10) VALUE IS 'AACTIVE      '.
    05 FILLER FIC X(10) VALUE IS 'RRETIRED     '.
    05 FILLER PIC X(10) VALUE IS 'TTERMINATED  '.
    05 FILLER PIC X(10) VALUE IS 'WWARNING     '.

01 STATUS-CODE-TABLE REDEFINES STATUS-CODE-TAB.
    05 STATUS-CODES OCCURS 4 TIMES.
       10 STATUS-CODE        PIC X.
       10 STATUS-CODE-DESC   PIC X(14).

01 CODE-INDEX               PIC 9.
01 IN-CODE                  PIC X.

PROCEDURE DIVISION.
START-PAR.
    DISPLAY 'ENTER EMPLOYEE STATUS CODE: '.
    ACCEPT IN-CODE.
    SEARCH STATUS-CODES VARYING CODE-INDEX
           AT END DISPLAY 'CODE NOT FOUND, PLEASE REENTER'
                  GOTO START-PAR.
           WHEN STATUS-CODE(CODE-INDEX) = IN-CODE
                DISPLAY 'STATUS-CODE-DESC(CODE-INDEX).
```

Fig. 8-8. Code to clear text display example.

In the code/cleartext display example the user is asked to enter a status code. Once entered, the code is compared to the values in the STATUS-CODE table. If a match is made the codes complete text is displayed to the user to help ensure that the correct code was entered. If the entered code does not match a value in the table, an error has occurred and an appropriate message is displayed.

TABLES AS A TEMPORARY HOLDING PLACE

There are times when it is advantageous to collect many records of information before writing that information to a file. A common use of this need is a general ledger journal entry screen. In the accounting world transactions must balance (debits must equal credits). Many journal entry input programs store the incoming information in tables until the user states that the entry is finished. Once complete, the program checks to see if the debits equal the credits. If they are equal the entire transaction is written to disk and the table is emptied in preparation for the next transaction. Figure 8-9 illustrates this process.

The program is divided into transaction level processes and entry level processes. To understand this distinction you must first understand the difference between transactions and entries.

Figure 8-10 lists a transaction that contains two entries. That the first line (or entry) is to cash for $50, and the second line is to payroll expense, also for $50. To understand the program in Fig. 8-9, all you must understand is that for given transaction the total dollar value of the debits entry lines must equal the total dollar value of the credit entry lines. Further, in the program debits will be represented as positive numbers and credits will be represented by negative numbers. Therefore, the data in the

```
IDENTIFICATION DIVISION.

PROGRAM-ID.        TRANS.
AUTHOR.            ERIC P. BLOOM.
INSTALLATION.      BOSTON.
DATE-WRITTEN.      SEP, 1, 1985.
DATE-COMPILED.     SEP, 1, 1985.
SECURITY.          NONE.

ENVIRONMENT DIVISION.

CONFIGURATION SECTION.
SOURCE-COMPUTER.    IBM.
OBJECT-COMPUTER.    IBM.

INPUT-OUTPUT SECTION.
FILE CONTROL.

      SELECT   TRANS-FILE ASSIGN TO "TRANS.MST".

DATA DIVISION.
FILE CONTROL.

FD TRANS-FILE.
   RECORD CONTAINS 76 CHARACTERS
   LABEL RECORDS ARE OMITTED
   DATA RECORD IS TRANS-RECORD.

01 TRANS-REC          PIC X(76).

WORKING-STORAGE SECTION.

01 TRANS-AREA.
   05 TRANS-TABLE OCCURS 100 TIMES.
      10 TRANS-NO                  PIC X(5).
      10 TRANS-PERIOD              PIC X(5).
      10 TRANS-ACCOUNT             PIC X(5).
      10 TRANS-DESC                PIC X(20).
      10 TRANS-AMOUNT              PIC S9999V99.

01 CONTROL-FIELDS
   05 ANSWER                    PIC X.
   05 ARRAY-SIZE                PIC 999.
   05 ARRAY-INDEX               PIC 999.
   05 OUT-OF-RECS               PIC X.
   05 FOUND-IT                  PIC X.
   05 VALID-OPTION              PIC X
```

Fig. 8-9. Journal entry transaction input program listing.

```
    05  TRANS-CHECK                     PIC S9999V99.
    05  TRANS-CHECK-DISPLAY             PIC -,--9.99.

01  WS-FIELDS.
    05  WS-NO                           PIC X(5).
    05  WS-PERIOD                       PIC X(5).
    05  WS-ACCOUNT                      PIC X(5).
    05  WS-DESC                         PIC X(20).
    05  WS-AMOUNT                       PIC 9999V99.

PROCEDURE DIVISION.
START-PAR.
    PERFORM READ-PAR THRU READ-PAR-END.
    OPEN OUTPUT TRANS-FILE.
    PERFORM WRITE-PAR THRU WRITE-PAR-END.
    MOVE  0 TO ARRAY-SIZE.
    MOVE  0 TO ARRAY-INDEX.
    PERFORM MAIN-MENU-PAR THRU MAIN-MENU-PAR-END.
    CLOSE TRANS-PAR.
    STOP RUN.


MAIN-MENU-PAR.
    MOVE 'N' TO VALID-OPTION.
    DISPLAY ' '.
    DISPLAY '                        JOURNAL ENTRY SYSTEM'.
    DISPLAY '                             MAIN MENU'.
    DISPLAY ' '.
    DISPLAY '      1. ADD A NEW TRANSACTION'.
    DISPLAY '      2. CHANGE CURRENT TRANSACTION'.
    DISPLAY '      3. PURGE CURRENT TRANSACTION'.
    DISPLAY '      4. DISPLAY CURRENT TRANSACTION'.
    DISPLAY '      5. LIST CURRENT TRANSACTION'.
    DISPLAY '      E. EXIT SYSTEM'.
    DISPLAY ' '.
    DISPLAY '                   ENTER OPTION: '.
    ACCEPT ANSWER.
    IF ANSWER = '1' MOVE 'Y' TO VALID-OPTION
                    MOVE  0  TO ARRAY-SIZE
                    PERFORM NEW-ADD-PAR THRU NEW-ADD-PAR-END.
    IF ANSWER = '2' MOVE 'Y' TO VALID-OPTION
                    PERFORM SUB-MENU-PAR THRU SUB-MANU-PAR-END.
    IF ANSWER = '3' MOVE 'Y' TO VALID-OPTION
                    PERFORM PURGE-PAR THRU PURGE-PAR-END.
    IF ANSWER = '4' MOVE 'Y' TO VALID-OPTION
                    PERFORM WRITE-PAR THRU WRITE-PAR-END
                    PERFORM PURGE-PAR THRU PURGE-PAR-END.
    IF ANSWER = '5' MOVE 'Y' TO VALID-OPTION
                    PERFORM LIST-PAR THRU LIST-PAR-END
                        VARYING ARRAY-INDEX FROM 1 BY 1
                        UNTIL ARRAY-INDEX = ARRAY-SIZE.
```

```
        IF ANSWER = 'E' GOTO MENU-PAR-END.

        IF VALID-OPTION = 'Y' GOTO MENU-PAR.
        DISPLAY ' '.
        DISPLAY 'ERROR: ANSWER MUST BE 1,2,3,4,5 or E, PLEASE
                 REENTER'.
        DISPLAY ' '.
        GOTO MAIN-MENU-PAR.

MAIN-MENU-PAR-END.


NEW-ADD-PAR.
    ADD 1 TO ARRAY-SIZE.
    MOVE ARRAY-SIZE TO ARRAY-INDEX.
    DISPLAY 'ENTER TRANSACTION NUMBER ( or END to end ) :'.
    ACCEPT  TRANS-NO(ARRAY-INDEX).
    IF TRANS-NO(ARRAY-INDEX) = 'END'
        MOVE      SPACES TO TRANS-NO(ARRAY-INDEX)
        SUBTRACT 1 FROM ARRAY-SIZE
        GOTO      NEW-ADD-PAR-END.
    DISPLAY 'ENTER ACCOUNTING PERIOD :'.
    ACCEPT  TRANS-PERIOD(ARRAY-INDEX).
    DISPLAY 'ENTER ACCOUNT NUMBER : '.
    ACCEPT  TRANS-ACCOUNT(ARRAY-INDEX).
    DISPLAY 'ENTER ENTRY DESCRIPTION  '.
    ACCEPT  TRANS-DESC(ARRAY-INDEX).
    DISPLAY 'ENTER ENTRY AMOUNT ( - FROM CREDIT ) : '.
    ACCEPT  TRANS-AMOUNT(ARRAP-INDEX).
    GOTO NEW-ADD-PAR-END.
NEW-ADD-PAR-END.


PURGE-PAR.
    MOVE SPACES TO TRANS-AREA.
PURGE-PAR.


SUB-MENU-PAR.
    MOVE 'N' TO VALID-OPTION.
    DISPLAY ' '.
    DISPLAY '                        JOURNAL ENTRY SYSTEM'.
    DISPLAY '                        ENTRY UPDATE MENU'.
    DISPLAY ' '.
    DISPLAY '    1. ADD A NEW LINE ENTRY'.
    DISPLAY '    2. CHANGE LINE ENTRY'.
    DISPLAY '    3. DELETE A LINE ENTRY'.
    DISPLAY '    4. DISPLAY A LINE ENTRY'.
    DISPLAY '    5. LIST ENTIRE TRANSACTION'.
    DISPLAY '    E. EXIT SYSTEM'.
    DISPLAY ' '.
    DISPLAY '                    ENTER OPTION: '.
    ACCEPT ANSWER.
```

```
        IF ANSWER = '1' MOVE 'Y' TO VALID-OPTION
                        PERFORM ADD-PAR THRU ADD-PAR-END.
        IF ANSWER = '2' MOVE 'Y' TO VALID-OPTION
                        PERFORM CHANGE-PAR THRU CHANGE-PAR-END.
        IF ANSWER = '3' MOVE 'Y' TO VALID-OPTION
                        PERFORM DELETE-PAR THRU DELETE-PAR-END.
        IF ANSWER = '4' MOVE 'Y' TO VALID-OPTION
                        PERFORM DISPLAY-PAR THRU DISPLAY-PAR-END.
        IF ANSWER = '5' MOVE 'Y' TO VALID-OPTION
                        PERFORM LIST-PAR THRU LIST-PAR-END
                            VARYING ARRAY-INDEX FROM 1 BY 1
                            UNTIL ARRAY-INDEX = ARRAY-SIZE.
        IF ANSWER = 'E' GOTO SUB-MENU-PAR-END.

        IF VALID-OPTION = 'Y' GOTO SUB-MENU-PAR.
        DISPLAY ' '.
        DISPLAY 'ERROR: ANSWER MUST BE 1,2,3,4,5 or E, PLEASE
                REENTER'.
        DISPLAY ' '.
        GOTO SUB-MENU-PAR.

        SUB-MENU-PAR-END.


ADD-PAR.
        ADD 1 TO ARRAY-SIZE.
        MOVE ARRAY-SIZE TO ARRAY-INDEX.
        DISPLAY 'ENTER TRANSACTION NUMBER :'.
        ACCEPT  TRANS-NO(ARRAY-INDEX).
        DISPLAY 'ENTER ACCOUNTING PERIOD :'.
        ACCEPT  TRANS-PERIOD(ARRAY-INDEX).
        DISPLAY 'ENTER ACCOUNT NUMBER : '.
        ACCEPT  TRANS-ACCOUNT(ARRAY-INDEX).
        DISPLAY 'ENTER ENTRY DESCRIPTION  '.
        ACCEPT  TRANS-DESC(ARRAY-INDEX).
        DISPLAY 'ENTER ENTRY AMOUNT ( - FROM CREDIT ) : '.
        ACCEPT  TRANS-AMOUNT(ARRAP-INDEX).
ADD-PAR-END.


CHANGE-PAR.
        PERFORM FIND-PAR THRU FIND-PAR-END.
        PERFORM LIST-PAR THRU LIST-PAR-END.
        DISPLAY 'ENTER NEW VALUE TO UPDATE OR <CR> TO LEAVE
                VALUE UNCHANGED'.
        DISPLAY ' '.

        DISPLAY 'ENTER TRANSACTION NUMBER : '.
        ACCEPT WS-TRANS-NO.
        IF WS-TRANS-NO NOT = SPACES MOVE WS-TRANS-NO TO
            NAME(ARRAY-INDEX).
```

```
      DISPLAY 'ENTER ACCOUNTING PERIOD : '.
      ACCEPT WS-TRANS-PERIOD.
      IF WS-TRANS-PERIOD NOT = SPACES
          MOVE WS-TRANS-PERIOD TO TRANS-PERIOD(ARRAY-INDEX).

      DISPLAY 'ENTER ACCOUNT NUMBER : '.
      ACCEPT WS-TRANS-ACCOUNT.
      IF WS-TRANS-ACCOUNT NOT = SPACES
          MOVE WS-TRANS-ACCOUNT TO TRANS-ACCOUNT(ARRAY-INDEX).

      DISPLAY 'ENTER ENTRY DESCRIPTION : '.
      ACCEPT WS-TRANS-DESC.
      IF  WS-TRANS-DESC NOT = SPACES
           MOVE WS-TRANS-DESC TO TRANS-DESC(ARRAY-INDEX).

      DISPLAY 'ENTER ENTRY AMOUNT : '.
      ACCEPT WS-TRANS-AMOUNT.
      IF WS-TRANS-AMOUNT NOT = SPACES
          MOVE WS-TRANS-AMOUNT TO TRANS-AMOUNT(ARRAY-INDEX).

CHANGE-PAR-END.

DELETE-PAR.
      PERFORM FIND-PAR THRU FIND-PAR-END.
      IF FOUND-IT = 'Y' MOVE '-----` TO TRANS-NO(ARRAY-INDEX).
DELETE-PAR-END.

LIST-PAR.
      DISPLAY TRANS-NO(ARRAY-INDEX), ' ',
              TRANS-PERIOD(ARRAY-INDEX),' ',
              TRANS-ACCOUNT(ARRAY-INDEX), ' ',
              TRANS-DESC(ARRAY-INDEX),' ',
              TRANS-AMOUNT(ARRAY-INDEX).
LIST-PAR-END.

FIND-PAR.
      DISPLAY 'ENTER ACCOUNT NUMBER : '.
      ACCEPT WS-TRANS-ACCOUNT.
      MOVE 'N' TO FOUND-IT.
      PERFORM FIND-1-PAR THRU FIND-1-PAR-END
              VARYING ARRAY-INDEX FROM 1 BY 1
              UNTIL ARRAY-INDEX = ARRAY-SIZE OR FOUND-IT = 'Y'.
      IF FOUND-IT = 'N' DISPLAY 'NOT FOUND'.

FIND-PAR-END.

FIND-1-PAR.
      IF TRANS-ACCOUNT(ARRAY-INDEX) = WS-TRANS-ACCOUNT
          DISPLAY ' '
          PERFORM LIST-PAR THRU LIST-PAR-END
```

```
            DISPLAY ' '
            DISPLAY 'IS THIS IT ( Y or N) : '
            ACCEPT FOUND-IT.
    FIND-1-PAR-END.


    READ-PAR.
            OPEN INPUT TRANS-FILE AT END MOVE 'Y' TO OUT-OF-RECS.
            MOVE 0 TO ARRAY-SIZE.
            READ TRANS-FILE AT END MOVE 'Y' TO OUT-OF-RECS.
            IF OUT-OF-RECS NOT = 'Y'
                PERFORM READ-2-PAR THRU READ-2-PAR-END UNTIL
                        OUT-OF-RECS = 'Y'.
            CLOSE TRANS-FILE.
    READ-PAR-END.


    READ-1-PAR.
        ADD 1 TO ARRAY-SIZE.
        MOVE TRANS-REC TO TRANS-TABLE(ARRAY-SIZE).
        READ TRANS-FILE AT END MOVE 'Y' TO OUT-OF-RECS.
    READ-1-PAR-END.


    WRITE-PAR.
      MOVE O TO TRANS-CHECK.
      PERFORM BAL-PAR THRU BAL-PAR-END
              VARYING ARRAY-INDEX FROM 1 BY 1 UNTIL
                      ARRAY-INDEX = ARRAY-SIZE.
      IF TRANS-CHECK = 0
         PERFORM WRITE-PAR THRU WRITE-PAR-END
              VARYING ARRAY-INDEX FROM 1 BY 1 UNTIL
                      ARRAY-INDEX = ARRAY-SIZE
      ELSE
         MOVE TRANS-CHECK TO TRANS-CHECK-DISPLAY
         DISPLAY ' '
         DISPLAY 'ERROR: DEBITS DO NOT MATCH CREDITS BY: ',
                   TRANS-CHECK-DISPLAY
         DISPLAY ' '.
    WRITE-PAR-END.


    WRITE-1-PAR-END.
      IF TRANS-ACCOUNT(ARRAY-INDEX) NOT = '-----'
         WRITE TRANS-REC FROM TRANS-ARRAY(ARRAY-INDEX).
    WRITE-1-PAR-END.


    BAL-PAR.
      ADD TRANS-AMOUNT(ARRAY-INDEX) TO TRANS-CHECK.
    BAL-PAR-END.
```

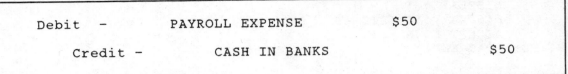

```
     Debit   -        PAYROLL EXPENSE            $50

        Credit  -          CASH IN BANKS                   $50
```

Fig. 8-10. A general ledger transaction example.

dollar amount files must net zero for the entire entry.

When the journal entry transaction program begins to execute three things happen. First, TRANS-FILE is opened for input, the file is read into TRANS-ARRAY, and TRANS-FILE is closed. Second, TRANS-FILE is opened for output, which deletes its records and is refilled by writing the entire contents of TRANS-ARRAY back to disk. This is done to allow records to be added to the end of the file. Some compilers allow a sequential file to be opened in an "append" mode which allows the program to add records to the end of the file without going through the reading and writing process. The third process is the display of the main menu, where the program pauses from execution in anticipation of user input. The menu displayed is shown in Fig. 8-11.

If option 1 on the menu is selected TRANS-ARRAY is purged and NEW-ADD-PAR is performed. This paragraph makes the assumption that all transactions will have at least two entries. Therefore, rather then continually ask the user if more lines are to be added, it just continues to ac-

cept data until told to do otherwise. In contrast to this paragraph, ADD-PAR assumes that once the entry has been initially loaded only one or two additions will be needed. Thus, after each addition control automatically returns to the submenu. Figure 8-12 shows the execution of the initial add option.

If the second menu option is selected the submenu is displayed. This menu lets the user add, modify, and display individual entry line items in the transaction. The submenu is shown in Fig. 8-13, and is explained in great detail in the array methodology section of Chapter 9.

Option 3 of the main menu is the purge transaction function that lets the user delete the transaction currently under development and thus contained in TRANS-ARRAY. The entire array is cleared in one step by moving spaces to TRANS-AREA and setting ARRAY-SIZE and ARRAY-INDEX to zero. In effect, the transaction was deleted because it was not placed on disk by the save option.

Option 4 is the save option, which places the array contents in TRANS-FILE and saves the

```
                     JOURNAL ENTRY SYSTEM
                          MAIN MENU



           1. ADD A NEW TRANSACTION
           2. CHANGE CURRENT TRANSACTION
           3. PURGE CURRENT TRANSACTION
           4. DISPLAY CURRENT TRANSACTION
           5. LIST CURRENT TRANSACTION
           E. EXIT SYSTEM

                     ENTER OPTION:
```

Fig. 8-11. Journal entry main menu screen.

```
ENTER TRANSACTION NUMBER ( or END to end ) : 123

ENTER ACCOUNTING PERIOD : 09/85

ENTER ACCOUNT NUMBER : 001

ENTER ENTRY DESCRIPTION : CASH FROM BOSTON BANK.

ENTER ENTRY AMOUNT ( - FROM CREDIT ) : -50



ENTER TRANSACTION NUMBER ( or END to end ) : 123

ENTER ACCOUNTING PERIOD : 09/85

ENTER ACCOUNT NUMBER : 375

ENTER ENTRY DESCRIPTION : WEEKLY PAYROLL EXPENSE

ENTER ENTRY AMOUNT ( - FROM CREDIT ) : 50
```

Fig. 8-12. Journal entry input example.

transaction. Remember, the file is already open for output because of the reading and writing processes performed at the beginning of the program's execution. Also, after the array contents are copied to disk the array is emptied to safeguard against saving the same transaction twice.

The fifth option displays the entire transaction on the screen. This is the same function performed by option 5 on the submenu. This option is offered twice to save the user from having to continually go back to the main menu during editing to display the entire transaction.

The "E" option will exit the main menu, close the transaction file, and exit the program.

```
            JOURNAL ENTRY SYSTEM
            ENTRY UPDATE MENU


    1. ADD A NEW LINE ENTRY
    2. CHANGE LINE ENTRY
    3. DELETE A LINE ENTRY
    4. DISPLAY A LINE ENTRY
    5. LIST ENTIRE TRANSACTION
    E. EXIT SYSTEM

            ENTER OPTION:
```

Fig. 8-13. Journal entry program submenu.

QUESTIONS

1. What is a table?

2. What is the function of an OCCURS clause?

3. What is the purpose of the ASCENDING KEY and INDEXED BY clauses?

4. In what two ways can data tables be loaded?

5. How are tables used in data validation?

6. How do tables assist in the date conversion process?

7. How are tables used to assist in the check-writing process?

8. What is a data dictionary?

9. Describe the menu structure used in Fig. 8-9.

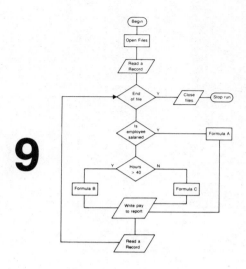

9

Sequential File Processing

Most business applications require the ability to store and modify information, which may be a list of posted general ledger transactions, a list of all inventoried merchandise, or the quotations of yesterday's stock prices. These groups of diverse information have one thing in common: they are all stored in data files. A data file is a collection of related information stored on disk or tape under a common name.

There are two primary types of data files—sequential files and random access files. A sequential file must be read in order, one record at a time, similar to a movie. To see the third act you must either watch or fast-forward through the first two screens. Random access files have the capability to go directly to the needed data. This access method is similar to the idea of post office boxes: the customer can take information from POB 10 without opening the first nine boxes.

There are two primary methods that can be used to update sequential files—the two-tape method and the array manipulation method.

TWO-TAPE UPDATE METHOD

The two-tape update method is very commonly used in industry to update files in a batch processing mode. It is performed by sorting the master file and transaction file in the same order, based on a common key field. Once sorted the two files are read into the program one record at a time, matching up the master file records with its transactions. When a match is made the master file record is modified or deleted as stated in the transaction record. Then the updated master file record is written to the new master file; this process continues until both files are out of records. Figure 9-1 is a conceptual view of this process.

Figure 9-2 is a listing of a working update program. To simplify the example assume that the two input files have already been sorted in employee number order. A master file update program should generate four reports: an old master file report, a new master file report, a transaction report and an error report. The old master file report should look exactly like the new master file report generated

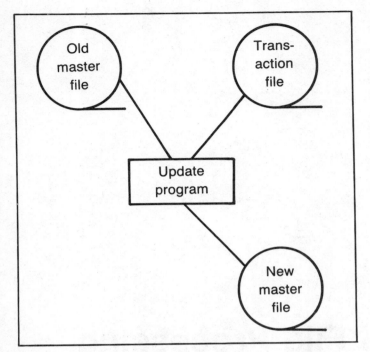

Fig. 9-1. Two-Tape update method.

```
IDENTIFICATION DIVISION.

    PROGRAM-ID.       TWOFILE.
    AUTHOR.           ERIC P. BLOOM.
    INSTALLATION.     BOSTON.
    DATE-WRITTEN.     SEP, 1, 1985.
    DATE-COMPILED.    SEP, 1, 1985.
    SECURITY.         NONE.

    ENVIRONMENT DIVISION.

    CONFIGURATION SECTION.
    SOURCE-COMPUTER.   IBM.
    OBJECT-COMPUTER.   IBM.

    INPUT-OUTPUT SECTION.
    FILE CONTROL.

        SELECT OLD-MASTER-FILE ASSIGN TO "OLDMAST.DAT".
        SELECT NEW-MASTER-FILE ASSIGN TO "NEWMAST.DAT".
        SELECT TRANS-FILE      ASSIGN TO "TRANS.DAT".

    DATA DIVISION.
    FILE SECTION.
```

Fig. 9-2. Two-Tape update method listing.

```
FD  OLD-MASTER-FILE
    RECORD CONTAINS 61 CHARACTERS
    LABEL RECORDS ARE OMITTED
    DATA RECORD IS OLD-MASTER-REC.

01  OLD-MASTER-REC.
    05  OLD-EMP-NO              PIC X(5).
    05  OLD-EMP-NAME            PIC X(30).
    05  OLD-EMP-SSN             PIC X(11).
    05  OLD-GROSS-YTD           PIC 9(5)V99.
    05  OLD-HOULY-WAGE          PIC 999V99.
    05  OLD-NO-OF-EXEMPS        PIC 99.
    05  OLD-OVERTIME-FLAG       PIC X.


FD  NEW-MASTER-FILE
    RECORD CONTAINS 61 CHARACTERS
    LABEL RECORDS ARE OMITTED
    DATA RECORD IS NEW-MASTER-REC.

01  NEW-MASTER-REC.
    05  NEW-EMP-NO              PIC X(5).
    05  NEW-EMP-NAME            PIC X(30).
    05  NEW-EMP-SSN             PIC X(11).
    05  NEW-GROSS-YTD           PIC 9(5)V99.
    05  NEW-HOULY-WAGE          PIC 999V99.
    05  NEW-NO-OF-EXEMPS        PIC 99.
    05  NEW-OVERTIME-FLAG       PIC X.

FD  TRANS-FILE
    RECORD CONTAINS 62 CHARACTERS
    LABEL RECORDS ARE OMITTED
    DATA RECORD IS TRANS-REC.

01  TRANS-REC.
    05  TRANS-EMP-NO            PIC X(5).
    05  TRANS-CODE              PIC X.
    05  TRANS-EMP-NAME          PIC X(30).
    05  TRANS-EMP-SSN           PIC X(11).
    05  TRANS-GROSS-YTD         PIC 9(5)V99.
    05  TRANS-HOULY-WAGE        PIC 999V99.
    05  TRANS-NO-OF-EXEMPS      PIC 99.
    05  TRANS-OVERTIME-FLAG     PIC X.


01  MAST-OUT-OF-RECS           PIC X.
01  TRANS-OUT-OF-RECS          PIC X.



PROCEDURE DIVISION.
```

```
START-PAR.
    OPEN INPUT  OLD-MASTER-FILE, TRANS-FILE.
    OPEN OUTPUT NEW-MASTER-FILE.
    PERFORM READ-MASTER-PAR THRU READ-MASTER-PAR-END.
    PERFORM READ-TRANS-PAR THRU READ-TRANS-PAR-END.
    PERFORM DISPATCH-PAR THRU DISPATCH-PAR-END.
    CLOSE OLD-MASTER-FILE, TRANS-FILE, NEW-MASTER-FILE.
    STOP RUN.

DISPATCH-PAR.
    IF TRANS-OUT-OF-RECS = 'Y'
        PERFORM COPY-MAST-PAR THRU COPY-MAST-PAR-END
            UNTIL MAST-OUT-OF-RECS = 'Y'
        GOTO MAIN-PAR-END.
    IF MAST-OUT-OF-RECS = 'Y'
        PERFORM FINISH-TRANS-PAR THRU FINISH TRANS-PAR-END
            UNTIL TRANS-OUT-OF-RECS = 'Y'
        GOTO MAIN-PAR-END.

    IF OLD-EMP-NO = TRANS-EMP-NO
        PERFORM EQUAL-PAR THRU EQUAL-PAR-END
    ELSE IF OLD-EMP-NO > TRANS-EMP-NO
        PERFORM GREATER-PAR THRU GREATER-PAR-END
    ELSE PERFORM LESS-PAR-END.

    GOTO DISPATCH-PAR.

DISPATCH-PAR-END.

EQUAL-PAR.
    IF TRANS-CODE = 'D'
        PERFORM READ-MASTER-PAR THRU READ-MASTER-PAR-END
        PERFORM READ-TRANS-PAR THRU READ-TRANS-PAR-END
    ELSE IF TRANS-CODE = 'C'
        PERFORM CHANGE-PAR THRU CHANGE-PAR-END
    ELSE IF TRANS-CODE = 'A'
        DISPLAY 'ERROR: ADD CAN NOT BE PERFORMED. RECORD EXISTS'
        PERFORM READ-TRANS-PAR THRU READ-TRANS-PAR-END
    ELSE
        DISPLAY 'ERROR: TRANSACTION CODE NOT VALID'.

EQUAL-PAR-END.

CHANGE-PAR.
    IF TRANS-EMP-NAME NOT = SPACES
        MOVE TRANS-EMP-NAME TO NEW-EMP-NAME.
    IF TRANS-SSN NOT = SPACES
        MOVE TRANS-SSN TO NEW-SSN.
    IF TRANS-GROSS-YTD NOT = 0
        MOVE TRANS-GROSS-YTD TO NEW-GROSS-YTD.
```

```
        IF TRANS-HOURLY-WAGE NOT = 0
            MOVE TRANS-HOURLY-WAGE TO NEW-HOURLY-WAGE.
        IF TRANS-NO-OF-EXEMPS NOT = 99
            MOVE TRANS-NO-OF-EXEMPS TO NEW-NO-OF-EXEMPS.
        IF TRANS-OVERTIME-FLAG NOT = SPACES
            MOVE TRANS-OVERTIME-FLAG TO NEW-OVERTIME-FLAG.

        PERFORM READ-TRANS-PAR THRU READ-TRANS-PAR-END.

        IF TRANS-EMP-NO NOT = NEW-EMP-NO
            WRITE NEW-EMP-NO
            PERFORM READ-MASTER-PAR THRU READ-MASTER-PAR-END.

CHANGE-PAR-END.

GREATER-PAR.
    IF TRANS-CODE = 'A'
        WRITE NEW-MASTER-REC.
        MOVE TRANS-EMP-MO TO NEW-EMP-NO
        MOVE TRANS-EMP-NAME TO NEW-EMP-NAME
        MOVE TRANS-SSN TO NEW-SSN
        MOVE TRANS-GROSS-YTD TO NEW-YTD
        MOVE TRANS-HOURLY-WAGE TO NEW-HOURLY-WAGE
        MOVE TRANS-NO-OF-EXEMPS TO NEW-NO-OF-EXEMPS
        MOVE TRANS-OVERTIME-FLAG TO NEW-OVERTIME-FLAG
        WRITE NEW-MASTER-REC
        MOVE OLD-MASTER-REC TO NEW-MASTER-REC
        PERFORM READ-TRANS-PAR THRU READ-TRANS-PAR-END
    ELSE
        DISPLAY 'ERROR - BAD TRANSACTION CODE'
        PERFORM READ-TRANS-PAR THRU READ-TRANS-PAR-END.

GREATER-PAR-END.

LESS-PAR.
    WRITE NEW-MASTER-REC.
    PERFORM READ-MASTER-PAR THRU READ-MASTER-PAR-END.
LESS-PAR-END.


COPY-MAST-PAR.
    WRITE NEW-MAST-REC.
    PERFORM READ-MASTER-PAR THRU READ-MASTER-PAR-END.
COPY-MAST-PAR-END.

FINISH-TRANS-PAR.
    IF TRANS-CODE = 'A'
        MOVE TRANS-EMP-MO TO NEW-EMP-NO
        MOVE TRANS-EMP-NAME TO NEW-EMP-NAME
        MOVE TRANS-SSN TO NEW-SSN
        MOVE TRANS-GROSS-YTD TO NEW-YTD
```

```
        MOVE TRANS-HOURLY-WAGE TO NEW-HOURLY-WAGE
        MOVE TRANS-NO-OF-EXEMPS TO NEW-NO-OF-EXEMPS
        MOVE TRANS-OVERTIME-FLAG TO NEW-OVERTIME-FLAG
        WRITE NEW-MASTER-REC
        PERFORM READ-TRANS-PAR THRU READ-TRANS-PAR-END
    ELSE
        DISPLAY 'ERROR: TRANSACTION CODE MUST BE "A"'
        PERFORM READ-TRANS-PAR THRU READ-TRANS-PAR-END.

FINISH-TRANS-PAR-END.

READ-MASTER-PAR.
    READ OLD-MASTER-FILE AT END MOVE 'Y' TO MAST-OUT-OF-RECS.
    MOVE OLD-MASTER-REC TO NEW-MASTER-REC.
READ-MASTER-PAR-END.

READ-TRANS-PAR.
    READ TRANS-FILE AT END MOVE 'Y' TO TRANS-OUT-OF-RECS.
READ-TRANS-PAR-END.
```

the last time the update program was run. Remember, this week's old master file was last week's new master file. Comparing these reports assures us that the most recent master file tape was used and that is was not modified since the last official update. The actual information and format of the report would greatly depend on the application being updated. However, it should in all cases include a record count and totals of numeric-oriented fields. Additionally, if appropriate, hash totals should also be calculated and printed.

The new master file report should include all the information contained in the new master file. This report has two functions—as a control check of the next update run and as a reference for the appropriate application user.

The transaction report should contain a list of all the processed transactions and the functions performed by those transactions. This list will serve as reference to the system administrators and also as an audit trail of master file modifications.

The error report provides a list of the transactions rejected by the update process. This report should include all transaction information, an explanation of the error, and if applicable, the master file record information that caused the error and the user who entered the transaction. With this in-

formation the application manager can locate, fix and re-enter incorrect transactions, identify users that need additional training, and isolate inadequate data entry validation techniques by reviewing the types of errors that re-occur.

The update program in Fig. 9-2 is logically divided into four sections: DISPATCH-PAR, EQUAL-PAR, GREATER-PAR and LESS-PAR.

DISPATCH-PAR acts as a controller and is used to pass control to the other sections of the program based on the relationship between the current master file and transaction file records. If the employee numbers are equal, control is passed to EQUAL-PAR. If the employee number in the master file is greater than its counterpart in the transaction file, GREATER-PAR is performed. If neither of these conditions are met, by definition the master file record employee number is less than the transaction record number and LESS-PAR is executed. Once in the secondary paragraphs, the software checks the transaction code to assess what function should be performed. "A" is for add, "C" is for change, and "D" is for delete.

EQUAL-PAR either changes or deletes the master file record as stated in the TRANS-CODE. If a delete is specified the new master file and transaction file records are retrieved. In effect, a master file record is deleted by not being written to the new master file. If a change is specified CHANGE-PAR is performed.

In CHANGE-PAR there is a series of IF statements which decide what should be changed in the master file. If a field in the transaction record is blank its corresponding field in the master file is not updated. If the field does have a value that value is passed forward to the master file. After the update takes place a new transaction record is retrieved. If this new transaction also updates the current master file record, processing continues and the paragraph ends. Otherwise the modified master file record is written to disk and a new master file record is read.

GREATER-PAR only performs an update if the TRANS-CODE is equal to A. Logically, a change or delete should not take place if the two employee numbers do not match. The addition is performed by zeroing out the information currently residing in NEW-MASTER-REC, moving the new transaction data to that record, and writing it to disk. The data originally contained in NEW-MASTER-REC is not lost. When a master file record is retrieved from the file it is immediately moved to NEW-MASTER-REC. Therefore, once the transaction information is written to disk this statement can again be executed, hence, reloading NEW-MASTER-REC.

The LESS-PAR paragraph is called only when the master file employee number is less than its transaction counterpart. In this situation master file records are just passed from the old master file to the new until an equal or greater-than situation occurs.

There is one facet of the program that has not yet been discussed. This is the program termination process. Sooner or later one of the input files will reach an end-of-file condition. When reached, the DISPATCH-PAR assesses which file is empty and performs either COPY-MAST-PAR or FINISH-TRANS-PAR to process the remaining records in the uncompleted file.

ARRAY MANIPULATION METHOD

The array manipulation method is similar to the technique used when developing word processing or spreadsheet-type software. When the program is executed the entire contents of the data file is read into an array (also know as a table) and is then modified on-line as specified by the user. Once the user has entered all the needed changes the update array is placed on disk, replacing the originally input version. Figure 9-3 is a working program that employs this technique to update a mailing list file.

The program listing is divided into many paragraphs, each of which performs a specific function. START-PAR is the first paragraph executed, with the function of ensuring that READ-PAR, MENU-PAR and WRITE-PAR are performed. READ-PAR opens and reads MAIL-FILE, loads its contents into the MAIL-TABLE array, and tracks the number of elements placed in the array by incrementing ARRAY-SIZE. After this process is complete MAIL-FILE is closed and control is passed back to START-PAR. The next paragraph executed is MENU-PAR, which provides the user with a menu that facilitates the update and display of the array-held data.

Figure 9-4 illustrates this menu. When the user selects an option, the IF statements in MENU-PAR analyze the entered value and transfer control to the appropriate paragraph for processing. Option 1 corresponds to paragraph ADD-PAR. This option and paragraph are used to add a new name to the mailing list. The addition is performed in the following way: First, ARRAY-SIZE is incremented by one. Remember, this is the variable that tracks the number of names contained in the array, therefore, if a name is added ARRAY-SIZE must also be increased by one. The value in ARRAY-SIZE is then moved to MAIL-INDEX, which is the subscript stating where in the array the new data should be placed. Since MAIL-INDEX was set to the incremented value of ARRAY-SIZE the new data will reside as the last name in the list. Finally, the user is prompted for the new information and it is entered into the appropriate array location. Figure 9-5 shows the user view of the add process.

Data is modified by selecting option 2 on the update menu, which in turn performs CHANGE-PAR. The first step of the change process is to

```
IDENTIFICATION DIVISION.

PROGRAM-ID.          MAIL.
AUTHOR.              ERIC P. BLOOM.
INSTALLATION.        BOSTON.
DATE-WRITTEN.        SEP, 1, 1985.
DATE-COMPILED.       SEP, 1, 1985.
SECURITY.            NONE.

ENVIRONMENT DIVISION.

CONFIGURATION SECTION.
SOURCE-COMPUTER.    IBM.
OBJECT-COMPUTER.    IBM.

INPUT-OUTPUT SECTION.
FILE CONTROL.

        SELECT   MAIL-FILE ASSIGN TO "MAILMAST.DAT".

DATA DIVISION.
FILE SECTION.

FD MAIL-FILE
    RECORD CONTAINS 76 CHARACTERS
    LABEL RECORDS ARE OMITTED
    DATA RECORD IS MAIL-REC.

01 MAIL-REC          PIC X(76).

WORKING-STORAGE SECTION.

01 MAIL-TABLE OCCURS 100 TIMES
    05 NAME                    PIC X(20).
    05 STREET-1                PIC X(20).
    05 STREET-2                PIC X(20).
    05 STATE                   PIC XX.
    05 ZIPCODE                 PIC X(9).

01 CONTROL-FIELDS
    05 ANSWER                  PIC X.
    05 ARRAY-SIZE              PIC 999.
    05 ARRAY-INDEX             PIC 999.
    05 OUT-OF-RECS             PIC X.
    05 FOUND-IT                PIC X.
    05 VALID-OPTION            PIC X

01 WS-FIELDS.
```

Fig. 9-3. Array update method program listing.

```
    05  WS-NAME                         PIC X(20).
    05  WS-STREET-1                     PIC X(20).
    05  WS-STREET-2                     PIC X(20).
    05  WS-STATE                        PIC XX.
    05  WS-ZIPCODE                      PIC X(9).

PROCEDURE DIVISION.
START-PAR.
    PERFORM READ-PAR THRU READ-PAR-END.
    PERFORM MENU-PAR THRU MENU-PAR-END.
    PERFORM WRITE-PAR THRU WRITE-PAR-END.
    STOP RUN.

MENU-PAR.
    MOVE 'N' TO VALID-OPTION.
    DISPLAY ' '.
    DISPLAY '                           MAIL LIST SYSTEM'.
    DISPLAY '                             UPDATE MENU'.
    DISPLAY ' '.
    DISPLAY '     1. ADD A NEW LABEL'.
    DISPLAY '     2. CHANGE CURRENT LABEL DATA'.
    DISPLAY '     3. DELETE A LABEL'.
    DISPLAY '     4. DISPLAY A LABEL'.
    DISPLAY '     5. LIST ALL LABELS'.
    DISPLAY '     E. EXIT SYSTEM'.
    DISPLAY ' '.
    DISPLAY '                 ENTER OPTION: '.
    ACCEPT ANSWER.
    IF ANSWER = '1' MOVE 'Y' TO VALID-OPTION
                    PERFORM ADD-PAR THRU ADD-PAR-END.
    IF ANSWER = '2' MOVE 'Y' TO VALID-OPTION
                    PERFORM CHANGE-PAR THRU CHANGE-PAR-END.
    IF ANSWER = '3' MOVE 'Y' TO VALID-OPTION
                    PERFORM DELETE-PAR THRU DELETE-PAR-END.
    IF ANSWER = '4' MOVE 'Y' TO VALID-OPTION
                    PERFORM DISPLAY-PAR THRU DISPLAY-PAR-END.
    IF ANSWER = '5' MOVE 'Y' TO VALID-OPTION
                    PERFORM LIST-PAR THRU LIST-PAR-END
                        VARYING ARRAY-INDEX FROM 1 BY 1
                        UNTIL ARRAY-INDEX = ARRAY-SIZE.
    IF ANSWER = 'E' GOTO MENU-PAR-END.

    IF VALID-OPTION = 'Y' GOTO MENU-PAR.
    DISPLAY ' '.
    DISPLAY 'ERROR: ANSWER MUST BE 1,2,3,4,5 or E,
             PLEASE REENTER'.
    DISPLAY ' '.
    GOTO MENU-PAR.

    MENU-PAR-END.
```

```
ADD-PAR.
    ADD 1 TO ARRAY-SIZE.
    MOVE ARRAY-SIZE TO ARRAY-INDEX.
    DISPLAY 'ENTER NAME (LAST, FIRST MI) : '.
    ACCEPT  LAST-NAME(ARRAY-INDEX).
    DISPLAY 'ENTER FIRST STREET ADDRESS :'.
    ACCEPT  STREET-1(ARRAY-INDEX).
    DISPLAY 'ENTER SECOND STREET ADDRESS'.
    ACCEPT  STREET-2(ARRAY-INDEX).
    DISPLAY 'ENTER STATE CODE'.
    ACCEPT  STATE(ARRAY-INDEX).
    DISPLAY 'ENTER ZIPCODE: '.
    ACCEPT ZIPCODE(ARRAP-INDEX).
ADD-PAR-END.

CHANGE-PAR.
    PERFORM FIND-PAR THRU FIND-PAR-END.
    PERFORM LIST-PAR THRU LIST-PAR-END.
    DISPLAY 'ENTER NEW VALUE TO UPDATE OR <CR> TO LEAVE
            VALUE UNCHANGED'.
    DISPLAY ' '.

    DISPLAY 'ENTER NAME ( LAST, FIRST, MI ): '.
    ACCEPT WS-NAME.
    IF WS-NAME NOT = SPACES MOVE WS-NAME TO NAME(ARRAY-INDEX).

    DISPLAY 'ENTER FIRST STREET ADDRESS '.
    ACCEPT WS-STREET-1.
    IF WS-STREET-1 NOT = SPACES MOVE WS-STREET-1 TO
        STREET-1(ARRAY-INDEX).

    DISPLAY 'ENTER SECOND STREET ADDRESS: '.
    ACCEPT WS-STREET-2.
    IF WS-STREET-2 NOT = SPACES MOVE WS-STREET-2 TO
        STREET-2(ARRAY-INDEX).

    DISPLAY 'ENTER STATE CODE : '.
    ACCEPT WS-STATE.
    IF WS-STATE NOT = SPACES MOVE WS-STATE TO STATE(ARRAY-INDEX).

    DISPLAY 'ENTER ZIPCODE '.
    ACCEPT WS-ZIPCODE.
    IF WS-ZIPCODE NOT = SPACES MOVE WS-ZIPCODE TO
        ZIPCODE(ARRAY-INDEX).

CHANGE-PAR-END.

DELETE-PAR.
    PERFORM FIND-PAR THRU FIND-PAR-END.
    IF FOUND-IT = 'Y' MOVE '-----` TO LAST-NAME(ARRAY-INDEX).
```

```
DELETE-PAR-END.

DISPLAY-PAR.
    PERFORM FIND-PAR THRU FIND-PAR-END.
    PERFORM LIST-PAR THRU LIST-PAR-END.
DISPLAY-PAR-END.

LIST-PAR.
    DISPLAY 'NAME     : ',NAME(ARRAY-INDEX).
    DISPLAY 'STREET   : ',STREET-1(ARRAY-INDEX).
    DISPLAY 'STREET   : ',STREET-2(ARRAY-INDEX).
    DISPLAY 'STATE    : ',STATE(ARRAY-INDEX).
    DISPLAY 'ZIPCODE  : ',ZIPCODE(ARRAY-INDEX).
LIST-PAR-END.

FIND-PAR.
    DISPLAY 'ENTER NAME ( LAST, FIRST, MI ) :'.
    ACCEPT WS-NAME.
    MOVE 'N' TO FOUND-IT.
    PERFORM FIND-1-PAR THRU FIND-1-PAR-END
            VARYING ARRAY-INDEX FROM 1 BY 1
            UNTIL ARRAY-INDEX = ARRAY-SIZE OR FOUND-IT = 'Y'.
    IF FOUND-IT = 'N' DISPLAY 'NOT FOUND'.

FIND-PAR-END.

FIND-1-PAR.
    IF NAME(ARRAY-INDEX) = WS-NAME
       DISPLAY ' '
       DISPLAY NAME(ARRAY-INDEX), ' ',STREET-1(ARRAY-INDEX)
       DISPLAY ' '
       DISPLAY 'IS THIS IT ( Y or N) : '
       ACCEPT FOUND-IT.
FIND-1-PAR-END.

READ-PAR.
    OPEN INPUT MAIL-FILE AT END MOVE 'Y' TO OUT-OF-RECS.
    MOVE 0 TO ARRAY-SIZE.
    READ MAIL-FILE AT END MOVE 'Y' TO OUT-OF-RECS.
    IF OUT-OF-RECS NOT = 'Y'
       PERFORM READ-2-PAR THRU READ-2-PAR-END UNTIL
               OUT-OF-RECS = 'Y'.
    CLOSE MAIL-FILE.
READ-PAR-END.

READ-1-PAR.
    ADD 1 TO ARRAY-SIZE.
    MOVE MAIL-REC TO MAIL-TABLE(ARRAY-SIZE).
    READ MAIL-FILE AT END MOVE 'Y' TO OUT-OF-RECS.
READ-1-PAR-END.
```

```
WRITE-PAR.
   OPER OUTPUT MAIL-FILE.
   PERFORM WRITE-PAR THRU WRITE-PAR-END
           VARYING ARRAY-INDEX FROM 1 BY 1 UNTIL
                   ARRAY-INDEX = ARRAY-SIZE.
   CLOSE MAIL-FILE.
WRITE-PAR-END.

WRITE-1-PAR-END.
   IF NAME(ARRAY-INDEX) NOT = '-----'
       WRITE MAIL-REC FROM MAIL-ARRAY(ARRAY-INDEX).
WRITE-1-PAR-END.
```

locate the record that must be changed. This is done by performing FIND-PAR. Once the record is found all information in the record is displayed. Then the user is prompted, one field at a time, to enter a new value or hit the return key to leave the value unchanged. Figure 9-6 shows the user view of the change process.

FIND-PAR is used by CHANGE-PAR, DELETE-PAR, and DISPLAY-PAR. Its function is to ask the user to enter the name of the desired record and search the table for a match. If a match is made, FOUND-IT is set to Y and ARRAY-INDEX is set to the array location at which the data was found.

DELETE-PAR deletes a name from the mailing list. This is done by executing FIND-PAR to locate the correct record, and placing dashes in the name field. Then, when the updates are complete and WRITE-PAR is performed, the records with dashes are not rewritten to disk and are therefore

deleted. Figure 9-7 shows the user view of the delete option.

Option 4 on the update menu executes DISPLAY-PAR. This paragraph simply performs two subparagraphs: FIND-PAR to find the appropriate data, and LIST-PAR to display the record's information. Figure 9-8 shows this option.

Option 5 on the menu lists all the names and addresses in the file by performing LIST-PAR while incrementing ARRAY-INDEX by one for each reiteration. This process continues until ARRAY-INDEX reaches the value contained in ARRAY-SIZE, thus ending the array. Figure 9-9 shows the output of the list option.

The change paragraph could have been written using a different technique. The process employed in the program steps the user through all the data fields of the selected record. This process is fine for files containing small numbers of fields, but would be unacceptable for files containing 10,

```
         MAIL LIST SYSTEM
          UPDATE MENU


   1.  ADD A NEW LABEL
   2.  CHANGE CURRENT LABEL DATA
   3.  DELETE A LABEL
   4.  DISPLAY A LABEL
   5.  LIST ALL LABELS
   E.  EXIT SYSTEM


          ENTER OPTION:
```

Fig. 9-4. Main update menu screen.

```
ENTER NAME (LAST, FIRST, MI ): Bloom, Eric P.
ENTER FIRST STREET ADDRESS: 5 MAIN STREET
ENTER SECOND STREET ADDRESS: Office 4A
ENTER STATE CODE: MA
ENTER ZIPCODE: 12345
```

Fig. 9-5. Add a label example.

```
ENTER NAME ( LAST, FIRST MI ): Bloom, Eric P.

Bloom, Eric P.        5 Main Street

IS THIS IT ( Y OR N ) : Y


   NAME     : Bloom, Eric p.
   STREET   : 5 Main street
   STREET   : Office 4A
   STATE    : MA
   ZIPCODE  : 12345

ENTER NEW VALUE TO UPDATE OR <CR> TO LEAVE VALUE UNCHANGED

   ENTER NAME ( LAST, FIRST MI ):
   ENTER FIRST STREET ADDRESS :
   ENTER SECOND STREET ADDRESS:
   ENTER STATE CODE:
   ENTER ZIPCODE:
```

Fig. 9-6. Change option example.

```
ENTER NAME ( LAST, FIRST MI ): Bloom, Eric P.

Bloom, Eric P.        5 Main Street

IS THIS IT ( Y OR N ) : Y
```

Fig. 9-7. Delete option example.

20 or even 50 data records. The alternate process, shown in Fig. 9-10, uses a menu-type approach.

The program listing places the data field names in a menu. When executed, the user selects the par-ticular field that must be updated and the system prompts the user for just that option. In fact, if this approach is used the programmer can also use the small field input paragraphs as part of the ADD

```
           ENTER NAME ( LAST, FIRST MI ): Bloom, Eric P.

    Bloom, Eric P.        5 Main Street

    IS THIS IT ( Y OR N ) : Y


        NAME     : Bloom, Eric p.
        STREET   : 5 Main street
        STREET   : Office 4A
        STATE    : MA
        ZIPCODE  : 12345
```

Fig. 9-8. Display option example.

```
    NAME     : Bloom, Eric p.
    STREET   : 5 Main street
    STREET   : Office 4A
    STATE    : MA
    ZIPCODE  : 12345


    NAME     : Smith, John J.
    STREET   : 7 Clove Drive
    STREET   :
    STATE    : MA
    ZIPCODE  : 02345


    NAME     : Jackson, Mike s.
    STREET   : 10 Marsh Ave.
    STREET   : Apt 25
    STATE    : NY
    ZIPCODE  : 32190
```

Fig. 9-9. List option example.

```
MENU-PAR.
  DISPLAY ' '
  DISPLAY '                MAIL LIST SYSTEM'.
  DISPLAY '                CHANGE MENU'.
  DISPLAY ' '
  DISPLAY '     1. NAME'.
  DISPLAY '     2. FIRST STREET ADDRESS'.
  DISPLAY '     3. SECOND STREET ADDRESS'.
  DISPLAY '     4. STATE CODE'.
```

Fig. 9-10. Alternate change process listing.

```
      DISPLAY '     5. ZIPCODE'.
      DISPLAY '     E. EXIT CHANGE MENU'.
      DISPLAY ' '
      DISPLAY '               ENTER OPTION:'
      ACCEPT ANSWER.

          IF ANSWER = '1' MOVE 'Y' TO VALID-OPTION
                  PERFORM NAME-PAR THRU NAME-PAR-END.
          IF ANSWER = '2' MOVE 'Y' TO VALID-OPTION
                  PERFORM STREET-1-PAR THRU STREET-1-PAR-END.
          IF ANSWER = '3' MOVE 'Y' TO VALID-OPTION
                  PERFORM STREET-2-PAR THRU STREET-2-PAR-END.
          IF ANSWER = '4' MOVE 'Y' TO VALID-OPTION
                  PERFORM STATE-PAR THRU STATE-PAR-END.
          IF ANSWER = '5' MOVE 'Y' TO VALID-OPTION
                  PERFORM ZIPCODE-PAR THRU ZIPCODE-PAR-END.
          IF ANSWER = 'E' GOTO MENU-PAR-END.

          IF VALID-OPTION = 'Y' GOTO MENU-PAR.
          DISPLAY ' '.
          DISPLAY 'ERROR: ANSWER MUST BE 1,2,3,4,5 or E, PLEASE
                  REENTER'.
          DISPLAY ' '.
          GOTO MENU-PAR.
  MENU-PAR-END.

  NAME-PAR.
      DISPLAY 'ENTER NAME ( LAST, FIRST, MI ): '.
      ACCEPT WS-NAME.
      IF WS-NAME NOT = SPACES MOVE WS-NAME TO NAME(ARRAY-INDEX).
  NAME-PAR-END.

  STREET-1-PAR-END.
      DISPLAY 'ENTER FIRST STREET ADDRESS '.
      ACCEPT WS-STREET-1.
      IF WS-STREET-1 NOT = SPACES MOVE WS-STREET-1 TO
          STREET-1(ARRAY-INDEX).
  STREET-1-PAR-END.

  STREET-2-PAR.
      DISPLAY 'ENTER SECOND STREET ADDRESS: '.
      ACCEPT WS-STREET-2.
      IF WS-STREET-2 NOT = SPACES MOVE WS-STREET-2 TO
          STREET-2(ARRAY-INDEX).
  STREET-2-PAR-END.
  STATE-PAR.
      DISPLAY 'ENTER STATE CODE : '.
      ACCEPT WS-STATE.
      IF WS-STATE NOT = SPACES MOVE WS-STATE TO STATE(ARRAY-INDEX).
  STATE-PAR-END.
```

```
ZIPCODE-PAR.
    DISPLAY 'ENTER ZIPCODE '.
    ACCEPT WS-ZIPCODE.
    IF WS-ZIPCODE NOT = SPACES MOVE WS-ZIPCODE TO
        ZIPCODE(ARRAY-INDEX).
ZIPCODE-PAR-END.
```

```
            MAIL LIST SYSTEM'.
            CHANGE MENU'.

1.  NAME
2.  FIRST STREET ADDRESS
3.  SECOND STREET ADDRESS
4.  STATE CODE
5.  ZIPCODE
E.  EXIT CHANGE MENU

        ENTER OPTION:
```

Fig. 9-11. Change option menu.

option, thus saving the programmer from writing and testing two input procedures (one for add and one for change). Figure 9-11 is a picture of the user change screen.

QUESTIONS

1. What is a data file?

2. Describe the difference between sequential and random access files.

3. Describe the two-tape update method.

4. List and describe the reports that could be generated during the sequential file update process.

5. How can a good file update error report assist in the discovery of data entry problems?

6. What is the function of the dispatch paragraph in Fig. 9-2?

7. Describe the sequential file array update method.

8. In the array update method program shown in Fig. 9-3, what are the functions of ARRAY-SIZE and ARRAY-INDEX?

9. In Fig. 9-3, how is a record logically and physically deleted?

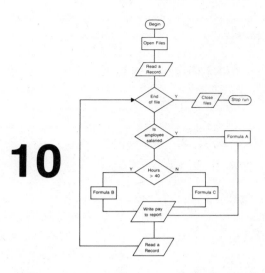

10

Report Generation

Report generation is a key aspect of a system's overall design and architecture. Systems include more than just application software and its host hardware. It includes the collection of raw data, the processing of that data, and the dissemination of processed information. Hardcopy (paper) reports are still a major component of data distribution. The reports serve many functions in a corporation—as reference to users, providing computerized information to those without on-line computer access, and providing an historical snapshot of days gone by.

This chapter will discuss the process required to create reports, as well as many of the details that assist users in reading and analyzing report information, including headings, record counts, page breaking, totals, subtotals, and suppressed printing.

All report programs, regardless of the information being reported, have the same basic programming structure. This structure, illustrated in Fig. 10-1, begins with things that only happen once, like opening files and initializing counters. Next is a loop that reads the file, places the data in the report, and calculates counters and totallers. Finally, when the program's looping process has completed the functions only done at the end of the report, like printing final totals and closing the files, are performed.

All reports have one thing in common: they all need data to process. Figure 10-2 is the data that shall be used throughout the chapter as input to the report programs. The data file will be called IN-FILE, and contains an employee number, employee name, the department in which the individual is assigned, and the employee's salary. Note that the file is sorted first by department and second by employee name.

Figure 10-3 is a simple report program that reads the input data file previously displayed and generates a simple report, shown in Fig. 10-4. This program will be used throughout the chapter as a basis for more sophisticated reporting processes.

In the first report program example (Fig. 10-3), there are a few major points of interest. First note that the output file record REP-REC is defined as 71 characters and has no specific format or detail. This is done because many formats will be printed

```
<===== OPEN FILES

<===== INITIALIZE VARIABLES

<===== PRINT FIRST HEADINGS

<===== READ FIRST RECORD


        <===== PERFORM CALCULATIONS

        <===== WRITE DATA TO REPORT

        <===== READ A NEW RECORD


<===== PRINT FINAL TOTALS

<===== CLOSE FILES

<===== END EXECUTION
```

Fig. 10-1. Report program structure.

to the file. These formats will be for report titles, headings, detail lines, subtotals and final counters and totals. These formats will be defined in the WORKING-STORAGE SECTION. The fields contained in IN-REC are not in the same order as the fields in DETAIL-REC. DETAIL-REC places the department name first, followed by the employee name, employee number, and hourly wage. The reason for the re-ordering is to highlight the way in which the report is sorted. The sorted fields should always be placed on the left-most side of the report in their order of priority. For example, this report is sorted first by department and then alphabetically within departments. Therefore, the printing order shown on the report is department, followed by employee name, followed by the remaining fields. If the report was sorted in employee number order, then DET-EMP-NO would have

```
00283Bloom, Eric P.          Accounting00475
03932Smith, Jonathan S.      Accounting00650
20003Tompson, William A.     Accounting00350
31212Conley, Steve J.        Computer  00626
65432Davis, John R.          Computer  00450
00421Olson, Kenny L.         Sales     00850
00534Patterson Sally D.      Sales     00750
04329Stone Samual T.         Sales     00325
05713Zide, Neal M.           Sales     00775
33321Jones, Allen F.         Training  00425
00094Wells Erwin T.          Training  00375
```

Fig. 10-2. Sample report input data file.

```
      IDENTIFICATION DIVISION.

      PROGRAM-ID.      SALREP.
      AUTHOR.          ERIC P. BLOOM.
      INSTALLATION.    BOSTON.
      DATE-WRITTEN.    SEP. 1, 1985.
      DATE-COMPILED.   SEP, 1, 1985.
      SECURITY.        NONE.

      ENVIRONMENT DIVISION.

      CONFIGURATION SECTION.
      SOURCE-COMPUTER.      IBM.
      OBJECT-COMPUTER.      IBM.

      INPUT-OUTPUT SECTION.
      FILE-CONTROL.

          SELECT IN-FILE ASSIGN TO 'PAYPAST.DAT'.
          SELECT REP-REC ASSIGN TO 'PAYREP.LIS'.

  DATA DIVISION.

  FILE SECTION.
  FD IN-FILE
     RECORD CONTAINS 45 CHARACTERS
     LABEL RECORDS ARE OMITTED
     DATA RECORD IS IN-REC.

  01 IN-REC.
     05 IN-EMP-NO          PIC X(5).
     05 IN-EMP-NAME        PIC X(25).
     05 IN-DEPT            PIC X(10).
     05 IN-SALARY          PIC 999V99.

  FD REP-FILE
     RECORD CONTAINS 71 CHARACTERS
     LABEL RECORDS ARE OMITTED
     DATA RECORD IS REP-REC.

  01 REP-REC               PIC X(71).

  WORKING-STORAGE.

  01 DETAIL-REC.
     05 DET-DEPT           PIC X(10).
     05 FILLER             PIC X(5).
     05 DET-EMP-NAME       PIC X(25).
```

Fig. 10-3. First report program example.

```
    05 FILLER                 PIC X(5).
    05 DET-EMP-NO             PIC X(5).
    05 FILLER                 PIC X(5).
    05 DET-SALARY             PIC 999V99.

01 OUT-OF-RECS                PIC X.

PROCEDURE DIVISION.
START-PAR.
    MOVE 'N' TO OUT-OF-RECS.
    OPEN INPUT  IN-FILE, OUTPUT REP-FILE.
    READ IN-FILE AT END MOVE 'N' TO OUT-OF-RECS.
    IF OUT-OF-RECS = 'N'
        PERFORM LOOP-PAR THRU LOOP-PAR-END UNTIL
                OUT-OF-RECS = 'Y'.
    CLOSE IN-FILE, OUT-FILE.
    STOP RUN.

LOOP-PAR.
    MOVE IN-EMP-NO      TO DET-EMP-NO.
    MOVE IN-EMP-NAME    TO DET-EMP-NAME.
    MOVE IN-DEPT        TO DET-DEPT.
    MOVE IN-SALARY      TO DET-SALARY.
    WRITE REP-REC FROM DETAIL-REC.
    READ IN-FILE AT END MOVE 'Y' TO OUT-OF-RECS.
LOOP-PAR-END.
```

been printed in the first column. Note the structure of the PROCEDURE DIVISION. Within START-PAR the files are opened, the first record is retrieved, and LOOP-PAR is performed. After all records have been processed the files are closed and the program ends. LOOP-PAR moves the data from IN-REC to DET-REC, writes DET-REC to REP-REC, and reads the next record. This process continues until IN-FILE is out of records, and the OUT-OF-RECS flag is set to Y. Figure 10-4 shows the report produced by the execution of this program.

```
Accounting    Bloom, Eric P.          00283    00475
Accounting    Smith, Jonathan S.      03932    00650
Accounting    Tompson, William A.     20003    00350
Computer      Conley, Steve J.        31212    00626
Computer      Davis, John R.          65432    00450
Sales         Olson, Kenny L.         00421    00850
Sales         Patterson Sally D.      00534    00750
Sales         Stone Samual T.         04329    00325
Sales         Zide, Neal M.           05721    00775
Training      Jones, Allen F.         33321    00425
Training      Wells Erwin T.          00094    00375
```

Fig. 10-4. Output from first report program.

As can be seen, the output of the first report program is far from professional quality. The second report program, shown in Fig. 10-5, will improve the report's appearance in three major areas: titles, headings, and format of the salary field. The title will be placed at the top of the report, centered on the first line of the page. The headings and underline will be placed after the title at the top of each detail column and the salary field will be redisplayed in a more readable format.

In Fig. 10-5 three programming changes were made. First, the picture clause in field DAT-SALARY was modified from 999V99 to ZZ9.99. This modification will change the way salary is printed on the report. ZZ means zero suppression; if the leading digits are zeros they will not be printed on the report. The other print change is the replacement of the V with a period, placed in the report at the specified location. It is used to denote the decimal place.

```
IDENTIFICATION DIVISION.

PROGRAM-ID.      SALREP.
AUTHOR.          ERIC P. BLOOM.
INSTALLATION.    BOSTON.
DATE-WRITTEN.    SEP. 1, 1985.
DATE-COMPILED.   SEP, 1, 1985.
SECURITY.        NONE.

ENVIRONMENT DIVISION.

CONFIGURATION SECTION.
SOURCE-COMPUTER.      IBM.
OBJECT-COMPUTER.      IBM.

INPUT-OUTPUT SECTION.
FILE-CONTROL.

    SELECT IN-FILE ASSIGN TO 'PAYPAST.DAT'.
    SELECT REP-FILE ASSIGN TO 'PAYREP.LIS'.

DATA DIVISION.

FILE SECTION.
FD IN-FILE
   RECORD CONTAINS 45 CHARACTERS
   LABEL RECORDS ARE OMITTED
   DATA RECORD IS IN-FILE.

01 IN-REC.
   05 IN-EMP-NO          PIC X(5).
   05 IN-EMP-NAME        PIC X(25).
   05 IN-DEPT            PIC X(10).
   05 IN-SALARY          PIC 999V99.
```

Fig. 10-5. Second report program example.

```
FD REP-FILE
   RECORD CONTAINS 71 CHARACTERS
   LABEL RECORDS ARE OMITTED
   DATA RECORD IS REP-REC.

01 REP-REC                    PIC X(71).

WORKING-STORAGE.

01 DETAIL-REC.
   05 DET-DEPT                PIC X(10).
   05 FILLER                  PIC X(5).
   05 DET-EMP-NAME            PIC X(25).
   05 FILLER                  PIC X(5).
   05 DET-EMP-NO              PIC X(5).
   05 FILLER                  PIC X(5).
   05 DET-SALARY              PIC ZZ9.99.


01 TITLE-1.
   05 FILLER PIC X(25) VALUE IS 'PROGRAM: REP001'.
   05 FILLER PIC X(25) VALUE IS 'EMPLOYEE MASTER LISTING'.
   05 FILLER PIC X(21).

01 HEADINGS-1.
   05 FILLER PIC X(10) VALUE IS 'DEPARTMENT'.
   05 FILLER PIC X(5).
   05 FILLER PIC X(25) VALUE IS 'EMPLOYEE NAME'.
   05 FILLER PIC X(5).
   05 FILLER PIC X(5) VALUE IS 'EMP NO.'.
   05 FILLER PIC X(5).
   05 FILLER PIC X(5) VALUE IS ' WAGE'.

01 HEADINGS-2.
   05 FILLER PIC X(10) VALUE IS '----------'.
   05 FILLER PIC X(5).
   05 FILLER PIC X(25) VALUE IS '-------------'.
   05 FILLER PIC X(5).
   05 FILLER PIC X(5) VALUE IS '-------'.
   05 FILLER PIC X(5).
   05 FILLER PIC X(5) VALUE IS '------'.


01 OUT-OF-RECS                PIC X.

PROCEDURE DIVISION.
START-PAR.
    MOVE 'N' TO OUT-OF-RECS.
    OPEN INPUT  IN-FILE, OUTPUT REP-FILE.
    READ IN-FILE AT END MOVE 'N' TO OUT-OF-RECS.
    PERFORM HEADINGS-PAR THRU HEADINGS-PAR-END.
```

```
        IF OUT-OF-RECS = 'N'
            PERFORM LOOP-PAR THRU LOOP-PAR-END UNTIL
                    OUT-OF-RECS = 'Y'.
        CLOSE IN-FILE, OUT-FILE.
        STOP RUN.

    LOOP-PAR.
        MOVE IN-EMP-NO       TO DET-EMP-NO.
        MOVE IN-EMP-NAME     TO DET-EMP-NAME.
        MOVE IN-DEPT         TO DET-DEPT.
        MOVE IN-SALARY       TO DET-SALARY.
        WRITE REP-REC FROM DETAIL-REC.
        READ IN-FILE AT END MOVE 'Y' TO OUT-OF-RECS.
    LOOP-PAR-END.

    HEADINGS-PAR.
        WRITE REP-REC FROM TITLE AFTER ADVANCING TOP-OF-FORM.
        WRITE REP-REC FROM HEADINGS-1 AFTER ADVANCING 2 LINES.
        WRITE REP-REC FROM HEADINGS-2 AFTER ADVANCING 1 LINES.
    HEADINGS-PAR-END.
```

The second change is the inclusion of the record definitions in the WORKING-STORAGE SECTION. These definitions (TITLE, HEADING-1, and HEADING-2) are used to define the format of the report title and column headings. This information is printed HEADINGS-PAR, which is called by START-PAR prior to the reading of IN-FILE.

Placing the statement that prints the first set of report headings in START-PAR was done to ensure that the titles are printed before the detail is written to the report file. Also, if IN-FILE is empty and LOOP-PAR is not performed, one set of headings will still be printed in the report file. This is important because if IN-FILE is empty, at least some-

Table 10-1. Output from Second Report Program.

```
PROGRAM: REP001              EMPLOYEE MASTER LISTING

DEPARTMENT          EMPLOYEE NAME              EMP NO      WAGE


Accounting          Bloom, Eric P.             00283       4.75
Accounting          Smith, Jonathan S.         03932       6.50
Accounting          Tompson, William A.        20003       3.50
Computer            Conley, Steve J.           31212       6.25
Computer            Davis, John R.             65432       4.50
Sales               Olson, Kenny L.            00421       8.50
Sales               Patterson Sally D.         00534       7.50
Sales               Stone Samual T.            04329       3.25
Sales               Zide, Neal M.              05721       7.75
Training            Jones, Allen F.            33321       4.25
Training            Wells Erwin T.             00094       3.75
```

thing identifiable has been printed, helping the programmer—the report was run but there was no data to process. In fact, some data processing shops require an ELSE clause on the IF statement that performs LOOP-PAR. This clause prints a message in the report file stating that IN-FILE was found and opened, but contained no data records. Table 10-1 shows the output of the second report program.

The output of the second report program still has some inadequacies. There are no page num-

bers, and even worse, there is no page break logic. In effect, this means the headings will print once at the beginning of the report and not at the top of any subsequent pages. An additional possible shortcoming is that the user may wish to sum the salary column. The program in Fig. 10-6 addresses these problems.

Several programming changes were incorporated, adding a page number to the title print line, counters to track page, and line counts and a totaler to calculate the total salary.

```
        IDENTIFICATION DIVISION.

PROGRAM-ID.        SALREP.
AUTHOR.            ERIC P. BLOOM.
INSTALLATION.      BOSTON.
DATE-WRITTEN.      SEP. 1, 1985.
DATE-COMPILED.     SEP, 1, 1985.
SECURITY.          NONE.

ENVIRONMENT DIVISION.

CONFIGURATION SECTION.
SOURCE-COMPUTER.      IBM.
OBJECT-COMPUTER.      IBM.

INPUT-OUTPUT SECTION.
FILE-CONTROL.

        SELECT IN-FILE ASSIGN TO 'PAYPAST.DAT'.
        SELECT REP-FILE ASSIGN TO 'PAYREP.LIS'.


DATA DIVISION.

FILE SECTION.
FD IN-FILE
    RECORD CONTAINS 45 CHARACTERS
    LABEL RECORDS ARE OMITTED
    DATA RECORD IS IN-REC.

01 IN-REC.
    05 IN-EMP-NO          PIC X(5).
    05 IN-EMP-NAME        PIC X(25).
    05 IN-DEPT            PIC X(10).
    05 IN-SALARY          PIC 999V99.
```

Fig. 10-6. Third report program example.

```
FD REP-FILE
    RECORD CONTAINS 71 CHARACTERS
    LABEL RECORDS ARE OMITTED
    DATA RECORD IS REP-REC.

01 REP-REC                  PIC X(71).

WORKING-STORAGE.

01 DETAIL-REC.
    05 DET-DEPT             PIC X(10).
    05 FILLER               PIC X(5).
    05 DET-EMP-NAME         PIC X(25).
    05 FILLER               PIC X(5).
    05 DET-EMP-NO           PIC X(5).
    05 FILLER               PIC X(5).
    05 DET-SALARY           PIC ZZ9.99.

01 TITLE-1.
    05 FILLER      PIC X(25) VALUE IS 'PROGRAM: REP001'.
    05 FILLER      PIC X(25) VALUE IS 'EMPLOYEE MASTER LISTING'.
    05 FILLER      PIC X(10).
    05 FILLER      PIC X(6) VALUE IS 'PAGE: '.
    05 PAGE-OUT    PIC ZZ9.

01 HEADINGS-1.
    05 FILLER PIC X(10) VALUE IS 'DEPARTMENT'.
    05 FILLER PIC X(5).
    05 FILLER PIC X(25) VALUE IS 'EMPLOYEE NAME'.
    05 FILLER PIC X(5).
    05 FILLER PIC X(5) VALUE IS 'EMP NO.'.
    05 FILLER PIC X(5).
    05 FILLER PIC X(5) VALUE IS ' WAGE'.

01 HEADINGS-2.
    05 FILLER PIC X(10) VALUE IS '----------'.
    05 FILLER PIC X(5).
    05 FILLER PIC X(25) VALUE IS '-------------'.
    05 FILLER PIC X(5).
    05 FILLER PIC X(5) VALUE IS '-------'.
    05 FILLER PIC X(5).
    05 FILLER PIC X(5) VALUE IS '------'.

01 SALARY-DISPLAY.
    05 FILLER       PIC X(30) VALUE IS 'TOTAL SALARY PER
                                    COMPANY HOUR: '.
    05 FILLER       PIC X(25).
    05 SALARY-OUT PIC ZZZ,ZZZ.99.

01 FLAGS-AND-COUNTERS.
```

```
      05  OUT-OF-RECS          PIC X.
      05  PAGE-NO              PIC 999.
      05  SALARY-NUM           PIC 9(5)V99.
      05  SALARY-OUT           PIC ZZZ,ZZ9.99.
      05  LINE-COUNT           PIC 99.

PROCEDURE DIVISION.
START-PAR.
      MOVE 'N'        TO OUT-OF-RECS.
      MOVE 0          TO SALARY-NUM.
      MOVE 0          TO PAGE-NO.
      OPEN INPUT  IN-FILE, OUTPUT REP-FILE.
      READ IN-FILE AT END MOVE 'N' TO OUT-OF-RECS.
      PERFORM HEADINGS-PAR THRU HEADINGS-PAR-END.
      IF OUT-OF-RECS = 'N'
          PERFORM LOOP-PAR THRU LOOP-PAR-END UNTIL
                    OUT-OF-RECS = 'Y'.
      WRITE REP-REC FROM HEADINGS-2.
      MOVE SALARY-NUM TO SALARY-OUT.
      WRITE REP-REC FROM SALARY-DISPLAY.
      CLOSE IN-FILE, OUT-FILE.
      STOP RUN.

LOOP-PAR.
      MOVE IN-EMP-NO        TO DET-EMP-NO.
      MOVE IN-EMP-NAME      TO DET-EMP-NAME.
      MOVE IN-DEPT          TO DET-DEPT.
      MOVE IN-SALARY        TO DET-SALARY.
      ADD IN-SALARY         TO SALARY-SUM.
      ADD 1                 TO LINE-NO.
      IF LINE-NUM > 55
          PERFORM HEADINGS-PAR THRU HEADINGS PAR-END.
      WRITE REP-REC FROM DETAIL-REC.
      READ IN-FILE AT END MOVE 'Y' TO OUT-OF-RECS.
LOOP-PAR-END.

HEADINGS-PAR.
      ADD 1           TO PAGE-NO.
      MOVE 5          TO LINE-COUNT
      MOVE PAGE-NO    TO PAGE-OUT.
      WRITE REP-REC FROM TITLE AFTER ADVANCING TOP-OF-FORM.
      WRITE REP-REC FROM HEADINGS-1 AFTER ADVANCING 2 LINES.
      WRITE REP-REC FROM HEADINGS-2 AFTER ADVANCING 1 LINES.
HEADINGS-PAR-END.
```

The page breaking logic starts at the very beginning of the program. In paragraph START-PAR, the page number variable, PAGE-NO. HEADINGS-PAR increments PAGE-NO by one, moves the calculated value to PAGE-OUT, prints the page title and headings, and sets LINE-COUNT to five. LINE-COUNT is used to track the number of lines printed on a page. As can be seen in LOOP-

PAR, LINE-COUNT is incremented by one each time a line of data is written to the report. When LINE-COUNT reaches a value of 55, HEADINGS-PAR is once again called, the counters are adjusted, and the headings are printed on the top of a new page.

The salary field is summed and printed with the help of two variables: SALARY-SUM and SALARY-OUT. SALARY-SUM is acting as a totaller and SALARY-OUT is contained in the SALARY-DISPLAY record and is being used to print the accumulated salary in an edited format.

SALARY-NUM is first referenced in START-PAR where it is initialized to zero. The initialization process is not required, but is a good programming practice to specifically assign variables a beginning value. The actual salary summation is done in LOOP-PAR. Here, each time a record is read from the file its salary value is added to SALARY-NUM. When all the records have been retrieved and written, SALARY-NUM is moved to SALARY-OUT and SALARY-DISPLAY is written to the report file.

Table 10-2 displays the report generated by the third report program. For the sake of size and example, the report was generated using four lines to a page.

Now let's add some bells and whistles. The next report enhancement will be to print the department name only once. The suppression of repeating department names will increase the readability of the report by showing the department breakdown more easily. Also, because this report contains salary information a footnote will be placed at the bottom of each page saying "confidential."

Figure 10-7 has been modified to include these new report features. Statements were added at various places to include the two suggested report enhancements. The department break logic required the addition of two new variables; LAST-DEPT and BLANK-LINE. LAST-DEPT is used to hold the name of the department previously printed. If the last department name matches the current department name, printing the department field is suppressed. If the departments do not match a change in department has occurred. Therefore, a line is skipped by writing REP-REC from DISPLAY-BLANK and the printing of department name is not suppressed.

To program the second needed enhancement, a footnote, a very simple procedure is used. HEADING-PAR is modified to include an IF state-

Table 10-2. Output from Third Report Program.

```
PROGRAM: REP001          EMPLOYEE MASTER LISTING   PAGE: 1

DEPARTMENT       EMPLOYEE NAME            EMP NO     WAGE

Accounting       Bloom, Eric P.           00283      4.75
Accounting       Smith, Jonathan S.       03932      6.50
Accounting       Tompson, William A.      20003      3.50
Computer         Conley, Steve J.         31212      6.25

PROGRAM: REP001          EMPLOYEE MASTER LISTING   PAGE: 2

DEPARTMENT       EMPLOYEE NAME            EMP NO     WAGE

Computer         Davis, John R.           65432      4.50
Sales            Olson, Kenny L.          00421      8.50
Sales            Patterson Sally D.       00534      7.50

TOTAL SALARY PER COMPANY HOUR:                      41.50
```

```
IDENTIFICATION DIVISION.

PROGRAM-ID.         SALREP.
AUTHOR.             ERIC P. BLOOM.
INSTALLATION.       BOSTON.
DATE-WRITTEN.       SEP. 1, 1985.
DATE-COMPILED.      SEP, 1, 1985.
SECURITY.           NONE.

ENVIRONMENT DIVISION.

CONFIGURATION SECTION.
SOURCE-COMPUTER.       IBM.
OBJECT-COMPUTER.       IBM.

INPUT-OUTPUT SECTION.
FILE-CONTROL.

       SELECT IN-FILE ASSIGN TO 'PAYPAST.DAT'.
       SELECT REP-FILE ASSIGN TO 'PAYREP.LIS'.


DATA DIVISION.

FILE SECTION.
FD IN-FILE
    RECORD CONTAINS 45 CHARACTERS
    LABEL RECORDS ARE OMITTED
    DATA RECORD IS IN-REC.

01 IN-REC.
    05 IN-EMP-NO            PIC X(5).
    05 IN-EMP-NAME          PIC X(25).
    05 IN-DEPT              PIC X(10).
    05 IN-SALARY            PIC 999V99.

FD REP-FILE
    RECORD CONTAINS 71 CHARACTERS
    LABEL RECORDS ARE OMITTED
    DATA RECORD IS REP-REC.

01 REP-REC                  PIC X(71).

WORKING-STORAGE.

01 DETAIL-REC.
    05 DET-DEPT             PIC X(10).
    05 FILLER               PIC X(5).
```

Fig. 10-7. Fourth report program example.

```
    05 DET-EMP-NAME            PIC X(25).
    05 FILLER                  PIC X(5).
    05 DET-EMP-NO              PIC X(5).
    05 FILLER                  PIC X(5).
    05 DET-SALARY              PIC ZZ9.99.

01 TITLE-1.
    05 FILLER       PIC X(25) VALUE IS 'PROGRAM: REP001'.
    05 FILLER       PIC X(25) VALUE IS 'EMPLOYEE MASTER LISTING'.
    05 FILLER       PIC X(10).
    05 FILLER       PIC X(6) VALUE IS 'PAGE: '.
    05 PAGE-OUT     PIC ZZ9.

01 HEADINGS-1.
    05 FILLER PIC X(10) VALUE IS 'DEPARTMENT'.
    05 FILLER PIC X(5).
    05 FILLER PIC X(25) VALUE IS 'EMPLOYEE NAME'.
    05 FILLER PIC X(5).
    05 FILLER PIC X(5) VALUE IS 'EMP NO.'.
    05 FILLER PIC X(5).
    05 FILLER PIC X(5) VALUE IS ' WAGE'.

01 HEADINGS-2.
    05 FILLER PIC X(10) VALUE IS '----------'.
    05 FILLER PIC X(5).
    05 FILLER PIC X(25) VALUE IS '-------------'.
    05 FILLER PIC X(5).
    05 FILLER PIC X(5) VALUE IS '-------'.
    05 FILLER PIC X(5).
    05 FILLER PIC X(5) VALUE IS '------'.

01 SALARY-DISPLAY.
    05 FILLER       PIC X(30) VALUE IS 'TOTAL SALARY PER
                                        COMPANY HOUR: '.
    05 FILLER       PIC X(25).
    05 SALARY-OUT PIC ZZZ,ZZZ.99.

01 BLANK-DISPLAY PIC X(71) VALUE IS SPACES.

01 FOOT-DISPLAY.
    05 FILLER PIC X(30).
    05 FILLER PIC X(20) VALUE IS '*** CONFIDENTIAL ***'.

01 FLAGS-AND-COUNTERS.
    05 OUT-OF-RECS             PIC X.
    05 PAGE-NO                 PIC 999.
    05 SALARY-NUM              PIC 9(5)V99.
    05 SALARY-OUT              PIC ZZZ,ZZ9.99.
    05 LINE-COUNT              PIC 99.
    05 LAST-DEPT               PIC X(10)
```

```
PROCEDURE DIVISION.
START-PAR.
    MOVE 'N'        TO OUT-OF-RECS.
    MOVE 0          TO SALARY-NUM.
    MOVE 0          TO PAGE-NO.
    OPEN INPUT  IN-FILE, OUTPUT REP-FILE.
    READ IN-FILE AT END MOVE 'N' TO OUT-OF-RECS.
    PERFORM HEADINGS-PAR THRU HEADINGS-PAR-END.
    IF OUT-OF-RECS = 'N'
        PERFORM LOOP-PAR THRU LOOP-PAR-END UNTIL
                OUT-OF-RECS = 'Y'.
    WRITE REP-REC FROM HEADINGS-2.
    MOVE SALARY-NUM TO SALARY-OUT.
    WRITE REP-REC FROM SALARY-DISPLAY.
    CLOSE IN-FILE, OUT-FILE.
    STOP RUN.

LOOP-PAR.
    MOVE IN-EMP-NO      TO DET-EMP-NO.
    MOVE IN-EMP-NAME    TO DET-EMP-NAME.
    MOVE IN-DEPT        TO DET-DEPT.
    MOVE IN-SALARY      TO DET-SALARY.
    ADD IN-SALARY       TO SALARY-SUM.
    ADD 1               TO LINE-NO.
    IF IN-DEPT = LAST-DEPT
        MOVE SPACES TO DET-DEPT
    ELSE
        WRITE REP-REC FROM BLANK-DISPLAY.
    MOVE IN-DEPT TO LAST-DEPT.
    IF LINE-NUM > 55
        PERFORM HEADINGS-PAR THRU HEADINGS PAR-END.
    WRITE REP-REC FROM DETAIL-REC.
    READ IN-FILE AT END MOVE 'Y' TO OUT-OF-RECS.
LOOP-PAR-END.

HEADINGS-PAR.
    ADD 1          TO PAGE-NO.
    MOVE 5         TO LINE-COUNT
    MOVE PAGE-NO   TO PAGE-OUT.
    IF PAGE-NO NOT = 1
        WRITE REP-REC FROM FOOT-DISPLAY AFTER ADVANCING 2 LINES.
    WRITE REP-REC FROM TITLE AFTER ADVANCING TOP-OF-FORM.
    WRITE REP-REC FROM HEADINGS-1 AFTER ADVANCING 2 LINES.
    WRITE REP-REC FROM HEADINGS-2 AFTER ADVANCING 1 LINES.
HEADINGS-PAR-END.
```

ment. This statement asks if the headings being printed are for the first page of the report. If it is page one, then no action is performed because the process has not yet reached the bottom of a page.

If is not page one, REP-REC is written from FOOT-DISPLAY, which contains the footnote message.

Table 10-3 is the output from the fourth report program. The report can be further enhanced to

Table 10-3. Output From Fourth Report Program.

```
PROGRAM: REP001            EMPLOYEE MASTER LISTING   PAGE: 1

DEPARTMENT         EMPLOYEE NAME              EMP NO      WAGE

Accounting         Bloom, Eric P.             00283       4.75
                   Smith, Jonathan S.         03932       6.50
                   Tompson, William A.        20003       3.50
Computer           Conley, Steve J.           31212       6.25
                   Davis, John R.             65432       4.50
Sales              Olson, Kenny L.            00421       8.50

                      *** CONFIDENTIAL ***

PROGRAM: REP001            EMPLOYEE MASTER LISTING   PAGE: 2

DEPARTMENT         EMPLOYEE NAME              EMP NO      WAGE

                   Patterson Sally D.         00534       7.50
                   Stone Samual T.            04329       3.25
                   Zide, Neal M.              05721       7.75
Training           Jones, Allen F.            33321       4.25
                   Wells Erwin T.             00094       3.75

TOTAL SALARY PER COMPANY HOUR:                          60.50
```

provide move functionality. This last report enhancement will subtotal salary by department. Figure 10-8 lists the report program as modified to include the new requirement.

The figure contains modifications in both the DATA DIVISION and PROCEDURE DIVISION.

The DATA DIVISION has three new additions: DEPT-SUB-1, DEPT-SUB-2, and DEPT-SUB-SUM. DEPT-SUB-1 and DEPT-SUB-2 are the print formats used to place the department subtotals in the report in a pleasing fashion. DEPT-SUB-SUM is used to sum the department salaries. The

```
IDENTIFICATION DIVISION.

PROGRAM-ID.       SALREP.
AUTHOR.           ERIC P. BLOOM.
INSTALLATION.     BOSTON.
DATE-WRITTEN.     SEP. 1, 1985.
DATE-COMPILED.    SEP, 1, 1985.
SECURITY.         NONE.

ENVIRONMENT DIVISION.

CONFIGURATION SECTION.
```

Fig. 10-8. Fifth report program example.

```
        SOURCE-COMPUTER.        IBM.
        OBJECT-COMPUTER.        IBM.

        INPUT-OUTPUT SECTION.
        FILE-CONTROL.

              SELECT IN-FILE ASSIGN TO 'PAYPAST.DAT'.
              SELECT REP-FILE ASSIGN TO 'PAYREP.LIS'.

        DATA DIVISION.

        FILE SECTION.
        FD IN-FILE
           RECORD CONTAINS 45 CHARACTERS
           LABEL RECORDS ARE OMITTED
           DATA RECORD IS IN-REC.

        01 IN-REC.
           05 IN-EMP-NO          PIC X(5).
           05 IN-EMP-NAME        PIC X(25).
           05 IN-DEPT            PIC X(10).
           05 IN-SALARY          PIC 999V99.

        FD REP-FILE
           RECORD CONTAINS 71 CHARACTERS
           LABEL RECORDS ARE OMITTED
           DATA RECORD IS REP-REC.

        01 REP-REC               PIC X(71).

        WORKING-STORAGE.

        01 DETAIL-REC.
           05 DET-DEPT           PIC X(10).
           05 FILLER             PIC X(5).
           05 DET-EMP-NAME       PIC X(25).
           05 FILLER             PIC X(5).
           05 DET-EMP-NO         PIC X(5).
           05 FILLER             PIC X(5).
           05 DET-SALARY         PIC ZZ9.99.


        01 TITLE-1.
           05 FILLER    PIC X(25) VALUE IS 'PROGRAM: REP001'.
           05 FILLER    PIC X(25) VALUE IS 'EMPLOYEE MASTER LISTING'.
           05 FILLER    PIC X(10).
           05 FILLER    PIC X(6) VALUE IS 'PAGE: '.
           05 PAGE-OUT  PIC ZZ9.

        01 HEADINGS-1.
           05 FILLER PIC X(10) VALUE IS 'DEPARTMENT'.
```

```cobol
       05 FILLER PIC X(5).
       05 FILLER PIC X(25) VALUE IS 'EMPLOYEE NAME'.
       05 FILLER PIC X(5).
       05 FILLER PIC X(5) VALUE IS 'EMP NO.'.
       05 FILLER PIC X(5).
       05 FILLER PIC X(5) VALUE IS ' WAGE'.

   01 HEADINGS-2.
       05 FILLER PIC X(10) VALUE IS '----------'.
       05 FILLER PIC X(5).
       05 FILLER PIC X(25) VALUE IS '-------------'.
       05 FILLER PIC X(5).
       05 FILLER PIC X(5) VALUE IS '-------'.
       05 FILLER PIC X(5).
       05 FILLER PIC X(5) VALUE IS '------'.

   01 SALARY-DISPLAY.
       05 FILLER       PIC X(30) VALUE IS 'TOTAL SALARY PER
                                           COMPANY HOUR: '.
       05 FILLER       PIC X(25).
       05 SALARY-OUT PIC ZZZ,ZZZ.99.

   01 BLANK-DISPLAY PIC X(71) VALUE IS SPACES.

   01 FOOT-DISPLAY.
       05 FILLER PIC X(30).
       05 FILLER PIC X(20) VALUE IS '*** CONFIDENTIAL ***'.

   01 DEPT-SUB-1.
       05 FILLER           PIC X(65).
       05 FILLER           PIC X(6) VALUE IS '------'.

   01 DEPT-SUB-2.
       05 FILLER           PIC X(65).
       05 DEPT-SUB-OUT      PIC ZZ,ZZZ.99.

   01 FLAGS-AND-COUNTERS.
       05 OUT-OF-RECS              PIC X.
       05 PAGE-NO                  PIC 999.
       05 SALARY-NUM               PIC 9(5)V99.
       05 SALARY-OUT               PIC ZZZ,ZZ9.99.
       05 LINE-COUNT               PIC 99.
       05 LAST-DEPT                PIC X(10)
       05 DEPT-SUB-SUM             PIC 9(5)V99.

   PROCEDURE DIVISION.
     START-PAR.
         MOVE 'N'       TO OUT-OF-RECS.
         MOVE 0         TO SALARY-NUM.
         MOVE 0         TO PAGE-NO.
```

```
          OPEN INPUT  IN-FILE, OUTPUT REP-FILE.
          READ IN-FILE AT END MOVE 'N' TO OUT-OF-RECS.
          PERFORM HEADINGS-PAR THRU HEADINGS-PAR-END.
          IF OUT-OF-RECS = 'N'
              PERFORM LOOP-PAR THRU LOOP-PAR-END UNTIL
                                    OUT-OF-RECS = 'Y'.
          WRITE REP-REC FROM HEADINGS-2.
          MOVE SALARY-NUM TO SALARY-OUT.
          WRITE REP-REC FROM SALARY-DISPLAY.
          CLOSE IN-FILE, OUT-FILE.
          STOP RUN.

      LOOP-PAR.
          MOVE IN-EMP-NO       TO DET-EMP-NO.
          MOVE IN-EMP-NAME     TO DET-EMP-NAME.
          MOVE IN-DEPT         TO DET-DEPT.
          MOVE IN-SALARY       TO DET-SALARY.
          ADD IN-SALARY        TO SALARY-SUM.
          ADD 1                TO LINE-NO.
          IF IN-DEPT = LAST-DEPT
             MOVE SPACES TO DET-DEPT
          ELSE
            IF  LAST-DEPT = SPACES
                NEXT SENTENCE
            ELSE
                MOVE DEPT-SUB-SUM TO DEPT-SUB-OUT
                WRITE REP-REC FROM DEPT-SUB-1
                WRITE REP-REC FROM DEPT-SUB-2
                MOVE 0 TO DEPT-SUB-SUM
                WRITE REP-REC FROM BLANK-DISPLAY.
          MOVE IN-DEPT    TO LAST-DEPT.
          ADD  IN-SALARY TO DEPT-SUB-SUM.
          IF LINE-NUM > 55
              PERFORM HEADINGS-PAR THRU HEADINGS PAR-END.
          WRITE REP-REC FROM DETAIL-REC.
          READ IN-FILE AT END MOVE 'Y' TO OUT-OF-RECS.
      LOOP-PAR-END.

      HEADINGS-PAR.
          ADD 1         TO PAGE-NO.
          MOVE 5        TO LINE-COUNT
          MOVE PAGE-NO  TO PAGE-OUT.
          IF PAGE-NO NOT = 1
              WRITE REP-REC FROM FOOT-DISPLAY AFTER ADVANCING 2 LINES.
          WRITE REP-REC FROM TITLE AFTER ADVANCING TOP-OF-FORM.
          WRITE REP-REC FROM HEADINGS-1 AFTER ADVANCING 2 LINES.
          WRITE REP-REC FROM HEADINGS-2 AFTER ADVANCING 1 LINES.
      HEADINGS-PAR-END.
```

Table 10-4. Output of Fifth Report Program.

```
PROGRAM: REP001              EMPLOYEE MASTER LISTING   PAGE: 1
DEPARTMENT          EMPLOYEE NAME              EMP NO      WAGE
─────────           ─────────────             ──────      ────

Accounting          Bloom, Eric P.             00283       4.75
                    Smith, Jonathan S.         03932       6.50
                    Tompson, William A.        20003       3.50
                                                          ──────
                                                          14.75

Computer            Conley, Steve J.           31212       6.25
                    Davis, John R.             65432       4.50
                                                          ──────
                                                          10.75

Sales               Olson, Kenny L.            00421       8.50
                    Patterson Sally D.         00534       7.50
                    Stone Samual T.            04329       3.25
                    Zide, Neal M.              05721       7.75
                                                          ──────
                                                          27.00

Training            Jones, Allen F.            33321       4.25
                    Wells Erwin T.             00094       3.75
                                                          ──────
                                                           8.00

─────────           ─────────────                         ──────
TOTAL SALARY PER COMPANY HOUR:                            60.50
```

PROCEDURE DIVISION enhancements were placed in the department break logic discussed in the last program version. This logic was expanded to include the printing of department subtotals. The new nested IF logic is testing to see if the current record is the first record in the file. LAST-DEPT will only have a value of spaces when there has been no previous record. Hence, the current record is the first record. This test must be made because the first record meets the department change logic criteria (LAST-DEPT NOT = IN-DEPT); however, department totals should not be printed.

In addition to the change made to the breaking logic an ADD statement was added. This statement adds in-salary TO dept-sub- sum. Remember, DEPT-SUB-SUM is only subtotalling; therefore, it must be set back to zero each time a department value is printed.

Table 10-4 lists the output of the fifth and last report program enhancement.

QUESTIONS

1. What role do reports play in the design of application software?

2. Describe the structure of most report programs.

3. Why is zero suppression used when printing numeric data?

4. How are report titles defined and printed?

5. What is page break logic and how is it used?

6. What are counters and totalers, and what role do they play in the report generation process?

7. Describe the process used to calculate and print page numbers.

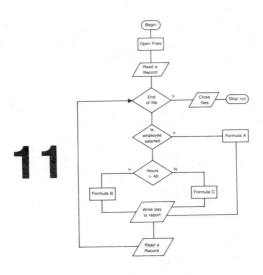

11

On-Line Systems

One of the strengths of todays computers is their ability to perform interactively with users through data entry screens, informational queries, department store cash registers, or other computer-related media. This chapter will deal with the techniques and processes that smooth user/computer interaction, a pre-requisite for a successful application software. In particular, the topics discussed will be menu-driven systems, transaction processing, data validation, on-line help, and cursor control.

Menu-driven systems are applications in which the user selects the desired function from options displayed on the screen. Transaction processing systems are software packages where the user enters a transaction code or name and the appropriate function is performed. Data validation is the process of analyzing input data to ensure its accuracy and correctness. On-line help is information that provides the user with instructions and insight about the application being executed. Cursor controlling is the process of moving the cursor from place to place around the screen. The *cursor* is the blinking line or box on the screen used to inform

the user where the next character will be placed.

MENU-DRIVEN SYSTEMS

Menus are by far the most commonly used application drivers. Their basic function is to navigate the operator from place to place in the application by providing short descriptions of the available options and letting the user select the appropriate action. Figure 11-1 is an example of a menu for an integrated accounting package.

Menu screens are generally divided into four sections: headings, options, input, and message display. The headings are the two or three lines on the top of the screen. Their function is to remind the user of his current location in the program. To help facilitate this mind jog, each menu heading should be unique, and clearly define the general purpose of the menu's options. For example, the main payroll menu should be titled something like: PAYROLL SUBSYSTEM MAIN MENU. The options are the choices displayed as possible actions to take. In Fig. 11-2, these are numbered from 1 to 4, and

```
       IAS001                    INTEGRATED ACCOUNTING SYSTEM
                                          MAIN MENU


                      1.  PAYROLL
                      2.  GENERAL LEDGER
                      3.  ACCOUNTS PAYABLE
                      4.  ACCOUNTS RECEIVABLE
                      E.  EXIT SYSTEM


                              ENTER OPTION:
```

Fig. 11-1. On-line menu example.

```
300    WORKING STORAGE.
310
351    01 ANSWER                      PIC X.
352    01 VALID-OPTION                PIC X.
353
400    PROCEDURE DIVISION.
401    START-PAR.
402        PERFORM MENU-PAR THRU MENU-PAR-END.
403        STOP RUN.
404
405    MENU-PAR.
406        MOVE 'N' TO VALID-OPTION.
407        DISPLAY ' '.
408        DISPLAY '                  INTEGRATED ACCOUNTING SYSTEM'.
409        DISPLAY '                          MAIN MENU'.
410        DISPLAY ' '.
411        DISPLAY '     1. PAYROLL'.
412        DISPLAY '     2. GENERAL LEDGER'.
413        DISPLAY '     3. ACCOUNTS PAYABLE'.
414        DISPLAY '     4. ACCOUNTS RECEIVABLE'.
415        DISPLAY '     E. EXIT SYSTEM'.
416        DISPLAY ' '.
417        DISPLAY '              ENTER OPTION: '.
418        ACCEPT ANSWER.
419        IF ANSWER = '1' MOVE 'Y' TO VALID-OPTION
420                        PERFORM PAYROLL-PAR THRU
                                  PAYROLL-PAR-END.
421        IF ANSWER = '2' MOVE 'Y' TO VALID-OPTION
422                        PERFORM GL-PAR THRU GL-PAR-END.
423        IF ANSWER = '3' MOVE 'Y' TO VALID-OPTION
424                        PERFORM AP-PAR THRU AP-PAR-END.
```

Fig. 11-2. Menu program logic.

```
425          IF ANSWER = '4' MOVE 'Y' TO VALID-OPTION
426                           PERFORM AR-PAR THRU AR-PAR-END.
427          IF ANSWER = 'E' GOTO MENU-PAR-END.
428

429          IF VALID-OPTION = 'Y' GOTO MENU-PAR.
430          DISPLAY ' '.
431          DISPLAY 'ERROR: ANSWER MUST BE 1,2,3,4 or E,
                       PLEASE REENTER'.
432          DISPLAY ' '.
433          GOTO MENU-PAR.
434     MENU-PAR-END.
```

E for exit. The input field is displayed as ENTER OPTION:. It is at this location the user enters the number associated with the desired function.

In many applications a line on the screen is designed as a message line. It's usually placed on the last line of the screen, but some applications place it at the top or even in the center. This line is used to display error messages, useful instructions, general correspondence, and other information that must be passed to the user.

Menu programs are composed of the DISPLAY statements, that print the headings and menu options; the ACCEPT statement, that lets the user input the desired option; the validation of the accepted value; and the logic that causes the appropriate option to be executed. Figure 11-2 is the programming logic required to drive a menu. This example does not include cursor controlling, and therefore must reprint the menu screen each time a value is entered or displayed.

Two variables are used in Fig. 11-2, ANSWER and VALID-OPTION. ANSWER contains the value input by the user. It is accepted in line 418 and is validated and acted upon in lines 419-427. VALID-OPTION is used as a program control flag. In line 406 it is set to N; then in lines 419-427 it is changed to Y if a valid answer is entered. The IF statement in line 429 states that if VALID-OPTION is equal to Y, go to MENU-PAR. If VALID-OPTION was never changed from N to Y the condition in line 429 would not be true and the error message in lines 430-432 would be printed.

TRANSACTION-DRIVEN SOFTWARE

Transaction driven programs are very similar to menu applications, with the exception that the possible options are not printed on the screen. These options may not be selected by entering a one digit code; they are selected by entering a three- to six-character mneumonic code. For example, ADDEMP may be the transaction code used to add a new employee to the master file. However, because these codes are not automatically displayed, a facility should be in place to, on request, list the possible options. A very commonly used technique to perform this display is to instruct the user to enter a question mark for a list of valid codes. Figure 11-3 is an example of a dispatch transaction screen for a payroll system.

Like the menu screen, this screen has meaningful headings, a data input location, and a line on the bottom to display messages to the user. It also contains a one-line instruction explaining that a list of possible transactions that can be obtained by entering a question mark.

The programming logic used to execute the selected transaction options may reside in either the main driver program or in separately called subprograms. Figure 11-4 can be used to perform the first option and execute transactions included in the main program. Figure 11-5 shows the logic needed to execute transactions with the logic contained in subprograms. As with Fig. 11-2, this program does not assume that the cursor can be moved from place to place on the screen. Therefore the headings and text are re-displayed each time a transaction is chosen.

The logic used in Fig. 11-4 is very similar to that used in Fig. 11-2. The most notable difference is the question mark option that provides the list

```
                        PAYROLL SUBSYSTEM
                MAIN TRANSACTION DISPATCH SCREEN


              ENTER TRANSACTION CODE:


      ENTER A QUESTION MARK ( ? ) FOR LIST OF POSSIBLE OPTIONS
```

Fig. 11-3. Transaction dispatch screen.

```
300     WORKING-STORAGE SECTION.
301
302     01 ANSWER                      PIC X.
303     01 VALID-OPTION                PIC X.
304
400     PROCEDURE DIVISION.
401     START-PAR.
402         PERFORM TRANS-PAR THRU TRANS-PAR-END.
403         STOP RUN.
404
405     TRANS-PAR.
406         MOVE 'N' TH VALID-OPTION.
407         DISPLAY ' '.
408         DISPLAY '                    PAYROLL SUBSYSTEM'.
409         DISPLAY '        MAIN TRANSACTION DISPATCH SCREEN'.
410         DISPLAY ' '.
411         DISPLAY '    ENTER TRANSACTION CODE: '.
412         DISPLAY ' '.
413         DISPLAY ' '.
414         DISPLAY 'ENTER A QUESTION MARK ( ? ) FOR LIST OF
                    VALID OPTIONS'.
415
416         ACCEPT ANSWER.
417
418         IF ANSWER = '?' MOVE 'Y' TO VALID-OPTION
419             PERFORM VALID-LIST-PAR THRU VALID-LIST-PAR-END.
420
421         IF ANSWER = 'ADDEMP' MOVE 'Y' TO VALID-OPTION
422         PERFORM ADD-EMPLOYEE-PAR THRU ADD-EMPLOYEE-PAR-END.
423
424         IF ANSWER = 'CHGEMP' MOVE 'Y' TO VALID-OPTION
425             PERFORM CHANGE-EMPLOYEE-PAR THRU
                        CHANGE-EMPLOYEE-PAR-END.
426
427         IF ANSWER = 'DELEMP' MOVE 'Y' TO VALID-OPTION
```

Fig. 11-4. Transaction-driven program logic.

```
428            PERFORM DELETE-EMPLOYEE-PAR THRU
                   DELETE-EMPLOYEE-PAR-END.
429
430     IF ANSWER = 'LISEMP' MOVE 'Y' TO VALID-OPTION
431            PERFORM LIST-EMPLOYEES-PAR THRU
                   LIST-EMPLOYEES-PAR-END.
432
433     IF ANSWER = 'CHECKS' MOVE 'Y' TO VALID-OPTION
434            PERFORM CHECKS-PAR THRU CHECKS-PAR-END.
435
436     IF ANSWER = 'EXIT  ' GOTO TRANS-PAR-END.
437
438     IF VALID-OPTION = 'Y' GOTO TRANS-PAR.
439     DISPLAY ' '.
440     DISPLAY 'ERROR: NOT A VALID OPTION, PLEASE REENTER
                   OPTION'.
441     DISPLAY'            OR ENTER QUESTION MARK ( ? ) '.
442     GOTO TRANS-PAR.
443
444  VALID-LIST-PAR.
445     DISPLAY ' '.
446     DISPLAY '              LIST OF VALID TRANSACTIONS'.
447     DISPLAY ' '.
448     DISPLAY '    CODE      FUNCTION'.
449     DISPLAY '    ------    --------'.
450     DISPLAY ' '.
451     DISPLAY '    ADDEMP    ADD A NEW EMPLOYEE '.
452     DISPLAY '    CHECKS    GENERATE PAYROLL CHECKS '.
453     DISPLAY '    CHGEMP    CHANGE EMPLOYEE INFORMATION '.
454     DISPLAY '    DELEMP    DELETE AN EMPLOYEE FROM THE
                   MASTER FILE '.
455     DISPLAY '    LISEMP    GENERATE AN EMPLOYEE LISTING '.
456     DISPLAY ' '.
457  VALID-LIST-PAR-END.
```

of valid options. In fact, this display technique is not limited to option lists, but can be used when automating manuals for computer-aided instruction or any other application with lines of textual display.

Figure 11-5 provides the logic needed to execute transactions contained in other COBOL programs. The advanced techniques used in this program could be used in the Fig. 11-4 example. Figure 11-5 uses a table to store information about the transaction options. The field OPTION-NAME contains the name of the options, as input by the user. The OPTION-PROGRAM field contains the name of the COBOL program needed to perform the transaction, and the OPTION-DESC field provides a short description of the transaction's function. The SEARCH command uses the table to compare the transaction options with the user entered value. When a match is made the associated OPTION-PROGRAM field is referenced in a CALL statement and the needed subprogram is executed. If a match is not found an error message is displayed and control is passed back to TRANS-PAR. The list of valid options is displayed by way of a loop. If the user enters a question mark, the DISPLAY-PAR paragraph is performed five times.

```
300    WORKING-STORAGE SECTION.
301    01 VALID-OPTIONS-TAB.
302       05 FILLER   PIC X(40)
303            VALUE IS 'ADDEMPPYADDEMPADD A NEW EMPLOYEE          '.
304       05 FILLER   PIC X(40)
305            VALUE IS 'CHECKSPYCHECKSGENERATE PAYROLL CHECKS '.
306       05 FILLER PIC X(40)
307            VALUE IS 'CHGEMPPYCHGEMPCHANGE EMPLOYEE DATA        '.
308       05 FILLER PIC X(40)
309            VALUE IS 'DELEMPPYDELEMPDELETE AN EMPLOYEE      '.
310       05 FILLER PIC X(40)
311            VALUE IS 'LISEMPPYLISEMPGENERATE EMPLOYEE LISTING'.
312
313    01 VALID-OPTIONS-TABLE REDEFINES VALID-OPTIONS-TAB.
314       05 VALID-OPTIONS OCCURS 5 TIMES.
315          10 OPTION-NAME              PIC X(6).
316          10 OPTION-PROGRAM           PIC X(8).
317          10 OPTION-DESC              PIC X(26).
318
319    01 OPTION-INDEX                   PIC 9.
320    01 ANSWER                         PIC X(6).
321
400    PROCEDURE DIVISION.
401    START-PAR.
402        PERFORM TRANS-PAR THRU TRANS-PAR-END.
403        STOP RUN.
404
405    TRANS-PAR.
406
407        DISPLAY ' '.
408        DISPLAY '                    PAYROLL SUBSYSTEM'.
409        DISPLAY '           MAIN TRANSACTION DISPATCH SCREEN'.
410        DISPLAY ' '.
411        DISPLAY '     ENTER TRANSACTION CODE: '.
412        DISPLAY ' '.
413        DISPLAY ' '.
414        DISPLAY 'ENTER A QUESTION MARK ( ? ) FOR LIST OF
                    VALID OPTIONS'.
415
416        ACCEPT ANSWER.
417
418        IF ANSWER = 'EXIT' GOTO TRANS-PAR-END.
419        IF ANSWER = '?' SET OPTION-INDEX TO 0
420                        PERFORM DISPLAY-PAR THRU
                                 DISPLAY-PAR-END 5 TIMES
421                        GOTO TRANS-PAR.
422
423        SEARCH VALID-OPTIONS VARYING OPTION-INDEX
```

Fig. 11-5. Transaction driver for called programs.

```
424                    AT END DISPLAY 'TRANSACTION NOT FOUND,
                               PLEASE REENTER'
425              WHEN OPTION-NAME(OPTION-INDEX) = ANSWER
426                    CALL OPTION-PROGRAM(OPTION-INDEX)
427                    NEXT SENTENCE.
428
429        GOTO TRANS-PAR.
430    TRANS-PAR-END.
431
432    DISPLAY-PAR.
433       SET OPTION-INDEX UP BY 1
434       DISPLAY OPTION-NAME(OPTION-INDEX),' - ',
                        OPTION-DESC(OPTION-INDEX)
435    DISPLAY-PAR-END.
```

Each time the paragraph executes the variable OPTION-INDEX is incremented and the option names and descriptions in the table are displayed.

DATA VALIDATION

Data validation procedures are employed to ensure the correctness of information input by on-line users. These procedures cannot stop the input of incorrect street addresses or fix the spelling of an employee's name, but they can perform routines that will check the reasonableness of input values. For example, the date "01/43/85" or the zipcode "ABCDE" would be flagged as invalid and the user required to re-input the data. There are many commonly-used techniques that can be used to find obvious errors: limit checks, combination checks, restrictive value checks, format checks, self-checking digit checks, relationship checks, and clear text verification checks.

Limit Checks

Limit checks verify that the value input is in a given range: for example, testing to ensure that the entered hourly wage is between $0-$25. If the user accidently enters a wage of $99 per hour instead of $9.90, the program would flag the problem and display an error message to the user. Figure 11-6 is a partial program containing the limit check logic.

In the limit check example, the hourly wage is input by the user and passed through an IF state-

ment. If the input value is in the specified range control drops through the IF statement to HOURLY-WAGE-PAR-END. If the input is out of range an error message is displayed and the user is asked to re-enter the data. The error message includes the range criteria of 0-25. Stating the edit criteria in the error message is a good programming practice, because it helps the user understand and correct the problem. Also, particularly in the case of salaries, prices, and other inflatable items, over a period of time the edit criteria may be changed; displaying the current range provides an early warning that a program change is needed, leaving plenty of time to make the modification.

Combination Checks

Combination checks are used to compare the values of two or more fields. For example, if by definition the first two digits of the employee number denotes the employee's department, the validation in Fig. 11-7 can be used to check the consistency of the two input data values.

The combination check in Fig. 11-7 asks the user to input the employee's department and employee number. The IF statement performs a test comparing DEPARTMENT-NO with EMPLOYEE-DEPT. If a match is made, the IF statement ends. Otherwise an error message is displayed and the user is asked to re-input both fields. In this example both fields are input at the same time. These fields could have been individually in-

```
      WORKING-STORAGE SECTION.

      01 HOURLY-WAGE              PIC 999V99.

      PROCEDURE DIVISION.

      START-PAR.
        PERFORM HOURLY-WAGE-PAR THRU HOURLY-WAGE-PAR-END.
        STOP RUN.

      HOURLY-WAGE-PAR.
        DISPLAY 'ENTER HOURLY WAGE : '.
        ACCEPT HOURLY-WAGE.
        IF HOURLY-WAGE < 0 OR HOURLY-WAGE > 25
            DISPLAY ' '
            DISPLAY 'ERROR: WAGE RATE IS NOT BETWEEN 0$ TO 25$'
            DISPLAY ' '
            GOTO HOURLY-WAGE-PAR.
      HOURLY-WAGE-PAR-END.
```

Fig. 11-6. Limit check example.

```
WORKING-STORAGE SECTION.

01 DEPARTMENT-NO              PIC XX.
01 EMPLOYEE-NO.
   05 EMPLOYEE-DEPT          PIC XX.
   05 FILLER                 PIC XXX.

PROCEDURE DIVISION.
START-PAR.
  PERFORM GET-DATA-PAR THRU GET-DATA-PAR-END.
  STOP-RUN.

GET-DATA-PAR.
  DISPLAY 'ENTER EMPLOYEE'S DEPARTMENT'.
  ACCEPT DEPARTMENT-NO.
  DISPLAY 'ENTER EMPLOYEE NUMBER'.
  ACCEPT EMPLOYEE-NO.

  IF DEPARTMENT-NO = EMPLOYEE-DEPT
     NEXT SENTENCE
  ELSE
     DISPLAY ' '
     DISPLAY 'DEPARTMENT NO. AND EMPLOYEE NO. ARE NOT CONSISTENT'
     DISPLAY ' '
     GOTO GET-DATA-PAR.
GET-DATA-PAR-END.
```

Fig. 11-7. Combination check example.

put and validated in separate paragraphs and then brought together for comparison.

Restrictive Value Checks

Restrictive value checks compare the input value with a list of acceptable options. The classic example of this type of test is the validation of sex code. There are only two possible options: M for male and F for female. Figure 11-8 is the first restricted value test example, and checks for a valid sex code. The second example, shown in Fig. 11-9, tests for valid days of the week.

The restricted value check illustrated in Fig. 11-8 is programmed in a fashion similar to the combination and limit check validations. The basic difference is the IF statement format and function. Here a compound IF statement is used to see if either of the appropriate values was entered. If a valid code was entered, then the NEXT SENTENCE clause ends IF statement processing. Otherwise the ELSE clause is performed and an error message is displayed.

There are instances where an input value may have one of many options. An example of this situation is the days of the week. The value entered must be one of seven values. The validation technique used in Fig. 11-8 would be cumbersome for seven options, therefore, an alternative format can be used. Figure 11-9 illustrates this format.

The second restricted value check example uses a SEARCH statement to assess the validity of INPUT-DAY. If INPUT-DAY matches a value found in the table WEEK-DAY, processing continues. If not, an error message is displayed and the user is asked to re-input a new value.

Format Checks

Format checks look in the entered value to ensure that it contains specified characters and conforms to pre-defined formats. For example, if all telephone numbers must be entered in the format 999-9999, a check should be made to see that the fourth character is a dash. Figure 11-10 illustrates the programming needed to perform this task.

When the figure is executed the user is asked to enter a telephone number. This number is ac-

```
WORKING-STORAGE SECTION.

01 SEX-CODE              PIC X.

PROCEDURE DIVISION.
START-PAR.
   PERFORM SEX-CODE-PAR THRU SEX-CODE-PAR-END.
   STOP RUN.

SEX-CODE-PAR.
   DISPLAY 'ENTER SEX CODE: '.
   ACCEPT SEX-CODE.
   IF SEX-CODE = 'M' OR SEX-CODE = 'F'
      NEXT SENTENCE
   ELSE
       DISPLAY ' '
       DISPLAY 'ERROR: SEX CODE MUST BE M or F, PLEASE REENTER'
       DISPLAY ' '
       GOTO SEX-CODE-PAR.
SEX-CODE-PAR-END.
```

Fig. 11-8. First restricted value check example.

162

```
WORKING-STORAGE SECTION.

01 DAY-INDEX              PIC 9.
01 INPUT-DAY             PIC XXX.
01 WEEK-DAY-TAB PIC X(21) VALUE IS 'SUNMONTUEWEDTHUFRISAT'.

01 WEEK-DAY-TABLE REDEFINES WEEK-DAY-TAB.
   05 WEEK-DAY OCCURS 7 TIMES PIC XXX.

PROCEDURE DIVISION.
START-PAR.
  PERFORM GET-DAY-PAR THRU GET-DAY-PAR-END.
  STOP RUN.

GET-DAY-PAR.
  DISPLAY 'ENTER DAY OF THE WEEK: '.
  ACCEPT INPUT-DAY.

  SEARCH WEEKDAY VARYING DAY-INDEX
     AT END DISPLAY ' '
             DISPLAY 'ERROR: NOT A VALID WEEK DAY,PLEASE REENTER'
             DISPLAY ' '
             GOTO GET-DAY-PAR
     WHEN WEEK-DAY(DAY-INDEX) = INPUT-DAY
             NEXT SENTENCE.

GET-DAY-PAR-END.
```

Fig. 11-9. Second restrictive value check example.

cepted into PHONE-NUMBER, which is divided into three sections: PHONE-EXCHANGE, PHONE-DASH and PHONE-EXTENSION. The division isolates the fourth character. Now that the fourth character can be individually referenced, it can be compared to the value – that is required in the format. Upon its validation, either an error message is displayed or processing continues.

Self-Checking Digit

The self-checking digit technique is used to assess the validity of numeric account numbers and codes. This procedure breaks the number into single digits, adds the digits together, and compares the sum to the right-most digit in the account number. If they match the number was input correctly.

If the numbers do not match, an input error has occurred. Figure 11-11 is a listing of the code needed to perform this check.

The self-checking digit example employs two variables, VENDOR-INPUT and VENDOR-SUM. VENDOR-INPUT is used to accept the user value. This variable is divided into six fields—the first five are actual vendor numbers, and the last character is the check field. VENDOR-SUM is used to total the five vendor code digits. The ones column of this field is then compared to the check digit field in VENDOR-INPUT. If the values are equal processing continues. Otherwise, an error message is displayed and the user is asked to once again enter a value.

The self-checking digit example uses very simple logic. In fact, this test will not detect transpo-

```
WORKING -STORAGE SECTION

01  INPUT-PHONE              PIC X(8).
01  PHONE-NUMBER.
    05  PHONE-EXCHANGE       PIC XXX.
    05  PHONE-DASH           PIC X.
    05  PHONE-EXTENSION      PIC X(4).

PROCEDURE DIVISION.
START-PAR.
   PERFORM GET-PHONE-PAR THRU GET-PHONE-PAR-END.
   STOP RUN.

GET-PHONE-PAR.
   DISPLAY 'ENTER PHONE NUMBER: '.
   ACCEPT INPUT-PHONE.

   IF PHONE-DASH = '-'
      NEXT SENTENCE
   ELSE
      DISPLAY ' '
      DISPLAY 'ERROR: NUMBER MUST BE IN THE FORMAT 999-9999'
      DISPLAY ' '
      GOTO GET-PHONE-PAR.

GET-PHONE-PAR-END.
```

Fig. 11-10. Format check example.

```
WORKING-STORAGE SECTION.

01  VENDOR-NUMBER.
    05  VENDOR-1         PIC 9.
    05  VENDOR-2         PIC 9.
    05  VENDOR-3         PIC 9.
    05  VENDOR-4         PIC 9.
    05  VENDOR-5         PIC 9.
    05  VENDOR-CHECK     PIC 9.

01  VENDOR-SUM.
    05  SUM-TENS         PIC 9.
    05  SUM-ONES         PIC 9.

PROCEDURE DIVISION.
   PERFORM GET-VENDOR-PAR THRU GET-VENDOR-PAR-END.
   STOP RUN.
```

Fig. 11-11. Self-checking digit example.

164

```
GET-VENDOR-PAR.
   DISPLAY 'ENTER VENDOR NUMBER: '.
   ACCEPT VENDOR-NUMBER.
   ADD VENDOR-1, VENDOR-2, VENDOR-3, VENDOR-4, VENDOR-5 GIVING
      VENDOR-SUM.

   IF VENDOR-CHECK = SUM-ONES
      NEXT SENTENCE
   ELSE
      DISPLAY ' '
      DISPLAY 'ERROR: NOT A VALID VENDOR NUMBER'
      DISPLAY ' '
      GOTO GET-VENDOR-PAR.

GET-VENDOR-PAR-END.
```

sitions or off-setting values. The actual routines used in industry are conceptually the same, but use more complex algorithms to calculate the value of the check digit. However, because of the complexity, a second program is needed. This program is used to originally generate valid account numbers.

Relationship Checks

Relationship checks compare the logical connection between variables. The most commonly used example of this technique is the relationship between sex code and civil code. If the user enters the sex code M for male, the civil title should be "Mr." or "Master." If the sex code is F for female, the title should be "Miss," "Mrs.," or "Ms." Figure 11-12 provides a program listing of this procedure.

Textual Verification Checks

Textual verification checks are helpful when entering employee numbers, vendor codes, and other fields that contain codes relating to descriptions or names. This process requires the user to enter the appropriate code. Then the computer looks up that code in a program table or data file. If the code is found the clear text description associated with that code (employee name, vendor name, job title, etc.) is displayed on the screen. The assumption is that the user will visually compare

the displayed text with the original document to ensure that the entered code matches the intended subject. If the expected result is displayed, processing continues; if not, the user will see the inconsistency and take appropriate action.

The textual verification check shown in Fig. 11-13 will perform its textual retrieval from a data table. If the text is received from a file on disk it would be advantageous to use a random access file. On-line searches through sequential files could take too long to process and significantly slow down the application. Also, if on a multi-user system a high volume of reads from disk could hurt the other user's performance.

In the textual verification example, note that if the code was found and the corresponding description was printed, no question was asked regarding the correctness of the value displayed. The assumption is made by the program that the user enters the correct value. Continually asking the user to verify the input would waste time and slow down the entry process. The program must contain the capability to change the original input for the event of an incorrectly entered value.

ON-LINE HELP INFORMATION

On-line help is information that provides the user with instructions and insight about the application being executed. This information should be accessible throughout the program and be displayed

```
WORKING-STORAGE SECTION.

01 SEX-CODE                     PIC X.

01 NAME.
   05 NAME-TITLE                PIC X(6).
   05 NAME-FIRST                PIC X(10).
   05 NAME-MIDDLE-INITIAL       PIC X.
   05 NAME-LAST                 PIC X(15).

PROCEDURE DIVISION.
START-PAR.
   PERFORM GET-TITLE-PAR THRU GET-TITLE-PAR-END.
   STOP RUN.

GET-TITLE-PAR.
   DISPLAY 'ENTER CIVIL TITLE: '.
   ACCEPT NAME-TITLE.
   IF (SEX-CODE = 'M' AND NAME-TITLE = 'MR.    ' ) OR
      (SEX-CODE = 'M' AND NAME-TITLE = 'MASTER' ) OR
      (SEX-CODE = 'F' AND NAME-TITLE = 'MISS  ' ) OR
      (SEX-CODE = 'F' AND NAME-TITLE = 'MRS.  ' ) OR
      (SEX-CODE = 'F' AND NAME-TITLE = 'MS.   ' )
      NEXT SENTENCE
   ELSE
      DISPLAY ' '
      DISPLAY 'ERROR: CIVIL TITLE DOES NOT MATCH SEX CODE'
      DISPLAY ' '
      GOTO GET-TITLE-PAR.

   GET TITLE-PAR-END.
```

Fig. 11-12. Relationship check example.

```
WORKING-STORAGE SECTION.

01 EMP-INDEX                    PIC 99.
01 INPUT-STATUS-CODE            PIC XXX.
01 EMP-TYPE-TAB.
   05 FILLER PIC X(30) VALUE IS 'FTHFULL TIME HOURLY      '.
   05 FILLER PIC X(30) VALUE IS 'FTSFULL TIME SALARIED    '.
   05 FILLER PIC X(30) VALUE IS 'PTHPART TIME HOURLY      '.
   05 FILLER PIC X(30) VALUE IS 'TSHTEMPORARY SUMMER HELP '.
   05 FILLER PIC X(30) VALUE IS 'OTHER TEMPORARY STATUS   '.

01 EMP-TYPE-TABLE REDEFINES EMP-TYPE-TAB.
```

Fig. 11-13. Textual verification example.

```
      05 EMP-TYPE OCCURS 5 TIMES.
         10 EMP-TYPE-CODE          PIC XXX.
         10 EMP-TYPE-DESC          PIC X(27).

  PROCEDURE DIVISION.
  START-PAR.
     PERFORM GET-EMP-STAT-PAR THRU GET-EMP-STAT-PAR-END.
     STOP RUN.

  GET-EMP-STAT-PAR.
     DISPLAY 'ENTER EMPLOYEE STATUS CODE: '.
     ACCEPT INPUT-STATUS-CODE.

     SEARCH EMP-TYPE VARYING EMP-INDEX
            AT END DISPLAY ' '
                    DISPLAY 'ERROR: STATUS CODE NOT FOUND.
                             PLEASE REENTER'
                    DISPLAY ' '
                    GOTO GET-EMP-STAT-PAR
            WHEN EMP-TYPE-CODE(EMP-INDEX) = INPUT-STATUS-CODE
                    DISPLAY EMP-TYPE-DESC(EMP-INDEX).

  GET-EMP-STAT-END.
```

upon user request. Also, the user's location in the program should dictate the subject of the information provided. Many applications let the user obtain help at any input prompt by entering a question mark. Figure 11-14 illustrates one method used to perform the help function.

In the first on-line help example a table is filled containing all the program help messages. Also, an IF statement follows each ACCEPT. The IF statements look for question marks; if a question mark is found, the data associated with the input field is displayed on the screen and the user is then asked to re-enter the value.

There are some applications that require the option to display a two- or three-page system overview. These overviews should be placed in a file and not in an on-line array. This is the kind of documentation that gets listed once by new users and is placed in the top left row for reference. By placing this text in a file and not in the program, the textual data is not called into primary computer memory each time the program is executed. This will allow your program to use less space and be

less of a burden to the computer's central processing unit (CPU). Figure 11-15 illustrates this display process.

CURSOR CONTROLLING

The cursor is the blinking dash or box on the screen used to inform the user where the next entered character will be printed. Cursor controlling is the process of moving the cursor from place to place on the screen.

COBOL compilers handle cursor addressing by special reserved words in the DISPLAY statement or by ignoring the issue. Cursor movement is performed for the second group by using the ENTER statement to execute subroutines in other programming languages.

The DISPLAY statement option is used in the COBOL compilers written by computer hardware manufacturers. Technically cursor addressing is performed by sending special instructions to the terminal's screen, and each manufacturer requires different screen instruction codes. Through the use of software, hardware manufacturers try to lock

```
WORKING-STORAGE SECTION.

01 EMP-NAME              PIC X(25).
01 EMP-ADDRESS           PIC X(25).
01 EMP-SEX-CODE          PIC X.
01 EMP-GROSS-PAY         PIC 9(5)V99.


01 HELP-TAB.
   05 FILLER PIC X(40) VALUE IS 'ENTER NAME IN LAST,
                                 FIRST MI FORMAT       '.
   05 FILLER PIC X(40) VALUE IS 'ENTER EMPLOYEE
                                 ADDRESS                    '.
   05 FILLER PIC X(40) VALUE IS 'ENTER A SEX CODE OF
                                 M or F                 '.
   05 FILLER PIC X(40) VALUE IS 'GROSS PAY MUST BE ON
                                 A YEARLY BASIS         '.

01 HELP-TABLE REDEFINES HELP-TAB.
   05 HELP OCCURS 4 TIMES PIC X(40).

PROCEDURE DIVISION.
START-PAR.
   PERFORM GET-NAME THRU GET-NAME-END.
   PERFORM GET-ADDRESS THRU GET-ADDRESS-END.
   PERFORM GET-SEX-CODE THRU GET-SEX-CODE-END.
   PERFORM GET-GROSS-PAY THRU GET-GROSS-PAR-END.
   STOP RUN.

GET-NAME-PAR.
   DISPLAY 'ENTER NAME: '.
   ACCEPT EMP-NAME.
   IF EMP-NAME = '?' DISPLAY HELP(1), GOTO GET-NAME-PAR.
GET-NAME-PAR-END.

GET-ADDRESS-PAR.
   DISPLAY 'ENTER ADDRESS: '.
   ACCEPT EMP-ADDRESS.
   IF EMP-ADDRESS = '?' DISPLAY HELP(2), GOTO GET-ADDRESS-PAR.
GET-ADDRESS-PAR-END.

GET-SEX-CODE-PAR.
   DISPLAY 'ENTER SEX CODE: '.
   ACCEPT EMP-SEX-CODE.
   IF EMP-SEX-CODE = '?' DISPLAY HELP(3), GOTO GET-SEX-CODE-PAR.
GET-SEX-CODE-PAR-END.

GET-GROSS-PAY-PAR.
   DISPLAY 'ENTER GROSS PAY: '.
   ACCEPT EMP-GROSS-PAY.
   IF EMP-GROSS-PAR = '?'DISPLAY HELP(4), GOTO GET-GROSS-PAY-PAR.
GET-GROSS-PAY-PAR-END.
```

Fig. 11-14. First on-line help example.

```
DATA DIVISION.

INPUT-OUTPUT CONTROL.
FILE SECTION.

FD HELP-FILE

01 HELP-REC          PIC X(80).

WORKING-STORAGE SECTION.

01 OUT-OF-RECS       PIC X.

PROCEDURE DIVISION.
START-PAR.
   OPEN INPUT HELP-FILE.
   MOVE 'N' TO OUT-OF-RECS.
   READ HELP-FILE AT END MOVE 'Y' TO OUT-OF-RECS.
   IF OUT-OF-RECS NOT = 'Y'
      PERFORM HELP-PAR THRU HELP-PAR-END UNTIL OUT-OF-RECS = 'Y'.
   CLOSE HELP-FILE.
   STOP RUN.

HELP-PAR.
   READ HELP-FILE AT END MOVE 'Y' TO OUT-OF-RECS.
HELP-PAR-END.
```

Fig. 11-15. Second on-line help example.

their customer base to their hardware, assuming that customers will not want to change hardware vendors because of the software ramifications.

Independent software vendors want their product to attain the highest possible appearance, and tend to keep away from areas that are hardware-vendor specific.

When using cursor controlling in an application, display the entire screen first and then move the cursor from place to place gathering data. This rule of thumb lets the user view the entire screen before beginning data input, and simplifies programming by getting all the screen DISPLAY statements out of the way at one time.

Figure 11-16 is an example data input screen. This screen will ask the user to enter the employee's name, address, telephone number and gross pay.

Figure 11-17 lists the program logic needed to execute the screen shown above. The cursor controlling is managed by an assembly language subroutine with two parameters. The first parameter specifies the horizontal row on which the cursor should be placed. The second parameter specifies the cursor's vertical column position. For example, "ENTER ASSEMBLY USING 5,40" places the cursor in the fifth row down and the 40th column across.

The logic needed to orchestrate cursor controlling can greatly expand the size of a program. The logic is divided into three types: data entry, error-display and field navigation. Data entry logic is the easiest to program and the simplest to follow. Its function is to place the cursor at the correct location on the screen in anticipation of user input. An example of this logic can be seen in paragraph

```
                    PAYROLL  SYSTEM
                EMPLOYEE  INPUT  SCREEN


            NAME        :

            STREET (1)  :

            STREET (2)  :

            STATE       :

            ZIP CODE    :


    S = SAVE + EXIT  !!  Q = QUIT  !!  < = UP  !!  > = DOWN
```

Fig. 11-16. Sample employee input screen.

```
WORKING-STORAGE SECTION.

01 EMPLOYEE-DATA.
    05 EMP-NAME            PIC X(30).
    05 EMP-STREET-1        PIC X(20).
    05 EMP-STREET-2        PIC X(20).
    05 EMP-STATE           PIC XX.
    05 EMP-ZIP             PIC X(9).

01 WS-EMPLOYEE-DATA.
    05 WS-NAME             PIC X(30).
    05 WS-STREET-1         PIC X(20).
    05 WS-STREET-2         PIC X(20).
    05 WS-STATE            PIC XX.
    05 WS-ZIP              PIC X(9).

01 IN-EMPLOYEE-DATA.
    05 IN-NAME             PIC X(30).
    05 IN-STREET-1         PIC X(20).
    05 IN-STREET-2         PIC X(20).
    05 IN-STATE            PIC XX.
    05 IN-ZIP              PIC X(9).

01 FLAGS-AND-CONTROL-FIELDS.
    05 WHERE-NEXT          PIC X(7).
    05 ERROR-FLAG          PIC X.

PROCEDURE DIVISION.
```

Fig. 11-17. Cursor-controlling sample program.

```
START-PAR.
    PERFORM DISPLAY-SCREEN-PAR THRU DISPLAY-SCREEN-PAR-END.
    PERFORM GET-DATA-PAR THRU GET-DATA-PAR-END
        UNTIL WHERE-NEXT = 'S' OR WHERE-NEXT = 'Q'.
    STOP RUN.

DISPLAY-SCREEN-PAR.
    ENTER ASSEMBLY CURSCREEN USING 1,30.
    DISPLAY 'PAYROLL SYSTEM'.
    ENTER ASSEMBLY CURSCREEN USING 2,25.
    DISPLAY 'EMPLOYEE INPUT SCREEN'.
    ENTER ASSEMBLY CURSCREEN USING 5,5.
    DISPLAY 'NAME        : '.
    ENTER ASSEMBLY CURSCREEN USING 7,5.
    DISPLAY 'STREET (1) : '.
    ENTER ASSEMBLY CURSCREEN USING 9,5.
    DISPLAY 'STREET (2) : '.
    ENTER ASSEMBLY CURSCREEN USING 11,5.
    DISPLAY 'STATE       : '.
    ENTER ASSEMBLY CURSCREEN USING 13,5.
    DISPLAY 'ZIP CODE   : '.
    ENTER ASSEMBLY CURSCREEN USING 23,5.
    DISPLAY 'S = SAVE + EXIT  !!   Q = QUIT  !!   < = UP  !
             !   > = DOWN'.
DISPLAY-SCREEN-PAR-END.


GET-DATA-PAR.
    IF WHERE-NEXT = 'NAME'
        PERFORM GET-NAME-PAR THRU GET-NAME-PAR-END.
    IF WHERE-NEXT = 'STREET1'
        PERFORM GET-STREET1-PAR THRU GET-STREET1-PAR.
    IF WHERE-NEXT = 'STREET2'
        PERFORM GET-STREET2-PAR THRU GET-STREET2-PAR-END.
    IF WHERE-NEXT = 'STATE'
        PERFORM GET-STATE-PAR THRU GET-STATE-PAR-END.
    IF WHERE-NEXT = 'ZIP'
        PERFORM GET-ZIP-PAR THRU GET-ZIP-PAR-END.
    IF CONTROL = 'S'
        MOVE WS-NAME      TO EMP-NAME
        MOVE WS-STREET1   TO EMP-STREET1
        MOVE WS-STREET2   TO EMP-STREET2
        MOVE WS-STATE     TO EMP-STATE
        MOVE WS-ZIP       TO EMP-ZIP
        MOVE SPACES       TO WS-NAME
        MOVE SPACES       TO WS-STREET1
        MOVE SPACES       TO WS-STREET2
        MOVE SPACES       TO WS-STATE
        MOVE SPACES       TO WS-ZIP.

    IF CONTROL = 'Q'
```

```
         MOVE SPACES        TO WS-NAME
         MOVE SPACES        TO WS-STREET1
         MOVE SPACES        TO WS-STREET2
         MOVE SPACES        TO WS-STATE
         MOVE SPACES        TO WS-ZIP.
   GET-DATA-PAR-END.

   GET-NAME-PAR.
      ENTER ASSEMBLY CURSCREEN USING 5,15.
      ACCEPT IN-NAME.
      IF IN-NAME = SPACES
         ENTER ASSEMBLY CURSCREEN USING 24,5
         DISPLAY 'ERROR: NAME IS REQUIRED FIELD, PLEASE RE-ENTER'
         GOTO GET-NAME-PAR.
      IF IN-NAME = 'S' GOTO GET-NAME-PAR-END.
      IF IN-NAME = 'Q' GOTO GET-NAME-PAR-END.
      IF IN-NAME = '<' ENTER ASSEMBLY CURSCREEN USING 24,5
                       DISPLAY 'ERROR: THIS IS THE TOP FIELD'
                       GOTO GET-NAME-PAR.
      IF IN-NAME = '>' MOVE 'STREET1' TO WHERE-NEXT
                       GOTO GET-NAME-PAR-END.
      MOVE IN-NAME TO WS-NAME.
      MOVE 'STREET1' TO WHERE-NEXT.
   GET-NAME-PAR-END.

   GET-STREET1-PAR.
      ENTER ASSEMBLY CURSCREEN USING 7,15.
      ACCEPT IN-STREET1.
      IF IN-STREET1 = 'S' GOTO GET-STREET1-PAR-END.
      IF IN-STREET1 = 'Q' GOTO GET-STREET1-PAR-END.
      IF IN-STREET1 = '<' MOVE 'NAME' TO WHERE-NEXT
                          GOTO GET-STREET1-PAR.
      IF IN-NAME = '>' MOVE 'STREET2' TO WHERE-NEXT
                       GOTO GET-STREET1-PAR-END.
      MOVE IN-STREET1 TO WS-STREET1.
      MOVE 'STREET2' TO WHERE-NEXT.
   GET-STREET1-PAR-END.

   GET-STREET2-PAR.
      ENTER ASSEMBLY CURSCREEN USING 9,15.
      ACCEPT IN-STREET2.
      IF IN-STREET2 = 'S' GOTO GET-STREET2-PAR-END.
      IF IN-STREET2 = 'Q' GOTO GET-STREET2-PAR-END.
      IF IN-STREET2 = '<' MOVE 'STREET1' TO WHERE-NEXT
                          GOTO GET-STREET2-PAR.
      IF IN-STREET2 = '>' MOVE 'STATE' TO WHERE-NEXT
                          GOTO GET-STREET2-PAR-END.
      MOVE IN-STREET2 TO WS-STREET2.
      MOVE 'STATE' TO WHERE-NEXT.
   GET-STREET2-PAR-END.
```

```
GET-STATE-PAR.
    ENTER ASSEMBLY CURSCREEN USING 11,15.
    ACCEPT IN-STATE.
    IF IN-STATE = 'S' GOTO GET-STATE-PAR-END.
    IF IN-STATE = 'Q' GOTO GET-STATE-PAR-END.
    IF IN-STATE = '<' MOVE 'STREET2' TO WHERE-NEXT
                      GOTO GET-STATE-PAR.
    IF IN-STATE = '>' MOVE 'ZIP' TO WHERE-NEXT
                      GOTO GET-STATE-PAR-END.
    MOVE IN-STATE TO WS-STATE.
    MOVE 'ZIP' TO WHERE-NEXT.
GET-STATE-PAR-END.

GET-ZIP-PAR.
    ENTER ASSEMBLY CURSCREEN USING 13,15.
    ACCEPT IN-ZIP.
    IF IN-ZIP = 'S' GOTO GET-ZIP-PAR-END.
    IF IN-ZIP = 'Q' GOTO GET-ZIP-PAR-END.
    IF IN-ZIP = '<' MOVE 'STATE' TO WHERE-NEXT
                    GOTO GET-ZIP-PAR.
    IF IN-ZIP = '>' MOVE 'NAME' TO WHERE-NEXT
                    GOTO GET-ZIP-PAR-END.
    MOVE IN-ZIP TO WS-ZIP.
    MOVE 'NAME' TO WHERE-NEXT.
GET-ZIP-PAR-END.
```

GET-NAME-PAR.

Once cursor controlling is employed, all data displays must be carefully placed and formatted, including error messages. Error messages are displayed using the following three-part process. First, the appropriate validation logic identifies an error. Second, ERROR-FLAG is set to Y, and the message is displayed on the screen. Finally, when a valid entry is entered the error message is deleted by overwriting the message line with spaces.

The field navigation logic is the most difficult and cumbersome to program. Its function is to move the cursor from field to field around the screen.

QUESTIONS

1. What is the function of program menus?
2. List and describe the parts of a menu screen.
3. What is the purpose of the screen message line?
4. Describe the programming logic used in menu programs.
5. What are transaction driven systems?
6. Describe and contrast the two transaction-processing design methods described in this chapter.
7. What is data validation, and why should it be performed?
8. What are limit validation checks, and how are they performed?
9. What are combination validation checks?
10. What is restrictive value checking?
11. Describe format check validations.
12. What is a self-checking digit?
13. What are relationship validation checks?
14. What is textual validation checking?
15. Describe the advantages of on-line help.

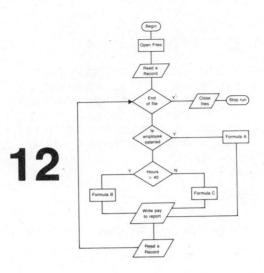

12

Inter-Program Communications

There are circumstances that require one COBOL program to execute a second COBOL program. This usually occurs because a program is so large that it becomes difficult to handle, or there is a specific function that must be performed by many programs.

The passing of control is orchestrated by the CALL and EXIT statements. CALL specifies the program that must be run and begins the execution process. The EXIT statement is placed in the subprogram and is used to return control from the subprogram to the original program.

The set of rules that must be followed to correctly perform this process differs from vendor to vendor. The primary difference between these processes is the way in which data is passed from place to place. Most vendors only require that the variables being passed are specified in the USING clause of the CALL statement, and in a USING clause affixed to the end of the PROCEDURE DIVISION line in the program being called.

Some vendors, however, have additional requirements. The most common of these require-

ments is the incorporation of a third area in the DATA DIVISION called the LINKAGE SECTION. This section defines the variables that will be passed from program to program. Compilers not requiring this section let linkage variables be defined in the WORKING-STORAGE SECTION like any other variable. Another approach occasionally taken is the inclusion of a run-time library that must be included during the program listing and loading process. The library is a set of special functions and language options not included as part of the standard COBOL compiler and linker. The routines generally contained in this library are placed there because they are seldomly used, and the vendor feels it is not necessary to continually reference them as part of the regular compilation process. Continued reference adds to the time needed to compile less sophisticated programs.

The examples used in this chapter will include only the USING clause. For information outlining the LINKAGE-SECTION and run-time options, refer to the COBOL reference manual that accompanied your compiler.

Figure 12-1 is a program that asks the user to enter a transaction code, executes the appropriate subprogram, and displays returned information to the screen.

When the program is executed, the user is asked to enter a transaction code. If the user enters A, program ATRANS is called. If the user enters B, BTRANS is called. Figure 12-2 is a listing of program ATRANS.

When this program is called, three variables are

```
DATA DIVISION.
WORKING-STORAGE SECTION.

01 TRANSACTION-CODE.
01 TRANS-A-DATE.
    05 A-NAME               PIC X(20).
    05 A-ADDRESS            PIC X(40).
    05 A-PHONE              PIC X(15).

01 B-HOURLY-WAGE            PIC 999V99.
01 B-NO-OF-DEDUCTIONS       PIC 99.

PROCEDURE DIVISION.
START-PAR.
    DISPLAY 'ENTER TRANSACTION CODE: '.
    ACCEPT TRANSACTION-CODE.
    IF TRANSACTION-CODE NOT = 'E'
        PERFORM LOOP-PAR THRU LOOP-PAR-END
            UNTIL TRANSACTION-CODE = 'E'.
    STOP RUN.

LOOP-PAR.
    IF TRANSACTION-CODE = 'A'
        CALL ATRANS USING TRANS-A-DATA
        DISPLAY 'NAME IS: ', A-NAME, A-ADDRESS, A-PHONE
    ELSE
        IF TRANSACTION-CODE = 'B'
            CALL BTRANS USING B-HOURLY-WAGE, B-NO-OF-DEDUCTIONS
            DISPLAY ' '
            DISPLAY B-HOURLY-WAGE, B-NO-OF-DEDUCTIONS
            DISPLAY ' '
        ELSE
            DISPLAY 'ERROR: TRANSACTION CODE MUST BE: '
            DISPLAY '           A = NAME AND PHONE INPUT'
            DISPLAY '           B = WAGE AND DEDUCTION INPUT'
            DISPLAY '           E = END RUN'
            DISPLAY ' '.

    DISPLAY 'ENTER TRANSACTION CODE: '.
    ACCEPT TRANSACTION-CODE.
LOOP-PAR-END.
```

Fig. 12-1. CALL menu program example.

```
DATA DIVISION.
WORKING-STORAGE SECTION.
01 TRANS-DATA.
   05 NAME              PIC X(20).
   05 ADDRESS           PIC X(40).
   05 PHONE             PIC X(15).


PROCEDURE DIVISION.
START-PAR.
   DISPLAY 'ENTER EMPLOYEE NAME: '.
   ACCEPT NAME.
   DISPLAY 'ENTER ADDRESS': '.
   ACCEPT ADDRESS.
   DISPLAY 'ENTER TELEPHONE NUMBER: '.
   ACCEPT PHONE.
   EXIT.
```

Fig. 12-2. ATRANS program listing.

passed from the main program to ATRANS. These variables are collectively named TRANS-A-DATA in the main program, and TRANS-DATA in the subprogram. The link between these two data areas is defined by the combination of the USING clause in the CALL statement in the main program and the USING clause in the PROCEDURE DIVISION declaration. The similarity in the variable names is not required by COBOL, but is considered a good programming practice to give linked variables common or identical names. These practices assist in the program's internal documentation and provide future programmers with a more clearly defined road map through the application.

Figure 12-3 contains a listing of program BTRANS. BTRANS is the second program called by the main menu program. The process used to call BTRANS is the same as that previously used to call ATRANS. The difference between these programs is the way the variables are passed. In ATRANS, one roll-up was passed containing three data fields. Here the fields are individually passed. When more than one variable is defined for passage, the order of the variables in the USING

Fig. 12-3. BTRANS program listing.

```
DATA DIVISION.
WORKING-STORAGE SECTION.
01 TRANSACTION-DATA.
   05 HOURLY-WAGE           PIC 999V99.
   05 NO-OF-DEDUCTIONS      PIC 99.

PROCEDURE DIVISION.
START-PAR.
   DISPLAY 'ENTER HOURLY WAGE: '.
   ACCEPT HOURLY-WAGE.
   DISPLAY 'ENTER NUMBER OF DEPENDENTS: '.
   ACCEPT NO-OF-DEPENDENTS.
   EXIT.                              .
```

176

clauses dictates which variables are linked. In the case of BTRANS, B-HOURLY-WAGE is linked to HOURLY-WAGE and B-NO-NO-DEPENDANTS is linked to NO-OF-DEPENDANTS.

QUESTIONS

1. What is inter-program communication?

2. What is the LINKAGE SECTION, and where is it placed in the program?

3. Describe the function of the USING clause and its role in the inter-program communication process.

4. What are the functions of the CALL and EXIT statements, and how are they used?

5. List and describe situations where program subroutining can be effectively used.

Appendix

Program Shells

In today's world of increasing programming labor costs and tightening departmental budgets, high programmer productivity is a must. One technique that can assist in maximizing this productivity is the use of program shells. Program shells are partially developed programs and modules that can be tailored to meet specific application needs. The shells that follow should be copied into a common programming library and modified to meet the programming conventions in the data processing department. Then, as the need arises, copy these programs into a development area for tailoring and use.

The program shells included in this appendix are:

☐ Complete Program Shell
☐ Simple Report Program
☐ Complex Report Program
☐ Two-tape Sequential File Update
☐ Sequential File Update by Array Manipulation
☐ On-Line Menu Module
☐ On-Line Transaction-Processing Call Module
☐ On-Line Validation Module

The program shell shown in Fig. A-1 does not contain file definitions or procedural logic, but it does include all required divisions, sections and paragraphs, thus saving the programmer from continually typing in the same code.

REPORT PROGRAMS

These report program shells can be used to develop simple reports, or as a starting point in the development of more complex report programs. A complete explanation of these programming techniques and the report generation process in general can be found in Chapter 10.

Figure A-2 contains the preliminary definitions and procedural logic needed to develop most simple report programs. This logic includes file definition, report formats, sequential file processing, and paging.

Figure A-3 lists a second report program shell containing more complex features. In addition to

178

the functionality described in Fig. A-2, this program shell contains subtotals, grand totals, and page foot titles.

TWO-TAPE SEQUENTIAL FILE UPDATE

The program shell in Fig. A-4 provides the basic logic needed to perform a sequential file update. There are three areas that should be considered when using this program. First, the program assumes that the master file and transaction file have been sorted in ascending order, based on some common key. Second, this program does not perform validations on the incoming transactions; and finally, an analysis should be conducted to assess what reports, if any, are needed to document the update process. Chapter 9, which discusses the update of sequential files, may provide some insight into updating report requirements.

A possible solution to the sorting and validation of data is the development of a second program that would sort and validate the incoming transactions and run prior to the master file update program. The advantage of a divide-and-conquer approach is that it minimizes each program's complexity, thus simplifying program development and improving the application's self-documenting properties (see Fig. A-4).

FILE UPDATE THROUGH ARRAY PROCESSING

The program shell in Fig. A-5 facilitates the update of sequential files through array manipulation. This process is discussed in depth in Chapter 9.

ON-LINE MENU MODULE

The program module shell in Fig. A-6 provides the logic needed to develop on-line menu applications. When using this module, the options to be performed by lines 419-427 should be paragraph names defined somewhere in the program. The processes used in this shell are discussed in Chapter 11 on on-line systems.

ON-LINE TRANSACTION-PROCESSING CALL MODULE

The transaction shell module shown in Fig. A-7 is explained in Chapter 11. Its function is to act as a focal point from which users can select and perform needed application functions.

ON-LINE VALIDATION MODULE

Figure A-8 is an on-line data validation procedure similar to those discussed in Chapter 11.

```
        IDENTIFICATION DIVISION.

        PROGRAM-ID.
        AUTHOR.
        INSTALLATION.
        DATE-WRITTEN.
        DATE-COMPILED.
        SECURITY.

        ENVIRONMENT DIVISION.

        CONFIGURATION SECTION.
        SOURCE-COMPUTER.
        OBJECT-COMPUTER.

        INPUT-OUTPUT SECTION.
        FILE-CONTROL.
```

Fig. A-1. Initial program shell.

```
        SELECT *** FILE *** ASSIGN TO *** FILE NAME GOES HERE ***
        SELECT *** FILE *** ASSIGN TO *** FILE NAME GOES HERE ***

DATA DIVISION.

FILE SECTION.
FD *** FILE NAME GOES HERE ***
    RECORD CONTAINS 80 CHARACTERS
    LABEL RECORDS ARE OMITTED
    DATA RECORD IS IN-REC.

01 *** RECORD NAME ***
    ***
    *** PLACE INPUT FILE RECORD LAYOUT HERE ***
    ***
```

```
        IDENTIFICATION DIVISION.

        PROGRAM-ID.
        AUTHOR.
        INSTALLATION.
        DATE-WRITTEN.
        DATE-COMPILED.
        SECURITY.

        ENVIRONMENT DIVISION.
        CONFIGURATION SECTION.
        SOURCE-COMPUTER.
        OBJECT-COMPUTER.

        INPUT-OUTPUT SECTION.
        FILE-CONTROL.

            SELECT IN-FILE      ASSIGN TO *** FILE NAME GOES HERE ***
            SELECT REP-FILE     ASSIGN TO *** FILE NAME GOES HERE ***

    DATA DIVISION.

    FILE SECTION.
    FD IN-FILE
        RECORD CONTAINS 80 CHARACTERS
        LABEL RECORDS ARE OMITTED
        DATA RECORD IS IN-REC.

    01 IN-REC.
        ***
        *** PLACE INPUT FILE RECORD LAYOUT HERE ***
        ***
```

Fig. A-2. Simple report program.

```
FD REP-FILE
    RECORD CONTAINS 80 CHARACTERS
    LABEL RECORDS ARE OMITTED
    DATA RECORD IS REP-REC.

01 REP-REC                     PIC X(*** 80 OR 132 CHARACTERS ***).

WORKING-STORAGE.

01 DETAIL-REC.
    ***
    *** REPORT DETAIL FORMAT GOES HERE ***
    ***

01 TITLE-1.
    ***
    *** REPORT TITLE FORMAT GOES HERE ***
    ***

01 HEADINGS-1.
    ***
    *** FIRST COLUMN HEADINGS GO HERE ***
    ***

01 HEADINGS-2.
    ***
    *** SUB COLUMN HEADINGS GO HERE ***
    ***

01 SALARY-DISPLAY.
    ***
    *** TOTAL LINE GOES HERE ***
    ***

01 FLAGS-AND-COUNTERS.
    05 OUT-OF-RECS             PIC X.
    05 PAGE-NO                 PIC 999.
    05 LINE-COUNT              PIC 99.
    ***
    *** OTHER FLAGS, COUNTERS AND TOTALERS GO HERE ***
    ***

PROCEDURE DIVISION.
START-PAR.
    MOVE 'N'      TO OUT-OF-RECS.
    MOVE 0        TO SALARY-NUM.
    MOVE 0        TO PAGE-NO.
    OPEN INPUT  IN-FILE, OUTPUT REP-FILE.
    READ IN-FILE AT END MOVE 'N' TO OUT-OF-RECS.
    PERFORM HEADINGS-PAR THRU HEADINGS-PAR-END.
```

```
        IF OUT-OF-RECS = 'N'
            PERFORM LOOP-PAR THRU LOOP-PAR-END UNTIL OUT-OF-RECS='Y'
        WRITE REP-REC FROM HEADINGS-2.
        ***
        ***   MOVING FINAL TOTALS TO FINAL TOTAL PRINTING AREA
              GOES HERE ***
        ***
        WRITE REP-REC FROM SALARY-DISPLAY.
        CLOSE IN-FILE, OUT-FILE.
        STOP RUN.

    LOOP-PAR.
        ***
        *** MOVE INPUT FIELDS TO OUTPUT FIELDS ***
        ***
        *** CALCULATE COLUMN TOTALERS HERE ***
        ***
        ADD 1                  TO LINE-NO.
        IF LINE-NUM > 55
            PERFORM HEADINGS-PAR THRU HEADINGS PAR-END.
        WRITE REP-REC FROM DETAIL-REC.
        READ IN-FILE AT END MOVE 'Y' TO OUT-OF-RECS.
    LOOP-PAR-END.

    HEADINGS-PAR.
        ADD 1         TO PAGE-NO.
        MOVE 5        TO LINE-COUNT
        MOVE PAGE-NO  TO PAGE-OUT.
        WRITE REP-REC FROM TITLE AFTER ADVANCING TOP-OF-FORM.
        WRITE REP-REC FROM HEADINGS-1 AFTER ADVANCING 2 LINES.
        WRITE REP-REC FROM HEADINGS-2 AFTER ADVANCING 1 LINES.
    HEADINGS-PAR-END.
```

```
    IDENTIFICATION DIVISION.

    PROGRAM-ID.
    AUTHOR.
    INSTALLATION.
    DATE-WRITTEN.
    DATE-COMPILED.
    SECURITY.

    ENVIRONMENT DIVISION.

    CONFIGURATION SECTION.
    SOURCE-COMPUTER.
    OBJECT-COMPUTER.
```

Fig. A-3. Complex report program shell.

```
      INPUT-OUTPUT SECTION.
      FILE-CONTROL.

            SELECT IN-FILE    ASSIGN TO *** FILE NAME GOES HERE ***
            SELECT REP-FILE   ASSIGN TO *** FILE NAME GOES HERE ***

      DATA DIVISION.
      FILE SECTION.

      FD IN-FILE
         RECORD CONTAINS 80 CHARACTERS
         LABEL RECORDS ARE OMITTED
         DATA RECORD IS IN-REC.

      01 IN-REC.
         ***
         *** INPUT RECORD FORMAT GOES HERE ***
         ***


      FD REP-FILE
         RECORD CONTAINS 80 CHARACTERS
         LABEL RECORDS ARE OMITTED
         DATA RECORD IS REP-REC.

      01 REP-REC                PIC X( *** 80 OR 132 CHARACTERS *** ).

      WORKING-STORAGE.

      01 DETAIL-REC.
         ***
         *** REPORT DETAIL LINE FORMAT GOES HERE ***
         ***

      01 TITLE-1.
         ***
         *** REPORT TITLE GOES HERE ***
         ***


      01 HEADINGS-1.
         ***
         *** FIRST COLUMN HEADINGS GOES HERE ***
         ***

      01 HEADINGS-2.
         ***
         *** COLUMN SUB HEADINGS GO HERE ***
         ***


      01 SALARY-DISPLAY.
```

```
    ***
    *** FORMAT OF COLUMN TOTALS GO HERE ***
    ***

01 BLANK-DISPLAY PIC X(71) VALUE IS SPACES.

01 FOOT-DISPLAY.
    ***
    *** PAGE FOOTING MESSAGE GOES HERE ***
    ***

01 DEPT-SUB-1.
    ***
    *** FIRST SUB TOTAL FORMAT LINE GOES HERE ***
    ***

01 DEPT-SUB-2.
    ***
    *** SUB TOTAL AMOUNT FORMAT PRINTED HERE ***
    ***

01 FLAGS-AND-COUNTERS.
    05 OUT-OF-RECS          PIC X.
    05 PAGE-NO              PIC 999.
    05 LINE-COUNT           PIC 99.
    05 LAST-DEPT            PIC X(10)
    ***
    *** OTHER FLAGS, COUNTERS AND TOTALERS GO HERE ***
    ***

PROCEDURE DIVISION.
START-PAR.
    MOVE 'N'      TO OUT-OF-RECS.
    MOVE 0        TO SALARY-NUM.
    MOVE 0        TO PAGE-NO.
    OPEN INPUT  IN-FILE, OUTPUT REP-FILE.
    READ IN-FILE AT END MOVE 'N' TO OUT-OF-RECS.
    PERFORM HEADINGS-PAR THRU HEADINGS-PAR-END.
    IF OUT-OF-RECS = 'N'
        PERFORM LOOP-PAR THRU LOOP-PAR-END UNTIL OUT-OF-RECS 'Y'.
    WRITE REP-REC FROM HEADINGS-2.
    ***
    *** FINAL TOTAL COMMANDS GO HERE ***
    ***
    WRITE REP-REC FROM SALARY-DISPLAY.
    CLOSE IN-FILE, OUT-FILE.
    STOP RUN.

LOOP-PAR.
    ***
```

184

```
      *** MOVE INPUT FIELDS TO OUTPUT FIELDS ***
      ***
      *** CALCULATE SUBTOTALS AND FINAL TOTALS HERE ***
      ***
      ADD 1                 TO LINE-NO.
      IF IN-DEPT = LAST-DEPT
         MOVE SPACES TO DET-DEPT
      ELSE
        IF   LAST-DEPT = SPACES
           NEXT SENTENCE
        ELSE
           ***
           *** PRINT SUBTOTALS AND SET THEM TO ZERO HERE ***
           ***
           WRITE REP-REC FROM BLANK-DISPLAY.
      MOVE IN-DEPT    TO LAST-DEPT.
      ADD   IN-SALARY TO DEPT-SUB-SUM.
      IF LINE-NUM > 55
         PERFORM HEADINGS-PAR THRU HEADINGS PAR-END.
      WRITE REP-REC FROM DETAIL-REC.
      READ IN-FILE AT END MOVE 'Y' TO OUT-OF-RECS.
LOOP-PAR-END.

HEADINGS-PAR.
      ADD 1         TO PAGE-NO.
      MOVE 5        TO LINE-COUNT
      MOVE PAGE-NO  TO PAGE-OUT.
      IF PAGE-NO NOT = 1
         WRITE REP-REC FROM FOOT-DISPLAY AFTER ADVANCING 2 LINES.
      WRITE REP-REC FROM TITLE AFTER ADVANCING TOP-OF-FORM.
      WRITE REP-REC FROM HEADINGS-1 AFTER ADVANCING 2 LINES.
      WRITE REP-REC FROM HEADINGS-2 AFTER ADVANCING 1 LINES.
HEADINGS-PAR-END.
```

```
IDENTIFICATION DIVISION.

PROGRAM-ID.
AUTHOR.
INSTALLATION.
DATE-WRITTEN.
DATE-COMPILED.
SECURITY.

ENVIRONMENT DIVISION.

CONFIGURATION SECTION.
```

Fig. A-4. Two-tape update method shell.

```
SOURCE-COMPUTER.
OBJECT-COMPUTER.

INPUT-OUTPUT SECTION.
FILE-CONTROL.

    SELECT

DATA DIVISION.
FILE SECTION.

FD OLD-MASTER-FILE
    RECORD CONTAINS 80 CHARACTERS
    LABEL RECORDS ARE OMITTED
    DATA RECORD IS OLD-MASTER-REC.

01 OLD-MASTER-REC.
    ***
    *** OLD MASTER FILE RECORD FORMAT GOES HERE ***
    ***

FD NEW-MASTER-FILE
    RECORD CONTAINS 80 CHARACTERS
    LABEL RECORDS ARE OMITTED
    DATA RECORD IS NEW-MASTER-REC.

01 NEW-MASTER-REC.
    ***
    *** NEW MASTER FILE RECORD FORMAT GOES HERE ***
    ***

FD TRANS-FILE
    RECORD CONTAINS 80 CHARACTERS
    LABEL RECORDS ARE OMITTED
    DATA RECORD IS TRANS-REC.

01 TRANS-REC.
    ***
    *** TRANSACTION FILE RECORD FORMAT GOES HERE ***
    ***


01 MAST-OUT-OF-RECS              PIC X.
01 TRANS-OUT-OF-RECS             PIC X.



PROCEDURE DIVISION.
START-PAR.
    OPEN INPUT  OLD-MASTER-FILE, TRANS-FILE.
    OPEN OUTPUT NEW-MASTER-FILE.
```

```
          PERFORM READ-MASTER-PAR THRU READ-MASTER-PAR-END.
          PERFORM READ-TRANS-PAR THRU READ-TRANS-PAR-END.
          PERFORM DISPATCH-PAR THRU DISPATCH-PAR-END.
          CLOSE OLD-MASTER-FILE, TRANS-FILE, NEW-MASTER-FILE.
          STOP RUN.

      DISPATCH-PAR.
          IF TRANS-OUT-OF-RECS = 'Y'
              PERFORM COPY-MAST-PAR THRU COPY-MAST-PAR-END
                  UNTIL MAST-OUT-OF-RECS = 'Y'
              GOTO MAIN-PAR-END.
          IF MAST-OUT-OF-RECS = 'Y'
              PERFORM FINISH-TRANS-PAR THRU FINISH TRANS-PAR-END
                  UNTIL TRANS-OUT-OF-RECS = 'Y'
              GOTO MAIN-PAR-END.

          IF OLD-EMP-NO = TRANS-EMP-NO
              PERFORM EQUAL-PAR THRU EQUAL-PAR-END
          ELSE IF OLD-EMP-NO > TRANS-EMP-NO
              PERFORM GREATER-PAR THRU GREATER-PAR-END
          ELSE PERFORM LESS-PAR-END.

          GOTO DISPATCH-PAR.

      DISPATCH-PAR-END.

      EQUAL-PAR.
          IF TRANS-CODE = 'D'
              PERFORM READ-MASTER-PAR THRU READ-MASTER-PAR-END
              PERFORM READ-TRANS-PAR THRU READ-TRANS-PAR-END
          ELSE IF TRANS-CODE = 'C'
              PERFORM CHANGE-PAR THRU CHANGE-PAR-END
          ELSE IF TRANS-CODE = 'A'
              DISPLAY 'ERROR: ADD CAN NOT BE PERFORMED. RECORD EXISTS'
              PERFORM READ-TRANS-PAR THRU READ-TRANS-PAR-END
          ELSE
              DISPLAY 'ERROR: TRANSACTION CODE NOT VALID'.

      EQUAL-PAR-END.

      CHANGE-PAR.
          ***
          *** MOVE TRANSACTION DATA TO MASTER FILE IF NEEDED USING THE
          *** EXAMPLE SHOWN BELOW:
          ***     IF TRANS-EMP-NAME NOT = SPACES
          ***         MOVE TRANS-EMP-NAME TO NEW-EMP-NAME.
          ***

          PERFORM READ-TRANS-PAR THRU READ-TRANS-PAR-END.

          IF TRANS-EMP-NO NOT = NEW-EMP-NO
```

```
            WRITE NEW-EMP-NO
            PERFORM READ-MASTER-PAR THRU READ-MASTER-PAR-END.

CHANGE-PAR-END.

GREATER-PAR.
    IF TRANS-CODE = 'A'
        WRITE NEW-MASTER-REC.
        ***
        *** MOVE TRANSACTION DATA TO MASTERFILE RECORD
        ***
        WRITE NEW-MASTER-REC
        MOVE OLD-MASTER-REC TO NEW-MASTER-REC
        PERFORM READ-TRANS-PAR THRU READ-TRANS-PAR-END
    ELSE
        DISPLAY 'ERROR - BAD TRANSACTION CODE'
        PERFORM READ-TRANS-PAR THRU READ-TRANS-PAR-END.

GREATER-PAR-END.

LESS-PAR.
    WRITE NEW-MASTER-REC.
    PERFORM READ-MASTER-PAR THRU READ-MASTER-PAR-END.
LESS-PAR-END.

COPY-MAST-PAR.
    WRITE NEW-MAST-REC.
    PERFORM READ-MASTER-PAR THRU READ-MASTER-PAR-END.
COPY-MAST-PAR-END.

FINISH-TRANS-PAR.
    IF TRANS-CODE = 'A'
        ***
        *** MOVE TRANSACTION FILE DATA TO MASTERFILE RECORD ***
        ***
        WRITE NEW-MASTER-REC
        PERFORM READ-TRANS-PAR THRU READ-TRANS-PAR-END
    ELSE
        DISPLAY 'ERROR: TRANSACTION CODE MUST BE "A"'
        PERFORM READ-TRANS-PAR THRU READ-TRANS-PAR-END.

FINISH-TRANS-PAR-END.

READ-MASTER-PAR.
    READ OLD-MASTER-FILE AT END MOVE 'Y' TO MAST-OUT-OF-RECS.
    MOVE OLD-MASTER-REC TO NEW-MASTER-REC.
READ-MASTER-PAR-END.

READ-TRANS-PAR.
    READ TRANS-FILE AT END MOVE 'Y' TO TRANS-OUT-OF-RECS.
    READ-TRANS-PAR-END.
```

```cobol
IDENTIFICATION DIVISION.

PROGRAM-ID.
AUTHOR.
INSTALLATION.
DATE-WRITTEN.
DATE-COMPILED.
SECURITY.

ENVIRONMENT DIVISION.

CONFIGURATION SECTION.
SOURCE-COMPUTER.
OBJECT-COMPUTER.

INPUT-OUTPUT SECTION.
FILE-CONTROL.

    SELECT

FD MAIL-FILE
   RECORD CONTAINS 80 CHARACTERS
   LABEL RECORDS ARE OMITTED
   DATA RECORD IS MAIL-REC.

01 MAIL-REC          PIC X( *** DEFINE RECORD LENGTH *** ).

WORKING-STORAGE SECTION.

01 MAIL-TABLE OCCURS 100 TIMES
   ***
   *** DEFINE RECORD LAYOUT HERE ***
   ***

01 CONTROL-FIELDS
   05 ANSWER                 PIC X.
   05 ARRAY-SIZE             PIC 999.
   05 ARRAY-INDEX            PIC 999.
   05 OUT-OF-RECS            PIC X.
   05 FOUND-IT               PIC X.
   05 VALID-OPTION           PIC X

01 WS-FIELDS.
   ***
   *** DEFINE WORKING AREA IN SAME FORMAT AS RECORD
       DESCRIPTION ***
   ***
```

Fig. A-5. Array update method program shell.

```
PROCEDURE DIVISION.
START-PAR.
     PERFORM READ-PAR THRU READ-PAR-END.
     PERFORM MENU-PAR THRU MENU-PAR-END.
     PERFORM WRITE-PAR THRU WRITE-PAR-END.
     STOP RUN.
MENU-PAR.
     MOVE 'N' TO VALID-OPTION.
     DISPLAY ' '.
     DISPLAY '                    *** SYSTEM TITLE GOES HERE ***
     DISPLAY '                       *** MENU TITLE GOES HERE ***
     DISPLAY ' '.
     DISPLAY '      1. ADD
     DISPLAY '      2. CHANGE      ***
     DISPLAY '      3. DELETE      *** MENU OPTIONS GO HERE ***
     DISPLAY '      4. DISPLAY     ***
     DISPLAY '      5. LIST
     DISPLAY '      E. EXIT SYSTEM'.
     DISPLAY ' '.
     DISPLAY '              ENTER OPTION: '.
     ACCEPT ANSWER.
     IF ANSWER = '1' MOVE 'Y' TO VALID-OPTION
                     PERFORM ADD-PAR THRU ADD-PAR-END.
     IF ANSWER = '2' MOVE 'Y' TO VALID-OPTION
                     PERFORM CHANGE-PAR THRU CHANGE-PAR-END.
     IF ANSWER = '3' MOVE 'Y' TO VALID-OPTION
                     PERFORM DELETE-PAR THRU DELETE-PAR-END.
     IF ANSWER = '4' MOVE 'Y' TO VALID-OPTION
                     PERFORM DISPLAY-PAR THRU DISPLAY-PAR-END.
     IF ANSWER = '5' MOVE 'Y' TO VALID-OPTION
                     PERFORM LIST-PAR THRU LIST-PAR-END
                        VARYING ARRAY-INDEX FROM 1 BY 1
                        UNTIL ARRAY-INDEX = ARRAY-SIZE.
     IF ANSWER = 'E' GOTO MENU-PAR-END.

     IF VALID-OPTION = 'Y' GOTO MENU-PAR.
     DISPLAY ' '.
     DISPLAY 'ERROR: ANSWER MUST BE 1,2,3,4,5 or E, PLEASE
             REENTER'.
     DISPLAY ' '.
     GOTO MENU-PAR.

     MENU-PAR-END.

ADD-PAR.
     ADD 1 TO ARRAY-SIZE.
     MOVE ARRAY-SIZE TO ARRAY-INDEX.
     ***
     *** ASK USER FOR INPUT OF NEW DATA RECORD USING PROCESS
             SHOWN BELOW
```

```
      ***           DISPLAY 'ENTER DATA : '.
      ***           ACCEPT  DATA-NAME(ARRAY-INDEX).
      ***
   ADD-PAR-END.

   CHANGE-PAR.
      PERFORM FIND-PAR THRU FIND-PAR-END.
      PERFORM LIST-PAR THRU LIST-PAR-END.
      DISPLAY 'ENTER NEW VALUE TO UPDATE OR <CR> TO LEAVE VALUE
               UNCHANGED'.
      DISPLAY ' '.

      ***
      *** ASK USER FOR FIELD CHANGES USING THE PROCESS SHOWN BELOW
      ***        DISPLAY 'ENTER DATA: '.
      ***        ACCEPT WS-NAME.
      ***
   CHANGE-PAR-END.

   DELETE-PAR.
      PERFORM FIND-PAR THRU FIND-PAR-END.
      IF FOUND-IT = 'Y' MOVE '-----` TO LAST-NAME(ARRAY-INDEX).
   DELETE-PAR-END.

   DISPLAY-PAR.
      PERFORM FIND-PAR THRU FIND-PAR-END.
      PERFORM LIST-PAR THRU LIST-PAR-END.
   DISPLAY-PAR-END.

   LIST-PAR.
      ***
      *** DISPLAY ALL FIELDS FOR A GIVEN RECORD USING ARRAY-INDEX AN
      *** SHOWN BELOW:
      ***     DISPLAY 'DATA     : ',DATA-NAME(ARRAY-INDEX).
      ***
   LIST-PAR-END.

   FIND-PAR.
      DISPLAY 'ENTER *** VALUE OF KEY DATA FIELD :'.
      ACCEPT WS-DATA-NAME.    *** NAME OF KEY DATA FIELD ***
      MOVE 'N' TO FOUND-IT.
      PERFORM FIND-1-PAR THRU FIND-1-PAR-END
              VARYING ARRAY-INDEX FROM 1 BY 1
              UNTIL ARRAY-INDEX = ARRAY-SIZE OR FOUND-IT = 'Y'.
      IF FOUND-IT = 'N' DISPLAY 'NOT FOUND'.

   FIND-PAR-END.

   FIND-1-PAR.
      IF *** DATA-NAME*** (ARRAY-INDEX) = *** WS-DATA-NAME ***
```

```
            DISPLAY ' '
            DISPLAY   **** DISPLAY APPROPRIATE DATA FIELDS ***
            DISPLAY ' '
            DISPLAY 'IS THIS IT ( Y or N) : '
            ACCEPT FOUND-IT.
    FIND-1-PAR-END.

    READ-PAR.
            OPEN INPUT MAIL-FILE AT END MOVE 'Y' TO OUT-OF-RECS.
            MOVE 0 TO ARRAY-SIZE.
            READ MAIL-FILE AT END MOVE 'Y' TO OUT-OF-RECS.
            IF OUT-OF-RECS NOT = 'Y'
                PERFORM READ-2-PAR THRU READ-2-PAR-END UNTIL
                        OUT-OF-RECS = 'Y'.
            CLOSE MAIL-FILE.
    READ-PAR-END.

    READ-1-PAR.
          ADD 1 TO ARRAY-SIZE.
          MOVE MAIL-REC TO MAIL-TABLE(ARRAY-SIZE).
          READ MAIL-FILE AT END MOVE 'Y' TO OUT-OF-RECS.
    READ-1-PAR-END.

    WRITE-PAR.
        OPER OUTPUT MAIL-FILE.
        PERFORM WRITE-PAR THRU WRITE-PAR-END
                VARYING ARRAY-INDEX FROM 1 BY 1 UNTIL
                        ARRAY-INDEX = ARRAY-SIZE.
        CLOSE MAIL-FILE.
    WRITE-PAR-END.

    WRITE-1-PAR-END.
        IF  *** DATA-NAME *** (ARRAY-INDEX) NOT = '-----'
            WRITE MAIL-REC FROM MAIL-ARRAY(ARRAY-INDEX).
    WRITE-1-PAR-END.
```

```
    300   WORKING STORAGE.
    310
    351   01 ANSWER                    PIC X.
    352   01 VALID-OPTION              PIC X.
    353
    400   PROCEDURE DIVISION.
    401   START-PAR.
    402       PERFORM MENU-PAR THRU MENU-PAR-END.
    403       STOP RUN.
    404
    405   MENU-PAR.
```

Fig. A-6. Menu program shell.

```
406          MOVE 'N' TO VALID-OPTION.
407          DISPLAY ' '.
408          DISPLAY '              *** SYSTEM NAME GOES HERE ***
409          DISPLAY '              *** MENU NAME GOES HERE ***
410          DISPLAY ' '.
411          DISPLAY '    1. ***
412          DISPLAY '    2. *** PLACE MENU OPTIONS HERE ***
413          DISPLAY '    3. ***
414          DISPLAY '    4.
415          DISPLAY '    E. EXIT SYSTEM'.
416          DISPLAY ' '.
417          DISPLAY '              ENTER OPTION: '.
418          ACCEPT ANSWER.
419          IF ANSWER = '1' MOVE 'Y' TO VALID-OPTION
420                          PERFORM *** OPTION-1 ***
421          IF ANSWER = '2' MOVE 'Y' TO VALID-OPTION
422                          PERFORM *** OPTION-2 ***
423          IF ANSWER = '3' MOVE 'Y' TO VALID-OPTION
424                          PERFORM *** OPTION-3 ***
425          IF ANSWER = '4' MOVE 'Y' TO VALID-OPTION
426                          PERFORM *** OPTION-4 ***
427          IF ANSWER = 'E' GOTO MENU-PAR-END.
428
429          IF VALID-OPTION = 'Y' GOTO MENU-PAR.
430          DISPLAY ' '.
431          DISPLAY 'ERROR: ANSWER MUST BE 1,2,3,4 or E, PLEASE
                     REENTER'.
432          DISPLAY ' '.
433          GOTO MENU-PAR.
434     MENU-PAR-END.
```

```
WORKING-STORAGE SECTION.
01 VALID-OPTIONS-TAB.
   ***
   ***   PLACE TRANSACTION DATA HERE IN FORMAT SHOWN BELOW;
   ***       05 FILLER  PIC X(40)
   ***             VALUE IS 'ADDEMPPYADDEMPADD A NEW EMPLOYEE      '.

01 VALID-OPTIONS-TABLE REDEFINES VALID-OPTIONS-TAB.
   05 VALID-OPTIONS OCCURS 5 TIMES.
       10 OPTION-NAME              PIC X(6).
       10 OPTION-PROGRAM           PIC X(8).
       10 OPTION-DESC              PIC X(26).

01 OPTION-INDEX                    PIC 9.
01 ANSWER                          PIC X(6).
```

Fig. A-7. Transaction driver for called program shell.

```
PROCEDURE DIVISION.
START-PAR.
     PERFORM TRANS-PAR THRU TRANS-PAR-END.
     STOP RUN.

TRANS-PAR.

     DISPLAY ' '.
     DISPLAY '                        PAYROLL SUBSYSTEM'.
     DISPLAY '                MAIN TRANSACTION DISPATCH SCREEN'.
     DISPLAY ' '.
     DISPLAY '     ENTER TRANSACTION CODE: '.
     DISPLAY ' '.
     DISPLAY ' '.
     DISPLAY 'ENTER A QUESTION MARK ( ? ) FOR LIST OF VALID
             OPTIONS'.

     ACCEPT ANSWER.

     IF ANSWER = 'EXIT' GOTO TRANS-PAR-END.
     IF ANSWER = '?' SET OPTION-INDEX TO 0
                     PERFORM DISPLAY-PAR THRU DISPLAY-PAR-END
                           5 TIMES
                     GOTO TRANS-PAR.

     SEARCH VALID-OPTIONS VARYING OPTION-INDEX
            AT END DISPLAY 'TRANSACTION NOT FOUND, PLEASE
                    REENTER'
          WHEN OPTION-NAME(OPTION-INDEX) = ANSWER
               CALL OPTION-PROGRAM(OPTION-INDEX)
               NEXT SENTENCE.

     GOTO TRANS-PAR.
TRANS-PAR-END.

DISPLAY-PAR.
    SET OPTION-INDEX UP BY 1
    DISPLAY OPTION-NAME(OPTION-INDEX),' - ',
            OPTION-DESC(OPTION-INDEX).
DISPLAY-PAR-END.
```

```
WORKING-STORAGE SECTION.

01 SEX-CODE              PIC X.

PROCEDURE DIVISION.
START-PAR.
```

Fig. A-8. Restricted value check shell.

```
      PERFORM SEX-CODE-PAR THRU SEX-CODE-PAR-END.
      STOP RUN.

  SEX-CODE-PAR.
      DISPLAY 'ENTER *** ENTER NAME OF DISPLAY TITLE HERE ***
      ACCEPT SEX-CODE.
      ***
      *** PLACE IF STATEMENT EDIT CRITERIA AS SHOWN BELOW
      ***      IF SEX-CODE = 'M' OR SEX-CODE = 'F'
      ***
          NEXT SENTENCE
      ELSE
          DISPLAY ' '
          DISPLAY 'ERROR: *** PLASE ERROR MESSAGE HERE ***
          DISPLAY ' '
          GOTO SEX-CODE-PAR.
  SEX-CODE-PAR-END.
```

Index

Other Bestsellers From TAB

☐ **PROGRAMMING WITH dBASE III® PLUS—Prague and Hammitt**

Packed with expert programming techniques and short-cuts, this is an essential guide to Aston Tate's newest version of its dBASE relational database manager for the IBM® PC™. It includes all the practical, use-it-now advice and guidance beginning PC users are looking for . . . as well as power programming techniques that will allow more advanced users to increase productivity while sharply reducing application development time. 384 pp., 150 illus. 7″ × 10″.

Paper **$21.95**   Hard **$29.95**
Book No. 2726

☐ **PROGRAMMING WITH R:BASE® 5000—Prague and Hammitt**

Picking up where user's manuals leave off, Prague and Hammitt guide you through all the many capabilities offered by R:base 5000, and show you how to adapt these capabilities for your own applications needs. In fact, the authors cover everything from how to use basic R:base tools to using R:base 5000 as a complete programming language for writing your own applications programs. 400 pp., 266 illus. 7″ × 10″.

Paper **$19.95**   Hard **$28.95**
Book No. 2666

☐ **TURBO PASCAL® PROGRAMMING, WITH APPLICATIONS—Wortman**

Using a series of 26 ready-to-use, practical business and financial applications written for the IBM PC™, XT™, AT® , and compatibles, Wortman lets you experience the features of Turbo Pascal firsthand. Most importantly, all the programs are completely formatted and explained so that you can easily understand and customize them. So whether you're a beginner who wants to see what Turbo Pascal is capable of, or if you've already discovered the remarkable capabilities of this language and want more applications code, you'll find a wealth of invaluable, new programming techniques and ideas. 256 pp., 26 illus. 7″ × 10″.

Paper **$17.95**   Hard **$23.95**
Book No. 2627

☐ **469 PASCAL PROBLEMS WITH DETAILED SOLUTIONS—Veklerov**

Now this unique self-teaching guide makes it amazingly easy even for a novice programmer to master Pascal. With a total of 469 problems ranging from the most basic to advanced applications, the guide provides a unique learning opportunity for anyone who wants hands-on understanding of the Pascal language and its programming capabilities. 224 pp., 23 illus. 7″ × 10″.

Paper **$14.95**   Hard **$21.95**
Book No. 1997

☐ **THE ILLUSTRATED DICTIONARY OF MICROCOMPUTERS—2nd Edition—Hordeski**

Little more than a decade after the introduction of the first microprocessors, microcomputers have made a major impact on every area of today's business, industry, and personal lifestyles. The result: a whole new language of terms and concepts reflecting this rapidly developing technology . . . and a vital need for current, accurate explanations of what these terms and concepts mean. Michael Hordeski has provided just that in this completely revised and greatly expanded *new* second edition of *The Illustrated Dictionary of Microcomputers*! 368 pp., 357 illus. 7″ × 10″.

Paper **$14.95**   Hard **$24.95**
Book No. 2688

☐ **SERIOUS PROGRAMMING IN BASIC**

Practical techniques for writing better applications programs in BASIC for the Apple® , Commodore® 64/128, IBM® PC, or PC-compatibles! Includes a wealth of subroutines and short programs to illustrate the principles of sound program development and help form the basis of your own subroutine library! It's a sourcebook that can change your whole outlook on program development! 224 pp., 153 illus. 7″ × 10″.

Paper **$14.95**   Hard **$21.95**
Book No. 2650

☐ **DATA COMMUNICATIONS AND LOCAL AREA NETWORKING HANDBOOK**

With data communications and LANs being the area of greatest growth in computers, this sourcebook will help you understand what this emerging field is all about. Singled out for its depth and comprehensiveness, this clearly-written handbook will provide you with everything from data communications, standards and protocols to the various ways to link together LANs. 240 pp., 209 illus. 7″ × 10″.

Hard **$25.00**   Book No. 2603

☐ **PROGRAMMING WITH dBASE III®**

With this excellent sourcebook at your side, using dBASE III is a snap! You'll discover how to take advantage of all this fourth generation software's data handling capabilities *plus* learn how to unlock the power of dBASE III as a complete programming language! Also includes an appendix detailing the differences between dBASE II and dBASE III, with full instructions for using dConvert—the utility program used to convert dBASE II programs to dBASE III! 304 pp., 215 illus. 7″ × 10″.

Paper **$17.95**   Book No. 1976

Other Bestsellers From TAB

JORDAN, MARSH
ILLUSTRATED CATALOG OF 1891
An Unabridged Reprint

BY

Jordan, Marsh and Company

A Joint Publication of
THE ATHENAEUM OF PHILADELPHIA
AND
DOVER PUBLICATIONS, INC., NEW YORK

Published in Canada by General Publishing Company, Ltd., 30 Lesmill Road, Don Mills, Toronto, Ontario.
Published in the United Kingdom by Constable and Company, Ltd., 3 The Lanchesters, 162–164 Fulham Palace Road, London W6 9ER.

This Athenaeum of Philadelphia/Dover edition, first published in 1991, is an unabridged republication of the *1891 Price List and Fashion Book*, published by Jordan, Marsh and Company, Boston. A preface and a publisher's note have been added.

Manufactured in the United States of America
Dover Publications, Inc., 31 East 2nd Street, Mineola, N.Y. 11501

Library of Congress Cataloging-in-Publication Data

Price list and fashion book.
    Jordan, Marsh illustrated catalog of 1891: an unabridged reprint / Jordan, Marsh and Company.
       p.   cm.
    Reprint. Originally published: Boston : Jordan, Marsh and Company, 1891, under title: Price list and fashion book.
    Includes index.
    ISBN 0-486-26738-5 (pbk.)
    1. Jordan, Marsh and Company—Catalogs. 2. Department stores—Boston (Mass.)—Catalogs. I. Jordan, Marsh and Company. II. Title.
    HF5465.U635B676   1991
    974'.041—dc20   91-4674
                                                           CIP

PREFACE TO THE ATHENAEUM/DOVER EDITION

THIS REPRINT EDITION of an 1891 Jordan, Marsh catalog is one in a series of reprints of books and trade catalogs published by special agreement between The Athenaeum of Philadelphia and Dover Publications, Inc. The objective of this series is to make available to the greatest possible audience rare and often fragile documents from the extensive collections of The Athenaeum in sturdy and inexpensive editions.

The Athenaeum of Philadelphia is an independent research library with museum collections founded in 1814 to collect materials "connected with the history and antiquities of America, and the useful arts, and generally to disseminate useful knowledge." It is housed in a handsomely restored National Historic Landmark building near Independence Hall in the heart of the historic area of Philadelphia.

As the collections expanded over the past 175 years, The Athenaeum refined its objectives. Today the library concentrates on nineteenth- and early twentieth-century social and cultural history, particularly architecture and interior design where the collections are nationally significant. The library is freely open to serious investigators, and it annually attracts thousands of readers: graduate students and senior scholars, architects, interior designers, museum curators and private owners of historic houses.

In addition to 130,000 architectural drawings, 25,000 historic photographs and several million manuscripts, The Athenaeum's library is particularly rich in original works on architecture, interior design and domestic technology. In the latter area the publications of manufacturers and dealers in architectural elements and interior embellishments have been found to be particularly useful to design professionals and historic house owners who are concerned with the restoration or the recreation of period interiors. Consequently, many of the reprints in this series are drawn from this collection. The Athenaeum's holdings are particularly strong in areas such as paint colors, lighting fixtures, wallpaper, heating and kitchen equipment, plumbing and household furniture.

The modern Athenaeum also sponsors a diverse program of lectures, chamber music concerts and exhibitions. It publishes books that reflect the institution's collecting interests, and it administers several trusts that provide awards and research grants to recognize literary achievement and to encourage outstanding scholarship in architectural history throughout the United States. For further information, write The Athenaeum of Philadelphia, East Washington Square, Philadelphia, PA 19106-3794.

ROGER W. MOSS
Executive Director

PUBLISHER'S NOTE

AT THE TIME this catalog was originally published, Jordan, Marsh and Company had already been in business for forty years.

The company began in 1851 when Eben Jordan and Benjamin Marsh opened a small wholesale dry-goods business, Jordan & Marsh. With the addition of new investors the following year, the name was changed to Jordan, Marsh and Company, the title it retained until 1901 when the name was changed to Jordan Marsh Company.

The business prospered, and soon included a retail store as well as the wholesale operation. Several times over the next few years, it was found necessary to move to larger quarters. In the early 1860s, the retail store moved to Washington Street, one of Boston's main shopping streets; by 1871, the wholesale division was located nearby. The business continued to prosper and grow, moving into neighboring sites in the area. The building shown on the back cover of the catalog, built in the 1880s, was at the corner of Washington and Avon Streets.

Jordan, Marsh and Company carried much more than just basic necessities. India Cashmere Valley Shawls could be purchased for from $150 to $500, gentlemen's smoking jackets were available in a variety of fabrics and the store had an entire department devoted to "Sporting Outfits for Polo, Lawn Tennis, Yachting, Base Ball, Lacrosse, and Rowing." Imported merchandise was common—the store had the "exclusive right to sell at retail in Boston the Black Silk Ribbons of the well-known Lyons Manufacturers, 'Les Fils' de C. J. Bonnet & Co"; some of the fabrics for boys' suits were "made exclusively for Jordan, Marsh & Co., by one of the leading manufactories of Galashiel, Scotland"; and the store's Fleur de Lis Corsets were "made by the best hands in Paris."

The store's return policy was liberal, promising "perfect satisfaction given, or money refunded," while customers encountering difficulties, no matter how small, were urged to contact the complaint bureau.

As stated in the catalog, the store had a mailing list of 100,000 names. While many of these customers undoubtedly shopped in person, the store boasted a "fully equipped mail-order department" offering "Prompt service. Utmost care in selection. Errors promptly remedied whenever they occur" and "Satisfaction guaranteed." The catalog particularly emphasizes the mail-order customer, claiming, "One can often trade with us through our mail-order department much cheaper than by a personal visit, as traveling costs more than a letter." Today, mail-order shopping has become extremely popular. That the same thing was true one hundred years ago can be seen by glancing through these pages.

PRICE LIST and FASHION BOOK

JORDAN MARSH and COMPANY

BOSTON

. . 1891 . .

OUR PARIS MODEL.

(1500 FRANCS.)

PRICE, $55.00. This costume was imported by us especially for our catalogue, and is from the celebrated house of Sara Mayer, Paris. It being one of the newest models, our intention is to copy the same at less than half the cost (1500 francs). Price, $55.00, in any material at $1.50 per yard. The bodice is quite elaborate, it being trimmed with fancy gold braid and six dozen of tiny gilt buttons. The bodice is of the new length, and in this price costume is a great novelty. The skirt is elegantly draped med with the same braid as bodice. Skirt is made up on silk, and bodice satteen. See measurement page 21 for instructions as to si

FOR INDEX SEE LAST PAGE.

Write nothing but your order for goods on this sheet.	**ORDER SHEET.**	If you want samples, use the sample sheet below.

No. 9.

To Jordan, Marsh & Co.

BOSTON, MASS.

....189

Send by (State whether by Open or Registered Mail, Express, or Freight)..

the goods, in quantities and at prices as per following order, viz.:

Quantity.	DESCRIPTION OF GOODS.	Date of Catalogue.	Page in Catalogue.	Number in Catalogue.	Dollars.	Cents.

CONTINUE YOUR ORDER ON THE OTHER SIDE OF THIS SHEET.

Total,...

Amount for Postage, Expressage, etc.,......................................

Enclosed find (Check, P.O. Order, Postal Note, Express M.O.) ....for $.........

Name,...

Post-office,...

County,...

State,...

NOTE.—Please state whether we shall substitute, in case any of the goods ordered have been closed out of stock, we guaranteeing to take back the same, defraying express expense, if unsuitable or unsatisfactory.

☞ We will investigate and rectify any error in the filling of an order, if made known to us. If an order is not satisfactorily filled we will refund the money. If too much money is sent us, the excess is returned.

SAMPLE SHEET.

Please send to the address below samples of ....

Name,...

Post-office,...

County,...

State,...

ix

CONTINUE YOUR ORDER HERE.

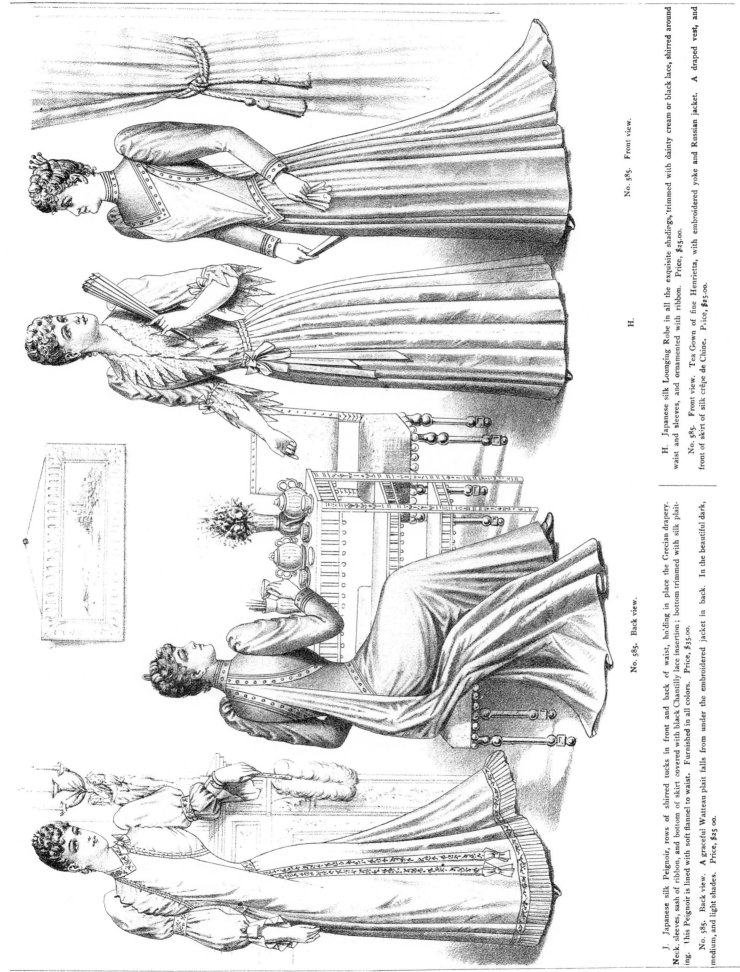

No. 585. Front view.

H.

No. 585. Back view.

H. Japanese silk Lounging Robe in all the exquisite shadings, trimmed with dainty cream or black lace, shirred around waist and sleeves, and ornamented with ribbon. Price, $25.00.

No. 585. Front view. Tea Gown of fine Henrietta, with embroidered yoke and Russian jacket. A draped vest, and front of skirt of silk crêpe de Chine. Price, $25.00.

J. Japanese silk Peignoir, rows of shirred tucks in front and back of waist, holding in place the Grecian drapery. Neck, sleeves, sash of ribbon, and bottom of skirt covered with black Chantilly lace insertion; bottom trimmed with silk plaiting. This Peignoir is lined with soft flannel to waist. Furnished in all colors. Price, $35.00.

No. 585. Back view. A graceful Watteau plait falls from under the embroidered jacket in back. In the beautiful dark, medium, and light shades. Price, $25.00.

THE MERCANTILE HEART OF NEW ENGLAND.

No. 607.

No. 501.

No 506.

No. 109.

No. 101.

No. 100.

No. 503.

No. 607.   French Silk Surah, in figures and stripes, trimmed with velvet ribbon, fancy basque.   Price, $17.50.
No. 501.   Cashmere Suit, in all colors, trimmed with velvet collar and cuffs.   Price, $6.50.
No 506.   All Wool Black Henrietta, richly embroidered with cord and soutache, and silk sleeves in basque.   Price, $18.00.
No. 109.   Striped and Plaid Cheviot, all wool, in all colors.   Price, $13.50.

No. 101.   Fancy Check Suit, in six colors, neatly trimmed with velvet collar and cuffs.   Price, $7.00.
No. 100.   All Wool Fine Plaid Suit, nicely trimmed, with buttons to match.   Price, $11.00.
No. 503.   Fine Cashmere Suit, handsomely trimmed, with silk ribbon to match, in all colors.   Price, $12.00.

No. 33. Handsome suit, made of fine quality faille française, with choice quality of passementerie ornaments on waist and skirt. Price, $30.00.

No. 31. Handsome suit, made of all wool ladies' sacking, in all shades. Points on waist and skirt, trimmed with large silk buttons. Price, $11.00.

No. 62. Elegant suit, made of fine moiair brilliantine in all shades. Embroidery on waist and both sides of skirt. Price, $12.00.

No. 33. Black Cashmere Suit; plaited skirt, revers, collar, and cuffs, and panel on skirt, of faillé française. Price, $11.00.

No. 76. Very handsome suit, made of French twilled cloth, in tan and brown combination. Waist and skirt embroidered in a neat design, as shown in cut. Price, $22.50.

No. 28. Handsome suit, made of cashmere, in all colors, elaborate embroidery on waist and skirt, as shown in cut. Price, $10.50.

No. 56. Tailor-made suit of imported check material, handsomely trimmed, with silk braid on waist and skirt. Price. $20.00.

No. 108.

No. 106.

No. 5746.

No. 5751.

No. 5607.

No. 5740.

No. 5709.

No. 5746.   Homespun, in all colors, plain skirt, with stitching, trimmed with silk cord and buttons.   Price, $13.50.

No. 108.   Tailor-made Tricot Suit, in all the latest shades, trimmed with small buttons, and bound with silk braid.   Price, $11.00.

No. 106.   Tailor-made Tricot Suit, trimmed with Hercules and soutache braid and large crochet buttons.   Price, $14.00.

No. 5709.   Plain Ladies' Cloth, with black gimp and surah trimmings.   Price, $27.50.

No. 5740.   Silk Lace, with surah lining, and profusely trimmed with ribbon.   Price, $40.00.

No. 5607.   Surah Waist, fine quality, trimmed with four-inch black lace gimp.   Price, $12.00.

No. 5751.   Black All Wool Cashmere, elaborately trimmed with gros-grain ribbon.   Price, $20.00.

No. 5708.

No. 5794.

No. 5823.

No. 5793.

No. 5791.

No. 5790.

No. 5790. Mixed Cloth Suiting, with brown cloth trimming and three rows of gold soutache braid. Long skirt waist. Price, $22.50.

No. 5791. Camel's Hair Stripe. Collar and girdle, plain and steel trimming. Skirt bias, with fan plaiting. Price, $36.50.

No. 5793. Light Tan Scotch Suiting, skirt coat, sleeves of plain and steel trimming. Price, $35.00.

No. 5823. Striped Camel's Hair, bias skirt, slashed square, faced with silk. Double-breasted waist, large pearl buttons. Skirt of waist faced with silk. Price, $30.00.

No. 5794. Striped Scotch Suiting, silver trimming, Louis XIV. coat, striped sleeves. Price, $38.00.

No. 5708. Serge Suiting, Louis XIV. coat, vest trimmed with soutache and ornament trimming. Price, $25.00.

No. 708.   No. 723.   No. 715.   No. 725.   No. 709.   No. 718.   No. 705.

No. 708. Suit of broken check goods, all wool, with stitching and silk braid. The skirt is made with a long plain drapery, slashed at the bottom, stitched and bound with the braid and falling over a plaiting. The waist is b und, vest is stitched, revers bound and ornamented with large buttons. Price, $18.50.

No. 723. Suit of all wool checked material. The skirt on the bias is plain, all the fulness being gathered in the plaited back. Vest of the goods on the bias has a plait on both sides of it ornamented with buttons. Price, $12.50.

No. 715. Suit of alpaca, trimmed with faille plaiting around bottom of skirt. Plaited vest, revers, rolling collar, and cuffs, of faille. Price, $13.50.

No. 725. Costume of brilliantine, with plaitings and a gimp with Milan drops. Plaiting edges the draperies all around. The waist is also finished at the bottom with a plaiting and gimp. There are narrow plaitings down the front of waist edged with the gimp. Back of waist similarly trimmed. Price, $21.00.

No. 709. Costume of a very fine serge with velvet and surah. The plain skirt has a fold of velvet around the bottom. A plaited vest of surah, revers of velvet, and a double row of velvet buttons from the waist. Trimming jacket effect. Price, $22.50.

No. 718. Costume in Henrietta cloth with faille. Gros grain ribbon and passementerie with Milan drops. Three narrow plaitings and loops of ribbon around the long straight drapery. The ribbon in loops edges the waist. Yoke of faille in front of waist is edged with the passementerie. The back of waist is plaited. Price, $25.00.

No. 705. Costume of shepherd plaid, trimmed with faille and passementerie. Draped skirt has two plaits of faille and a panel of the passementerie on one side. Folds of faille and goods also. A revers-shaped piece of passementerie forms the waist trimming. Price, $27.50.

No. 702. No. 729. No. 707. No. 741. No. 701. No. 713. No. 710.

No. 702. Suit made of tricot. The front of skirt is slightly draped. Sides are plaited. The front of waist shows plaits, each being stitched. Collar and cuffs are made of faille in a contrasting shade. Price, $11.50.

No. 729. Suit of checked ladies' cloth, bound with silk braid in a contrasting shade. There is a fan of plaits on one side of the skirt bound with the braid, one of the plaits having buttons and button-holes the entire length. The waist has folds of the cloth in front bound with the braid. There is a revers to one side, which is bound and ornamented with buttons and buttonholes. The sleeves have buttons and buttonholes the entire length. Price, $20.00.

No. 707. Suit of a pin-checked material, trimmed with a fancy-edged braid. Five clusters of braid at the bottom of plain skirt arranged as shown in accompanying cut, braid on waist corresponding to skirt. Folds of goods form the waist. Price, $20.00.

No. 741. Suit of fine imported challie, trimmed with velvet to match the color of the design. The skirt has three small flounces around the bottom, each with a piping of velvet. The waist has olds of challie and velvet down the front, with small bows of velvet, giving a pretty finish. Shirred pieces of the challie coming from sides of waist end in the front with a piping of velvet. The back of waist is trimmed with velvet. Price, $22.50.

No. 701. Suit made of ladies' cloth, trimmed with afancy edge; silk braid, straight skirt with five rows of braid around the bottom, ending in spirals in front. The waist is trimmed, back and front, with the braid in graduated lengths to correspond to skirt. Braid similarly arranged on collar and sleeves. Price, $16.50.

No. 713. Suit of mohair, trimmed with narrow velvet ri'bon. The front of skirt has the ribbon in graduated lengths, two rows around p'aits on the sides. The ribbon is arranged yoke shape on the waist. Price, $13.50.

No. 710. Costume of Henrietta cloth, trimmed with faille in a contrasting shade. There is a plaiting of faille under the drapery, which falls over it in scallops. Waist similarly plaited and slashed, also a plaited vest and shirred zouave of the faille. Price, $25.00.

No. 33.

No. 26.

No. 67.

No. 36.

No. 52.

No. 35.

No. 60.

No. 33. Ladies' suit, made of mohair brilliantine in gray mixture. Skirt and waist trimmed with fine silk braid. Price, $11.75.

No. 26. Cashmere suit, made in all shades. Embroidery on waist and around bottom of skirt. Price, $10.50.

No. 67. Combination suit of tan and brown camel's hair, all wool. Waist trimmed with silk cord, made after a Paris sample. Price, $16.50.

No. 36. Stylish suit, made of extra quality brilliantine, large horn buttons on waist and skirt. Price, $13.50.

No. 52. Very stylish suit, made in all wool English plaid in five different shades. Skirt made with bias front and straight back. Price, $12.50.

No. 35. Elegant suit, made of real mohair brilliantine. Double row of buttons on waist, plaiting on bottom of skirt. Price, $13.50.

No. 60. Elegant suit, with plaited skirt, made of fine mohair brilliantine, in all shades, passementerie gimp trimming on waist. Price, $9.50.

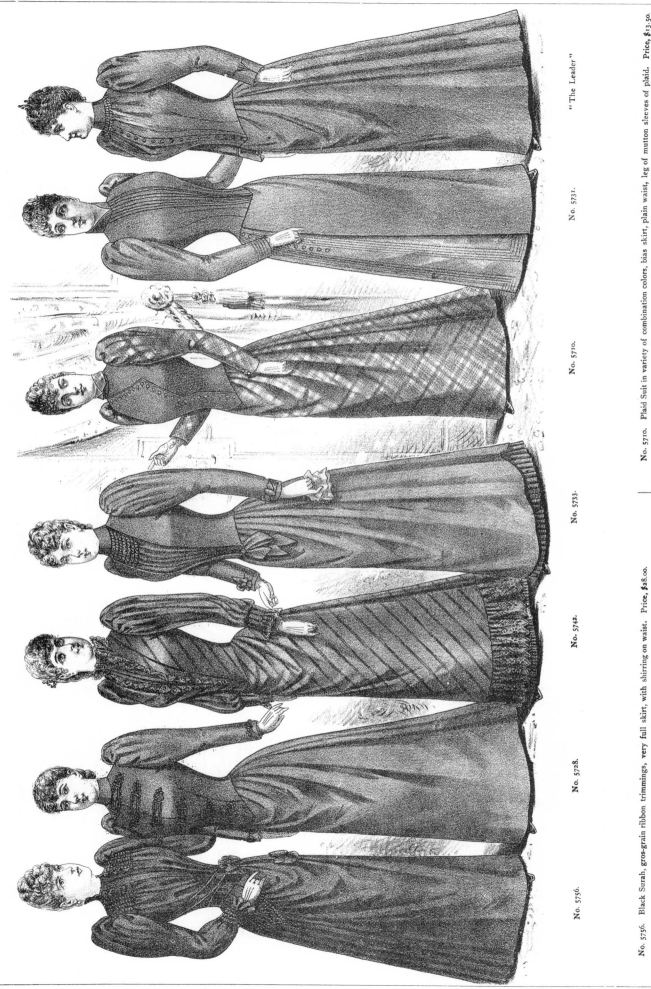

No. 5756. Black Surah, gros-grain ribbon trimmings, very full skirt, with shirring on waist. Price, $28.00.

No. 5728. Cheviot Suiting, bias skirt, black frog trimmings. Price, $20.00.

No. 5742. Black Lace Striped Surah, with lace trimmings, bias skirt. Price, $40.00.

No. 5733. Fine Qual't. Henrietta, English draped skirt, gros-grain ribbon trimmings and plaiting of material. Price, $27.50.

No. 5710. Plaid Suit in variety of combination colors, bias skirt, plain waist, leg of mutton sleeves of plaid. Price, $13.50.

No. 5731. Navy Blue Serge, with tan combination, blue soutache braid and crochet buttons. Price, $17.50.

"The Leader" is a black faille silk of a superior quality and handsome lustre. It is simply made, but 18 yards of silk are used in the making. Price, $25.00.

No. 5756.   No. 5728.   No. 5742.   No. 5733.   No. 5710.   No. 5731.   "The Leader"

559. **Surah Waist with Yoke and Medicis Collar.** Yoke and sleeves lined with lawn. Price, $6.50.

3040. A Silk Surah Waist, in black and colors. Embroidery is in self colors. An embroidered belt goes with it, which does not appear in the cut. Price, $10.50.

513. **Cheviot Shirt Waist** of Cotton Shirting Cheviot. Body, plain color. Cuffs, collar, and belt of stripe. Comes in pink, blue, brown, and gray. Price, $1.50.

3007. Surah Silk Waist in black and colors. Price, $8.50.

501. Surah Silk Waist, lined throughout with lawn, in black and colors. Price, $9.00.

527. Blazer Jacket with new effects in collar and pockets, fine serge. In white, black, navy, and tan, etc. Price, $4.00.

521. Blazer Jacket Reefer of Serge, with handsome cord ornaments. Full line of colors. Price, $6.00.

3001. Is the latest and most useful outing suit, the waist being of Surah, and the skirt of Wool outing material, in stripes and plaids or plain white. They can be sold separately or as a complete suit. Price of waist, $8.50 Price of skirt, $9.50.

3. Correct English Reefer, in navy, black, and tan Ladies' cloth. Price, $5.00.

2. The London Blazer. Made in stripe crêpe cloth. Price, $1.00.

1. The Newport. Made of Ladies' navy blue and black cloth. Price, $2.50.

4. Yachting Jacket, made in cream, navy, black, and tan flannel, with contrasting colored edging and buttons. Price, $6.50.

65. Black Open Reefer Jacket. Made of fine Cheviot cloth, edged all round with black and gold mixed cord, entire fronts lined with silk serge, very stylish. Comes also in tan, navy, and blue. Price, $12.00.

5. Black Stockinette Jacket. Fine quality, revers front, vest effect, handsome soutache braiding, tailor made. Price, $8.50.

THE MERCANTILE HEART OF NEW ENGLAND.

170. Black Blazer with Shawl Collar. Vest faced with Sicilian silk. Also in tan and navy. Price, $8.50.

187. Black Cheviot Reefer Jacket with Medicis collar. Collar and sleeves braided with fancy gold braiding, and one-sided ornaments. Also in navy and tan. Price, $13.50.

516. Tan Cloth Jacket. Marie Antoinette collar, embroidered Zouave style. Also in black and navy. Price, $10.50.

101. Black Stockinette Jacket. Single-breasted, plaited back. Medicis collar. Price, $4.00.

183. Black Cheviot Jacket. Marie Antoinette collar. Notched revers. Price, $6.00.

160. Black Cheviot Vest Front Jacket. With notched collar. Vest faced with Regence silk, bound with braid. Also in tan and navy. Price, $12.00.

514. Ladies' Tan Cloth Cape. Tight fitting back, feather edge, Medicis collar, with fancy gold embroidery. Also in black and navy. Price, $15.00.

1559. Double-breasted Reefer. Made out of fine Cheviot, Sicilian collar, embroidered with silk, lined half way with silk, pearl buttons. Price, $12.00.

513. Tan Vecuna Cloth, Double Cape. With embroidered Medicis collar. Also in black and navy. Price, $5.50.

164. Tan Cheviot Blazer. With shawl collar, edged with gold cord. Also in black and navy. Price, $8.50.

345. Flannel Blazer. in black and navy. Price, $2.50.

1494. Revers Front Vest Jacket. Made of Wool Cheviot, stitched edges. Price, $7.00.

411. Cotton Flannel Blazer. In variety of stripes and colors. Price, $2.00.

218. Navy Cloth Blazer. Royal collar, with white embroidery and cord and tassel. Price, $4.00.

1516. Double-breasted Tight Fitting Jacket. Made out of Wool Cheviot, bound with braid. Price, $5.50.

No. 116.   No. 159.   No. 703.   No. 235.   No. 115.

No. 180.   No. 619.   No. 504.   No. 617.   No. 133.

No. 608.   No. 45.   No. 22.   No. 615.   No. 625.

No. 116.   Black Stockinette Jacket.   Vest front, Shawl Collar, piped with braid.   Price, $12.
No. 159.   Tight fitting, Stockinette Jacket with Sailor Collar.   27 inches long.   Price, $9.00.
No. 703.   Imported Beaded Cape.   Beaded fringe, silk lined.   Price, $5.50.
No. 235.   Reefer.   Made of fine striped tennis cloth.   Cloth facing, trimmed with white ivory buttons, assorted colors.   Price, $5.00.
No. 115.   Black Stockinette Jacket.   Im. Shawl Collar, piped with braid.   Plaited back. $10.
No. 180.   Reefer Jacket, made of fine Stockinette.   Price, $11.00.
No. 619.   Long vest front Cape, tight fitting back, made of Tan Broadcloth, handsomely embroidered in tan and gold.   Comes in blue, black, and pearl gray.   Price, $12.50.
No. 504.   Tan Ladies' Cloth Cape, with embroidered Medicis Collar, gathered at the neck, also in black and navy.   Price, $4.00.
No. 617.   Extra long Roman Cape, made of Tan Kersey cloth, handsomely embroidered all around in tan and gold silk cording to match, high Medicis Collar.   Price, $12.00.

No. 133.   Fancy revers front, with Shawl Collar, trimmed and piped with silk braid, made of fine Stockinette cloth.   Price, $8.50.
No. 608.   Long Cape, fine knife plaiting and pointed yoke front and back, made of pearl gray cloth, handsomely embroidered in silver tinsel, very elaborate.   Price, $5.00.
No. 45.   Black Reefer Jacket, made of extra fine Cheviot cloth, entire Shawl Collar, faced with heavy Renaissance silk, handsomely embroidered with fine silk cording, silk crochet loops for fastening.   Price, $12.50.
No. 22.   Black Reefer Jacket, made of fine English Cheviot, double-breasted, with side pockets.   Price, $8.50.
No. 615.   Long English Cape, made of fine tan broadcloth, elaborately braided in tan and gold, three plaits running from shoulder in front and back, newest effect.   Price, $8.50.
No. 625.   Long Bernhardt Cape, tight fitting, pointed back, made of tan broadcloth, handsomely embroidered front and back in tan and gold, new and stylish.   Price, $7.50.

No. 66.

No. 1405.

No. 102.

No. 1403.

No. 86B.

No. 131.

No. 156.

No. 1416.

No. 154.

No. 3.

No. 120.

No. 93.

No. 58.

No. 92.

No. 68.

No. 66. Blue Open-front **Reefer**, made of English kersey, handsomely embroidered in gold mixed cording down entire front, edged all around with fine silk cord. Price, $15.00.

No. 1405. Black Worsted Diagonal Cloth Wrap, very elaborately braided with fine silk cording, all silk and mohair fringe, very handsome and stylish. Price, $15.00.

No. 102. Black Blazer Jacket, made of a very fine cheviot cloth. Price, $12.50.

No. 1403. Black Cheviot Wrap, handsomely braided with fine silk cording, trimmed with imported silk and worsted fringe of a superior quality. Price, $13.50.

No. 86B. Black Blazer-shape Jacket, made of finest quality English wide wale diagonal cloth, with fancy black and gold mixed girdle. Price, $15.00.

No. 131. Black Stockinette Jacket, good quality, with revers fronts. Price, $4.50.

No. 156. Black Jacket, made of diagonal corkscrew material, revers fronts, vest effect. Welt seams, tailor-made. Price, $6.50.

No. 1416. Black Clay Diagonal Wrap, lined throughout with fine silk serge, garment braided all over very handsomely, and trimmed with fine bullion fringe. Price, $20.00.

No. 154. Black Jacket, made of clay diagonal coating, tailor-made. Price, $7.50.

No. 3. Black Stockinette Jacket, fine quality, revers fronts, vest effect, handsomely braided with silk cording, tailor-made. Price, $7.50.

No. 120. Blazer Jacket, made of fine striped, all wool heavy flannel, handsome girdle, cloth-faced, very stylish. Price, $4.00.

No. 93. Black Reefer Jacket, made of cheviot cloth, edged all round with black and gold cord, shawl collar, new side pockets. Price, $7.00.

No. 58. Black Jacket, made of gray homespun cloth, tailor-made. Price, $5.50.

No. 92. Reefer Jacket, made of tan cheviot cloth, edged all round with tan and gold mixed cord to match, handsome ornaments, side pockets. Price, $8.50.

No. 68. Open-front Reefer Jacket, made of fine tan broadcloth, handsomely embroidered in tan and gold cording, also girdle to match, lined half way back with fine tan silk serge, Price, $18.00.

No. 220. No. 510. No. 168. No. 103. No. 115.

No. 201. No. 185. No. 329. No. 530. No. 342. No. 331. No. 303. No. 110.

No. 220. Misses' Blazers, sizes 14 to 16 years. Made from light and dark tan Cloakings, roll collar with lapel, fastened in front with frog. Price, all sizes, $6.50.

No. 510. Child's Reefer. Navy and red flannel, plain, double-breasted, notched collar, unlined, navy buttons. 4 to 12 years. All sizes, $4.00.

No. 168. Miss's Jacket, sizes 14 to 16 years. Made from navy blue Basket Cloth, collar, cuffs, pocket, and front made of gray material to match, the edges all trimmed with cord. All sizes, $10.75.

No. 103. Child's Reefer, in sizes from 4 to 12 years. Cut double-breasted, from blue and tan Cloakings, with double collar and cuffs, the under collar and cuff being blue with tan body or tan with blue body, both edged with cord to match, silver buttons.

Sizes,	4,	6,	8,	10,	12,
Prices,	$4.25,	4.50,	4.75,	5.00,	5.25.

No. 115. One-piece Sailor Suit of all Wool Flannel, trimmed with white Hercules braid. In navy blue and red flannel.

Years,	4,	6,	8,	10,	12,	14,
Prices,	$5.00,	5.50,	6.00,	6.50,	7.00,	7.50.

No. 201. Miss's Two-piece Dress. Fancy plaid, with velvet bodice, revers, standing collar, and cuffs, gathered sleeves, back of waist plaited. 12 to 18 years.

Sizes,	12,	14,	16,
Prices,	$13.50,	14.50,	15.50.

No. 185. Two-piece Miss's Suit of Fancy Mixture, set off with contrasting shades of Cashmere, elaborately trimmed with braid. In tan mixture and gray mixture.

Years,	14,	16,
Prices,	$12.50,	13.50.

No. 329. Mixed Twills. Plain full skirt from yoke, square collar, full silk sleeves over cloth sleeves. Handsome woven silk girdle. Collar and cuffs corded. 8 to 14 years.

Sizes,	8,	10,	12,	14,
Prices,	$15.00,	15.50,	16.00,	16.50.

No. 530. Child's Reefer. Mixed Cassimere, double-breasted, notched collar, unlined. 4 to 12 years. All sizes, $4.50.

No. 342. Fancy Striped Imported Materials. Medici collar and ruff, faced with surah. Edging of collar and ruff. also girdle, of tinsel mixed cord. Pearl ball buttons. 4 to 12 years.

Sizes,	4,	6,	8,	10,	12.
Prices,	$13.50,	14.25,	15.00,	15.75,	16.50.

No. 331. Child's Gretchen, in sizes from 8 to 14 years. Made with yoke and cape, from light and dark tan goods, trimmed with braid, loose front and girdle.

Sizes,	8,	10,	12,	14,
Prices,	$9.00,	9.50,	10.00,	10.50.

No. 303. Child's Gretchen, in sizes from 6 to 14 years. Made with jacket front, from blue and tan diagonal goods, combined with plain goods to match, sailor collar, shirred skirt with girdle, edges trimmed with cord.

Sizes,	6,	8,	10,	12,	14,
Prices,	$10.50,	11.00,	11.50,	12.00,	12.50.

No. 110. Elegant Two-piece Striped Tennis Costume, with vest, revers, collar, and cuffs of white flannel, trimmed with soutache to match material. In blue and white, and red and white striped tennis flannel.

Years,	10,	12,	14,	16,
Prices,	$10.00,	10.50,	11.00,	11.50.

No. 206.   No. 122.   No. 312.   No. 100.   No. 193.   No. 177.   No. 124.   No. 232.   No. 111.   No. 318.   No. 150.   No. 106.   No. 462.

No. 206. Miss's Reefer, sizes 14 to 16 years. Cut double-breasted, from fine imported plaid goods, roll collar with lapel. All sizes, $10.00.

No. 122. Child's Reefer, in sizes from 6 to 14 years. Cut double-breasted, with roll collar and lapel, from fine imported plaid goods, and navy blue basket goods.
Size 6, $6.75; size 8, 7.00; size 10, 7.25; size 12, 7.50; size 14, 8.00.

No. 193. One-piece Dress of all Wool Cashmere, with unique waist front, sash back, and soutache trimmed. In navy, tan, havana brown, gray, and rose.
4 years, $7.50; 6 years, 8.25; 8 years, 9.50; 10 years, 10.25; 12 years, 11.00; 14 years, 11.75.

No. 312. Fancy Checks. Single-breasted, with frogs and olives, no buttons. Full sleeves. Five rows soutache braid on collar and cuffs. Zouave jacket outlined in braid. 4 to 12 years.
Size 4, $8.50; size 6, 9.00; size 8, 9.50; size 10, 10.00; size 12, 10.50.

No. 124. Child's Dress. Combination of plain tricot and fancy mixed goods. Eyelet and cord ornamentation on waist and cuffs, full sleeves, shawl collar, sash with fringed ends in bow at back. 4 to 12 years.
Size 4, $7.50; size 6, 8.00; size 8, 8.50; size 10, 9.00; size 12, 9.50.

No. 100. Child's Dress. Fancy mixtures, with blouse of plain tricot under Zouave jacket effect. Combination soutache braid on cuffs, yoke, jacket, and collar, two rosettes at back. 4 to 12 years.
Size 4, $7.00; size 6, 7.50; size 8, 8.00; size 10, 8.50; size 12, 9.00.

No. 177. One-piece Dress of Fancy Mixture, trimmed with braid, with yoke, belt, and cuffs of Cashmere, in contrasting shades. Rosette finish at back. In tan mixture and gray mixture.
4 years, $5.00; 6 years, 5.50; 8 years, 6.00; 10 years, 6.50; 12 years, 7.00; 14 years, 7.50.

No. 232. Miss's Three-piece Dress. A particularly new, novel, and pleasing effect, in fancy Scotch mixtures. Skirt plain front, plaited back, edged with mixed braid. Round French waist, buttoning on side, leg of mutton sleeves. Front of neck, cuffs, and front of waist line trimmed with two rows fancy braid, back of waist terminating in braided coat-tail effect.
The jacket (a novel addition) is made sleeveless, silk-lined, tailor-made, rolling collar, and side pockets.
The jacket being worn gives a very effective street costume, or, if not worn, the result is a handsome house dress. 12 to 18 years.
Size 12, $23.00; size 14, 25.00; size 16, 26.00.

No. 111. Child's 4 Cape Gretchen. Very light weight, made of small English all Wool checks, shirred skirt, brass button,
Size 4, $7.50; size 6, 8.00; size 8, 8.50; size 10, 9.00; size 12, 9,50; size 14, 10.00.

No. 318. Child's Cloak. Plain Cheviot, double-breasted, deep Byron collar, fine Pearl buttons, full sleeves, box-plaited skirt. Collar, cuffs, and pocket laps braided in contrasting colors. 8 to 14 years.
Size 8, $15.00; size 10, 15.75; size 12, 16.50; size 14, 17.25.

No. 150. Child's all Wool Cashmere Dress, with Fedora of white or canary Cashmere, collarette and cuffs. Sash back. In rose, sage green, tan, gray, and light brown.
4 years, $7.00; 6 years, 7.50; 8 years, 8.00.

No. 106. Child's Reefer, in sizes from 4 to 14 years. Made double-breasted, from gray and light and dark tan Cloakings, with large sailor collar and lapel, full cuffs, all edged with cord to match, gold buttons.
Size 4, $4.75; size 6, 5.00; size 8, 5.25; size 10, 5.50; size 12, 6.00; size 14, 6.25.

No. 462. Misses' Reefing Jacket in all Wool Kerseys. Blue, back, tan, and red. Satin-faced, revere and 4 silk ornaments. Sizes, 12, 14, 16 years. All sizes, $7.50.

Nos. 13 and 14.

No. 1.

No. 2.

No. 3.

No. 5.

No. 4.

No. 6.

No. 7.

No. 8.

No. 9.

No. 15.

Nos. 10 and 11.

No. 12.

Nos. 16 and 17.

No. 1. Hub Suit. Strictly all wool. Sizes, 5 to 16 years. We are New England agents for this celebrated suit. Price, $5.00.

No. 2. "The Harvard." Three-button Cutaway Suit, with Vest, from 10 to 16 years, in Scotch mixtures, Cheviots, blue and black Diagonals. Prices, $7.00, 8.00, 10.00, 12.00, 14.00.

No. 3. Boys' Suit with Vest, in Scotch Mixtures, blue Tricot, and Diagonal. Can be worn with shirt waist or white vest. Sizes, 4 to 10 years. Prices, $5.00, 6.00, 8.00, 10.00.

No. 4. A beautiful assortment of Imported Cotton Sailor Suits, in combinations of stripes and plain colors. Also, white, with blue or red collars and cuffs. Sizes, 4 to 10 years. Prices, $3.00, 4.00, 5.00, 6.00.

No. 5. Boys' Zouave Suits, in Velvet, Tricot, and Scotch mixtures, to be worn with fancy blouse. Sizes, 4 to 10 years. Prices for Velvet and Tricot, from $8.00 to 12.00; do. for mixtures, $5.00, 6.00, 7.00, 8.00. We have an endless variety of fancy Blouses to be worn with these suits, $1.75 to 6.00. Colored Blouses, $1.00.

No. 6. Boys' Two-piece Kilt Suits. Sizes, 3 to 6 years. Plain colors, checks, and fancy mixed materials. Prices ranging from $5.00 to 12.00, according to style and quality.

No. 7 This cut represents a pretty wash dress for boys, with dark blue blouse and percale skirt, with collar and cuffs to match. Price, $1.75, 2.00.

No. 8. Double-breasted Suit, in handsome Scotch mixtures. 6 to 16 years. Prices, $6.00, 8.00, 10.00.

No. 9. Single-breasted Suit with patch pockets, in plain and Scotch mixtures. 6 to 16 years. Prices, $5.00, 6.00, 7.00, 8.00, 10.00.

Nos. 10 and 11. Stout and extra stout suits for fat boys. We make a specialty of these suits in both 2 and 3-piece suits, made and trimmed in the best manner. 8 to 16 years. 2-piece suits, $8.00, 10.00, 12.00. 3-piece suits, $10.00, 12.00, 14.00. Extra pants, one-third price of suit.

No. 12. Norfolk Suit in all wool materials. Sizes, 4 to 10 years. Prices, $5.00 to 10.00.

Nos. 13 and 14. Boys' Star Shirt Waists. Prices, 50c., 75, $1.00, 1.50 each. Our assortment of these waists includes an exhaustless variety of patterns of the latest productions, in Percale and Linen. Unlaundered waists, 25 and 50 cents each.

No. 15. Ladies' Star Shirt Waists, in fancy Percales, with either standing or roll-over collar, straight or turn-over cuff. Sizes, 30 to 38 in. bust measure. Price, $1.50, all sizes. We have secured this season a large assortment of Ladies' Shirts, modelled after the celebrated Star pattern, and made from the newest and daintiest French and Scotch Flannels in the market. We have these in sizes from 30 to 42 in. bust measure. Prices, $3.00, 3.50.

Nos. 16 and 17. Flannel Blouse and Waist. Every style of Boys' Flannel and Cheviot Blouses. Prices, $1.00, 1.50, 2.00. French Flannel, $2.50.

"Hub Combination."

No. 1.   No. 2.   No. 3.   No. 4.   No. 13.

No. 5.   No. 7.

No. 6.

MEASUREMENT
FOR
BOYS' SUITS.

Coat.

Length of sleeve (1 to 2
and 3).
Around the breast, under
arm, over vest (4).

Short Pants.

Around waist (5).
Outside length of pants
(5 to 6).
Height.
Age.
For long pants, take
inside seam to 7.
These same measures
answer for Overcoats.

No. 8.   No. 9.   No. 10.   No. 11.   No. 12.

No. 1.   Boys' Covert Coat, in blue, black, gray, and brown.   A very natty garment.
9 to 18 years.   Prices, $8.00, 10.00, 12 00, 14 00.

No. 2.   Boys' Spring Reefers.   Sizes, 4 to 15 years.   In navy blue, $5.00; in gray and
brown mixed, $3.50, 5.00; in Scotch plaids, $6.00, 8.00, 10.00.

No. 3.   Boys' Single Breasted Sack Overcoat, in plain and fancy materials.   Suitable for
spring and fall wear.   Sizes, 12 to 18 years.   Prices, $9.00 to 16.00.

No. 4.   Boys' Sack Suits.   Ages, 14 to 18 years.   (Long Pants.)   We have them in broken
checks, Cassimeres, plain Cheviots, plaids and stripes, blue and black Diagonal, in all grades
Prices range from $8.00 to 18.00.

No. 5.   Sailor Suit, in blue and black English Serge, made with regular shirt sleeve and extra
wash-over collar, in blue with white trimmings.   Sizes, 4 to 10 years.   Prices, $6.50, 7.50, 8.00.

No. 6.   Boys' Sailor Suits, in Flannel and Serge.   Great variety of styles.   Blue, gray,
and brown.   Range in price, $1.50, 2.50, 3.50, 5.00, 6.00.

No. 7.   "Avon Suit."   Double-breasted, round corners.   This suit made in handsome
Scotch mixtures, and is very desirable.   6 to 16 years.   Prices, $5.00, 6.00, 7.00, 8.00, 10.00,
12.00.

No. 8.   Boys' Kilts with Zouave Jackets, in velvet and cloths, with lawn or silk blouses.
Prices, $8.00, 10.00, 12.00, 14.00.   Also, separate lawn blouses in various styles, ranging in
prices from $1.75 to 6.00.   Sizes, 3 to 6 years.

No. 9.   Boys' Double-breasted Long Pant Suits, made in same materials as figure No. 4.
A very desirable style this season.   14 to 18 years.   Prices, $10.00 to $22.00.

No. 10.   Boys' Cape Overcoats.   Ages, 3 to 7 years.   In plaids and stripes, plain or plaited,
in both foreign and domestic goods.   Prices, $4.00, 5.00, 6.00, 8.00, 10.00, 12.00.

No. 11.   Boys' Jersey Suits in several styles.   3 to 10 years.   Prices, $4.00, 5.00, 6.00.
Jersey Waists or Blouses, striped or plain.   Prices, $2.25, 2.50, 2.75, according to age.   Jersey
Sashes, in blue, black, or red.   Price, $1.50.

No. 12.   Youths' three-buttoned Cutaway Suit, with skirt coat, in blue and black clay
Diagonal.   16 to 20 years.   Prices, $18.00 and 20.00.   Coat and vest of same for mixed trousers,
Price, $15.00.

No. 13.   "Hub Combination."   Price, $5.00.   Sizes, 4 to 15 years.   Consists of Suit, extra
Pants, and Cap, to match, in all-wool materials.   We have a variety of patterns in fine mixtures
and checks.   Cut plaited, 4 to 10 years; plain Jacket, 10 to 15 years.

Boys' Odd Long Pants.   14 to 18 years.   In plaids and stripes.   Prices, $2.00, 3.00, 4.00,
5.00.

Boys' Odd Short Pants.   4 to 16 years.   Prices, 50 and 75c.   All wool, $1.00, 1.50, 2.00.

REMARKS.

We have for this season imported direct the finest line of Scotch Cheviots, which we will
manufacture into our finest grade of Suits and Reefers at prices that cannot be equalled.   These
goods are made from pure selected Australian Wool, long staple, perfectly fast color.   Weight,
19 oz. to the yard.

Special designs made exclusively for Jordan, Marsh & Co., by one of the leading manufactories of Galashiel, Scotland.

These goods are made into Norfolk Suits, 4 to 10 years; Single-breasted Suits, 6 to 16 years;
Double-breasted Suits, with Reefers to match, 6 to 16 years; Suits with Vests, 11 to 16 years;
Long Pant Suits, 15 to 18 years.

P.S.—We guarantee all our Boys' Suits to be just as represented.   Perfect satisfaction
given, or money refunded.

No. 1. $3.50.

No. 2. $6.00,

No. 3. $4.00

No. 4. $5.00.

No. 5. $5.00,

No. 6. $6.50.

No. 7. $5.00,

No. 8. $5.00.

MILLINERY.

In ordering these hats, state with the number color desired, and we will send exact copies. Trimmed hats from $5.00 to 50.00, copied from imported French pattern hats, always in stock.

As we import everything in the millinery line that fashion requires, and buy in very large quantities, we are enabled to offer the trade, both wholesale and retail, the best goods at lowest possible prices, resulting often in a saving of over fifty per cent.

We carry an extensive line of leghorn flats, for ladies, misses, and children, from $1.00 to 4.50. The $1.00 grade in black is a special bargain this year.

French flowers in natural and fancy mountings, gold mixtures, wreaths, and flowers of all kinds for corsage trimmings and dress garnitures.

Roses, 25c. per dozen and upwards.
Red poppies, 10c. per dozen and upwards.
French montures, 25c.
Imported daisy wreaths, all colors, 15c.
Buttercup wreaths, 25c.
Lilacs, all colors, 6 sprays in a bunch, $1.00 per bunch.
Splendid line of black flowers, in plain and jetted specialties.
Ostrich feathers, French, German, and American goods, 50c. and upwards.

THE MERCANTILE HEART OF NEW ENGLAND.

BOLERO   NEWPORT   ROXBURG

GLENDOWER   MARJORIE   DIANA

MARLBORO   JOCKEY   SIREN   ARTLESS

OLIVIA   QUEEN   VIENNA   WESTON

PRINCESS   ALENE   RITA   DELL

ALICE

ENGLISH SAILOR   ELITE   GEM   ROSITA

The above cuts represent a few of the leading shapes for the SPRING AND SUMMER SEASON of 1891.

In plain Milan braid...........................at 50c, 75c, $1.00, 1.25, 1 50 | In fancy braids............... ....at 38c, 50c, 75c, $1.00 to 3.00
With fancy edges................................at 75c, $1.00, 1.25 and 1.50 | Rough and Ready Straw Sailors...................... .... at 19c

Mountain Leghorn Shade Hat, 15c.

Fayal Hats; most comfortable shade hats, on account of their light weight. In the natural color, black or white, at 25 cts. each. Can be rolled up and packed away without injury to the hat.

THE MERCANTILE HEART OF NEW ENGLAND.

No. 1904.

No. 1933.

No. 1936.

No. 1938.

No. 1915.

No. 1916.

No. 1909.

No. 1904. Striped and plaid Gingham Wrapper, with plaited front from the shoulder to the waist. Price, $3.00.

No. 1933. Finest Scotch Gingham, with a robe of plain material to match, in pink, light blue, gray, navy, and old rose. Price, $4.50.

No. 1936. Printed French Sateen Wrapper, with a plain sateen robe. Shirred on to a pointed yoke. Black, navy, white, and gobelin grounds. Price, $5.00.

No. 1938. Printed French Sateen Wrapper, trimmed with embroidery to match. Ribbon bows on the shoulder and at the waist, with tucked sateen robe from the shoulders. Black, navy, gobelin, and light grounds. Price, $6.50.

No. 1915. Very fine Swiss Embroidery Wrapper, with tucked robe and tucked Watteau. Edging ruffle around the bottom, and ribbon rosettes at the neck and waist. Price, $11.00.

No. 1916. Printed French Challie Wrapper, in the latest designs, with plain cashmere robe and trimmings. Silk feather stitching on cuffs, collar, revers, and bodice. Price, $12.00.

No. 1909. Figured and Striped English Debeige Wrapper, with plain cashmere robe. Silk feather stitching on cuffs, collar, and bodice. In brown, gray, navy, old rose, and black. Price, $5.50.

SPRING AND SUMMER, 1891.

Rules for Self-measurement

FOR

COSTUMES MADE TO ORDER ONLY.

The following rules for self-measurement will be found a valuable guide to those of our customers who purpose ordering by mail. If accurate measures are taken as illustrated, we can assure a perfect fit; but, in order to avoid the possibility of a mistake made either by our patrons or ourselves, we should prefer that a waist already made and worn should be sent in every instance when possible.

CATALOGUE COSTUMES AND GARMENTS.

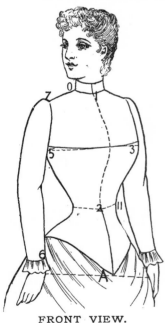

COSTUMES.

Bust measure and length of skirt in front.

TEA GOWNS.

Bust measure and length in front from neck to bottom of skirt.

CLOAKS AND JACKETS.

Bust measure only.

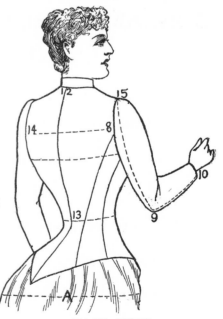

FRONT VIEW.

1, around the neck.
1 to 2, neck to waist.
3 to 5, bust, to be taken all around under arms.
5 to 6, length of sleeve inside.
O to 7, length of shoulder.
3 to 11, from under arm to waist.
11, size of waist, all around.
A.—Around hips.

BACK VIEW.

Waist.—12 to 13, length of back to waist.
8 to 14, across back.
15 to 9, shoulder to elbow.
9 to 10, elbow to wrist.
Skirt.— Length in front from waist.
Length in back from waist.
Belt measure.

WE keep on hand a large assortment of all Catalogue Suits and Garments in every size from 32-inch inch to 46-inch bust. Should extra large sizes be required, we should have to charge a trifle more pro rata. It occasionally happens that special sizes have to be made. In such cases a week's delay is unavoidable.

THE MERCANTILE HEART OF NEW ENGLAND.

FOR TRAVELLING AND OUTING.

THE CUNARDER.

THIS represents one of the most stylish and comfortable garments for yachting ever produced. A similar garment is an absolute necessity for those travelling abroad; and, in consequence of the increased demand this year, we have enlarged our stock with all the different grades of English Mackintoshes, and everything to be had in domestic manufacture. o o o o o o o o o o o

THE DEVONSHIRE

Two elegant Styles, - - $7.50, 10.50.

Price, $3.50.

GOSSAMER RUBBER DEPARTMENT.

Alligator * * * * *

Misses' Waterproof Circulars, - - $1.25, $1.50

"   "   Peasant, with Cape, - 2.00

"   "   Westminster, - - 3.00

Boys' Light-weight Waterproofs, - - 1.50

Ladies' Plain Circulars, - - - 1.25, 1.50

"   Checks and Stripes, Peasant or Circular, 2.75

Showerproof Garments, - - - 5.00, 6.50

* * * * Waterproof.

Price, $2.00.

A large stock of Imported Mackintoshes in all styles always on hand at $12.00, 16.50, 18.50, 20.00, and upwards.

This is our trade-mark for one of the greatest bargains ever offered in a Gossamer Rubber Waterproof. It is manufactured for us alone, and under our special supervision. The shape is perfectly new, has all the latest improvements, is guaranteed perfectly waterproof, and fully worth $3.00.

THE MERCANTILE HEART OF NEW ENGLAND.

SILKS, VELVETS, SATINS, AND PLUSHES.

SPRING SEASON, 1891.

PLAIN AND PRINTED SILKS.

Now Complete. Our importation of Plain and Printed China, India, Corea, and Tonquin Silks, Plain Colored Crepes, Figured Crepes, Plain and Striped Wash Silks, and Plain and Figured Surah Silks. Never before has such a UNIQUE and EXTENSIVE STOCK of ORIGINAL and EXCLUSIVE designs and colorings been offered in Boston. Should you make a selection from our importations for the season of 1891, your dress cannot become common, as we have ordered only limited quantities of each combination.

PLAIN AND PRINTED INDIA AND CHINA SILKS.

Printed India Silks in all the very latest colorings, and printed on entirely new, original, and exclusive designs.

SPECIAL VALUES.

20-inch Printed India Silks, ...	$0.49
22-inch " " "	.69
27-inch " " "	1.00
27-inch " " "	1.25

PRINTED TUSSOR AND COREA SILKS.
Both in Light Grounds and Dark Effects.

LATEST EFFECTS IN PLAID SURAH SILKS.

20-inch Plaid and Stripe Surah Silks, ...	$0.69
24-inch " " " "	1.00

WASH SILKS.

Both in Stripes, Checks, and Plaids, the Popular Fabric of the Spring Season of 1891.

SPECIAL VALUES.

22-inch Stripe and Plaid Wash Silks, ...	$0.69
24-inch " " " "	1.00

For Blouses, Waists, Costumes, Skirts, Shirts, and Lawn Tennis Dresses or Yachting Costumes, these fabrics will be universally worn. You can wash them like a piece of white cotton.

PLAIN COLORED CHINA SILKS AND INDIA SILKS.

In all the latest colors, including Black and Plain White.
For a light, cool summer costume, we know of no fabric to equal this fashionable article.

SPECIAL VALUES.

22-inch Plain India and China Silks, ...	$0.69
27-inch " " "	.75

HIGH ART PRINTED CHINA SILKS, FOR DECORATIVE PURPOSES.

SPECIAL VALUES.

20-inch High Art Printed China Silks, . . .	$0.49
24-inch " " " . . .	.75
27-inch " " " . . .	.85

FASHION NOTES.

LATEST ADVICES FROM THE LEADING DRESSMAKERS OF EUROPE.

As fashion dictates, Silks will be more popular than any other class of fabrics that will be offered for the Spring and Summer Season, as all the leading dressmakers of Paris, Berlin, Vienna, and other fashionable centres are positively making by far more Silk Costumes this season than for years.

WORTH,

of Paris, predicts that more Silk Dresses will be worn this season than in the palmiest days of Silk Costumes; and he recommends nothing else.

BLACK SILKS.

OUR CHOICE AMERICAN BLACK SILKS.

The progressive spirit shown in the manufacture of these goods is fast bringing them up to the acknowledged standard of foreign productions. Indeed, all connoisseurs give them the preference to-day for their superb wearing qualities and perfect finish.

HEADQUARTERS IN THE UNITED STATES FOR AMERICAN SILKS.

NOTE.—*The List Prices for our great Leaders are guaranteed the lowest of any house in America.*

19-in. wide, . . .	$0.65	22-in. wide, . . .	$0.87
20-in. " . . .	.75	23-in. " . . .	1.00
20-in. " . . .	.87½	22-in. " . . .	1.25
21-in. " . . .	1.00	22-in. " . . .	1.50
22-in. " . . .	1.00	22-in. " . . .	1.75
24-in. " . . .	1.00	22-in. " . . .	2.00

JORDAN, MARSH & CO. FAMILY SILKS.

22-in. wide, . .	$1.00	22-in. wide, . .	$1.50
24-in. " . .	1.00	22-in. " . .	1.75
22-in. " . .	1.25	22-in. " . .	2.00

BELLON BLACK LYONS SILKS.

20-in. wide, $0.75, ordinarily worth $1.00			24-in. wide, $1.50, ordin'ly worth $1.87½			
20-in. "	1.00,	" "	1.25	24-in. "	1.75, " "	2.25
21-in. "	1.25,	" "	1.50	24-in. "	2.00, " "	2.50
22-in. "	1.50,	" "	2.00	24-in. "	2.25, " "	2.75
24-in. "	1.00,	" "	1.25	24-in. "	2.50, " "	3.00
24-in. "	1.25,	" "	1.62½	24-in. "	3.00, " "	4.00

OUR OWN MARIE ANTOINETTE BLACK SILKS.

22-in. wide, . . .	$1.00	22-in. wide, . . .	$1.75
22-in. " . . .	1.25	22-in. " . . .	2.00
22-in. " . . .	1.50		

CASHMERE ALEXANDER BLACK SILKS.

21-in. wide, . . .	$1.00	24-in. wide, . . .	$1.00
22-in. " . . .	1.25	24-in. " . . .	1.25
22-in. " . . .	1.50	24-in. " . . .	1.50
22-in. " . . .	1.75	24-in. " . . .	1.75

C. J. BONNET & CIE. BLACK SILKS.

21-in. wide, . . .	$1.00	23-in. wide, . . .	$1.75
21-in. " . . .	1.25	23-in. " . . .	2.00
22-in. " . . .	1.50	24-in. " . . .	2.25
22-in. " . . .	1.75	24-in. " . . .	2.50
22-in. " . . .	2.00	24-in. " . . .	3.00

GUINET & CIE. BLACK SILKS.

20-in. wide, . . .	$1.00	22-in. wide, . .	$1.75
21-in. " . . .	1.25	22-in. " . .	2.00
22-in. " . . .	1.50		

OUR CHALLENGE BLACK SILKS.

24-in. wide, . . .	$1.00	22-in. wide, . . .	$1.50
22-in. " . . .	1.25	Best values ever retailed in America.	

BLACK FAILLE FRANCAISE SILKS.

21-in. wide, . . .	$0.69	24-in. wide, . . .	$0.89
21-in. " . . .	.79	24-in. " . . .	1.00
22-in. " . . .	.89	24-in. " . . .	1.25
22-in. " . . .	1.00	24-in. " . . .	1.50
22-in. " . . .	1.25	24-in. " . . .	1.75
22-in. " . . .	1.50	24-in. " . . .	2.00

BLACK SATIN RHADAMES.

20-in. wide, . . .	$0.69	24-in. wide, . . .	$0.89
20-in. " . . .	.75	24-in. " . . .	1.00
21-in. " . . .	1.00	24-in. " . . .	1.10
21-in. " . . .	1.25	24-in. " . . .	1.25
22-in. " . . .	1.50	24-in. " . . .	1.50
22-in. " . . .	1.75	24-in. " . . .	1.75
22-in. " . . .	2.00	24-in. " . . .	2.00

THE MERCANTILE HEART OF NEW ENGLAND.

BLACK SATIN DUCHESS SILKS.

21-in. wide,	$1.00	24-in. wide,	$1.50
22-in. "	1.25	24-in. "	2.00
22-in. "	1.50	24-in. "	2.50
23-in. "	1.75	24-in. "	3.00
23-in. "	2.00	24-in. "	4.00

BLACK ARMURE ROYAL SILKS.

20-in. wide,	$0.75	21-in. wide,	$1.25
20-in. "	1.00	22-in. "	1.50

BLACK PEAU DE SOIE SILKS.

20-in. wide,	$1.00	23-in. wide,	$1.25
21-in. "	1.25	23-in. "	1.50
22-in. "	1.50		

BLACK FAMILY SURAH SILKS.

20-in. wide,	$0.49	24-in. wide,	$0.69
20-in. "	.69	24-in. "	.89
21-in. "	.75	24-in. "	1.00
22-in. "	.69	24-in. "	1.00
22-in. "	.79	24-in. "	1.25
23-in. "	.89	24-in. "	1.50

BLACK AMERICAN SURAH SILKS.

20-in. wide,	$0.59	24-in. wide,	$0.69
21-in. "	.69	24-in. "	.89
23-in. "	.79	24-in. "	1.00
24-in. "	1.00	24-in. "	1.25

FACTS THAT WILL REPAY ALL TO CONSIDER.

The question with you is where to get the best value for your money. The question with us is how best to do justice to our reputation,—how to meet the requirements of every one of our customers in such a way that the business connection between us will be a lasting one. It would not pay us to lose a single customer by disappointing the high expectations that are justly held of us. We make a special study of the needs of our patrons, and our long experience enables us to do this as well from a letter describing what they desire as if they could come personally to inspect the goods.

COLORED SILK DEPARTMENT.

COLORED GROS GRAIN SILKS.

20-in. wide,	$0.75	20-in. wide,	$1.00

COLORED FAILLE FRANCAISE.

20-in. wide,	$1.00	22-in. wide,	$1.50
21-in. "	1.25		

COLORED SURAH SILKS.

20-in. wide,	$0.69	24-in. wide,	$0.85
21-in. "	.75	24-in. "	1.00
24-in. "	.85		

COLORED ARMURE ROYAL SILKS.

20-in. wide,	$1.00	22-in. wide,	$1.50

COLORED SATIN RHADAMES.

20-in. wide,	$0.75	22-in. wide,	$1.25
21-in. "	1.00		

COLORED SATIN DUCHESS.

22-in. wide,	$1.50	24-in. wide,	$2.00

COLORED MOIRE SILKS.

22-in. wide,	$1.00	22-in. wide,	$1.50

EVENING SILKS.

SILKS FOR WEDDINGS AND BALLS.

20-in. wide,	$1.00	22-in. wide,	$1.50
22-in. "	1.25	22-in. "	2.00

FANCY NOVELTIES IN SILKS.

20-in. wide,	$0.75	22-in. wide,	$1.25
22-in. "	1.00		

SATIN DEPARTMENT.

19 and 20 in. Satin,	$0.50	20-in. Black Satin,	$0.75
20 and 22 in. "	1.00	22-in. "	1.00
18-in. Black Satin,	.50	22-in. "	1.25

LARGEST STOCK IN AMERICA
OF
RICH PARIS NOVELTIES,

In all the very latest combinations, ranging from the simple, plain effects to the most wonderful and elegant productions of the looms of the Old World. If you want a combination for a Silk or Woollen Fabric, send us a sample, and we will send by return mail the proper effect to combine.

BLACK and WHITE SURAH SILKS, FOULARDS, PONGEE and CHINA SILKS,

In Stripes, Figures, Checks, Plaids, and Polka Dots.
For elderly ladies or those confined to mourning, you cannot help making a selection from our enormous collection. Prices in every instance guaranteed the lowest.

DOMESTIC SILK NOVELTIES,

In Surahs, Satin Finished Effects, and Gros Grains, both in Brocades, Stripes, and Plaids. In our new collection we offer only the very latest combinations for costumes, skirts, and trimmings.

PLUSH DEPARTMENT.

16-in. Colored Silk Plushes,	$0.39	24-in. Colored Silk Plush,	$1.00
18-in. " " "	.49	24-in. " " "	1.25
18-in. " " "	.69	24-in. " " "	1.50
28-in. " " "	.79	24-in. " " "	1.75
20-in. " " "	1.25	24-in. " " "	2.00
21-in. " " "	1.50		

BLACK SILK PLUSHES.

18-in. wide,	$0.59	24-in. wide,	$1.00
18-in. "	.75	24-in. "	1.25
18-in. "	1.00	24-in. "	1.50
18-in. "	1.25	24-in. "	1.75
22-in. "	1.50	24-in. "	2.00

COSTUME SILK PLUSHES.

22-in. wide,	$1.50	24-in. wide,	$1.50
24-in. "	2.00	24-in. "	2.00
24-in. "	1.00	24-in. "	2.50

SILK PLUSHES FOR FANCY WORK.

16-in. wide,	$0.39	24-in. wide,	$1.00
18-in. "	.49	24-in. "	1.25
18-in. "	.69	24-in. "	1.50

VELVETEEN DEPARTMENT.
COLORED SILK FINISHED VELVETEENS.

20-in. wide,	$0.50	22-in. wide,	$1.00
21-in. "	.75		

BLACK SILK FINISHED VELVETEENS.

20-in. wide,	$0.37½	22-in. wide,	$1.00
20-in. "	.50	24-in. "	1.25
21-in. "	.75		

IMPORTANT NOTICE.

To all who request, we will send samples FREE of charge, asking only that the KIND OF GOODS, RANGE OF PRICES, and COLORS WANTED, be explicitly stated, so that we can send you just what you want, instead of a great lot of samples, which are of no use to you, and which cost us considerable money.

THE MERCANTILE HEART OF NEW ENGLAND.

VELVETS.

BLACK SILK VELVETS.

17-in. wide, ... $0.75	22-in. wide, ... $1.00
17-in. " 1.00	22-in. " 1.25
18-in. " 1.00	24-in. " 1.50
18-in. " 1.25	24-in. " 1.75
18-in. " 1.50	24-in. " 2.00
19-in. " 2.00	24-in. " 5.50

COLORED SILK VELVETS.

16-in. wide, ... $0.75	19-in. wide, ... $1.00
18-in. " 75	19-in. " 1.25
18-in. " 1.00	19-in. " 1.50
18-in. " 1.25	19-in. " 2.00

BLACK AND COLORED LYONS SILK VELVETS.

20-in. Colored, . . . $4.00	24-in. Colored, . . . $5.00
20-in. " . . . 5.00	27-in. " . . . 7.50
20-in. " . . . 6.00	27-in. " . . . 10.00

BLACK ALL SILK VELVETS.

20-in. wide, ... $3.00	27-in. wide, ... $5.00
20-in. " 4.00	27-in. " 6.00
20-in. " 5.00	27-in. " 7.00
24-in. " 5.00	27-in. " 8.00
24-in. " 6.00	27-in. " 9.00

COLORED COSTUME VELVETS.

22-in. wide, ... $2.00	18-in. wide, ... $2.00
22-in. " 3.00	22-in. " 2.00

FOR FANCY WORK. We have in stock this season the largest collection of popular Fabrics, both in Plain and Printed effects. Send for samples.

The Popular Fabric of the Season.

COLORED CREPE DE CHINE.

22-in. wide, ... $1.00	24-in. wide, ... $1.50
24-in. " 1.25	

In the largest and most exquisite line of light and dark shades ever offered by any house in the United States.

LINING SILK DEPARTMENT.

Black Lining Silks, . . $0.50	Colored Lining Silks, . . $0.50
" " " . . .75	" " " . . .75

MATTERS CONCERNING THE LARGEST DEPARTMENT IN OUR ESTABLISHMENT.

SILKS.

Never in the history of our business have we made such strenuous efforts to place before our patrons the greatest values in Silks, Velvets, Satins, and Plushes to be found on this continent. Being universally acknowledged the headquarters in America for Silks, all who will investigate our collection will pronounce this assertion beyond contradiction. If you do not find mentioned in this Catalogue what you want, write for samples, as we carry in stock every known weave in Silk Fabrics, many of which we have omitted to advertise, owing to limited space.

JORDAN, MARSH & CO.

BUTTONS.

Buttons form an essential part of a fashionable gown (or garment) this season. All styles are used, both large and small, Crochet, Jet, Gilt, Metal, Steel, Pearl, Buffalo Horn, Ivory, and Pearl and Steel combinations. Fancy buttons are the leading feature of the Spring novelties. We will send sample of buttons, if desired (the same to be returned).

GILT BUTTONS.

French gilt buttons, both ball or flat, 25, 37½, 42, 50, and 62½c. per dozen (according to size).
Engraved, triple plate, gilt or silver, 25, 37½, 42, and 50c.
Gilt or silver buttons, ball shape or flat, 10, 12½, 15, 17, and 20c. per doz.
Fine riveted steel (dress sizes), 50, 62½, 75c., $1.00 to 2.50 per doz.
Pearl and steel, 50, 62½, 75, 87½c., $1.00, 1.25 to 6.00 per doz.
Miniature buttons (large sizes), $15.00 per doz.
Pearl buttons (both "sew through" or shank, for tailor gowns, jackets, etc.), 25, 37½, 42c. per doz. (small sizes). Large, 42, 62½, 75, 87½c., $1.00, 1.25, 1.50 to 12.00 per doz.
Pearl buttons (for wash dresses), 12½, 15, 20, 25, 37½ to 75c. per doz.
Enamelled (dress sizes), $1.00, 1.50, and 2.00 per doz.
Large, $4.00 and 5.00 per doz.
Sterling silver (ball shape, 18 line), $6.00 per doz.
Sterling silver, fine cut and engraved (24 line and 28 line), $6.00, 7.00, 7.50 to 10.50 per doz.
Engraved metal button, 10, 12½, 15, 20, 33, 37½c., to $1.00 per doz.
Engraved pearl button, 25, 37½, 42, 50, 75c., to $1.00 per doz.

JET BUTTONS.

Jet, diamond cut, both ball shape or flat (dress sizes), 25, 37½, 42, 50, 62½, 75, 87½c., and $1.00 per doz.
"Riveted jet improved," 25, 37½, and 50c. per doz.
Fancy jet, 25, 37½, 42, 50, and 62½c. per doz.
Fine jet, with riveted steel points, 25, 37½, 42, 50, 62½, and 75c. per doz.
Pressed jet, 10 to 20c. per doz.
Mat jet (for mourning), 12½, 20, 25, 37½, 42 to $1.50 per doz.

CROCHET BUTTONS.

Colored crochet, pure silk, hand made (ball shape), 42c. per doz. (these are made to our order, and all the very latest shades).
Colored crochet, pure silk, hand made, flat or ball shape, 30c. per doz.
Colored crochet (large sizes), $1.25 per doz.
Black silk crochet, dress sizes (ball or flat), 20, 25, 37½, 42, 50, 62½, 75, 87½c. per doz.
Black silk crochet, large sizes, 75c., $1.00, 1.50, 2.00, 2.50, 3.00 to 8.00 per doz. (according to size and pattern).
Black silk crochet, large sizes (square shape), $1.25, 1.50, 1.75, 2.00, 2.50, 3.00, and 4.00 per doz.
Black beaded crochet, ball shape or flat, 42, 50, 62½, 75, 87½c., and $1.00 per doz. (dress sizes). Large sizes, $1.00, 1.50, 2.00, 2.50 to 4.00 per doz.

OLIVES.

Black silk crochet olives, 75, 87½c., $1.00, 1.25, 1.50, 2.00, 2.50 per doz.
Black Mohair Olives, 25, 37½, 50c. per doz.
Colored silk olives (small sizes), 50c. per doz.
Colored silk olives (large sizes), 62½, 75c per doz.
Colored mohair olives, 37½c. per doz.

BRAID BUTTONS.

Colored silk braid buttons, 22 line, 10c. per doz.; 28 line, 15c. per doz.
Colored mohair, 22 line, 10c. per doz.; 28 line, 15c. per doz.
Black silk braided buttons, 20, 25, 37½, 42 to 50c. per doz.
Mohair braid buttons (black), 12½, 15, 20, 25 to 75c. per doz.
Silk, bombazine, and lasting buttons, 8, 12½, 15, 20, 25 to 50c. per doz.
Black velvet buttons, 15, 20, 25 to 50c. per doz.

BUFFALO HORN BUTTONS.

Ball shape or flat, 25, 37½, 50, 62½c. to $1.00 per doz.
Tailor buttons, in all the new effects (both horn and ivory), 12½, 15, 20, 25, 37½, 42, 50, 62½, 75, and 87½c.
White or natural pearl, 10, 12½, 15, 20, 25 to 87½c.
White pearl (ball shape), fine engraved, 25, 37½, 42, 50, 62½, 75, and 87½c. per doz.
Shirt buttons, 12½, 15, 20, and 25c. per doz.
Bone (for underwear), 20, 25, 37½, and 75c. per gross.
Lace buttons, 6, 8, 10, 12½, 20 to 37½c. per doz.
Linen buttons, 6, 8, 10, 12½c. per doz.
Boot buttons, 13c. per gross.
Ivory buttons, for wash dresses, all colors, 10c. per card of two dozen (by card only).
Special.—We have had made a book of linen buttons, 6 doz. in the book, of various sizes, for 10c. each.
Leather buttons. The latest Paris novelty, 37½ to 87½c. per doz.

BUCKLES.

Clasps, Buckles, and Slides.—We are constantly adding all the late novelties.
Metal Clasps.—13, 20, 25c. each.
Pearl Clasps.—38, 50, 75c. to $1.50 each.
Oxidized, Bronze, or Silver Clasps.—62½, 75, 87½c., $1.00, 1.50, 1.75, and 2.00 each.
Enamelled or Jewelled Clasps.—$1.50, 1.75, 2.00 to 3.00 each.
Sterling Silver Buckles.—$3.00, 4.00, 5.00, 6.00 to 9.00 each (according to weight).
Rolled Gold Buckles (on white metal).—62½, 75c., $1.00, 1.50 to 4.00 each.
Pearl Buckles (white, snail, or natural).—42, 50, 62½, 75c. to $3.00 each.
Steel Buckles.—25, 37½, 50, 75c., $1.00 to 3.00 each (according to size and quality).
Rhinestone Buckles.—$1.00, 1.50, 2.00, 3.00 to 8.00 each.
SPECIAL.—A Late Paris Novelty.—A large Hook and Eye, silver, gold, or oxidized, $1.38 each.
In ordering above goods, please state the length desired; also, whether slide or buckle.

CARPETINGS AND RUGS.

CARPETINGS.

For the present spring trade we have in stock a superb assortment of

GOBELINS

. . . AND . . .

AXMINSTERS

in the most delicate soft tints, suited to the finest furnishings of the Drawing Room and Parlor, ... $2.25 per yard.

ENGLISH WILTONS

$3.00 per yard.

BIGELOW AND LOWELL WILTONS

$2.25 and 2.50 per yard.

BODY BRUSSELS.

We have secured over 70 private designs in **Bigelow, Lowell,** and other leading makes of Brussels Carpetings, with ⅝ Borders, ... Prices, $1.25, 1.35, and 1.50 per yard.

SMITH'S MOQUETTES

In all the newest colorings, ... $1.65 per yard.

AGRA CARPETING

$1.00 per yard.

INGRAIN CARPETING

In an almost endless variety of the Lowell Manufacturing Co., at . . . . 75c per yard. Likewise other Ingrain Carpets from . . 25 to 50c per yard.

ROXBURY TAPESTRIES.

We carry every pattern of these famous floor coverings at the very lowest price.

CHINA MATTINGS.

Our direct importation has just landed, and is of a most superior quality of sound, fresh straw, in white and fancy, at 12½ to 50c per yard.

OIL CLOTHS AND LINOLEUMS

In all widths.

ENGLISH BRUSSELS.

28 private designs with beautiful borders, only $1.75 per yard.

We shall give to the Carpet Department our most earnest attention, and will endeavor to make it the leading branch of our mammoth establishment.

ORIENTAL RUGS

Of a very large variety in regular sizes and odd shapes to fit any corridor, hall, or room, in

PERSIANS,

MECCAS,

CARABAGHS,

GHIORDES,

DAGHESTANS,

AND CASHMERES.

Send for one of our Daghestan Rugs at . . . . . $10.00.

SCOTCH ART SQUARES.

Very durable and inexpensive.

2½ yards by 3 yards,	. . . .	$3.00
3 " " 3 "	. . . .	3.50
3 " " 4 "	. . . .	4.00
3½ " " 4 "	. . . .	4.50

ALL WOOL KENSINGTON ART SQUARES.

2½ yards by 3 yards,	. . . .	$6.75
3 " " 3 "	. . . .	8.25
3 " " 3½ "	. . . .	9.50
3 " " 4 "	. . . .	11.00
4 " " 4 "	. . . .	14.75
4 " " 5 "	. . . .	18.50

SMYRNA RUGS

Of every size, including whole carpets at popular prices.

SCOTCH BRUSSELS RUGS.

36 inches square, ... only 58c each.

BRUSH MATS

All sizes and prices, ... from 50c to $4.00 each.

CARPET SWEEPERS.

$3.50 each.

THE MERCANTILE HEART OF NEW ENGLAND.

"LOWELL"

WILTONS,

BRUSSELS,

INGRAINS.

FOR MORE THAN A HALF-CENTURY

LOWELL CARPETS

HAVE BEEN ACKNOWLEDGED

BY ALL TO BE THE BEST.

THE WORD "LOWELL" APPEARS IN CAPITAL LETTERS in the back of Lowell Wilton and Body Brussels at every repeat of the pattern.

LOOK CAREFULLY to the trade-marks, and be sure you get the genuine "Lowell" Carpets.

THE LOWELL INGRAINS are wound upon a hollow stick, which the U.S. Court decided to be a valid trade mark. The stick is in two solid pieces, with the name of the LOWELL MANUF'G CO. Stamped within.

Beware of Imitations.

These goods are invariably full width, and may be had in a large variety of designs, which for technique and coloring are unequalled, rendering them especially appropriate for artistic homes.

The grade has never been lowered, and the Company unhesitatingly challenge comparison with the production of any manufacturer in the world.

"LOWELL"

COTTONS.

BLEACHED AND UNBLEACHED, ALSO SHEETS AND PILLOW SLIPS.

WE can assure our patrons that the best values in Cotton will always be found with us, our stock comprising a full line of Bleached, Half Bleached, and Unbleached, from one yard wide to full sheeting widths.

BLEACHED COTTONS.

36 inches wide,	5, 6¼, 7, 8, 9, 10, 11, 12½, and 15c per yard.
42 " "	10, 11, 12½, 14, and 15c per yard.
45 " "	12½, 14, 15, 16, and 17c per yard.
48 " "	18c per yard.
50 " "	16, 18, and 19c per yard.
54 " "	18 and 20c per yard.
63 " "	20, 22, 27, and 37½c per yard.
72 " "	22, 24, 31, and 47c per yard.
81 " "	25, 26, 33, and 50c per yard.
90 " "	27, 28, 29, 35, and 53c per yard.
99 " "	45 and 60c per yard.
108 " "	50c per yard.

Please state when ordering if **Fine, Medium,** or **Heavy Weight** Cotton is desired.

TWILLED BLEACHED COTTON.

36 inches wide,	12½, 14, and 17c per yard.
81 " "	35c per yard.
90 " "	37½c per yard.

DOUBLE WARP BLEACHED COTTON.

36 inches wide,	12½ and 15c per yard.
81 " "	35c per yard.
90 " "	37½c per yard.

UNBLEACHED COTTON.

36 inches wide,	5, 6¼, 7, 8, and 9c per yard.
40 " "	7, 8, 9, and 10c per yard.
42 " "	10 and 11c per yard.
45 " "	11, 12½, and 14c per yard.
49 " "	14 and 15c per yard.
54 " "	16 and 17c per yard.
58 " "	18 and 20c per yard.
67 " "	20 and 22c per yard.
78 " "	22 and 24c per yard.
87 " "	25 and 26c per yard.

Please state when ordering if **Fine, Medium,** or **Heavy Weight** Cotton is desired.

LONSDALE CAMBRIC.

36 inches wide, 12½c per yard.

BERKLEY CAMBRIC.

36 inches wide, 14 and 16c per yard.

COTTON SHEETS AND PILLOW SLIPS.

Pillow Slips, "Androscoggin Cotton," well made, size 20 x 37 inches, 30c per pair.

Pillow Slips, "Alexander Cotton," well made, size 20 x 37 inches, 34c per pair; 22 x 37 inches, 40c per pair.

Pillow Slips, "Langdon Cotton," well made, size 20 x 37 inches, 40c per pair; 22 x 37 inches, 50c per pair.

Pillow Slips, "Fruit of the Loom Cotton," well made, size 20 x 37 inches, 40c per pair; 22 x 37 inches, 50c per pair.

Pillow Slips, "Wamsutta Cotton," well made, size 24 x 37 inches, 68c per pair; 25 x 37 inches, 72c per pair; 27 x 37 inches, 76c per pair.

Bolster Slips, "Fruit of the Loom Cotton," well made, size 18 x 74 inches, 35c each; 20 x 74 inches, 40c each; 22 x 74 inches, 45c each.

Bleached Sheets, "Pequot Sheeting," well made, size 1¾ x 2½ yards, $1.24 per pair; 2 x 2½ yards, $1.38 per pair; 2¼ x 2⅝ yards, $1.40 per pair; 2½ x 2⅝ yards, $1.50 per pair.

Unbleached Sheets, "Pequot Sheeting," well made, size 67 x 90 inches, $1.24 per pair; 78 x 95 inches, $1.38 per pair; 87 x 95 inches, $1.50 per pair.

Our sheets are finished with three and one inch hem. Pillow and Bolster slips finished with three inch hem.

Orders for large or small quantities promptly filled.

Special sizes made to order.

Colored Cheese Cloth, 36 inches wide, 12½c per yard. Extra fine quality. Largely used for evening dresses and fancy costumes.

SOUDAN OR COLORED CHEESE CLOTH.

24 inches wide, 6¼c per yard.

These goods are extensively used for decorative purposes, taking the place of the more expensive bunting. They are also used for fancy draperies. Samples will be sent on application. We have them in the following shades: Light, Medium, and Dark Blue, Cream, Corn, Old Gold, Cardinal, Light and Medium Pink, Mikado, Rose Pink, Shrimp, Red, Black, White, Navy Blue, Absinthe, Fawn, Nile Green, Lavender, Ecru, Medium Green.

CURTAIN SCRIM.

40 inches wide, 5 and 10c per yard, all Cream Ground, Woven Lace Work.

PRINTED PONGEE.

A close imitation of China Silk, 32 inches wide, 15c per yard.

These goods have a special adaptability for curtain draperies, side-lights, short curtains, etc., taking the place in many cases of the genuine silk.

COLORED DRESS GOODS.

WE are unquestionably the leaders and headquarters in the United States for COLORED DRESS GOODS. We have for the spring and summer of 1891 one of the Largest and Best Selected Stocks that it has been our pleasure to place before the public. We wish to call *Special Attention* to our large stock of every conceivable material known in Imported Dress Fabrics. It has been our aim to make this season far eclipse any ever before attempted.

NOVELTIES.

We have opened the largest and most complete line of high grade novelties ever imported. They are in all the choice combinations, both all wool and silk and wool, from the French, German, and English manufacturers. The majority of these goods are exclusive, and contain only one dress pattern each.

EMBROIDERED DRESS PATTERNS.

We shall offer this season a superb variety of combinations and colorings. Prices range from $7.50 to 50.00.

HIGH ART NOVELTIES.

We shall show all the newest styles and weaves in stripes, plaids, diagonal weaves, polka dots effects. Prices, from $1.25 to 2.50 per yard.

CAMEL'S HAIR,

Including plain colors and mixtures, with the long hair attached. Also in the natural or self-color. Prices, from 50c. to $2.50 per yard. Widths, 36 to 50 inches.

BROADCLOTHS

In a splendid variety of shades, for tailor-made dresses, 50 inches wide. Prices, $1.25, 1.50, 2.00, 2.50, and 2.75 per yard.

OUR CELEBRATED BARJEON WOOL HENRI-ETTAS AND CASHMERES.

In these beautiful materials we are pleased to announce that we shall offer the most extensive assortment of all the new and desirable colorings that have ever been shown. No comments on these goods are necessary, for they are justly celebrated and favorably known from Maine to California. The 50c. quality, 40 inches wide; the 75c., $1.00, and 1.25 quality are full 45 inches wide. We call particular attention to the quality we are offering at 75 cents, full 45 inches wide.

SILK WARP HENRIETTAS,

Embracing all the new and desirable colorings, 40 inches wide. Prices, $1.00 and 1.25 per yard.

FIFTY-INCH COSTUME CLOTHS,

In all the new and stylish spring styles, in mixtures, plaids, stripes, and bouclé effects, for street dresses. Prices, $1.00, 1.25, 1.50, 2.00, and 2.50 per yard.

SILK AND WOOL LANSDOWN.

The effect of this beautiful material for evening wear is of the richest description, combining as it does a rich, silky sheen, with splendid wearing qualities. These goods we are showing in a larger scope of colorings than ever before, including cream and ivory white, and a full line of tints and delicate shades. Width, 40 inches. Price, $1.25 per yard.

THE MERCANTILE HEART OF NEW ENGLAND.

INDIA TWILLS AND SERGES.

A full line of colors and splendid value. The 50c. quality, 38 and 40 inches wide; the 75c. and $1.00, 38 to 46 inches wide.

ALL WOOL CREPE DE CHINE,

In both street and evening shades. Prices, 75c. and $1.00 per yard. 40 inches wide.

BEIGES,

In all colors. Prices, 50, 75c., and $1.00. Width, 40 to 50 inches.

BEDFORD CORDS.

This is an entirely new weave this season, and destined to become one of the most popular fabrics for ladies' dresses. Width, 40 to 50 inches. Prices, $1.25, 1.50, 2.00, 2.50 per yard.

COLORED GRENADINES.

The indications are for the coming season that Black Ground Grenadines, with bright colored figures and spots, will be very popular. We shall show large lines of them, ranging from $1.00 to 3.00 per yard.

SPECIAL.

We always carry in stock large lines of low-priced **Dress Goods**, ranging in prices from 12½, 15, 17, 19, 25, 29, 37½, and 50c., consisting of plaids, stripes, mixtures, checks, plain goods, and in fact everything in low-priced Dress Goods.

ENGLISH MOHAIRS AND BRILLIANTINES

Will be very popular this season. For durability these goods are unexcelled. All the new and plain colors, gray and brown mixtures. Also, brocades, stripes, checks, and fancy weaves. Widths, 27 to 54 inches. Prices, 25, 29, 37½, 50, 62½, 75c., and $1.00 per yard.

We call attention to the line of

ENGLISH MOHAIRS

that we shall retail this season at 29c. per yard. These are in plaids, checks, stripes, plain colors. Also, gray and brown mixtures. In fact, 40 different styles and colorings.

EVENING, PARTY, AND WEDDING DRESS GOODS,

Consisting of **Albatross, Nun's Veiling, Lansdowns, Henriettas, Wool Crapon Grenadines,** and all kinds of **Dress Goods** for evening wear. Prices, 50c. to $1.50 per yard.

IMPORTED WASH-DRESS FABRICS.

We shall display this season for inspection the largest and most varied assortment of these beautiful fabrics which we have ever shown, selected from all the new and original designs of the most celebrated manufacturers of Europe.

French Sateens, Scotch Zephyr Ginghams, Linen Lawns, Printed India Linens, Figured Jaconets, and **Plain** and **Figured Organdie Muslins.**

We call attention to the new style **Jacquard Sateen,** in black and colored ground, with printed figures.

We are displaying a handsome line of **Zephyr Ginghams,** at 17 and 25c. per yard.

P. S.—Samples of all of the above goods sent *free* on application.

LININGS.

Cambrics, in all shades, in soft finish and glazing.

Silesias, in American and English, 10, 12½, 15, 20, 25, and 30c yard.

Fancy Silesias, in striped, checked, brocaded, and watered, for ladies' waist lining. These linings are being used very much, and add to the finish of a dress. 15, 20, 25, 33, 37½, and 50c yard.

Double-faced Lining, for Buntings and Black Silks. The goods come black on one side, and white and fancy on the other; this, as a lady will see, makes them very desirable for black dresses. 15, 20, 25, 33, and 37½c yard.

Also in Cambric. 8, 10, and 12½c yard.

Canvas, in black, white, brown, and slate, for dress facings, 17, 20, and 25c yard.

Crinoline, in checked and plain, white, black, and slate, 8, 10, 12½, 15, and 25c yard.

Wiggin, black, white, and slate, 10 and 12½c yard.

Bunting, for flags, 18 inches, red, white, and blue, 25c yard.

Cotton Sateens, in all shades, 40 inches wide. A lining very much used for quilt linings. 25 and 33c yard.

Hair Cloth, 16, 17, 18 inches wide, 20, 25, 33, 37½, and 50c yard.

A new thin lining, namely, Percaline, in all shades, 36 inches, 15, 17, and 25c yard.

All Wool Moreen, for skirts, 24 inches wide, in all shades, 50c yard.

All Wool Serge, for skirts, 50c yard.

Wool Wadding, dark and white, 20c sheet.

Cotton Wadding, black and white, 4c sheet.

Black Lastings, 27 inches wide, 20, 25, 37½, and 50c yard.

Black Lastings, 54 inches wide, 75, 87½c, $1.00, 1.25, 1.50, 1.62½, 1.75 yard.

A MODEL WAIST LINING.

THE MOSCHCOWITZ.

We have tried all kinds of linings and all kinds of charts, and our decision centres down to the MOSCHCOWITZ, which is simply without equal. Send us your correct bust measurement (measuring slightly above the bust under the arms, drawing the measure tighter than the dress is going to fit), and we will send you a marked lining, either in black, white, medium light, or dark shade gray, that will fit to perfection. Kindly state what shade or size you want. Following are the sizes and prices:—

Sizes, 27 x 28, 29 x 30, 31 x 32, 33 x 34, 39c; 35 x 36, 37 x 38, 39 x 40, 45c; 41 x 42, 43 x 44, 48c.

27-inch Lastings, in all shades, to match spring and summer dress goods, 37½ and 50c yard.

Levantines, in black, white, and fancy shades. Goods used for waist linings, part silk and linen. 50, 62½, and 75c yard.

Lining Silks, in plain and twilled, all shades, 50, 62½, and 75c yard. Fancy Striped and Checked Silk and Satin Linings for coats.

We also carry a full line of Tailors' Trimmings, such as lastings, satins, and silk sleeve linings, 25c to $2.00 yard.

Fast Black Cambrics and Silesias that do not change color. Cambrics, 7 and 10c; silesias, 15, 20, and 25c yard.

Nursery Sheeting, in the following widths and prices: 3-4 wide, 50c yard; 4-4 wide, 75c yard; 5-4 wide, $1.00 yard; 6-4 wide, $1.25 yard.

Also Rubber Sheets, for nursery use. 3-4 square, 38c; 4-4 square, 75c; 5-4 square, $1.25; 6-4 square, $1.75.

EXTRA.—We make special inducements to dressmakers purchasing linings, and our stock is complete.

THE MERCANTILE HEART OF NEW ENGLAND.

BLACK DRESS GOODS.

IN this department we are prepared to show the largest and most complete line of All Wool and Silk and Wool, both plain and fancy weaves, ever imported. Carefully selected from all the leading English, French, and German manufacturers.

In connection with the All Black, our patrons will find a magnificent line of Black and White and Half Mourning Dress Goods.

ENGLISH MOHAIRS,
BRILLIANTINES,
SICILIANS,
AND MOHAIR TAMISE,

In all the Newest Plain and Fancy Effects in Blacks and Grays.

These are among the most stylish materials for this season. The fact that these goods can be used equally well for house, street, or travelling wear, makes them extremely desirable. Widths, 27 to 54 inches. Price, 25, 37½, 50, 62½, 75c., $1.00, 1.25 up to 2.00 per yard.

Pure silk and wool Henrietta Cloth, width 40 inches. Price, $1.00, 1.25, 1.37½, 1.50, 2.00, 2.50 up to 5.00 per yard.

Our Celebrated "Barjeon" Black Cashmere. Controlled exclusively by us. This make is ntoed for its heavy weight and elegant finish and splendid wearing qualities. Width, 38 to 46 inches. Price, 50, 62½, 75, 87½c., $1.00, 1.25, 1.50 up to 2.50 per yard.

Thibets and Merinos. Width, 44 to 46 inches. Price, $1.00, 1.25, 1.50, 2.00 per yard.

All Wool Henrietta Silk Finish. Width, 46 inches. Price, 75c., $1.00, 1.25, 1.50 per yard.

French India Twills. Width, 38 to 46 inches. Price, 50, 62½, 75, 87½c., $1.00, 1.25, 1.50 per yard.

English, French, German Diagonals and Serges. Width, 38 to 46 inches. Price, 75, 87½c., $1.00, 1.25, 1.50, 1.75, 2.00 per yard.

French Foulé. Width, 38 to 46 inches. Price, 75c., $1.00, 1.25 per yard.

Drap d'Alma, all wool, and silk and wool. Width, 38 to 46 inches. Price, 75c, $1.00, 1.25, 1.50, 1.75, 2.00, 2.50 per yard.

English, French, and German Stripes and Cords. Width, 38 to 44 inches. Price, 75c., $1.00, 1.25, 1.50 per yard.

Sebastopol, Rayé, and Brocades. Width, 40 to 44 inches. Price, 75c., $1.00, 1.25, 1.50 per yard.

English, French, and German Broadcloths. Width, 44 to 54 inches. Price, 75c., $1.00, 1.25, 1.50, 1.75, 2.00, 2.50, 2.75, 3.00, 3.50 per yard.

Tricots. Width, 38 to 54 inches. Price, 50, 62½, 75c., $1.00, 1.25, 1.50, 2.00, 2.50 per yard.

Lastings. Width, 27 to 54 inches. Price, 25, 37½, 50, 75c., $1.00, 1.25, 1.50 per yard.

Nun's Veilings for Veils. We always carry a full line, both all wool and silk and wool, with border, both the celebrated B. Priestly & Co. and Ecroyd's make. Width, 40 to 44 inches. Price, 75c., $1.00, 1.25, 1.50, 1.75, 2.00, 2.50, 3.00, 3.50, 4.00 per yard.

Courtauld's English Crapes. For Veils and Trimming. We keep a full line constantly in stock. Price, 75c. to $10.00 per yard.

Drap-d'Été. Width, 46 inches. Price, $2.00, 2.50, 3.00, 3.50, 4.00, 4.50 per yard.

Cashmere Biarritz. Width, 40 to 44 inches. Price, 75c., $1.00, 1.25, 1.50 per yard.

Nun's Serge. Width, 38 to 56 inches. Price, 50, 75c., $1.00, 1.25, 1.50 per yard.

Nun's Cord. Width, 40 to 44 inches. Price, $1.00, 1.25, 1 50, 2.00 per yard.

Camel's Hair. A full line of light and medium weights, for dresses and wraps. Width, 40 to 52 inches. Price, 75c., $1.00, 1.25, 1.50, 1.75, 2.00, 2.50 up to 6.00 per yard.

We also wish to state that our patrons will always find a full and complete line of plain and fancy effects of the celebrated B. Priestly & Co. manufacture, Bradford, England.

Venetian Crape Cloth. Width, 40 to 44 inches. Price, 75c., $1.00, 1.25, 1.50, 2.00 per yard.

Plain All Silk Grenadine. Width, 22 to 42 inches. Price, 75, 87½c., $1.00, 1.25, 1.50, 1.75, 2.00, 2.50 per yard.

Brocaded and Fancy Grenadines. Width, 18 to 24 inches. Price, 37½, 50, 62½, 75c., $1.00 per yard.

Brocaded, Figured, and Striped All Silk Grenadines. Width, 22 to 24 inches. Price, $1.00, 1.25, 1.50, 1.75, 2.00, 2.50, 3.00 per yard.

Silk and Wool Plain Hernani. Width, 21 to 24 inches. Price, 50, 62½, 75c., $1.00, 1.25, 1.50, 1.75, 2.00 per yard.

Plain and Embroidered Silk Muslins. Width, 22 to 24 inches. Price, 75c., $1.00, 1.25, 1.50, 1.75, 2.00, 2.50 per yard.

Plain Crepe de Chine, All Silk. Width, 22 to 24 inches. Price, $1.25, 1.50, 1.75, 2.00, 2.50 per yard; 46 inches, $3.50, 4.00, 4.50, 5.00, 6.00, 6.50 per yard.

Silk and Wool Crépon. Width, 24 inches. Price, $1.00, 1.25, 1.50, 1.75, 2.00 per yard; 44 inches, $2.50, 3.00, 3.50 per yard.

Brocaded and Figured Crêpe de Chine. Width, 22 to 24 inches. Price, $2.00, 2.50, 3.00 up to 9.00 per yard.

Plain Nun's Veiling, all wool, for dresses. Width, 40 to 44 inches. Price, 50, 62½, 75c., $1.00, 1.25 per yard.

All Wool and Silk and Wool Tamise. Width, 40 to 42 inches. Price, 50, 62½, 75c., $1.00, 1.25, 1.50, 1.75, 2.00 per yard.

All Wool Batiste. Width, 40 to 42 inches. Price, 50, 62½, 75c., $1.00, 1.25 per yard. Silk and Wool, $1.00, 1.25, 1.50, 1.75, 2.00 per yard.

Albatross Cloth, all wool. Width, 38 to 44 inches. Price, 50, 62½, 75c., $1.00 per yard.

Plain and Fancy Bunting. Width, 38 to 42 inches. Price, 50c. to $1.00 per yard.

Checked and Striped Grenadine, all wool. Width, 38 to 42 inches. Price, 75c., $1.00 per yard.

HOSIERY.

LADIES' FAST BLACK COTTON HOSIERY.

No.   Per pair.
X110. Ladies' Black Cotton Hose, fast color, every pair warranted, . $0.25
X111. Ladies' Black Cotton Hose, our celebrated fast dye, every pair
    warranted, ...37½
X112. Ladies' Fast Black Cotton Hose, extra fine quality, warranted not
    to crock or stain, ...50
X115. Ladies' Black Cotton Hose, extra fine quality, stainless dye, . .75
X116. Ladies' Black English Cotton Hose, very fine quality, warranted
    not to stain, ... 1.00 and 1.25

LADIES' COLORED COTTON HOSE.

X117. Ladies' Cotton Hose, light and dark grounds, with fancy stripes
    and boot patterns, sizes 8 to 10, ... $0.25
X118. Ladies' Fancy Cotton Hose, stripes and boot patterns, new designs, .37½
X119. Ladies' extra fine quality Fancy Cotton Hose, including all the
    latest styles, ...50
X120. Ladies' Solid Colored Cotton Hose, light and dark shades, . .25
X121. Ladies' Solid Colored Cotton Hose, mode and tan shades, .37½
X122. Ladies' Solid Colored Cotton Hose, fine quality, ...50
X123. Ladies' Solid Colored Cotton Hose, extra fine quality, mode and
    tan shades, ...75

LADIES' LISLE HOSE.

X124. Ladies' Colored Lisle Hose, ... $0.37½
X125. Ladies' Colored Lisle Hose, fine quality, plain and drop stitch, . .50
X126. Ladies' Colored 4-thread Lisle Hose, all desirable shades, . .75
X127. Ladies' Colored C. G. Paris Lisle Hose, mode, tan, and slates, 1.00
X128. Ladies' Black Lisle Hose, fast dye, ...37½
X129. Ladies' Black Lisle, warranted fast color, ...50
X130. Ladies' Black Lisle Hose, fine quality, warranted not to crock, .75
X131. Ladies' Black C. G. Lisle Hose, split sole, ... 1.00
X132. Ladies' Black C. G. Paris Lisle Hose, ... 1.25
X133. Ladies' Unbleached Lisle Hose, ...37½ and .50
X135. Ladies' Fancy Lisle Hose, in all the newest styles and combina-
    tions, ...50, .75, 1.00, 1.25, 1.50, 1.75, and 2.00

UNBLEACHED BALBRIGGAN HOSE.

X136. Ladies' Balbriggan Hose, heavy, light, and medium weight, $0.25
X137. Ladies' Balbriggan Hose, fine quality, ...37½
X138. Ladies' fine Balbriggan Hose, silk clocked, ...50
X139. Ladies' extra superfine Balbriggan Hose, silk clocked, . .75
X140. Ladies' Real Irish Balbriggan Hose, . 1.00, 1.25, 1.50, and 2.00

OUTSIZE COTTON AND LISLE HOSE.

X141. Ladies' Outsize Unbleached Cotton Hose, . $0.37½, .50, and .62
X142. Ladies' Outsize Colored Cotton Hose, . . .37½, .50, and .75
X143. Ladies' Outsize Black Cotton Hose, warranted fast, .37½, .50, and .75
X144. Ladies' Outsize Black Lisle Hose, ...75
X145. Ladies' Outsize Colored Lisle Hose, mode, tan, and slates, . .75
X146. Ladies' Outsize Unbleached, ...75 and 1.00
X147. Ladies' Outsize Black C. G. Lisle, ... 1.50

OPERA HOSE.

X148. Ladies' Unbleached Cotton Opera Hose, . . . $0.62½, .75
X149. Ladies' Unbleached Lisle Opera Hose, ... 1.00
X150. Ladies' Colored Cotton Opera Hose, ...75
X151. Ladies' Black Lisle Opera Hose, warranted fast color, . 1.25
X152. Ladies' Colored Lisle Opera Hose, all shades, . . 1.25
X153. Ladies' Colored Plated Silk Opera Hose, all shades, . 1.50
X154. Ladies' Black and Colored Cotton Opera Hose, extra fine, . 1.00

LADIES' SILK HOSE.

X155. Ladies' Black Plated Silk Hose, fast dye, ... $0.75
X156. Ladies' Black English Spun Silk Hose, ... 1.00
X157. Ladies' Black English Spun Silk Hose, fine quality,
    1.25, 1.37, 1.50, 1.75, 2.00, and 2.25
X158. Ladies' Black Bright Silk Hose, . 2.00, 2.50, 3.25, 3.50, and 4.50
X159. Ladies' White and Cream Silk Hose, ... 4.00
X160. Ladies' Colored Silk Hose, all desirable shades, . 1.00, 1.50, and 2.75
X161. Ladies' Colored Bright Silk Hose, clocked, all desirable shades, 3.50
X162. Ladies' Bright Silk Hose, lace fronts, cream, pink, sky, white, lav-
    ender, garnet, and black, ... 4.50
X163. Ladies' Fancy Bright Silk Hose, latest Paris styles, elegant com-
    binations, ... from $3.50 to 12.00
X164. Ladies' Outsize Plated Silk Hose, black and colored, . . 1.50
X165. Ladies' Outsize English Spun Silk (black only), . . . 2.25
X166. Ladies' Black Derby Ribbed English Spun Silk, . . . 3.50

CHILDREN'S COTTON HOSIERY.

X167. Black Ribbed Cotton Hose, size 6 to 9½, warranted fast color, $0.25
X168. Black Ribbed Cotton, heavy weight, size 6 to 9½, warranted fast
    color, ...37½
X169. Black 7 x 1 and 2 x 1 Ribbed Cotton Hose:

Sizes,	6,	6½,	7,	7½,	8,	8½,	9,	9½
Price,	$0.37½.	.37½.	.42,	.42,	.50,	.50,	.55,	.62½

X170. Black Ribbed Extra Heavy Double Knee:

Sizes,	6,	6½,	7,	7½,	8,	8½,	9,	9½
Price,	$0.42,	.42,	.50,	.50,	.55,	.55,	.62,	.75

X171. Black French Corduroy, best quality :

Sizes,	7,	7½,	8,	8½,	9,	9½
Price,	$0.62½,	.75,	.87½,	1.00,	1.12½,	1.25.

X172. Misses' Fast Black English Derby Ribbed Cotton Hose :

Sizes,	5,	5½,	6,	6½,	7,	7½,	8,	8½,	9,	9½
Price,	$0.50,	.50,	.55,	.55,	.62½,	.62½,	.70,	.75,	.75,	.75

X173. Misses' Black English Derby Ribbed Cotton Hose, full-fashioned,
    fast color :

Sizes,	5,	5½,	6,	6½,	7,	7½,	8,	8½,	9
Price,	$0.62½,	.75,	.87½,	1.00,	1.12,	1.25,	1.25,	1.37,	1.50

X174. Misses' Plain Black Cotton Hose, fast color, all sizes,
    $0.25, .37½, .50, and .75
X175. Boys' 5 x 3 Ribbed Fast Black Cotton Hose, linen sole, warranted
    not to crock or stain :

Sizes,	6,	6½,	7,	7½,	8,	8½,	9,	9½
Price,	$0.33,	.37½,	.42,	.50,	.50,	.50,	.50,	.55

CHILDREN'S LISLE HOSE.

X176. Misses' Plain Black Lisle Hose, all sizes, warranted not to stain, $0.37½
X177. Misses' Plain Black Lisle Hose, warranted not to stain, . .50
X178. Misses' Ribbed Lisle Hose, fast black, and new tan shades :

Sizes,	6,	6½,	7,	7½,	8,	8½,	9
Price,	$0.50,	.50,	.55,	.55,	.62½,	.62½,	.75

INFANTS' HOSIERY.

X179. Infants' Black Cotton Hose, fast dye, . . $0.25, 37½, and .50
X180. Infants' White Cotton Socks, ...25 and .37½
X181. Infants' White Cotton ¾ Hose, ...25 and .37½
X182. Infants' White Merino Socks, all sizes, ...37½
X183. Infants' White Merino ¾ Hose, ...50
X184. Infants' White Merino Hose, ...50
X185. Infants' Black Cashmere ¾ Hose, all sizes, . .33, .42, and .50
X186. Infants' Black Cashmere Hose, all sizes, . . .37½ and .50
X187. Infants' Colored and Black ¾ Spun Silk Hose, ...75
X188. Infants' Black Spun Silk Socks, ...62½

CHILDREN'S SILK HOSIERY.

X189. Misses' Black Plated Silk Hose, fast color, . . $0.50 to .75
X190. Misses' Black English Spun Silk Hose, split sole :

Sizes,	4,	4½,	5,	5½,	6,	6½,	7,	7½,	8,	8½
Price,	$1.00,	1.00,	1.12½,	1.12½,	1.25,	1.25,	1.37½,	1.37½,	1.50,	1.50

X191. Misses' Black English Spun Silk Hose :

Sizes,	4,	4½,	5,	5½,	6,	6½,	7,	7½,	8,	8½
Price,	$0.38,	.38,	.50,	.50,	.55,	.55,	.55,	.62½,	.62½,	.75

X200. Boys' and Misses' Black Ribbed Silk Hose :

Sizes,	5,	5½,	6,	6½,	7,	7½,	8,	8½,	9,	9½
Price,	$1.12,	1.25,	1.37,	1.50,	1.62,	1.75,	1.87,	2.00,	2.25,	2.50

X201. Misses' and Boys' Black Ribbed Silk Hose, fine quality :

Sizes,	6,	6½,	7,	7½,	8,	8½,	9,	9½
Price,	$2.00,	2.25,	2.50,	2.75,	3.00,	3.25,	3.50,	3.50

GENTLEMEN'S HOSIERY.

X202. Drab and Brown Mixed Seamless Half Hose, heavy and light
    weight, ... $0.12½
X203. Fancy Striped Cotton Half Hose, unbleached and mode grounds,
    all sizes, ...25
X204. Solid Colored Cotton Half Hose, mode, tan, and slates, . .25
X205. Unbleached Cotton Half Hose (our celebrated 1470), . .25
X206. Unbleached Cotton Half Hose, heavy weight, ...25
X207. Shawknit Cotton Half Hose, light and heavy weight, . .25
X208. "Snow Black" Shawknit, ...50
X209. Fancy Striped English Cotton Half Hose, choice styles, . .37½
X210. Solid Colored English Cotton Half Hose, ...37½
X211. Fancy Cotton Half Hose, superior quality, ...50
X212. Plain Cotton Half Hose, superior quality, ...50
X213. Plain and Fancy Cotton Half Hose, ...75
X214. Plain and Fancy Cotton Half Hose, extra fine, . 1.00 and 1.25
X215. Our Warranted Fast Black Cotton Half Hose, extra fine quality,
    . . . . .25, .37½, and .50
X216. Genuine Irish Balbriggan Half Hose, . .50, .75, 1.00, and 1.25
X217. Plain and Fancy Lisle Half Hose, . . .50, .75, 1.00, and 1.25
X218. Black Lisle Half Hose, fast color, ...50 and .75
X219. Black and Colored Plated Silk Half Hose, ...75
X220. Black Spun Silk Half Hose, ... 1.50 and 2.00
X221. Black and Colored Bright Silk Half Hose, 2.00, 2.50, 3.00, and 3.50
X222. Novia Silk Half Hose, light and heavy weight, . 1.50 and 2.50

MERINO HALF HOSE.

X223. Domestic Merino Half Hose, ... $0.25 and .37½
X224. English Merino Half Hose, ...50 and .75
X225. Summer Weight Cashmere Half Hose, . . .50, .75, and 1.00

BICYCLE HOSE.

X226. Gentlemen's All-wool Bicycle Hose, black, . . $1.00 and 1.25
X227. Gentlemen's Genuine Scotch Wool, in black, all sizes, . 1.50
X228. Gentlemen's French Corduroy Cotton, in black, extra fine quality,
    all sizes, ... 1.25
X229. Gentlemen's Fast Black 7 x 1 Ribbed Cotton, all sizes, . .75
X230. Gentlemen's Unbleached Cotton, long and ¾ Hose, all sizes, .62½ and .75

THE MERCANTILE HEART OF NEW ENGLAND.

FLANNELS.

EMBROIDERED FLANNELS.

Our line this season surpasses all our previous efforts for beauty of design, artistic work of Embroidery, fine quality of Silk Twist and Flannel, and especially low price of any previous years.

For an Infant it is 1½ to 1¾ yards; for a Child, 1¼ to 1½ yards; for a Lady, 2 to 2½ yards. Prices, in white, 62½, 75, 87½c, to $3.00 per yard.

In colored, red and gray shaker, embroidered in scarlet, cardinal, and blue, 75, 87½c, to $1.25 per yard.

Opera Flannel Embroidered, light blue with self, pink embroidered with self, at $1.00 and 1.25 per yard.

WHITE FLANNELS.

A full line of the best standard makes, celebrated for their washing and wearing qualities, in all widths and grades.

All Wool, 27 inches wide, 37½, 42, 45, 50, 55, and 62½c per yard; 30 inches wide 45, 50, 55, 62½, 75, and 87½c per yard; 34 inches wide, 50, 55, 62½, 75, 87½c, and $1.00 per yard; 42 inches wide, 80, 87½c, $1.00, 1.12½, and 1.25 per yard.

Silk and Wool, 30 inches wide, 87½c per yard; 34 inches wide, $1.00 per yard.

Cotton and Wool Mixed, 27 inches, 25, 30, 33⅓, and 37½c per yard; 30 inches, 25, 30, 37½, and 45c per yard; 34 inches, 37½, 45, and 50c per yard.

Domets, Cotton and Wool, 27 inches, 12½, 17, 20, 25, 33⅓, and 37½c per yard; 30 inches, 17, 20, 25, 30, 33⅓, and 37½c per yard; 34 inches, 25, 30, 37½, 45, and 50c per yard.

Shaker Domets, 27 inches, 10, 12½, 17, 20, and 25c per yard.

Swan's-down Flannel for Infants' Squares, 36 inches, 75, 87½c, and $1.00 per yard.

Art Flannels for Infants' Squares, 27 inches, $1.25 per yard.

All Wool Shaker Flannels, 30 inches, 37½c per yard; 34 inches, 50 and 62½c per yard.

Angola Twilled Flannels, 22 inches, 25c per yard.

All Wool Gauze Flannel, 30 inches, 50 and 62½c per yard; 34 inches, 62½ and 75c per yard.

Lawn Tennis Twilled Suiting Flannel, Cream, White, Cotton and Wool, 27 inches, 25, 30, and 37½c per yard; 54 inches, 62½ and 75c per yard.

All Wool, 27 inches, 50c per yard; 54 inches, 87½c, $1.00, and 1.25 per yard.

FANCY FLANNELS.

In Foreign and Domestic Flannels we have the most complete line ever shown. Scotch Flannels for Ladies' and Children's Dresses.

Gentlemen's Fancy Shirts and Pajamas, 30 inches wide, from 25 to 62½c per yard.

French Printed Flannels, stripes and dots, so stylish for Ladies and Children, in or out door wear, 27 inches wide, at 62½ and 75c per yard.

French Cashmere, Twilled Flannels, plain colors, 27 inches wide, 62½c per yard.

French Twilled Woven Striped Flannels, for Ladies' Dressing Sacks and Wrappers, and steamer wear, 26 inches wide, at 67c per yard.

Wash Silks, the latest fabrics for Ladies' blouse waist, and shirts and for Gents' fine shirts. It is a Cotton Warp with Silk filling in fancy stripes and plain colors, 30 inches wide, at 62½c per yard.

Lawn Tennis Flannels, all grades of Silk Striped Flannels, 30 inches wide, in many colorings, at 50c per yard.

FLANNELS — PYRENEE SUITINGS.

Our New Make of Tennis Striped Flannels, in all the New Scotch effects and finish, the finest line ever brought out for spring and summer wear, for Ladies' and Children's Suits and Wrappers, and Gents' and Boys' Shirts and Pajamas. Is 29 inches wide, and being Cotton and Wool is unshrinking. Price, 37½c per yard.

FANCY FLANNELS.

Opera Flannels, all colors, 25 inches, 37½c per yard.

Cashmere Twilled, all colors, 26 inches, 50c per yard.

Imperial Eider Down Flannels, 36 inches, all shades, 75c per yard.

Jersey Striped Flannels, 25 inches wide, 62½c per yard.

All Wool Navy Blue Twilled Flannels, 27 inches, 25, 33⅓, 37½, to 62½c per yard. (The 50 and 62½c qualities are pure Indigo dye.)

The Original Outing Cloth, in stripes and plaids, 27 inches, 12½c per yard, over 50 styles.

Twilled Grays and Mixtures for Blouses and Shirtings, 27 inches wide, from 25 to 45c per yard.

Bathing Suit Flannels from 12½ to 50c per yard.

Colored Cotton Flannels, single faced, 27 inches wide, 12½ and 20c per yard, all shades. Double faced, 30 inches, 25c all shades.

Table Plush for Dining Tables, under the cloth saves both table and cloth, 50 and 63 inches wide, 37½, 50, 62½, 75, and 87½c per yard.

Felt for Ironing Boards, 36 inches wide, 50c per yard; 72 inches wide, $1.00 per yd.

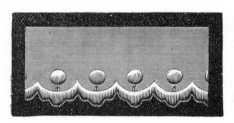

No. 12. $0.62½.

No. 4. $0.87½.

No. 14. $0.87½.

No. 9. $1.75.

No. 10. $2.00.

No. 13. $0.75.

No. 7. $1.25.

THE MERCANTILE HEART OF NEW ENGLAND.

EMBROIDERED FLANNELS.

Street Floor, Rear.

We can only display a few of the many patterns we carry in stock; and, as we cut no samples, if we should happen to be out of any pattern, or you wish something different, please state price, and we will send the best pattern we have for the money. If not satisfactory, it can be returned.

No. 1. $1.50.

No. 16. $1.25.

No. 2. $1.25.

No. 17. $0.87½.

No. 8. $1.50.

No. 5. $0.87½.

No. 6. $1.00.

No. 14. $0.87½.

No. 15. $1.00.

No. 3. $1.00.

No. 11. $1.00.

THE MERCANTILE HEART OF NEW ENGLAND.

WOOLLENS.

Street Floor, Rear, Avon St. Entrance.

NO lady will have cause to complain, this season, of difficulty in selecting a suitable cloth for a becoming Spring and Summer outside garment. Plain colors will be largely used in the make-up of outside garments, and late advices state that they will be more popular than anything else.

Mixed Woollen goods in plaid and mixtures shaded to a nicety, and interwoven with a fine silk thread of pleasing character, will be very popular for long New-markets.

FINE CLOTHS
For   and
Ladies, Children,   Gentlemen.

EXCLUSIVE DESIGNS, NOTABLE FOR ORIGINALITY AND TASTE.

The latest English and French importations in fine Woollen materials, suitable for Tailor-made Suits, Garments, Riding Habits, etc. Samples post-free.

Black Dolman Cloth of novelties with raised stripes and small flowers will be very stylish; also fancy weaves, of which we shall show an immense variety of beautiful designs.

Broadcloths and Amazon Cloths for full costumes will be very popular.

For Gentlemen and Boys, **Pin Checks and Mixtures** will be used for nobby business suits, as well as the **Scotch Suitings** in fine mixtures.

We invite ladies and gentlemen to examine the largest stock of **Superior Quality Woollens**, collected from the best European and American Manufacturers, ever shown by us.

Broadcloths, different quality, 52 to 54 inch, from $1.25, 1.50, 2.00, 2.50, 3.00, 3.50, 4.00, 4.50, 5.00 to 6.00.

Doeskins, 6-4. Prices, $3.00, 4.00, 4.50 to 5.00.

Police Cloth, 6-4 wide. $1.75, 2.00, 2.50, 3.00 to 4.00.

Blue Yacht, 6-4 wide. $2.00, 2.50, 3.00 to 5.00.

Blue and Black Cheviots, 6-4. $2.00, 2.50, 3.00 to 3.50.

Black and Blue Diagonals for Gents' Suits, 6-4 wide. $2.00, 2.50, 3.00, 3.50, 4.00 to 5.00.

Black and Blue Whipcord. $3.50, 4.00 to 5.00.

Blue, Black, and Brown Pique, 6-4 wide. From $3.50, 4.00, 4.50 to 5.00.

Also a fine line of **Black Broadcloth** for gents' dress suits, from $3.50 to 6.00 per yard.

We have taken special care to select a fine line of

HABIT CLOTHS,

in all new shades, 6-4 wide. $1.50, 2.00, 2.50, 3.00, 3.50, 4.00, 4.50 to 5.00.

Tricot Cloths, 6-4 wide, $3.50 to 5.00.

Black Camel's Hair, $2.00, 2.50, 3.00 to 4.00.

Kersey Cloths in all shades, $2.00, 2.50, 3.00 to 4.00.

French and German Cloakings, in all the latest novelties. $1.50, 2.00, 2.50, 3.00, 3.50, 4.00 to 6.00.

We have this season a fine assortment of all the new and popular mixtures and plaids of **Scotch Cheviots**, in rich colorings, for ladies' garments in all qualities, 6-4 wide.

Prices, $1.50, 2.00, 2.50, 3.00, 3.50, 4.00 to 5.00.

Domestic Cloakings in all the leading makes. $1.25, 1.50, 2.00, 2.50, 3.00, 3.50, 4.00 to 5.00.

Plain Waterproof Cloths, 6-4 wide. 75c., $1.00, 1.25.

Plaid, Blue and Green, 6-4 wide. $1.25.

Infants' White Cloakings. $2.50 to 3.00.

White Lawn Tennis Cloths, 6-4. $1.75, 2.00, 2.50.

We call particular attention to the most varied assortment of **English, French, and German Suitings** for gentlemen. We feel that all who examine these elegant goods will find no difficulty in making a selection. All 6-4 wide. $2.00, 2.50, 3.00 to 4.00.

Waterproof Cloth, a very large assortment of plaids and stripes of the very latest spring styles. Price, $1.00, 1.25 per yard.

Domestic Cloakings of all the leading makes, in fancy mixtures and plaid. $1.25, 1.50, 2.00, 2.50, 3.00, 3.50, 4.00 to 5.00.

54-inch Lawn Tennis Cloths for street and mountain wear, in plaids of all the latest colorings, made exclusive to our order and not to be found in any other store in Boston. Our price, $2.00 per yard.

Domestic Suitings of all the leading makes, in fancy mixtures, 6-4 wide. $1.50, 2.00, 2.50, 3.00, 4.00 to 5.00.

We call particular attention to our ¾ **Cassimeres**, all wool, for boys' wear, in fine mixtures and plaids, at very low prices. 50, 62½, 75c., $1.00, 1.25.

We call attention to our new line of **Corduroys** for Spring, in all the new shades and best quality silk finish, at 75c. and $1.00 per yard.

SHAWLS.

India Cashmere Valley Shawls, $150, 200, 250, 300, 500

India Filled Umritzer Shawls, $25, 35, 50, 60, 75, 100

Embroidered India Chudda Shawls, $10, 12, 15, 20, 25, 30, 35, 40, 50

India Chudda Shawls,—long, in all colors, $8, 10, 12, 15, 20, 25, 30, 35

India Chudda Shawls,—square, in all colors, $4, 5, 6, 8, 10, 12, 15, 20, 25

Paisley, Broché, or French Cashmere Shawls,—long, $10, 12, 15, 20, 25, 30, 35, 50. Square, $5, 6, 7, 8, 10, 12, 15, 20, 25

Indienne, or Imitation of India Shawls, $10, 12, 15, 20, 25, 30, 35, 40, 50

Velvet Beaver Shawls, with knotted fringes, in gray, brown, tan, black, &c., $1.50, 2, 2.50, 3, 4, 5, 6, 7, 8, 9, 10, 12, 15

Himalayan Shawls.—Soft and warm, but heavy.—In plain gray, black, brown, tan, fancy checks, plaids, &c. $5, 6.50, 7.50, 10, 12, 15

English and Scotch Camels' Hair Shawls, for riding, travelling, and steamer wraps, $3.50, 4, 5, 6, 7, 9, 10

Real Scotch Shawls, in Clan plaids, grays, browns, etc.—Long, $8, 10, 12

" " " " " " " Square, $5, 6, 10

Fancy Silk and Wool Shawls, for opera and evening wear, in a choice assortment of colors, $3.50, 5, 8, 10, 12, 15

Persian Shawls, pure silk and wool, $5, 6, 8, 10, 12, 15

Canton Crepe Shawls, large size, richly embroidered, with deep fringe, $25, 30, 35, 40, 50, 75, 100

China Silk Shawls, handsomely embroidered, with knotted fringe: 42 inches square, $7.50; 48 inches square, 10; 52 inches square, 12; 60 inches square, 15; 64 inches square, 20.

English and French Chudda Shawls, all colors, $1.50, 2, 2.50, 3.50, 5

Plain Cashmere Shawls, all the desirable shades, $1, 1.50, 2, 2.50, 3.50

Shetland Shawls, Foreign and Domestic, all the fashionable colors, $0.50, .75, 1, 1.50, 2, 2.50, 3.50, 5

Hand-knit worsted Shawls, 50 to 60 inches square, all colors, $2, 2.50, 3, 3.50

Imported Berlin Honey-comb Shawls, $1, 1.25, 1.50, 2, 2.50, 3.50, 5

Tinsel Shawls, with Gilt and Satin Stripes, for evening wear, $2.50, 3, 4, 5, 6

Pure Silk Shawls, in Shell and other choice patterns, $2.50, 3.50, 4, 5, 6, 7.50, 8, 10, 12

Domestic Wool Shawls, all colors: 4 yards long by 2 yards wide, $3, 4, 5, 6, 7, 8; 2 yards square, 1.50, 2, 2.50, 3, 3.50, 4, 5.

All Wool Shoulder Shawls: 35 inches square, $0.50, .75, 1; 40 inches square, 1.25; 47 inches square, 1.75, 2.50.

MOURNING SHAWLS.

Plain Black Merino or Thibet Shawls: 4 yards long by 2 yards wide, $6, 7, 8, 9, 10, 12, 15, 18, 20, 25, 30, 35; 2 yards square, $3.50, 4, 5, 6, 7, 8, 9, 10, 12.

Plain Black Cashmere Shawls: 4 yards long by 2 yards wide, $3, 4, 5, 6, 7, 8, 9, 10; 2 yards square, $1, 1.25, 1.50, 2, 2.50, 3, 3.50, 4, 4.50, 5, 6.

Plain Black Wool Shawls: 4 yards by 2 yards, $4, 5, 6, 7, 8, 9, 10, 12; 2 yards square, $2, 2.50, 3, 3.50, 4, 5, 6.

CARRIAGE ROBES.

Heavy Mohair Plush Robes, all colors, including plain dark green, seal brown, black and fancy colors, $2.50, 3.50, 4, 5, 6, 7, 8, 9, 10, 12, 15, 20, 25. Also, Fine Imported Plush Robes, $25, 30, 35, 40, 50. Heavy Wool Robes, $3, 3.50, 4, 5, 6, 7.50, 8.50. Plain Wool Robes to match carriage linings, in green, blue, brown, wine, black, etc., $1.50, 2.50, 3.50, 5, 7.50, 8, 10, 12.

STEAMER RUGS AND TRAVELLING SHAWLS FOR LADIES AND GENTLEMEN,

in Scotch, English, and American Goods, $5, 6, 7, 8, 9, 10, 12, 15, 20, 25, 50.

BLACK EMBROIDERED FICHUS.

A complete line, comprising the largest and choicest assortment of patterns to be found in America, many of them our own exclusive designs, $1, 2, 3, 5, 6, 8, 10, 12, 15, 18, 20, 25, 30, 35, 40, 50.

GENTLEMEN'S GLOVES

For Street or Driving and Evening Wear.

We have determined to supply the BEST GLOVE to be had for the money, and these are made to our own special order and for us exclusively. They are strong, flexible, neat fitting, and every pair warranted.

CHEVREAU.

Chevreau, $1.50 per pair.

2 Button Dress Kid Glove, manufactured by Perrin Frères, of Grenoblé, France.

This brand of glove we shall keep in tans, modes, white, and opera shades, suitable for parties or theatre wear. Fit and quality guaranteed.

KHEDIVE.

Khedive, $1.25 per pair, Fowne's make. 1 Button, Patent Fastening, Embroidered Back, Street Glove.

Manufactured exclusively for us by Fowne Brothers, of London.

As we intend to make this brand our leader for this season, we have taken especial care in having the fit correct. We shall have these gloves in two lengths of fingers. Men with short fingers should be sure and call for the *Cadet* sizes.

HYDE PARK.

$2.00 per pair.

TREFOUSSE MAKE.

2 Button, Best Quality, Pique Sewn Walking Gloves. Made by Trefousse & Co. and Perrin Frères.

These gloves are made of the very best quality kid skins, and every pair warranted.

FOWNE'S
CRAVEN TAN GLOVES.

$1.75 per pair

Suitable for street or driving.

MOCHA.

2 Button Patent Fastening Undressed Kid Gloves, with the Orleans point on the back. The correct glove for spring and summer wear. $1.37½.

Gentlemen's Lisle Gloves, in black, white, and colors, 25c.

Gentlemen's Best Lisle Gloves, in colors, 50c.

Gentlemen's Taffeta Gloves, in Black and colors, 62½c.

LENOX.

(Embroidered.) $1.25 a pair.

PERRIN FRERES.

A glove made especially for youth's wear, of good quality of dogskin, in 1 and 2 button length, with embroidered and spear-point backs.

MEN'S FOSTER KID GLOVES.

2 Hook William,	.	$1.25
2 " Fowler,	.	1.50
2 " Fosterina,	.	2.00

In Overseam and Pique Sewn, with the new one row embroidery on the backs.

BLANKETS.

Full line of Summer Blankets, 11-4, at $3.50, 4.00, 5.00 per pair. 12-4, at $6.00, 7.00, and 8.00 per pair. In red, blue, and old gold borders.

A full assortment of wool and all wool blankets always on hand, in all sizes: 10-4, $0.75, 1.00, 1.50, 2.00, 3.00, 4.00, and 5.00 per pair. 11-4, $2.00, 2.50, 3.00, 3.50, 4.00, 5.00, 6.00, 7.00, 8.00, and 10.00 to 25.00. 12-4, $4.00, 5.00, 6.00, 7.00, 8.00, 10.00, 12.00 to 25.00 per pair. Special inducements given to buyers for hotels and summer houses.

A fine assortment of Crib Blankets constantly in stock, in all the latest novelties, from $1.50 per pair to $6.00 per pair.

GRAY AND FANCY BLANKETS,

10-4, $1.00, 1.50, 2.00, 2.50, and 3.00. 11-4, $1.50, 2.00, 2.50, 3.00, 4.00, 5.00.

These goods are used very extensively for Ladies' Wrappers and camping purposes.

HORSE CLOTHING.

We make a specialty in this department during the summer months to carry a full assortment of Linen Sheets and Coolers, together with a full line of Carriage Robes and Dusters at special prices.

COMFORTERS.

A full assortment continually on hand, prices $0.75, 1.00, 1.25, 1.50, 2.00, 2.50, 3.00, 4.00.

QUILTS.

Marseilles and Crochet.

We have a large variety of Quilts in all the popular prices. Marseilles Quilts from $1.25, 2.00, 2.50, 3.00, 3.50, 4.00.

In imported, $4.00, 5.00, 6.00, 7.00, 8.00, 10.00. Also a Mitcheline in all the latest colorings, at $3.00 each.

Crochet Quilts, $0.65, .75, .87½, 1.00, 1.25, 1.50. Also a full line of Crib Quilts, both Marseilles and Crochet.

TABLE AND PIANO COVERS.

We have a large and varied assortment of Velours, Turcoman, Tapestry, and Piano Covers, viz: 6-4, Velours at $4.50, 6.00, 8.00, 10.00, and 14.00. 8-4, $7.00, 10.00, 14.00. 10-4, $10.00, 14.00, 18.00.

TAPESTRY COVERS.

6-4, $1.00, 1.25, 1.50, and 2.00. 8-4, $2.50, 3.00. 10-4, $2.50, 3.00, and 4.00. 12-4, $3.50, 5.00, and 9.00.

TURCOMAN COVERS.

6-4, $1.25, 1.50, 2.00, 3.50. 6-4, Fringed, $2.50 and 3.00. 8-4, $3.00, 3.50, and 4.00. 8-4, Fringed, $5.00. 10-4, $4.50, 5.00, 7.00. 10-4, Fringed, $7.00.

PIANO COVERS.

We have constantly on hand a variety of Billiard Cloth Piano Covers, in green, and dark and light wine shades, with old gold and colored embroidery, at $3.50, 4.00, 5.00, 6.00, 7.00, 8.00, 9.00.

Turcoman Covers at $6.00, 7.00, 8.00, and 9.00.

Velours, $14.00, 15.00, 16.00, 20.00. The Turcoman and Velours Covers will be in all the popular shades. A novelty for upright Pianos will be a plain Turcoman with deep knotted fringe, at $7.50, also Plush, at $4.00, 5.00, 9.00, 10.00, 11.00, and 12.00.

THE MERCANTILE HEART OF NEW ENGLAND.

GLOVES.

One Side of our Glove Counter., Centre of Street Floor.

Ladies' Gauntlet Wrist Driving Gloves, $1.50.

MISSES' KID GLOVES.

4 Button or 5 Hook Lacing Gloves,	$1.00, 1.25
4 Button or 5 Hook Dogskin Gloves,	1.50
1 or 2 Button Youths' Street Gloves,	1.25
2 Button Youths' Kid Gloves,	1.25

SUEDE GLOVES.

As Suède Gloves are the most stylish gloves worn at present, we take great pleasure in announcing the fact that we have secured the control of a first-class glove, both in quality and fit, which we do not hesitate to warrant in every particular. Prices are very low for this Suède Glove, as we intend to make it our leader this season.

4 Button or 7 Hook,			$1.25
6 "			1.50
8 "	Mousquetaire, with Foster Hook at wrist,		1.60
12 "	"		2.00
16 "	"		2.75
20 "	"		3.50
24 "	"		4.00
30 "	"		4.50

LADIES' LACE MITTS.

Lace Top, Pure Silk Mitts, colors and black,		$0.25
" " " " "		.37½
" " " " "		.50
" " " " "		.62½
Children's Lace Top, Silk Mitts, colors and black,		.25, .37½
11 inch Jersey Wrist, Pure Silk Mitts,		.50
11 " " " " Best,		.75
15 " " " " "		1.00

Opera and White Silk Mitts and Gloves, for evening wear, from 10 to 30 button length, Jersey wrist. Prices from $1.25 to 2.00 per pair.

FABRIC GLOVES.

30 Button Silk Mitts, $1.50.

6 Button Length, Jersey Top, Colors and Black, Taffeta Gloves,						$0.25
6 "	"	"	"			.37½
6 "	"	"	"	Best Quality,		.50
6 "	"	"	"			.62½
6 "	"	"	Pure Silk Gloves,			.50
6 "	"	"	"			.75
6 "	"	"	"	English make,		1.00
6 "	"	"	Lisle Gloves,			.25
6 "	"	"	Frame-made Lisle Gloves,			.37½
6 "	"	"	Best Frame-made Lisle Gloves,			.50
Children's Lisle Gloves,	"	"				.25 to .37½
Children's Taffeta Gloves,	"	"				.37½ to .50

LONG SILK GLOVES FOR EVENING WEAR.

12 Button, . . $1.00   20 Button, . . $1.50   30 Button, . . $2.00

BIARRITZ GLOVES

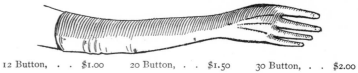

Are the most sensible glove worn by the ladies of to-day. We are prepared to show the best line of these gloves, as we have paid special attention to get the fit and quality correct. Price, $1.00 per pair.

CHAMOIS GLOVES,

In white and natural color. A sensible glove, to be worn at the seashore, and also for driving purposes. 6 button length, $1.00.

DOGSKIN GLOVES

Are the most sensible gloves to be worn at this season as they are comfortable and stylish. We recommend them, as they will outwear two pair of other gloves. We are prepared to show the best line of these gloves, as we have paid special attention to get the fit and quality correct.

4 Button,			$1.00
4 " or 7 Hook,			1.50
4 " 7 " best quality,			1.75

THE MERCANTILE HEART OF NEW ENGLAND.

KID GLOVES.

During the past ten years greater improvements in Kid Gloves have been made than ever before. The greatest is undoubtedly the mode of fastening by Foster's lacing hooks.

Ten years ago the old and imperfect system of buttoning was almost universal; to-day it is almost obsolete.

By the Foster system Gloves are easily and rapidly laced, producing a perfect fit, regardless of the size of wrist.

Five years ago we secured the sole agency for these goods; to-day we have the largest Glove department in the United States.

A good article is always imitated, and we are compelled to caution our customers against base imitations of the Foster hook.

The genuine goods are manufactured by the well-known firm of Foster, Paul & Co., at Grenoble, France, and Berlin, Prussia.

Each pair is stamped with one of the annexed Trade Marks, and we add list of Prices.

   **TRADE**      **MARKS**   

PRICE LIST.

DESCRIPTION.	SEWING.	HOOKS.	WILLIAM.	FOWLER.	FOSTERINA.
GLACE, LADIES',	OVERSEAM,	5	$1 00	$1 50	$2 00
" "	"	7	1 25	1 75	2 00
" "	"	10	1 50	2 00	2 50
" "	PIQUE,	7	1 50	1 75	2 00
" MISSES',	OVERSEAM,	5	1 00	1 25	1 50
" MEN'S,	"	3	1 25	1 50	2 00
" "	PIQUE,	3	1 50	1 75	2 00
" "	SADDLERS,	3	1 25	1 50	2 00
SUEDE, LADIES',	OVERSEAM,	5	1 00	1 25	1 50
" "	"	7	1 25	1 50	1 75
" "	"	10	1 50	1 75	2 00
" "	PIQUE,	7	1 25	1 50	2 00
" MEN'S,	"	3	1 25	1 50	2 00
" LADIES',	OVERSEAM,	8 IN.	1 50	1 75	2 00
" "	"	16 "	......	......	3 25
" "	"	24 "	......	......	4 00
" "	"	30 "	......	......	5 00

BEWARE OF IMITATIONS.

LINENS.

Bleached Damask, 58 in., 37½c; 60 in., 50c; 64 in., 62½ and 75c; 66 in., 75 and 87½c; 68 in., 75 and 87½c.

Double Satin Damask, in the latest and handsomest designs, with Napkins to match, in two sizes.

Heavy Double Damask, 72 in., $1.00 yard. Napkins to match, ⅝ size, $2.25; ¾ size, $3.50 doz.

Extra Heavy Double Satin Damask, 68 and 72 in., $1.25 yard. ⅝ Napkins to match, $2.50; ¾ Napkins, $3.50 doz.

Heavy Double Satin Damask, 68 and 72 in., $1.50 yard. ⅝ Napkins, $3.00; ¾ Napkins, $4.50 doz.

Very Fine Double Satin Damask, 72 in., $1.75 yard. ⅝ Napkins to match, $3.50; ¾ Napkins to match, $5.50 doz.

We have a full line of extra wide Damasks, prices from $1.75 to 3.50 yard.

Cream Damask, 54 in., 25c; 58 in., 37½c; 60 in., 50c; 66 in., 62½ and 75c; 72 in., $1.00 and 1.25 yard.

Cream Damask, red border, 58 in., 37½c; 60 in., 50c; 66 in., 62½c; 72 in., $1.00 and 1.25 yard.

Bleached Table Cloths. This being by far the most important branch of our housekeeping department, therefore we pay particular attention to have always on hand the most desirable and latest designs, and the best values that can possibly be offered for first-class goods.

Bleached Damask Cloths, 2 x 2 yds., $2.50, 3.00, 4.00, 5.00, and 5.50 each.

2 x 2½ yds., $2.75, 3.25, 4.00, 4.50, 5.00, and up to $10.00 each.

2 x 3 yds., $3.00, 4.00, 4.50, 5.00, 5.50, 6.50, 7.50, 8.50, 9.50, 10.50, and upwards.

2 x 3½ yds., $4.00, 4.50, 5.00, 5.75, 6.50, 7.50, 8.50, 10.00, 12.00, 13.50, and upwards.

2 x 4 yds., $5.00, 6.00, 7.50, 9.00, 11.00, 12.50, 15.00, 17.00, and upwards.

2½ x 2½ yds., from 5.00 to 17.00.

2½ x 3 yds., from $6.50 to 20.00.

2½ x 3½ yds., from $7.50 to 25.00.

2½ x 4 yds., from $8.00 to 30.00.

Bleached Napkins. Breakfast size, "all linen," 50, 75, 87½, $1.00 doz.

⅝ Bleached Napkins, $1.25, 1.50, 1.75, 2.00, 2.25, 2.50, 3.00, 3.50, 4.00, 5.00, 6.50, 7.50, and upwards.

¾ yd. Bleached Dinner Napkins, $1.25, 1.50, 1.75, 2.00, 2.50, 3.00, 3.50, 4.00, 4.50, 5.50, 6.00, 7.00, 8.50, 10.00, 12.00, 13.50, 15.00, and up to 24.00 doz.

Fringed Lunch Cloth, plain white and fancy borders, sizes from 2 to 4 yds., prices from $1.50 to 7.50 each.

Doilies, or fringed napkins, in plain white and fancy colored borders, prices from $1.00 to 6.50 doz.

Also a full assortment of Tray Cloths, Finger Bowl Doilies, Doilies for dentists' use, etc.

Carving Cloths and Slips from 50c to $2.50 each.

Turkey Red Damask, 54 in., 25c; 58 in., 37½c; 60 in., 50, 62½, 75c; 68 in., 75 and 87½c yard.

Fancy Tabling, Turkey and Green, Turkey and Blue, 56 in., Turkey and Green, 42c; 60 in., "Imported," 75c; 68 in. Turkey and Red and Turkey and Blue, 87½c.

Cardinal Damask, 60 in., 62½ and 75c; 66 in., best quality, $1.00 yard.

Toilenette Checks and Stripes, 60 in. check, 75c; 64 in. check, $1.00; 60 in. stripe, 87½c; 64 in. stripe, $1.00 yard.

Turkey Red Cloths, fringed, 5-4, 38c; 6-4, 75c; 7-4, $1.00; 8-4, 1.35; 8-10, 1.65, 8 x 12, 1.85; 8 x 14. 2.25; 8 x 16, 3.00.

Extra Heavy Superior Turkey Red Cloths, 2 x 2 yds., $2.00; 2 x 2½ yds., 2.50; 2 x 3 yds., 3.00; 2 x 3½ yds., 3.50; 2 x 4 yds., 4.00.

Cardinal Cloths, plain red, white, and black borders, 5-4, 50c; 6-4, $1.13; 7-4, 1.38; 8-4, 1.50; 8-10, 2.00; 8-12, 2.50; 8-14, 3.00; 8-16, 3.50.

Extra Heavy Superior Cardinal Cloths, 8-4, $2.50; 8-10, 3.00; 8-12, 3.50; 8-14, 4.00; 8-16, 4.50.

Extra Fine Cotton Diaper, 18 in., 70c piece; 20 in., 80c piece; 22 in., 90c piece; 24 in., $1.00 piece of 10 yards.

Diaper Linen, 10 yards in each piece, sold by the piece only: 18 in., $1.00, 1.25, 1.50, 1.75, 2.00, and 2.50; 20 in., $1.25, 1.50, 1.75, 2.00, 2.50, and 3.00; 22 in., $1.50, 1.75, 2.00, 2.50, 3.00, and 3.50; 24 in., $1.75, 2.00, 2.50, 3.00, and 3.50; 26 in., $2.50, 3.00, 3.50, and 4.00.

Diaper Cotton, 18 in., 50c per piece of 10 yards; 20 in., 65c per piece of 10 yards; 22 in., 75c per piece of 10 yards; 24 in., 87½c per piece; 27 in., $1.00 per piece.

Linen Sheeting. Our Stock of Linen Sheetings and of Pillowcase Linens is unusually large, and comprises the very best makes of Scotch, German, Belgian, Barnsley, and Irish goods: 2 yards wide sheeting, 87½c and $1.00 yard; 2¼ yards wide sheeting, 87½c, $1.00, and 1.25 yard; 2½ yards wide sheeting, 87½c, $1.00, 1.25, 1.50, 1.75, and 2.00 yard; 2¾ yards wide sheeting, $1.20 to 2.50 yard; 3 yards wide sheeting, $2.00 and 3.00 yard.

Hemstitched Linen Pillow-cases. Price, $1.25, 1.50, 1.75, 2.00, and 2 50 per pair.

Pillow-case Linen, 40 in., 50, 67, 75, 87½c, and $1.00 yard; 42 in., 50, 62½, 75, 87½, and $1.00 yard; 45 in., 50, 62½, 75, 87c, and $1.00 yard; 50 in., 75, 87½c, $1.00, and 1.25 yard; 54 in., 75, 87½c, $1.00, and 1.25 yard.

4-4 Fronting Linen in three grades, fine, medium, and heavy. Prices from 25c to $1.25 yard.

Crumb Cloths, brown, 2½ yards square, $2.00 each; 2½ x 3, 2.50; 2½ x 3½, 3.00; 2½ x 4, 3.50; 3 x 3, 3.00; 3 x 3½, 3.50; 3 x 4, 4.00. Slate, 2½ x 2½ yards, $2.25 each; 2½ x 3, 2.75; 2½ x 3½. 3.25; 2½ x 4, 3.75; 3 x 3, 3.25; 3 x 3½, 3.75; 3 x 4, 4.25.

Crumb Damask by the yard, 2½ yards wide, brown, 75c; 3 yards wide, brown, 87½c and $1.00; 2½ yards wide, slate, 87½c; 3 yards wide, slate, $1.00.

Red Check, 2½ x 2½ yards, $3.00 each; 2½ x 3, 3.50; 2½ x 3½, 4.00; 2½ x 4, 4.50; 3 x 3, 4.00; 3 x 3½, 4.50; 3 x 4, 5.00.

Red Check Crumb Damask, by the yard, 2½ yards wide, $1.00; 3 yards wide, $1.37½.

Towels. Huck Towels, 10, 12½, 20, 25, 37½, and 50c each.

Bath Sheets, extra heavy, 50 x 76 in., $2.00 each; 60 x 80 in., 3.00.

An endless assortment of Fancy Turkish Towels used for tidies. Prices, 15, 25, and 37½c each.

A full assortment of Damask Towels, plain white and fancy colored borders. Prices range from 12½c to $3.00 each.

Huckabuck Toweling, white and loom, 16 in., 12½, 15, 18, 20c; 18 in., 12½, 15, 18, 20, and 25c; 20 in., 20, 25, 30, and 37½c; 22 in., 25, 33⅓, 37½, and 50c; 24 in, 37½ and 50c; 26 in., 50, 62½, and 75c yard.

Glass Toweling, red and blue checks, 18 in., 10, 12½, 15, and 18c; 20 in., 12½, 15, 20, and 25c; 22 in., 20 and 25c; 24 in., 25 and 30c; 26 in., 25 and 37½c yard.

Stair Linens, 16 in., 16c; 18 in., 18c; 20 in., 20c; 22 in., 25c yard.

Crashes of every grade and quality, Russia, Irish, Barnsley, Scotch, plain and twilled. Price from 5 to 25c yard.

Hemstitched Set, consisting of 1 table-cloth and 1 dozen dinner napkins. Four sizes, 2 to 4 yards in length. Prices from $14.00 to 18.50 per set.

Toilenette Plaid Tea Cloths,
2 x 2 yards, $2.25   2 x 3 yards, $3.25
2 x 2½ " 2.75   2 x 3½ " 3.75

72-in. Bleached Double Satin Damask, $1.75 per yard.
⅝ Napkins to match, $3.50 doz.
¾ " " " 5.50 "

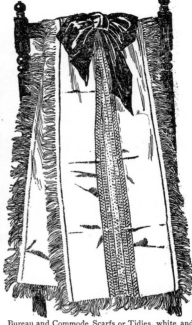

Bureau and Commode Scarfs or Tidies, white and fancy colored centres.
18 inches by 54 inches . from $0.50 to 1.25 each.
18 " 63 " . " .75 to 1.50 "
18 " 72 " . " .87½ to 2.00 "

Fruit D'Oyleys, in buff, pink, blue, $2.25 per doz.

72-inch Bleached Double Satin Damask, $1.75 per yard. Napkins to match, $3.50 and 5.50 doz.

24 Bleached D'Oyleys, red border, $1 to $3 doz.

72-in. Bleached Double Satin Damask, $1.50 yard. ⅝ Napkins to match, $3.00 doz.; ¾ Napkins to match, $4.50 doz.

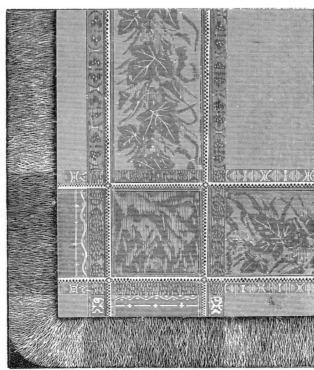

Colored Bordered Sets. Price with open-work borders, 2 x 2½, $6.50; 2 x 3, 7.50; 2 x 3½, 8.50. Plain Borders, 2 x 2½, 5.50; 2 x 3, 6.50; 2 x 3½, 7.50.

72-in. Bleached Double Satin Damask, $1.25 yard. ⅝ Napkins to match, $2.50 doz.; ¾ Napkins to match, $3.50 doz.

THE MERCANTILE HEART OF NEW ENGLAND.

RIBBONS.

We are pleased to inform you that we have had conferred upon us the exclusive right to sell at retail in Boston the Black Silk Ribbons of the well-known Lyons Manufacturers, "Les Fils" de C. J. Bonnet & Co. These Ribbons are made of the Finest French Silk, and the cocoons are carefully selected on the manufacturers' own premises, the thread spun and thrown, and the ribbons woven in the manufacturers' own establishment. The goods are from beginning to end under scrupulous supervision, and the result is a ribbon of the greatest possible perfection.

We can strongly recommend these ribbons to y u as being especially suitable for a high-class millinery and dress-making trade, and none are genuine unless they bear the above well-known trade-mark and the manufacturers' signature.

We ea nestly solicit from you an order for this ribbon.

Black Horse, Plain Black, Gros Grain.

No.	Width (in.)	Per piece	Per yard	No.	Width (in.)	Per piece	Per yard
5	1	$1.75	$0.18	16	2½	$4.75	$0.50
7	1¼	2.25	.25	22	3	5.25	.55
9	1½	2.90	.30	30	3½	5.75	.60
12	2	3.75	.40	40	4	6.25	.60

Red Horse, Heavy Black, Gros Grain.

No.	Width (in.)	Per piece	Per yard	No.	Width (in.)	Per piece	Per yard
2	½	$0.75	$0.08	16	2½	$3.50	$0.37½
3	¾	1.20	.12½	22	3	4.00	.42
5	1	1.40	.15	30	3½	4.75	.50
7	1¼	1.80	.20	40	4	5.50	.55
9	1½	2.40	.25	50	4½	6.50	.70
12	2	2.90	.30	60	5	7.50	.80

Blue Horse, with narrow Satin Edge.

No.	Inch wide	Per piece	Per yard
5	1	$1.75	$0.18
7	1¼	1.90	.20
9	1½	2.40	.25
12	2	3.00	.33
16	2½	3.75	.40
22	3	4.25	.45
30	3½	4.75	.50

Fancy Patterns in Black Ribbons.

No.	Inches wide	Per piece	Per yard
22	3	$3.50	$0.37½
30	3½	3.75	.39
40	3¾	4.50	.48

A special line of Checked Patterns.

No. 30, ... 3½ inches wide, $3.25 per piece, $0.35 per yard.

FINE FRENCH GROGRAIN · OUR OWN & COMPANY.

Fine French Gros Grain Ribbon, from ½ to 4 inches wide, manufactured expressly for us, in over one hundred different shades. Manufactured from the finest Italian silk, in colors and black.

No.	Inch wide	Per piece	Per yard
2	½	$0.75	$0.08
3	¾	.95	.10
5	1	1.20	.12½
7	1¼	1.45	.15
9	1½	1.90	.20
12	2	2.40	.25
16	2½	2.90	.30
22	3	3.65	.37½

Anticipating the great demand for Velvet Ribbons for dress trimmings this season, we have made very large contracts for these goods, and will have and carry the whole season a very extensive line, both in satin backs and linen backs, at the following low prices: —

Black Linen Back Velvet Ribbons. This celebrated brand only, G. F.

No.	Inch wide	Per piece	Per yard
1½	¼	$0.45	
1¾	⅜	.52	
2	½	.58	
2½	½	.70	
3	⅝	.75	
3½	¾	.95	$0.10
4	¾	1.05	.11
4½	⅞	1.20	.12
5	⅞	1.25	.12½
5½	1	1.38	.15
6	1¼	1.50	.16
6½	1⅜	1.75	.18
7	1½	2.00	.22
8	1⅝	2.25	.25
9	1¾	2.50	.28
10	2	2.75	.30
12	2¼	3.00	.32
14	2½	3.25	.35
16	2¾	3.50	.37½
18	2⅞	3.75	.40
20	3	4.50	.48
30	3½	6.25	.65

P. S.— From No. 1½ to 3 we sell by the piece only, all warranted 11 yards, full measure.

Colored Linen Back Velvet Ribbons.

No.	Inch wide	Per piece	Yards
4	⅞	$1.00	10
5	1	1.25	10
7	1¼	1.50	10
9	1½	2.00	10
12	2	2.50	10

Sold by the piece only.

Colored Satin Back Velvet Ribbons.

No.	Inch wide	Per piece	Per yard
4	⅞	$1.50	$0.18
5	1	2.00	.25
7	1¼	2.50	.28
9	1½	3.00	.35
12	2	3.75	.42
16	2½	4.50	.50
22	3	6.50	.75

Black Satin and Velvet Ribbons.

No.	Inch wide	Per piece	Per yard
1	¼	$0.75	$0.08
2	½	1.00	.12½
3	¾	1.25	.15
4	⅞	2.00	.22
5	1	2.25	.25
7	1¼	2.75	.30
9	1½	3.00	.33
12	2	3.25	.35
16	2½	3.75	.40
22	3	6.50	.70
30	4	8.50	.90

Our regular standard qualities of Satin and Gros Grain Ribbons, extra line of widths and shades, in colors and black. First quality.

No.	Inch wide	Per piece	Per yard
1	¼	$0.35	$0.04
2	½	.65	.07
3	¾	.85	.09
5	1	1.20	.12½

No. 7, ... 1¼ inches wide, $1.40 per piece, $0.15 per yard.
" 9, ... 1½ " " 1.75 " .18 "
" 12, ... 2 " " 2.25 " .25 "
" 16, ... 2½ " " 2.75 " .28 "
" 22, ... 3 " " 3.25 " .35 "
" 60, ... 5 " " 4.75 " .48 "

Second quality Satin and Gros Grain Ribbons, in colors and black.
No. 5, 1 in. wide, $0.95 pc., $0.10 yd. No. 12, 2 in. wide, $1.90 pc., $0.20 yd.
" 7, 1¼ " 1.20 " .12½ " " 16, 2½ " 2.25 " .25 "
" 9, 1½ " 1.40 " .15 " " 22, 3 " 2.75 " .29 "

Fine Gros Grain, with satin edges, promises to be a most desirable ribbon for the season.

Finest quality Satin Edge Gros Grain, colors and black.
No. 1, ... ¼ inch wide, $0.25 per piece, $0.03 per yard.
" 2, ... ½ " " .75 " .08 "
" 3, ... ¾ " " .90 " .10 "
" 5, ... 1 " " 1.20 " .12½ "
" 7, ... 1¼ " " 1.45 " .15 "
" 9, ... 1½ " " 1.90 " .20 "
" 12, ... 2 " " 2.40 " .25 "
" 16, ... 2½ " " 2.90 " .30 "
" 22, ... 3 " " 3.50 " .37½ "
" 30, ... 3½ " " 4.25 " .45 "
" 40, ... 4 " " 4.75 " .50 "
" 60, ... 5 " " 5.75 " .60 "

Our standard make of Black Satin Edge Gros Grain.
No. 5, 1 in. wide, $1.10 pc., $0.12 yd. No. 16, 2½ in. wide, $2.40 pc., $0.25 yd.
" 7, 1¼ " 1.20 " .13 " " 22, 3 " 2.90 " .30 "
" 9, 1½ " 1.60 " .17 " " 30, 3½ " 3.25 " .35 "
" 12, 2 " 2.00 " .21 " " 40, 4 " 3.75 " .40 "

~ALL SILK ~
WARRANTED 10 YARDS.
REGISTERED FEBY 21, 84
Manufactured by JOHN ERSKINE & Co.

Satin Edge Gros Grain, in colors and black.
No. 2, ½ in. wide, $0.45 piece, $0.05 yd.
" 3, ¾ " " .75 " .08 "
" 5, 1 " " .95 " .10 "
" 7, 1¼ " " 1.20 " .12½ "
" 9, 1½ " " 1.40 " .15 "
" 12, 2 " " 1.90 " .20 "
" 16, 2½ " " 2.20 " .23 "
" 22, 3 " " 2.40 " .25 "

Crown Edge Moire Ribbons, blacks only.
No. 16, ... 2½ inches wide, $2.40 per piece, $0.25 per yard.
" 22, ... 3 " " 3.25 " .35 "

Cordena Ribbons, black, white, and cream only.
No. 4, ... 1 inch wide, $1.62 per piece, $0.17 per yard.

Fancy Ribbons, very fine quality, in several choice patterns, manufactured expressly for us.
No. 30, ... 3½ inches wide, $4.50 per piece, $0.48 per yard.
" 40, ... 4 " " 4.75 " .50 "

Special line of Colored Surah Sash Ribbons, colors and black.
13 inches wide, ... $0.98 per yard.

Our regular standard quality Colors and Black Satin Edge Gros Grain Sash Ribbons, with Satin Edges.
8 inches wide, ... $1.00 per yard.
9 " " . . . . 1.25 "
11 " " . . . . 1.50 "

Black Faille de Lyon Satin and Gros Grain. This is one of the best Ribbons made. Warranted to give entire satisfaction.
No. 5, 1 in. wide, $1.50 pc., $0.16 yd. No. 12, 2 in. wide, $2.40 pc., $0.25 yd.
" 7, 1¼ " 1.75 " .18 " " 16, 2½ " 3.25 " .30 "
" 9, 1½ " 2.00 " .22 " " 22, 3 " " " "

Plain Black Gros Grain Ribbons, superior manufacture.
No. 1, ¼ in. wide, $0.25 pc., $0.03 yd. No. 9, 1½ in. wide, $1.90 pc., $0.20 yd.
" 1½, ⅜ " .40 " .05 " " 12, 2 " 2.40 " .25 "
" 2, ½ " .75 " .08 " " 16, 2½ " 2.90 " .30 "
" 3, ¾ " .90 " .10 " " 22, 3 " 3.25 " .35 "
" 4, ⅞ " 1.25 " .12 " " 30, 3½ " 4.00 " .42 "
" 5, 1 " 1.40 " .15 " " 40, 4 " 4.50 " .50 "
" 7, 1¼ " 1.65 " .17 "

Black Gros Grain, a very fine domestic ribbon.
No. 2, ... ½ inch wide, $0.60 per piece, $0.07 per yard.
" 3, ... ¾ " " .75 " .08 "
" 5, ... 1 " " 1.00 " .11 "
" 7, ... 1¼ " " 1.25 " .13 "
" 9, ... 1½ " " 1.50 " .16 "
" 12, ... 2 " " 1.90 " .20 "
" 16, ... 2½ " " 2.25 " .25 "
" 22, ... 3 " " 2.80 " .30 "

Special line of Faille Francaise, in colors and black.
No. 16, ... 2½ inches wide, $3.25 per piece, $0.35 per yard.
" 22, ... 3 " " 4.50 " .48 "

Special bargains in Black Gros Grain Sash Ribbons.
8 inches wide, ... $0.69 per yard.
9 " " . . . . .89 "
12 " " . . . . 1.00 "

Picot Edge Gros Grain, black, white, and cream only.
No. 2, ... ½ inch wide, $0.75 per piece, $0.08 per yard.
" 3, ... ¾ " " .90 " .10 "
" 5, ... 1 " " 1.25 " .13 "
" 7, ... 1¼ " " 1.40 " .15 "
" 9, ... 1½ " " 1.90 " .20 "
" 12, ... 2 " " 2.40 " .25 "
" 16, ... 2½ " " 2.90 " .30 "

Great variety of Fringed Sashes, in black and colors.

4½ yards long, ... $3.50
5 " Surah, . . . 5.50
5 " Fancy, . . . 10.00
5 " " " . . . 12.00
5 " " " . . . 15.00
5 " " " . . . 20.00

P. S.—The $5.50 quality is plain Surah, with satin and picot edges, manufactured expressly for us, and is a most beautiful Sash for the price.

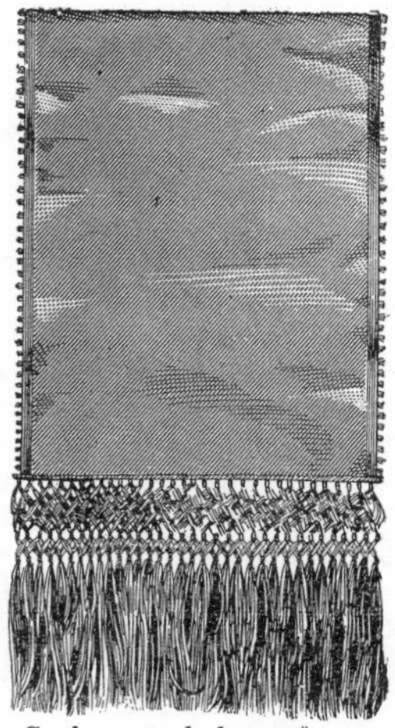

Sash, 5 yards long, $5.50.

A full assortment of all the Clan Sashes, with fringed ends, to match the Tartan.

Black Satin Edge Gros Grain. "Value for the price." This ribbon beats the world.
No. 2, ½ inch wide, $0.50 piece, $0.06 yard.
" 3, ¾ " " .65 " .07 "
" 5, 1 " " .75 " .10 "
" 7, 1¼ " " 1.00 " .12½ "
" 9, 1½ " " 1.25 " .14 "
" 12, 2 " " 1.50 " .17 "
" 16, 2½ " " 2.00 " .22 "
" 22, 3 " " 2.40 " .25 "
" 30, 3½ " " 2.90 " .30 "

Loop Edge Ribbons, in colors and black, and black with colored loops.
No. 5, ... 1 inch wide, $1.90 per piece, $0.20 per yard.

Special line of Colored Sashes, Gros Grain, with Moire stripes.
9 inches wide, ... $1.00 per yard.

Black Satin and Gros Grain Sash Ribbons.
5 inches wide, $4.50 piece, $0.48 yard. 7 inches wide, $7.00 piece, $0.75 yard.
8 " " 8.50 " .87 " 9 " " 9.00 " 1.00 "
10 " " 11.50 " 1.25 "
13-inch Clan Sash Ribbon, ... $7.29 per yard.

Black Gauze Ribbons, in carefully selected patterns, several exclusive designs.
2 inches wide, $2.25 piece, $0.25 yard. 2½ inches wide, $2.95 piece, $0.30 yard.
3 " " 3.25 " .35 " 3½ " " 3.75 " .40 "

Special line of very fine French Faille, manufactured expressly for the millinery trade.
4 inches wide, ... $4.00 per piece, $0.45 per yard.

Our Bargain Counter for Ribbons. Ribbons in all widths at about one-half their real value.

GENTLEMEN'S FURNISHING GOODS.

OUR GREAT SOVEREIGN SHIRT.

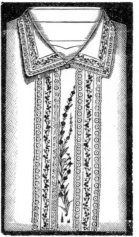

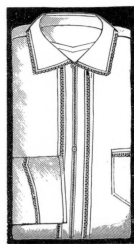

MEN'S WHITE SHIRTS. (Unlaundered.)

Our Great "Sovereign" Shirt needs no commendation from us, as it advertises itself. Made from Utica Nonpareil cotton, 2200 solid linen bosoms and wristbands, sectional yokes, 39 inches long, extra large bodies. Sizes, 13½ to 19 inches. We guarantee this to be the best shirt in the United States, and give the following three reasons why it is:—

1st. It is known as the great Balfour Shirt, therefore the workmanship is as near perfection as possible. 2d. The materials used are carefully selected, only the finest grades of cottons and linens being used in their manufacture. 3d. The grading of sizes is exact, being made with OUR OWN SECTIONAL YOKE, thus insuring a perfect fitting shirt. Price, $1.00 each.

Our "Champion" Shirt, made from Wamsutta cotton, 1800 linen bosoms, 36 inches long, hand-made buttonholes. Sizes, 14 to 17 inches. Price, 75c. each.

Our "J., M. & Co." Shirt, made from good cotton, 3-ply set-in linen bosoms, reinforced front and back. Sizes, 14 to 17 inches. Price, 65c. each.

Our "America" Shirt, made from Langdon cotton, 3-ply linen bosoms and wristbands, reinforced back and front. Price, 50c. each.

Remember we manufacture our own shirts, therefore we save you all intermediate profits.

Our "64 C" Shirt, made open back and front, closed neck bands, good cotton, 3-ply linen bosoms and wristbands. Sizes, 13½ to 17 inches. Price, 50c. each.

Our "Excelsior" Shirt, open back and front, closed neck band, New York Mills cotton, 2000 linen bosoms, hand-made buttonholes. Sizes, 13½ to 17 inches. Price, 75c. each.

Our "O. B. & F." Shirt, made from New York Mills Cotton, 2200 solid linen bosoms, linen neck band and wristbands. Sizes, 13½ to 17 inches. Price, $1.00 each.

Our "30" Shirt, open front, Wamsutta cotton, 2000 linen bosoms and wristbands, full size bodies, 36 inches long. Sizes, 13½ to 17 inches. Price, $1.00 each.

Our "Full Dress" Shirt, made from best cottons, finest linens, open back and front, laundered in the best manner. This shirt is cut by an artist, and made by our custom shirt operators. A full line always in stock, ready for immediate use. Sizes, 14 to 18 inches. Price, $1.50 each.

No. 9. Made from twilled cotton, full size bodies, well made. Sizes, 15 to 17 inches. Price, 75c. each.

Remember we manufacture our own shirts, consequently they are reliable in size, fit, and workmanship.

No. 10. Made from first quality Pepperell Jean, extra large bodies, hand-made buttonholes. Sizes, 15 to 19 inches. Price, $1.00 each.

No. 11. Made from Wamsutta cotton, 54 inches long, hand-made buttonholes, yoke back, felled seams. Sizes, 15 to 19 inches. Price, $1.00 each.

No. 12. Made from first quality Pepperell Jean, 60 inches long, extra large bodies. Sizes, 15 to 19 inches. Price, $1.12½.

No. 13. Fancy trimmed Night Shirts, good cotton, nice trimmings, full size. Sizes, 15 to 17 inches. Price, 50c. each.

No. 14. Fancy Trimmed Night Shirts, first quality cottons, neat and desirable styles of trimmings, in red, white, or blue. Sizes, 15 to 17 inches. Price, 75c. each.

No. 15. Fancy Trimmed Night Shirts, Wamsutta cotton, in silk embroidered and Cash trimmings. A choice assortment of elegant designs. Sizes, 15 to 18 inches. Price, $1.00 each.

No. 16. Fancy Trimmed Night Shirts, in the latest styles of trimming, elegantly made, the latest styles of coloring, in prices ranging from $1.25 to 3.00 each.

MEN'S NIGHT SHIRTS.

No. 8. Made from good cotton, 52 inches long, full size bodies, collar and pocket. Sizes, 15 to 17 inches. Price, 50c. each.

FLANNEL AND NEGLIGE SHIRTS.

No. 7 C. Men's Gray Mixed Flannel Shirts, medium weight, button front, with collar and pocket. Sizes, 15 to 17 inches. Price, $1.50 each.

No. 9 C. Men's Flannel Overshirts, made from Stanley suitings, in light, medium, and dark gray, brown, olive, and tan shades, button front, with collar and pocket. Sizes, 15 to 17 inches. Price, $2.00 each.

No. 11 C. Men's Flannel Overshirts, made from Assabet flannel, all shades, button front, collar, and pocket. Sizes, 15 to 17 inches. Price, $2.25 each.

No. 13 C. Men's Fancy Silk Stripe Flannel Shirts, in stripes and checks, neat designs, choice colorings, button front, collar and pocket. Sizes, 14½ to 17 inches. Price, $2.75 each.

No. 14 C. Men's French Flannel Overshirts. All the latest designs, stripes, and checks. Prices, $1.50, 2.00, 2.50, 3.00 to 5.00 each.

Men's English Madras Outing Shirts, in carefully selected and exclusive patterns. Prices, from $1.50 to 3.50 each.

Men's Cheviot Shirts, in hundreds of different patterns, collar and pocket. Prices, $0.75, 1.00, 1.25, 1.50, 2.00 to 2.25 each.

SILK SHIRTS.

An immense assortment of the best styles in Silk Outing Shirts. Prices, from $3.00 to 10.00 each.

GENTLEMEN'S LINEN COLLARS AND CUFFS.

All Collars and Cuffs sold by us are PURE LINEN.

LINEN COLLARS.

Our "J., M. & Co." 200 series 4-ply pure linen, in 25 different styles, 15c. each; $1.50 dozen. Our "Owl Brand," in 10 of the latest styles Turn-down 4-ply Pure Linen Collars, 20c. each; $2.00 dozen. The celebrated "Barker Brand" of Linen Collars and Cuffs, of which we are the sole agents in Boston. "Barker's" 4-ply All Linen Collars, in 19 of the latest styles, 19c. each; $2.20 dozen.

LINEN CUFFS.

Roman, Norman, and Saxon. Round and square corners, 5-ply pure linen. Sizes, 9½ to 11½, 20c. each; $2.00 dozen.

Our Great "Owl Brand" Cuffs. California, round corners; India, round and cut-away; Persia, square corners; Laconia Link Cuff, round corners; Inglesia Link Cuff, square corners. These cuffs are 4-ply pure linen, hand-made buttonholes, and are A1. 33⅓c. pair; $3.50 dozen.

THE MERCANTILE HEART OF NEW ENGLAND.

Charmer and Badger. Round and square corners, 25c. pair; $2.75 dozen.
Wexford Link Cuff, square corners. Sizes, 9½ to 11½, 25c. pair; $2.75 dozen.
"Royal Brand" 5-ply All Linen Cuffs, 50c. pair.
Reversible, three buttonholes, 25c. pair; $2.75 dozen.

SHIRT BOSOMS (for Insertion).

4-ply linen, 20, 25, 33⅓, 37½, 50c. each.   Cuffs (to sew on), 15c. pair; 3-ply linen.

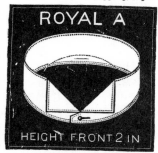

ROYAL A — HEIGHT FRONT 2 IN

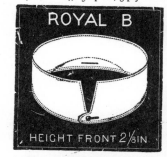

ROYAL B — HEIGHT FRONT 2⅛ IN

ROYAL C — HEIGHT FRONT 2 IN

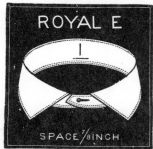

ROYAL E — SPACE ⅞ INCH

OUR "ROYAL BRAND" of 5-ply All Linen Collars, in 8 of the latest styles, hand-made buttonholes, are the best made, at 25c. each.

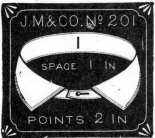

J. M. & CO. Nº 201 — SPACE 1 IN — POINTS 2 IN

J. M. & CO. Nº 200 — POINTS 2 IN

J. M. & CO. Nº 202 — SPACE 1¼ IN — POINTS 2 IN

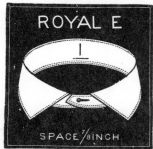

J. M. & CO. Nº 203 — SPACE ½ IN — POINTS 2¼ IN

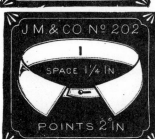

J. M. & CO. Nº 209 — SPACE ¾ IN — HEIGHT FRONT 1⅛ IN

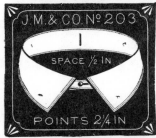

J. M. & CO. Nº 205 — HEIGHT IN BACK 1¾ IN — HEIGHT FRONT 2 IN

J. M. & CO. Nº 204 — SPACE ½ IN — HEIGHT FRONT 2¼ IN

J. M. & CO. Nº 207 — SPACE ¾ IN — HEIGHT FRONT 2 IN

J. M. & CO. Nº 206 — SPACE 1¼ IN — HEIGHT FRONT 2 IN

J. M. & CO. Nº 208 — HEIGHT IN BACK 1½ IN — HEIGHT FRONT 1⅞ IN

These Collars are 4 ply pure linen, and are made expressly for Jordan, Marsh & Co. 15c. each; $1.50 dozen.

SPECIAL Nº 3

SPECIAL Nº 7

SPECIAL STANDING COLLARS.

Our Jordan, Marsh & Co. Specials No. 1, No. 2, No. 3, No. 4, No. 5, No. 6, No. 7. These specials are 4-ply pure linen, hand-made buttonholes, and equal in every respect to collars sold at 25c. each.   20c. each; $2.00 dozen.

OWL BRAND — VIRGINIA.

Our Owl Brand of Pure Linen Collars is known all over this country. They are well made, and the quality of linen used is first-class; and a trial order will convince all gentlemen that the Owl Brand are the best fitting collars ever produced.

OWL BRAND — SERVIA.

PAVONIA — HEIGHT FRONT 1⅞ IN

GARCIA

OWL BRAND

WIDTH 3¾ IN — NORMAN.

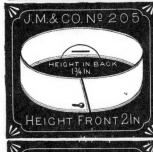

WIDTH 3⅝ IN — SAXON.

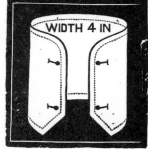

WIDTH 4 IN — ROMAN.

SAXON. These Cuffs are 20c. pair; $2.00 dozen. **ROMAN.**

WATERPROOF AND CELLULOID COLLARS AND CUFFS.

Men's Collars, 25c. each; $2.75 dozen.   Men's Cuffs, 50c. pair; $6.00 dozen.
Ladies' Collars, 25c. each; $2.75 dozen.   Ladies' Cuffs, 50c. pair; $6.00 doz.

THE MERCANTILE HEART OF NEW ENGLAND.

GENTLEMEN'S NECKWEAR.

Gentlemen's Silk Scarfs, in Tecks, Puffs, and Four-in-hands, newest patterns and largest assortment, at 25c.

Gentlemen's Silk Scarfs, in Tecks, Puffs, and Four-in-hands, 50c.

Gentlemen's Silk Scarfs, in Tecks, Puffs, and Four-in-hands, the very newest combinations, made in the correct shapes, 75c., $1.00, 1.25 to 2.50.

BLACK SILK NECKWEAR.

We have made a specialty of Black Silk and Satin Neckwear for years, and we offer only the best goods.

Black Silk Scarfs, in Knots, Puffs, Flats, and Four-in-hands, $0.50, .75, 1.00, 1.25, 1.50.

Black Silk Square for elderly gentlemen, $1.50, 2.00, 2.50, 3.00 to 5.00.
Black Silk Bows, 15, 25, 37½, and 50c.
Black Silk String Ties, ¾ to 1½ inches, 25c.
Black Silk String Ties, all widths, $0.37½, .50, .62½, .75 to 1.50.

WHITE SILK AND SATIN NECKWEAR.

White Silk and Satin Scarfs, in Knots, Puffs, and Four-in-hands, $0.25, .50, .75 to 2.50.
White Silk and Satin String Ties, $0.25, .50 to 1.25.
White Silk and Satin Bows, 12½, 25, 37½ to 50c.

WHITE LAWN TIES.

White Lawn String Ties, $0.25, .50, .75, 1.00 per dozen.
White Lawn String Ties, 12½, 25, 37½c. each.
White Lawn Dress Bows, 12½, 25, 30 to 50c. each.

DE JOINVILLE SCARFS.

Gentlemen's De Joinvilles or long Scarfs, 42 inches long, 5 to 7 inches wide, $0.75, 1.00, 1.25, 1.50 to 5.00.
We devote more space and carry at all seasons of the year the largest assortment of Neckwear of any retail house in *America*.

GENTLEMEN'S SUSPENDERS.

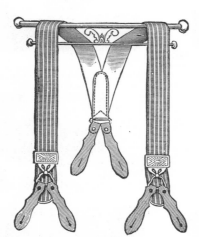

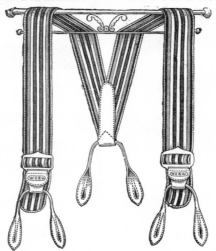

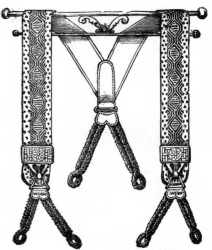

No. 1. Men's Plain and Fancy Elastic Web Suspenders, with or without drawers supporters, 25c. pair.

No. 2. Men's Suspenders, in plain and fancy elastic webs, with silk or leather ends, at 50c. pair.

No. 3. Men's Suspenders, in plain and fancy elastic webs, with silk or leather ends, at 75c. pair.

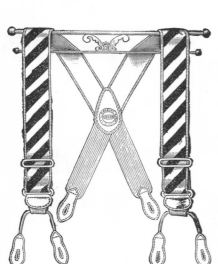

No. 4. Men's Plain and Fancy Silk Suspenders, with kid or silk ends to match, at $1.50, 1.75, 2.00 to 2.50 pair.

No. 5. Men's Silk Braces, hand embroidered, in all colors, suitable for presents, at $2.50, 3.00, 3.50 to 8.00 pair.

No. 6. Men's Fine Imported Elastic Web Suspenders, with kid or silk ends, at 75c., $1.00, 1.25, and 1.50 pair.

Men's Plain and Fancy Elastic Web Suspenders, with or without drawers supporters. No. 1, 25c. pair.
Men's Suspenders, in plain and fancy elastic webs, with silk or leather ends. Nos. 2 and 3, at 50c. pair.
Men's Fine Imported Elastic Web Suspenders, with kid or silk ends. No. 6, at $0.75, 1.00, 1.25, and 1.50 pair.
Men's Plain and Fancy Silk Suspenders, with kid or silk ends to match. No. 4, at $1.50, 1.75, 2.00 to 2.50 pair.

Men's Silk Braces, hand-embroidered, in all colors, suitable for presents. No. 5, at $2.50, 3.00, 3.50 to 8.00 pair.

HOSE SUPPORTERS.

Gentlemen's Hose Supporters, in cotton, 25c. pair.
Gentlemen's Hose Supporters, in silk, 50c. pair.
Gentlemen's Drawers Supporters, in nickel, 10c. pair.
Gentlemen's Arm Bands, 10, 15, and 25c. pair.

THE MERCANTILE HEART OF NEW ENGLAND.

BOYS' FURNISHINGS.

ONE of the most important features in our immense Men's Furnishing Department is the section set apart for "The Boys," where everything in the line of Boys' Furnishings is kept. Particular and special attention is devoted to this branch. All the latest styles in men's goods are at once copied and made suitable for boys.

BOYS' SHIRTS.

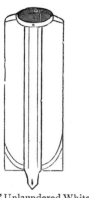

Boys' Unlaundered White Shirts, 50, 75c.   Boys' Night Shirts, 50c.   Boys' Flannel Shirts, $1.00, 1.25, 1.50, 1.75.

Boys' White Unlaundered Shirts, open back, ... $0.50
Boys' White Unlaundered Shirts, open back and front, .   .   .50
Boys' White Unlaundered Shirts, ...75
Boys Laundered White Shirts, ...75, 1.00
Boys' Night Shirts, plain white, .   .   .50
Boys' Night Shirts, fancy trimmed, .   .75, 1.00, 1.25, 1.50
Boys' Flannel Shirts, in plain and fancy flannels, button and loop front,
                          $1.00, 1.25, 1.50, 1.75

BOYS' NECKWEAR.

Boys' Knot and Puff Scarf, .   . $0.25, .50, .75
Boys' Windsor Ties, .   .25, .37½, .50, .75, 1.00
Boys' Bows, .   .   .10, .15, .25

All the latest styles in Neckwear reproduced for the boys.

BOYS' SUSPENDERS.

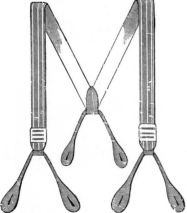

Boys' Suspenders, 25, 50, 75c. pair.   Boys' Suspenders, 25 and 50c.
Boys' Elastic Web Suspenders, .   . $0.25, .50, .75
Boys' Silk Suspenders, .   .   1.00, 1.25, 1.50
Boys' Silk Embroidered Suspenders, .   1.75, 2.00, 2.50

We are Headquarters for Boys' Furnishing Goods.

BOYS' COLLARS AND CUFFS.

It has always been a difficult matter to obtain suitable styles of linen collars and cuffs. We have given this special attention, and present the following styles, which are the latest in men's goods and copied for the boys:
Collars, 4-ply linen, ...15c.; $1.50 per dozen
Cuffs, 4-ply linen, .   .   20c. per pair; $2.00 per dozen

"OUR BOYS'" LATEST STYLES OF COLLARS AND CUFFS.

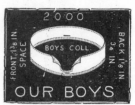

Note.— Everything made or designed for boys in Furnishings can be found in this department, as we make it a specialty.

BACK-SUPPORTING SHOULDER BRACE AND SUSPENDER
(for Men and Boys).

This Brace provides a firm yet flexible support for the back, from the hip to the shoulders, to which is attached at the waist a yielding belt, which helps to keep the back support in place. At the upper part are connected carefully constructed adjustable pads, so arranged as to draw the shoulders gently back without cutting or chafing under the arms, thus inclining the body to an erect position, correcting all tendency to stooping or round shoulders. Suspender attachments are also added for the trousers, which render other suspenders unnecessary.
No. B65. Boys', pair, ... $2.00
No. B66. Young men's, pair, .   .   .   2.25
No. B67. Men's pair, ...   2.50
On receipt of price, we will send this Brace by mail, postage paid, to any part of the United States.

OUR SPORTING SUIT FOR BASE BALL LAWN TENNIS & ALL OUT-DOOR SPORTS.

OUR SPORTING SUIT.

Our Sporting Suit of English Worsted Jersey, Stockings to match. Suitable for base ball, bicycling, Suit, the chest measure is all that is necessary

$4.62½ Per Suit.

consisting of Jersey, Knee-tights, and lawn tennis, etc. In ordering this

SPORTING OUTFITS for Polo, Lawn Tennis, Yachting, Base Ball, Lacrosse, and Rowing.

OUR SPORTING GOODS DEPARTMENT.

In our new extension we have set apart a special section for Sporting Clothes of all kinds, and this season we shall keep the most complete stock of these goods to be found in Boston. Estimates furnished to Base Ball, Tennis, Bicycle, and Yachting Clubs, and special prices given Tennis Coats and Trousers made to order at very reasonable prices. In all instances we guarantee a perfect fit.

Sporting Clothes for Polo, Lawn Tennis, Yachting, Base Ball, Lacrosse, and Rowing.

ENGLISH JERSEYS.

All colors and sizes. Colors warranted fast.

1st quality.	Ribbed collar and cuffs,	$4.25
1st quality.	Striped collar and cuffs,	4.25
1st quality.	Quarter sleeve,	4.00
1st quality.	Sleeveless,	3.50
2d quality.	English Jerseys, all colors and sizes, ribbed collars and cuffs,	2.50
2d quality.	Striped,	3.00
2d quality.	No collar,	2.00
2d quality.	No collar, quarter sleeve,	1.25
3d quality Jerseys.	All sizes in brown and blue,	1.50

TIGHTS. All colors and sizes.

1st quality.	English Worsted Knee Tights,	$2.75 and 3.00
1st quality.	Full Tights,	3.50
2d quality.	Knee Tights,	1.25, 1.50, and 2.00
2d quality.	Full Tights,	2.50

LAWN TENNIS AND YACHTING SHIRTS.

In English Worsted and Flannel.

1st quality. **Jersey Shirts.** Lace or button front, with collar, in all colors and sizes,	$4.25. 2d quality, 2.25
Colored Flannel Shirts, S. B.,	1.25, 1.50, 1.75, and 2.25
Blue Flannel Shirts, S. B.,	1.50, 1.75, and 2.00
Blue Flannel Shirts, D. B.,	1.62½, 1.87½, and 2.37½
Blue Flannel Shirts, laced,	2.00 and 2.50
Colored Flannel Shirts, laced,	1.50, 2.00, and 2.50
French Flannel Shirts, S. B.,	2.50 and 3.00
White Flannel Shirts, S. B.,	2.25
White Flannel Shirts, laced fronts,	2.50

In ordering, the size of collar worn is all that is necessary.

Bicycle Suits, in Cloth, Flannel, and Corduroy,	6.50 to 10.50

Estimates furnished to clubs.

We shall show this season a most complete line of Tennis and Outing Suits, all imported Flannels and Serges, and made in the best possible manner. We always keep a full line of Tennis Sashes, and in fact everything pertaining to Base Ball, Tennis, Yachting, etc.

TENNIS TROUSERS.

In plain white Flannel from $2.50 to 7.00. In fancy stripe and check, from $3.00 to 8.00 per pair.

TENNIS SUIT

(*i. e.*, coat and trousers to match), from $6.00 to $15.00 per suit.

TENNIS COATS.

In plain white, and all the different color stripes, from $1.50 to 6.50 each.

Our Importation this season in English Tennis Suits is large and very complete, embracing all the latest styles Tennis Coats and Trousers, direct from the leading European manufacturers.

THE MERCANTILE HEART OF NEW ENGLAND.

GENTLEMEN'S SMOKING JACKETS, BLANKET AND BATH WRAPS.

A full assortment of these goods may be found in this department at all seasons of the year.

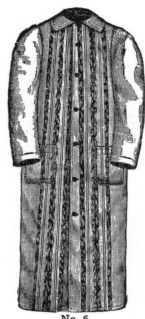

GENTLEMEN'S MACKINTOSH AND RUBBER COATS.

We keep a full line of Waterproof Coats all they ear round, our assortment being so large we can suit all who want RAIN PROTECTORS.

Men's Rubber Coats, all sizes, at $2.50 and 3.00 to 5.00.

Men's Mackintosh Coats, without Cape, $5.00, 7.50 to 15.00.

Men's Mackintosh Coats, with Cape, in large variety of patterns, at from $8.50, 11.00, 13.00, 15.00, 18.00, 23.00, to 30.00 each.

Boys' Rubber Coats, $2.50 to 4.00.

Boys' Mackintosh Coats, from $5.00 to 15.00 each.

These garments we warrant to be STRICTLY WATERPROOF.

Note.— In ordering any of the above goods, the chest measure is all that is required.

No. 5.

Gentlemen's Dressing Gowns, in whipcords, Venetian cloths and flannels, satin-trimmed collar, cuffs, and pockets, at $10.50, 12.00, 15.00 to 50.00 each.

Gentlemen's Dressing Gowns, all colors, in plain all wool flannels, at $7.50, 9.00, 10.00 each.

No. 6.

Gentlemen's Blanket and Bath Wraps, made from all wool blankets, in plain colors and fancy stripes and checks, similar in style to cut No. 6, at $5.00, 6.50, 8.00, 10.00 to 20.00 each.

GENTLEMEN'S PAJAMAHS.

(Night Suits.)

We carry in stock all the year round a large assortment of Pajamahs, or Night Suits, in madras, cheviots, flannels, silk, and silk and wool.

Madras, per suit 2 pieces, $2.50, 3.00, 3.50 to 5.00.

Cheviots, per suit 2 pieces, $2.00, 2.50, 3.00 to 5.00.

Flannels, per suit 2 pieces, $2.50, 3.00, 4.00, 5.00 to 8.00.

Silks, per suit 2 pieces, $5.00, 6.50, 8.00 to 20.00.

No. 1.

Gentlemen's Smoking or House Jackets, in plain tricot, brown, gray, navy blue, checks and plaids (No. 1), at $5.00 each.

Gentlemen's Smoking Jackets in plain colors, quilted lining, cord or satin edge. Sizes, 34 to 46, $6.50, 7.50, 8.50. (No. 2.)

Turkish Bath Wraps, our own importation. Prices, $4.00, 5.00, 6.00, 7.00, 8.00, 9.00, 10.00 to 20.00 each.

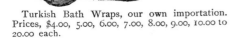

PAJAMA NIGHT SUITS.

No. 2.

Gentlemen's Smoking and House Jackets in fine all wool English cheviots and Scotch plaids and checks, not lined, made with button or frogs, with cord edge, similar in style to cut No. 1, at $6.50, 7.50, 8.50, 10.50 to 18.

CUSTOM SHIRT DEPARTMENT.

Our Work is Guaranteed.

Take Elevator in centre of store, street floor, for CUSTOM Shirt Department.

INSTRUCTIONS FOR SELF-MEASUREMENT.

......**Neck.**—Measure straight around the neck with fore-finger inside of tape.

......**Collar Worn.**—State size of Collar you wish to wear.

......**Chest.**—Close measurement **around** the body directly **under** the arms at D.

......**Waist.**—Close measure around the waist.

......**Length of Bosom.**—From top of Bosom, where it joins the yoke, as far down as required. Usual length, 14 to 15 inches.

......**Length of Shirt.**—From top of Bosom to about 4 inches above the knee.

......**Yoke.**—Straight across the back from B to B.

......**Sleeve.**—From C, around the point of elbow, to wrist joint, G, arm raised horizontally, as per cut.

......**Cuff or Band.**—Size around the largest part of hand.

......**Style of Bosom.**—As per number of cut.

......**Open Back Shirt or Open Front or both.**

☞ State whether you use Spiral Stud or Button Stud in Bosom, and how many. Whether you wish collar-stud front only or front and back, on neck band. If Cuffs, for Sleeve-buttons or plain ; if Bands, for Stud or Button.

Regular Style Bands.
1½ inch wide.

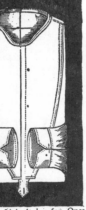

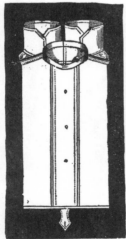

No. I. ½ inch lap for Open Back or Open Front—the leading style of Boston.

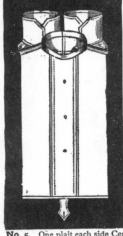

No. 5. One plait each side Center plait, either Open Front or Back. These are 25c. each, extra from regular price.

Regular Style Cuffs.
3½ inch wide.

No. 2. Box Plait Center, from 1 inch to 3 inches wide, as desired.

FINE SHIRTS TO ORDER

FOR BUSINESS, DRESS, AND EVENING WEAR.

We submit the following prices :—

A.—Shirt, $1.50. Made from G. B. Cotton. 2,000 Linen Bosom and Cuffs. Reinforced Front, Buttonholes and Gussets strictly hand-work. Silk woven Initial. Unlaundered.

B.—Shirt, $2.00. Made from Wamsutta Cotton. 2,100 Linen Bosom and Cuffs. Reinforced Front. Buttonholes and Gussets strictly hand-work. Silk woven Initials.

C.—Shirt, $2.50. Made from New York Mills Cotton. 2,200 Linen Bosom and Cuffs. Reinforced Front extending under the arm. Buttonholes and Gussets strictly hand-work. The Initials on this Shirt are hand-worked and made with great care.

D.—Shirt, $3.00. We take great pleasure in calling your attention to this Shirt, knowing it to be the "Best Shirt" made in the city. It is made from Grinnell Cotton. 2,300 Linen Bosom (extra heavy inter-linings), making a Solid Linen Bosom, Solid Linen Cuffs, Neck Bands and Tabs are all of the best Linen, and the Initials worked by hand extra fine. This Shirt is specially made for Full Dress and Evening Wear. Being cut on the latest French System, it cannot fail to please the most fastidious. $0.50 extra for Solid Linen Collars attached.

Collars and Cuffs. Particular attention will be given to this branch of the trade. We shall make two grades only. All Linen Collars and Cuffs made in the very best manner, **$5.50 per dozen.** Linen outside with Cotton Lining, Hand Buttonholes, etc., **$4.50 per dozen.** Any style of Collar carefully copied and adjusted to the form, attached to the Shirt or not. Other "makes" of Shirts carefully copied, altered to fit where a misfit has taken place, and repairing neatly done.

Pajahmas Suits Carefully Made to Order of Cotton, Calcutta Flannel, All-Wool Flannel, Fancy Silks, Zephyrs, Cheviots, and Linen.

Custom Underwear Carefully Cut to Measure, and made in the best possible manner.

Night Shirts of any material desired. Our Night Shirts are cut extra large in order to ensure perfect comfort and ease. All-Linen, $48 to $96 per dozen.

Night Shirts, $18 to $60 per dozen.

Our Cutting Department is in charge of the best of manufacturers, and we employ **ONLY THE BEST OF OPERATORS.**

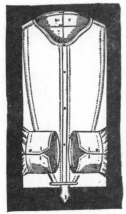

No. 3. 2 laps, ¼ inch wide; turned toward center, with ¾ inch space for studs.

Style of Round End Cuffs.

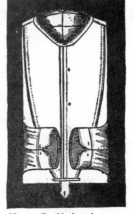

No. 4. Double lap; lower one ½ inch, with ¼ inch lap on top.

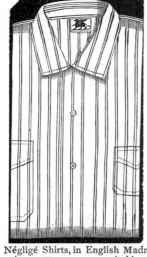

Men's Fine French Flannel Shirts, made in the best manner from select designs, at $2.25, 2.50, 2.75, 3.00 to 5.00 each.

Négligé Shirts, in English Madras, in nice patterns, very suitable for summer wear, at $1.50, 1.75, 2.00, 2.50.

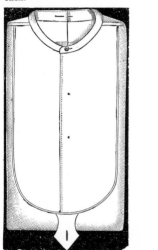

O. B. & F. Open Back and Front Shirts, 2000 solid linen bosoms, New York Mills cotton, perfect fitting. Unlaundered, $1.00 each; laundered, $1.25.

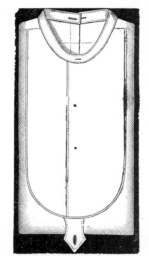

Our Excelsior, open back and front, closed neck band. Unlaundered, 75c.; laundered, $1.00.

Men's Plain and Twilled Flannel Shirts, made from Assabet and Stanley suiting, $2.00 and 2.25.

The trade-mark "faultless" represents the most varied and unique styles of Fancy Trimmed Night Shirts ever shown in America. We carry a full line at all seasons of the year at $0.50, .75, 1.00, 1.25, 1.50, 1.75, 2.00 to 3.50 each. All sizes.

TRUNKS AND BAGS.

"Our Special." Flat top, canvas covered and light weight. Has one deep tray with hat box. Grade A, linen lined; sizes, 30, 32, 34 inches. Prices, $7.00, 7.50, 8.00. Grade B, paper lined. Prices, $5.50, 6.00, 6.50.

"The Calaveras Trunk," metal covered, iron bottomed and bound. Hat box in the tray. Sizes, 28, 30, 32, 34 inches. Prices, $3.00, 3.37, 3.75, 4.00.

Purses, in many styles, at 5, 10, 25, 50c each. Cut represents Lady's four-pocket purse at 50c.

Canvas Extension Travelling Cases. The No. 1 quality, sizes, 14, 16, 18, 20, 22 inches. Prices, 50, 75c, $1.00, 1.25, 1.50.

Ladies' Pocket Books, with inside coin pocket, in grain and calfskin. Prices, 25c to $1.00.

Scrap Baskets, in combination of rush and willow, full size. Price, 25c.
Scrap Baskets, in green rush and willow. Various styles and sizes. Prices, 50c to $1.50. Work Baskets, in white and fancy colors. Prices, 25c to $1.00.
Nursery Baskets. Prices, 50, 62, 75, 87c.
Nursery Stands. Prices, $1.00 to 3.50.
Work Stands. Prices, $1.00 to 3.00.
Lunch Baskets. Prices, 20c to $1.50.
Small fancy toy or decorating baskets, in endless variety of size, style, and color. Prices, from 5 to 50c.

Grain Leather "Gladstone" Travelling Bags, opening wholly down. Color, brown only. Sizes, 14, 16, 18, 20 inches. Quality A, leather lined. Prices, $7.00, 7.50, 8.00, 8.50. Quality B, linen lined. Prices, $5.00, 5.50, 6.00, 6.50. Quality C, linen lined. Prices, $3.50, 4.00, 4.50, 5.00.

Steamer Trunks. Canvas covered, iron bound and bottomed, in sizes from 28 to 34 inches. Prices, from $3.50 to 5.00.
An extra quality of same, with sole leather corners and linen lining. Sizes, 30 to 36 inches. Prices, $6.00 to 7.50.

Sole Leather Blacking Sets, with patented Adjustable Handle Brush. Price, $1.37.

Grain Leather "Club" Satchel, for shopping or travelling. Colors, brown and black. Sizes, 10, 11, 12, 13, 14, 15, 16 inches. Kid lined: prices, $2.25, 2.62, 3.00, 3.25, 3.50, 3.75, 4.25. Linen lined: prices, $1.37, 1.62, 1.87, 2.12, 2.37, 2.62, 2.87. Imitation of Alligator Leather: prices, 75, 87c, $1.00, 1.12, 1.25, 1.50, 1.75.

Gentlemen's Strap Wallet, with bill fold in calf, grain, and seal. Price, 50c to $2.50.

Chatelaine Bags, in grain, seal, velvet, and antelope, mounted with various styles of frames. Prices from 50c to $3.50.

UPHOLSTERY AND DRAPERY DEPARTMENT.

IN order still farther to increase our already tremendous business in this department, we have made extra arrangements and used every effort at our command to place before the people of this country a stock of Upholstery and Art Fabrics that should attract the attention of every purchaser. These goods are manufactured for us by the leading manufacturers of England, France, Germany, and Switzerland, imported by us direct. Many of the designs and colorings are exclusively our own, and cannot be purchased elsewhere. Our aim has been, in selecting these fabrics, to produce art colors and artistic effects in low and medium-priced goods, as well as in the higher grades.

Our facilities for furnishing private residences, offices, steamboats, yachts, theatres, and hotels, are unexcelled. Practical men are sent to measure, and estimates furnished free of charge.

SPECIAL ORDERS.

We are prepared to show this season a larger line of art fabrics for special orders than has ever been our pleasure to offer our patrons. These goods comprise Brocatelles, Satin Derbys, Silk and Mohair Plushes, English and French Tapestries, single and double faced Velours, Satin Damask, and many rare French Novelties in latest designs and colorings, many of which are made expressly for us. Drapery and Furniture Fringes, Cords, Edgings, and Loops to match the above goods always to be found in our store. None but men of experience and practical designers are employed for all special order work. Measures taken and estimates given free of charge.

LACE CURTAINS.

Anticipating the great advance on these goods that must follow the passage of the New "Tariff Bill," we placed large orders with the Nottingham, Paris, and St. Gaul manufacturers, with the understanding that the goods should be manufactured for us during their dull season, thus enabling us to secure an extra discount from the manufacturers' regular prices. Every pair of Curtains was landed in this port at the old duty.

Our patrons will readily see that we are in a position to defy competition, even from the larger wholesale houses.

We predict the greatest season we have ever had. Parties ordering by mail from any of the prices quoted below or from cuts, we guarantee, will receive one of the best Curtains for the money that can be obtained in this country. All Curtains or other Upholstery and Drapery Goods so ordered can be returned at our expense, if not satisfactory, and money refunded.

Muslin Curtains will be carried in stock more this season than ever before, and present indications point to a large run on these goods. **Renaissance** and **Colbert Curtains** in lovely designs, in which some fine hand-work is displayed, will be popular with the most refined taste.

Brussels Curtains grow in demand each year. Prices being so much less than heretofore, the exquisite patterns and fine border-work tend to popularize them.

One of the features this season in Lace Curtains will be the increased use of Sash Curtains. These dainty little French curtains are very popular, and we shall carry in stock a full line, many of them to match full-length curtains, including Antique, Cluny, Irish Point, and Brussels, at $1.75, 2.00, 2.50, 3.00, 4.00, 5.00, 6.00, 7.00, 10.00, and up to 50.00 per pair.

Nottinghams.—50, 62½, 75, 87½c., $1.00, 1.25, 1.50, 1.75, 2.00, 2.50, 3.00, 4.00, 4.50, 5.00, 6.00, 7.00, 8.00 per pair.

Muslin.—$1.25, 1.75, 2.50, 3.00, 3.50, 4.00, 5.00, 8.00 per pair.

Antique.—$1.75, 2.00, 3.00, 4.00, 5.00, 6.00, 8.00, 10.00, 12.00, 15.00, 18.00, 20.00, to 40.00 per pair.

Cluny.—$2.00, 3.00, 4.00, 5.00, 6.00, 8.00, 10.00, 12.00, 15.00, 18.00, 20.00, to 40.00 per pair.

Swiss.—$4.00, 5.00, 6.00, 7.00, 8.00, 9.00, 10.00, 12.00, 15.00, 18.00, 20.00, to 40.00 per pair.

Brussels.—$12.00, 15.00, 18.00, 20.00, 22.00, 25.00, 30.00, to 75.00 per pair.

Renaissance.—$12.00, 15.00, 18.00, 20.00, 22.00, 25.00, 30.00, 35.00, 40.00, 50.00, 60.00, to 200.00 per pair.

Irish Point.—$3.50, 4.00, 5.00, 6.00, 7.00, 8.00, 9.00, 10.00, 11.00, 12.00, 13.50, 15.00, 17.00, 18.00, 20.00, 22.00, 25.00, to 50.00 per pair.

Madras Curtains, Cream.—$1.50, 1.75, 2.00, 2.50, to 5.00 per pair.

Cream and Gold.—$1.75, 2.00, 2.50, to 5.00 per pair.

Colored Madras.—$3.00, 3.50, 4.00, 5.00, to 12.00 per pair.

Arabian Crape.—$8.00, 10.00, 12.60, 15.00, 17.00, 20.00 per pair.

Silk Damask Curtains.—$8.00, 10.00, 12.00, 15.00, 16.00, 20.00, to 40.00 per pair.

Silk and Satin Band Curtains.—$4.00, 5.00, 6.00, 7.00, 8.00, 9.00, 10.00 per pair.

PORTIERES.

Having been successful in placing orders, both as regards prices, quantity, and material, we are bound to keep up the high standard we have reached on this line of goods. Buying in such quantities, we have been able to make our own prices, therefore we will give the benefit to our customers. We have photographed some of our special values, so that our customers living at a distance can more easily select.

Turcoman and Chenille Dado.—$2.00, 3.00, 3.50, and 4.00 per pair.

All Chenille, plain top, with beautiful floral dados, all new colors, $5.00, 6.00, and 7.00 per pair.

Plain Chenille, extra quality, with extra heavy fringe at both ends, 3 yards long and 50 inches wide, $5.50 per pair.

Figured Chenille, in all new and rich colorings, $8.50, 10.00, 12.00, and 15.00 per pair.

Chenille Throw-over Curtains, with dado and frieze, all new colors, extra heavy fringe at both ends, $6.00, 8.00, 9.00, 10.00, 12.00, 15.00, 18.00, and 20.00 per pair.

Silk Sheila.—In this line we are showing a beautiful assortment of private designs imported by us. Prices, $20.00, 25.00, 30.00, 40.00, 45.00, and 50.00 per pair.

Figured Double-faced Velours, extra quality, new and private designs. Price, $40.00 per pair.

CHINA SILKS.

New designs and new colorings, made expressly for Mantel Draperies, Bookcases, Bed Canopies, Screen Panels, and Sash Curtains.

Prices, 50, 75c., $1.00, and 1.25 per yard. These are exclusively our own designs, and surpass anything that we have ever shown. Fringes to match all colors.

Cream and Ecru Madras.—40 inches wide, 25c. per yard; 50 inches wide, 37½c. per yard.

Fancy Colored Madras.—25, 37½, 50, 75c., and $1.00 per yard. All our own importations.

FURNITURE COVERINGS.

Our assortment in this line embraces everything in coverings.

Ramie Cloth, 50 inches wide, 37½, 45, and 50c.

Petit Point, 50 inches wide, 50, 62½, 75, 87½c., and $1.00 per yard.

Spun Silk, 50 inches wide, 87½c., $1.00, 1.25, 1.50, 1.75, 2.00, to 3.50.

Silk and Wool Tapestries, 50 inches wide, $2.50, 2.75, 3.00, 3.50, 3.75, 4.00, 4.50, 5.00, to 10.00 per yard.

Satin-faced Tapestries, 50 inches wide, $2.50, 3.00, 3.50, 3.75, 4.00, 5.00, 7.00, 10.00, 12.00, and 15.00 per yard.

All-wool Tapestries, 50 inches wide, $2.50, 3.00, 4.00, 4.50, 5.00, 6.00, to 10.00 per yard.

Felts and Windsor Cloths, 72 inches wide, $1.00 per yard, all colors.

Billiard Cloths, 72 inches wide, $3.00 per yard.

Mohair Damask. These goods are taking the place of the old-fashioned reps, they being much better wearing goods, and are made in all the fashionable colors, 50 inches wide, $1.50 and 1.75 per yard.

Corduroys, 27 inches wide, $1.00 per yard, all colors.

Hair Cloth, 18 inches wide, 80c.; 24 inches, $1.00; 27 inches, 1.25; 30 inches, 1.50.

Crushed Plushes, 24 inches wide, all colors, $1.00, 1.12½, 1.25, 1.50, and 1.75 per yard.

Plain Mohair Plushes, best makes, all colors, 24 inches wide, $1.50 and 2.50 per yard.

Frieze Plush, 24 inches, all colors, $3.00 per yard.

Fancy Figured Plush, 24 inches wide, $2.50 per yard.

Silk Plushes, in all the new shades, 24 inches, $1.25, 1.50, 1.75, 2.00, 2.50, and 3.50 per yard; 54 inches, $6.00 per yard.

Silk Brocatelles, 50 inches wide, in all the new colors, $3.50, 5.00, 7.00, and 10.00 per yard.

Linen Velours, single-faced, 50 inches wide, $1.50, 1.70 and 2.25 per yard.

Linen Velours, double-faced, 50 inches wide, $1.75, 2.00, 3.00, and 4.00 per yard.

Turkish Satins, 50 inches wide, $1.50 and 2.00 per yard.

UPHOLSTERY TRIMMINGS.

Fringes, Cords, Tassels, and Gimps. We have on hand the most beautiful selection of trimmings ever shown in this city. Tassels and ball cotton fringe, 7c. per yard.

Cretonne Fringes to match any combination of colors, 10, 12½, 15, 25, 37½, and 50c. per yard.

Silk and Worsted Tassel Fringe in every conceivable color and combination, 10c. per yard.

Moss Edging, a very pretty trimming for Sofa Pillows, 25 and 50c. per yard.

Fancy Silk Tassel Fringes, 3 inches deep, just the thing for trimming Mantel Draperies, Piano Scarfs, and Tidies, 15 and 25c. per yard.

Silk Edging Fringes for Portières, 37½, 50, 75c., and $1.00 per yard.

Fancy Silk Drapery Fringes in all the new colors and designs, from 3 to 7 inches deep, 50, 62½, 75, 87½c., $1.00, 1.25, 1.50, 1.75, 2.00, 2.50, to 5.00 per yard.

We are showing a splendid line of Silk Tinsel Fringes, 15 to 24 inches deep, which are used as valances over Lace Curtains and Portières, $1.00, 1.50, 2.00, 2.25, 2.50, 2.75, 3.00, to 5.00 per yard.

Furniture Fringes to match all combinations of colors, 6 to 7 inches deep, 37½, 50, 75, 87½c., $1.00, 1.25, 1.50, 1.75, 2.00, and 2.50 per yard. No limit to the assortment.

Special orders intrusted to our care receive prompt attention.

THE MERCANTILE HEART OF NEW ENGLAND.

COTTON PLUSHES.

Single-faced, 12½c., all colors, 30 inches wide.
Double-faced, 25c., all colors, 30 inches wide.
Double-faced, figured, all colors, 25 and 30c., 30 inches wide.
Bed Pillows, Mattresses, and Ticks always on hand.
Down Sofa Pillows, 18 inches, 20 inches, 22 inches, and 24 inches; 87½c., $1.37½, 1.75, and 2.00 each.

WINDOW SHADES.

It is an acknowledged fact that we are the leading manufacturers and dispensers of Window Shades. Our orders during the past season have far surpassed those of any previous year in the history of our business. The reason is obvious: it is the natural outcome of first-class work. The largest line of Scotch and American Holland, tint cloth, and opaque, in all widths and colors, constantly on hand.

American Holland Shades, one yard wide and two yards long, with crescent or ring, and spring fixture, 30c.

Tinted Opaque, same width and length, 40c.

Scotch-finished Holland shades, finished complete, one yard wide and two yards long, best spring fixture and nickel ring, 50c.

Hand Tinted Shades, in any color, to match interior decorations, one yard wide and two yards long, finished with "Hartshorn" fixture, cord and ball attachment, 85c. All extra sizes proportionate in price.

Special prices made to factories, hotels, and stores.

Measures taken and estimates given free of charge.

Parties sending their own measures should give finished size, both length and width, and state whether the brackets are to be placed in the run of the window or on the casing.

Table Enamel Cloth.—5 x 4, 25c.; 6 x 4, 35c.

Shelf Enamel Cloth.—8c. per yard.

Cretonnes.—American, English, and French makes, an immense assortment to select from, 10, 12½, 17, 25, 37½, 50, 62½, 75, 85c., $1.00, 1.25, 1.75, 2.00, 2.25. Samples cheerfully sent to any address.

Curtain Poles.—Black walnut, ash, cherry, and ebonized, 5 feet long, all complete, with wood or brass trimmings, 25c. each. Best quality walnut, ash, cherry, and ebonized, 5 feet long, all complete, with brass trimmings, 75c. each. Extra lengths proportionate in price.

Brass Rods.—½-in., 3c. per foot.

Brass Poles.—⅝-in., ¾-in., 1-in., 1½-in., 2-in., all complete, 5 feet long, with ends, rings, and brackets, from 50c. to $5.00 each.

Loose Coverings.—Cotton Damask, 31 in. wide, 20c. Striped Linen, 36 in. wide, 25c.; 50 in. wide, 37½ and 50c. per yard.

We cut and make Loose Covers for a full set of furniture,—sofa, two easy-chairs, and three small chairs,—from all linen goods complete, with binding or inside seams, for $15.00.

PARLOR FURNITURE.

In connection with our Upholstery Department, we are showing some very fine Parlor Furniture, manufactured by us, and warranted to be the best that can possibly be made. These goods are shown in the cotton cover, so that parties can select their own coverings from our immense assortment, to match any interior decorations.

Furniture upholstered in a thorough manner, at very low prices. Goods called for and delivered free of charge, at any place within the limits of our free delivery system.

3-fold Screen, in antique oak, oak cherry, walnut, and ebony, all prices, from $2.50 to 25.00 each.

Fire Screens, in all woods, from $3.00 to 20.00 each.

The above goods are being used very extensively, and can be mounted by us in plain or figured China Silks and Art Muslins, in any colors, to match interior decorations, at a small cost.

AWNINGS.

We make a specialty of making and hanging Awnings of all kinds, for private residences, hotels, factories, or stores, employing only practical men. All work warranted. Prices much less than regular awning-makers' prices. We show about forty different styles of awning goods to select from. Prices from 15 to 37½c. per yard. Measures taken and estimates given free of charge.

Adjustable Window Screens, to fit all common-sized windows, 25, 30, and 40c. each. Parties ordering the above should always state the width of the windows.

Bed Canopies, in pink or white, all sizes, complete, with ceiling attachment, cord, and tassel. Prices, $1.25, 1.75, 2.00, 2.25, 2.50, 2.75, and 3.00 each.

No. 70. Plain Chenille Throwover Portières, extra quality, in all the new colors, 50 inches wide, 3 yards long. $5.50 per pair.

No. 70. Extra Quality Throwover Curtains, with beautiful dado and frieze, 3 yards long, 50 inches wide. $6.00 per pair.

No. 5. Silk Edging Fringe, 5 inches deep, for Scarfs, Tidies, Mantel Lambrequins, and all kinds of fancy work. 25c. yard.

No. 6. Silk Drapery Fringe, 5 inches deep, in all the new combination of colors. 75c. yard.

No. 1. Cotton Ball Edging Fringe, in white, cream, and mixed colors. 7c. yard.

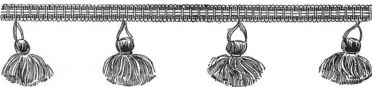

No. 2. Silk Edging Fringes, in all colors. 10c. yard.

No. 4. Silk Edging Fringe, made to match all colors, in plain or figured China Silks for Glass Curtains. 15c. yard.

No. 3. Silk Edging Fringe, to match all the new combinations in China Silks, for Glass Curtains, Tidies, Table or Mantel Scarfs. 25c. yard.

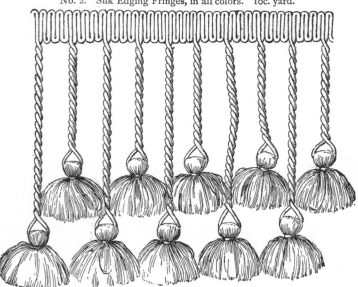

No. 7. Silk Drapery Fringe, 6 in. deep, in all colors. 62½c. yard.

No. 10. Worsted and Silk Furniture Fringe, 7 inches deep, with handsome overskirt, made in all colors to match the new combinations in silk and wool Tapestries, Brocatelles, or plain and figured Mohair Plushes. $1.00 yard.

No. 11. Overskirt Fringe, 12 inches deep, designed expressly to use as finish over the tops of lace curtains or heavy window draperies; made in all colors to match interior decorations. $1.00 yard.

No. 9. Worsted Fringe, 7 inches deep, with overskirt, in colors to match Tapestries, Brocatelles, and Mohair Plushes. 50c. yard.

THE MERCANTILE HEART OF NEW ENGLAND.

No. 100. Swiss Curtain, 50 in. wide, 3½ yds. long. $12.00 a pair.

No. 9007. Nottingham Brussels effect, 60 in. wide, 3½ yds. long, in écru or white $4.25 a pair.

No. 4024. Nottingham Curtain, in white only, 3½ yds. long, 60 in. wide. $3.00 per pair.

☞ We sell a single Portiere, but do not break a pair of Lace Curtains.

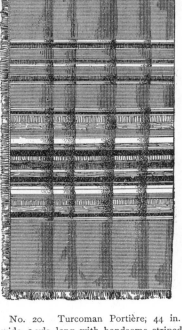

No. 30. Turcoman Portière, 50 in. wide, 3 yds. long, 36 in. solid Chenille dado, plain tops, in all the new colorings. $3.50 a pair.

No. 20. Turcoman Portière; 44 in. wide, 3 yds. long, with handsome striped dado, plain top, in all colors. $1.75 a pair.

No. 40. All Chenille Portières with beautiful floral dado, 50 in. wide, 3 yds. long, in all the new colorings. $5.00 a pair.

No. 50. Extra quality, all Chenille Portières, 50 in. wide, 3 yds. long, with beautiful floral dado, embracing all the new combinations of colors. $6.00 a pair.

THE MERCANTILE HEART OF NEW ENGLAND.

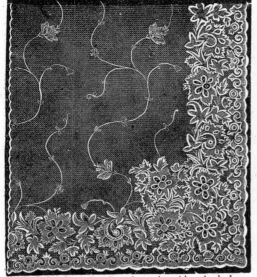

No. 10. Irish Point Curtain, 50 in. wide, 3½ yds. long. $5.00 a pair.

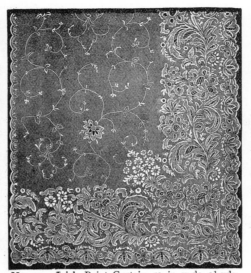

No. 11. Irish Point Curtain, 50 in. wide, 3½ yds. long. $9.00 a pair.

No. 10164. Nottingham Curtain, 3½ yds. long, 54 in. wide. $2.00 per pair in écru and white.

No. 13. Antique Curtain, 48 in. wide, 3 yds. long. $2.50 a pair.

No. 14. Antique Curtain, 50 in. wide, 3¼ yds. long. $3.75 a pair.

No. 7081. Nottingham Curtain, 3½ yds. long, 60 in. wide. $3.00 pair in écru and white.

No. 8056. Nottingham Curtain, 47 in. wide, 3 yds. long, in écru or white, taped edges. $1.15 a pair.

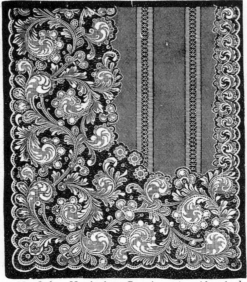

No. 8063. Nottingham Curtain, 52 in. wide, 3½ yds. long, in écru or white, taped edges. $1.40 a pair.

No. 4082. Nottingham Curtain, 53 in. wide, 3⅝ yds. long, in écru or white, taped edges. $1.50 a pair.

THE MERCANTILE HEART OF NEW ENGLAND.

SPRING AND SUMMER NOVELTIES.

IN this department can be found the largest and best assortment of fine quality Neck Ruche, and our prices are the lowest.

RUFFLING

SPRING AND SUMMER.

Fine Quality Hand-gathered Muslin de Soie Directoire Pleat Neck Ruche, suitable for Collar and Jabot, $1.00 to 2.50 per yard.

1352. Fine Quality Hand-gathered Silk Mull Neck Ruche, for plain and upright collars, cream, white, and black, 37½ and 50c. per yard.

1156. Fine English Crape, Directoire Pleat Neck Ruche, cream, white, black, red, and light blue, suitable for Collar and Jabot, $0.50 to 2.50 per yard.

1977. Double Row Silk Cord, on Silk Bolton Cloth, Cream, White, and Black Ruche, 25c. per yard.

2147. Double Row Crimp Silk Cord, on Silk Bolton Cloth, Cream, White, and Black Ruche, $0.25 per yard or 2.75 per dozen.

2324. Two Row Silk Loop Ruche, cream, white, and black, $0.12½ per yard or 1.40 per dozen.

2337. Three Row Silk Loop Edge Ruche, cream, white, and black, $0.25 per yard or 2.75 per dozen.

Imported Hand-embroidered Gilt and Silver Edge Neck Ruche, 50, 75, and 87½c. per yard.

1371. Duplex Crepe Lisse Ruche, two row, cream, white, and black, $0.25 per yard or 2.65 per dozen.

1477. Two Row Lace Edge, on Soft Finished Mull, Cream and White Ruche, 25 and 37½c. per yard.

2081. Single Row Puff Mull Neck Ruche, cream, white, and black, $0.25 per yard or 2.50 per dozen.

1347. Two Row Bolton Cloth, Cream, White, and Black Ruche, $0.20 and .25 per yard or 2.00 per dozen.

1348. Two Row Silk Scrim Ruche, cream, white, and black, $0.37½ per yard or 4.00 per dozen.

1873. Two Row Bolton Cloth Ruche, with fine tinsel edge, cream and white, 25c. per yard.

817. Double Row Full Soft Finish Mull Neck Ruche, cream, white, and black, 37½c. per yard.

450. Imported Crepe Lisse Neck Ruche, cream, white, and black, $0.25 per yard or 2.80 per dozen.

4532. Two Row Silk Bolton Cloth, with Gold or Silver Bead Edge, Ruche, 25, 37½ and 50c. per yard.

866. Single Row Heavy Cord, Cream, White, and Black Ruche, 25c. per yard.

1436. Three Row Fine Quality Crepe de Chine Ruche, cream, white, and black, 37½c. per yard.

257. Single Row Fine Soft Finish Puff Crepe Lisse Ruche, cream, white, and black, $0.25 per yard or 2.75 per dozen.

SKIRT PLAITINGS.

2061. Two Row Platt Val. Lace Edge Skirt Plaiting, cream and white, 8½ inches wide, 75c. per yard.

1941. Two Row Platt Val. Lace Edge Skirt Plaiting, 7 inches wide, 50c. per yard.

1804. Two Row Platt Val. Lace Edge Skirt Plaiting, cream and white, 5 inches wide, 37½c. per yard.

1572. Three Row Lace Edge Skirt Plaiting, cream, white, and black, 4½ to 5½ inches wide, 25c. per yard.

TOURIST RUFFLING.

1732. Fine Quality German Val. Lace Edge Tourist Ruche, 6 yards in box, 75c. per box.

1744. Fine Imitation Thread Lace Edge Tourist Ruche, 6 yards in a box, 50c. per box.

1720. Three patterns Fine Narrow Lace Edge Tourist Ruche, 6 yards in box, 25c. per box.

1801. Cream White and Black and White Silk Cord Edge Tourist Ruche, 6 yards in a box, 25c. per box.

MADE-UP LACES.

Black Spanish Guipure Lace Scarfs.—$0.75, 1.00, 1.25, 1.50, 2.00, 2.25.

Black Hand-run Spanish Lace Scarfs.—$3.50, 4.00, 5.00, 6.00, 7.50, 10.00, 12.50, 18.00.

Black Hand-run Spanish Lace Fichus.—$4.00, 5.00, 6.00, 7.50, 10.00, 15.00.

Real Duchesse Lace Collarettes.—$3.00, 5.00, 6.00.

Real Point Lace Collarettes.—$10.00, 25.00.

CHILDREN'S LACE COLLARS.

Children's Hand-made Torchon Lace Collars.—12½, 20, 25, 37½c.

Children's Hand-made Florentine Lace Collars.—$0.50, .62½, 1.00.

Children's Hand-made Crochet Lace Collars.—25, 37½c.

White Embroidered Mull Ties.—12½, 25c.

All Silk Windsor Ties, in plain colors.—25, 37½, 50c.

All Silk Windsor Ties, in stripes and plaids.—25, 37½, 50c.

VEILINGS.

Latest novelties in face Veil are the Tuxedo Nets, in single and double width, fancy mesh, and chenille spot, at 25, 37½, 50, 75c. per yard.

All the new designs in composition spots, black and colors, 27 inches wide, 50c. per yard.

Large and small chenille spot, in all colors, 27 inches wide, 50, 62½, 75c. per yard.

Plain Maline Nets, in every shade, 27 inches wide, 25, 37½c. per yard.

Fancy Thread Spot Veiling, 18 inches wide, plain and embroidered edges, $0.75, 1.00, 1.25 per yard.

Plain Brussels Net, single width, 25, 37½c.; double widths, 27 and 36 inches wide, $0.62½, .75, 1.00, 1.25 per yard.

Fancy border in Grenadine Veiling, in plain and chenille spots, in all colors, 17, 25c. per yard.

Sewing-silk Veiling, plain and striped edge, fine quality, 25c. per yard.

27 inches wide Point d Esprit, in black, écru, and white, 25, 50, 87½c. per yard.

BLACK LACES.

Chantilly Edges.—2 in. wide, 12½, 17c.; 3 in., 17, 20, 25c.; 4 in., 20, 25, 37½c.; 5 in., 37½, 50, 75c.

Point d'Bayeux Edges.—2½ in. wide, 25c.; 3 in., 37½c.; 4 in., 50c.: 5 in., 62½c.; 7 in., $1.00.

Spanish Guipure Edges.—2½ in. wide, 12½, 17c.; 3 in., 17, 20, 25c.; 4 in., 20, 25, 37½c.; 5 in., 25, 37½, 50c.

Hand-run Spanish Edges.—4 in. wide, $1.00; 5 in., $1.50; 7 in., $2.00.

Real Marquise Edges.—3 in. wide, $1.00, 1.25, 1.50; 4 in., $1.50, 2.00; 5 in., $2.00, 2.50.

Silk Duchesse Edges.—4 in. wide, 50c.; 5 in., 75c.; 7 in., $1.00; 9 in., $1.50.

Point d'Venise Edges.—3 in. wide, $0.75, 1.00; 4 in., $1.00, 1.50; 9 in., $1.50, 2.25; 15 in., $3.50, 4.50.

27-INCH WEB LACES.

Real Marquise —$7.50, 10.00.

Silk Duchess.—$4.00

42-INCH WEB LACE.

Real La Tosca Net.—$1.50, 2.00.

46-INCH WEB LACES.

Point d'Venise.—$7.50, 12.50.

Drapery Nets.—In stripes, figures, and spots, $0.75, 1.00, 1.25, 1.50, 1.75 2.00, 2.25, 2.50, 3.00, 4.00, 4.50 to 6.00.

72-INCH WEB LACE.

Real Brussels Net.—$2.00.

40-INCH FLOUNCES.

Chantilly —$1.00, 1.25, 1.50, 2.00, 2.50.

Marquise Chantilly.—$2.00, 2.50, 3.00.

Striped Flounces.—$2.50, 3.00, 3.50.

Real Marquise.—$9.00, 10.00, 12.50, 13.50.

WHITE REAL LACES.

Real Duchess Lace.—
  1 to 2 inches wide, $0.75, .87½, 1.00, 1.25, 1.50 per yard.
  2 to 3 inches wide, $1.50, 2.00, 2.25, 2.50, 3.00 per yard.

Real Valenciennes Lace.—
  ½ to 1 inch wide, $0.37½, .50, .62½, 1.00 per yard.
  1 to 4 inches wide, $1.25, 1.50, 2.00 to 5.00 per yard.

Real Point Lace.—
  1 inch wide, $2.50 to 3.50 per yard.
  1½ to 3 inches wide, $3.00 to 10.00 per yard.

Real H. M. Torchon Lace.—
  ½ to 1 inch wide, 5, 8, 10, 12½c. per yard.
  1½ to 2½ inches wide, 12½, 17, 20, 25 to 50c. per yard.

Real Medici Lace.—
  ½ to 1 inch wide, 6, 8, 10, 12½c. per yard.
  1½ to 3 inches wide, 12½, 17, 20, 25c. per yard.

Real Florentine Point Lace.—
  2 to 3 inches wide, 25, 37½, 50c. per yard.
  3½ to 5 inches wide, $0.62½ to 1.00.

WHITE IMITATION LACES.

German Valenciennes Lace.—
  ½ to 1 inch wide, 3, 4, 5, 8, 10c. per yard.
  1½ to 4 inches wide, 10, 12½, 17, 20, 25 to 50c. per yard.

Platt Val. Lace.—
  1 to 2 inches wide, 5, 8, 10c. per yard.
  2 to 6 inches wide, 10, 12, 17 to 25c. per yard.

Oriental Lace.—
  1 to 3 inches wide, 10, 12½ to 25c. per yard.
  4 to 7 inches wide, 12½, 17 to 50c. per yard.

Silk Fedora Lace.—
  1 to 2 inches wide, 12½, 17, 20 to 25c. per yard.
  2 to 9 inches wide, $0.25, .37½, .50 to 1.50 per yard.

Silk Chantilly Lace.—
1 to 2 inches wide, 12½, 17, 20c. per yard.
2½ to 5 inches wide, 25 to 50c. per yard.

Extra Fine Point de Gene Lace.—
1 inch wide, 25c. per yard.
2 to 2½ inches wide, 50, 62½c. per yard.
3 to 5 inches wide, $0.75 to 1.50 per yard.

Heavy Point de Gene Lace.—
1½ inches wide, 17, 25c. per yard.
2 to 5 inches wide, 25 to 50c. per yard.

WEB LACES IN WHITE.

Silk Chantilly.— 45 inches wide, $1.50, 2.00 per yard.
Spanish Web.— 27 inches wide, $2.00 per yard.
Fedora Web.— 27 inches wide, $1.50 per yard.
Wash Blonde.— 36 inches wide, 17, 20, 25, 37½c. per yard.
Silk Illusion.— 27 inches wide, 25c. per yard.
Silk Illusion.— 36 inches wide, 37½c. per yard.
Silk Illusion.— 72 inches wide, 75c. per yard.
Silk Illusion.— 108 inches wide, $1.00 per yard.
White and Black Crepe Lisse.— 36 inches wide, 50c. per yard.
White Cotton Point d'Esprit.— 27 inches wide, 25, 37½c. per yard.

HANDKERCHIEFS.

Gents' Plain Hemmed all Linen Handkerchiefs.— 8⅓, 10, 12½, 17, 25, 37½, 50c. each.

Gents' Plain Hemmed all Linen Handkerchiefs.— Extra large size, 25, 37½, 50c. each.

Gents' all Linen White Hemstitched Handkerchiefs.— 1 and 2 inch hems, 25, 37½, 50, 75c., $1.00 each.

Gents' all Linen White Hemstitched Handkerchiefs.— ½ inch hem, 25, 37½, 50c. each.

Gents' all Linen White Hemstitched Handkerchiefs.— Extra large size, 50, 75c., $1.00 each.

Gents' all Linen White Hemstitched Handkerchiefs.— In fancy boxes, ½ dozen in a box, $1.50.

Gents' all Linen Plain Hemstitched Handkerchiefs.— In fancy boxes, ½ dozen in a box, $1.50.

Gents' all Linen Hemstitched Colored Bordered Handkerchiefs.— 8⅓, 10, 12½, 25, 37½, 50c. each.

Gents' Plain Hemmed all Linen Handkerchiefs.— In printed and woven borders, 8⅓, 10, 12½c. each.

Gents' all Linen Mourning Hemstitched Handkerchiefs.— 25, 37½, 50c. each.

Gents' all Linen Hemstitched Initial Handkerchiefs.— 37½, 50c. each.

Gents' all Linen Hemstitched Initial Handkerchiefs.— In fancy boxes, ½ dozen in a box, $2.25, 3.00.

Gents' all Linen Hemstitched Unlaundered Initial Handkerchiefs.— 25c. each. A great bargain.

Ladies' all Linen Hemstitched Initial Handkerchiefs.— In 1 inch hems, 25, 37½, 50c. each.

Ladies' all Linen Hemstitched Unlaundered Initial Handkerchiefs.— 17c. each.

Ladies' all Linen Plain Hemmed Handkerchiefs.— 5, 6¼, 8⅓, 10, 12½c. each.

Ladies' all Linen White Hemstitched Handkerchiefs.— 8⅓, 10, 12½, 17, 25, 37½, 50c. each.

Ladies' all Linen White Hemstitched Handkerchiefs.— In ¼, ½, 1, and 2 inch hems, 12½, 17, 25, 37½, 50c. each.

Ladies' all Linen White Hemstitched Handkerchiefs.— Embroidered in dots, squares, tucks, and scalloped edge, 25c. each.

Ladies' French Hand-embroidered Handkerchiefs.— Hemstitched and scalloped edge, embroidered in white and colors, $0.25, .37½, .50, .75, 1.00, 1.25, 1.50, 1.75, 2.00 to 15.00.

Ladies' Mourning Handkerchiefs.—With solid black borders, ¼, ½, 1, and 2 inch hem, 12½, 25, 37½, 50c. each.

Ladies' Mourning Handkerchiefs.—With stripes, tucks, and embroidered edge, 25, 37½, 50c. each.

Ladies' Embroidered Mourning Handkerchiefs.— $0.25, .37½, .50, .75, 1.00, 1.25 to 2.00 each.

Ladies' Fancy Mourning Handkerchiefs.— 12½, 25c. each.

Children's Colored Bordered Handkerchiefs.— 5, 6¼, 8⅓, 12½, 25c. each.

Real Duchesse Lace Handkerchiefs.— $0.50, .75, 1.00, 1.50, 2.00, 2.50, 3.00, 3.50, 4.00, 4.50, 5.00, 6.00, 6.50, 7.00, 7.50, 8.00, 8.50, 9.00, 10.00 to 35.00.

Real Bretonne Lace Handkerchiefs.— $1.00 each.

Silk Handkerchiefs.— Plain and brocaded, in white and in colors, in all styles, $0.25 to 1.50 each.

Gents' Hemstitched China Silk Handkerchiefs.— $0.50, .62½, .75, 1.00 each.

Gents' Hemstitched Japanese Silk Handkerchiefs.— $0.50, .62½, .75, 1.00, 1.50 each.

Gents' Hemstitched Japanese Silk Handkerchiefs.—With colored borders, $0.50, .62½, .75, 1.00 each.

Gents' Black Silk Squares.— 28 to 40 inches, $1.25 to 2.75 each.

Gents' Silk Bandana Handkerchiefs.— $0.75, .87½, 1.00, 1.25 each.

Gents' Hemstitched Japanese Silk Handkerchiefs.—With the Initial, 75c. each.

Gents' Silk Mufflers.— In cream, white, and in colors, $0.75, 1.00, 1.25, 1.50, 1.75, 2.00, 2.25, 3.00 each.

Gents' Cashmere Mufflers.— In white and in colors, $0.37½ to $1.00.

HAMBURG EMBROIDERIES.

45-inch Flouncing.— In muslin, $0.50, .75, .87½, 1.00, 1.25, 1.50, 2.00, 2.50 per yard.

Muslin Flouncing.— 20 inches wide, $0.50, .62½, .75, .87½, 1.00, 1.25, 1.50 per yard.

Muslin Embroideries.— 2½ to 6 inches wide, $0.25, .37½, .50, .62½, .75, .87½, 1.00 per yard.

Muslin Insertion.— From ½ to 2 inches wide, 20, 25, 37½, 50 to 75c. per yard.

Nainsook Flouncing.— 20 inches wide, $1.00, 1.25, 1.50, 2.00, 2.50, 3.00 per yard.

Nainsook Edgings.— 2½ to 6 inches wide, $0.25, .37½, .50, .62½, .75, .87½, 1.00, 1.25, 1.50 per yard.

Narrow Nainsook Edgings.— ½ to 1½ inches wide, 12½, 20, 25, 37½, 50c. per yard.

Nainsook Insertion.— ½ to 2 inches wide, 25, 37½, 50, 62½, 75, 87½c. per yard.

Cambric Flouncing.— 45 inches wide, $0.50, .75, .87½, 1.00, 1.25, 1.50 to 2.00 per yard.

Cambric Flouncing.— 20 inches wide, $0.37½, .50, .62½, .75, .87½, 1.00 per yard.

Cambric Flouncing.— 10 to 15 inches wide, 25, 37½, 50, 62½, 75, 87½c. per yard.

Cambric Embroidery.— 2½ to 6 inches wide, 25, 37½, 50, 62½c. per yard.
Cambric Embroidery.— 1½ to 3 inches wide, 20, 25, 37½, 50, 62½c. per yard.
Cambric Edging.— ½ to 1½ inches wide, 5, 8, 10, 12½, 17, 20c. per yard.
Cambric Insertion.— ½ to 2 inches wide, 12½, 17, 20, 25, 37½, 50c. per yard.
Cambric Allover.— 20 inches wide, $0.62½, .75, .87½, 1.00, 1.25 to 3.50 per yard.

Muslin Allover.— 20 inches wide, $0.75, 1.00, 1.25 to 1.50 per yard.

APRONS.

Nurses' Lace Stripe Lawn Aprons.— 25c. each.
Nurses' Lace Stripe Lawn Aprons.— Large size, 50c. each.
Nurses' Large Size Lawn Aprons.—With three tucks, 25, 37½, 50c. each.
Nurses' Large Size Lonsdale Aprons.— With three tucks, 25, 37½, 50c. each.
Fine Lawn Aprons.— With wide insertion, $1.00 each.
Fine Embroidered Aprons.— $0.50, .75, 1.00 each.

WHITE GOODS.

Mousseline de Soie.—White, cream, pink, blue, yellow, salmon, lavender, gray, 45 inches wide, $1.00, 1.25 per yard.
Silk Mulls.— All the leading shades, 50 inches wide, $1.00 per yard.
Embroidered Silk Mulls.— All colors, 50 inches wide, $1.50, 2.50 per yard.
Figured and Spotted Swisses.— 32 inches wide, 25, 37½, 50c. per yard.
Swiss Muslin.— Plain, 32 inches wide, 12½, 17, 20, 25, 37½, 50c. per yard.
Linen Lawn.— 36 inches wide, $0.50, .62½, .75, 1.00, 1.75 per yard.
Victoria Lawn.— 32 inches wide, 10, 12½, 17, 20, 25, 37½, 50c. per yard.
India Linen.— 32 inches wide, 12½, 17, 20, 25, 37½, 50c. per yard.
Persian Lawn.— 32 inches wide, 25, 37½c. per yard.
Persian Lawn.— 32 inches wide, all colors, 25c. per yard.
Plain Nainsook.— 36 inches wide, 17, 20, 25, 33⅓, 37½, 42, 50c. per yard.
French Nainsook.— 48 inches wide, $0.37½, .42, .50, .62½, .75, 1.00 per yard.
Plaid and Check Nainsook.— 6¼, 8, 10, 12½, 17, 20, 25, 37½c. per yard.
Fancy Lace Striped Lawns.—With black and colored embroidered spots, 50c. per yard.
Fancy Lace Check Lawns.— 27 inches wide, all white, 17, 25, 30, 37½, 50c. per yard.
Embroidered Piques.—White and colored, 25, 37½, 50c. per yard.
Fleece-lined Piques.— 37½, 50, 62½, 75c. per yard.
Tucked Skirtings.— 25, 37½, 50c. per yard.
Allover Tuckings.— From 1-16 to 1 inch broad, $0.25, .37½, .50, .62½ to 2.00 per yard.
Fancy Allover Tuckings.— In revers and lace effects, $0.37½, .50, .62½, .75 to 2.00 per yard.
Tarlatan.—White, 50 inches wide, 12½, 17, 20, 25, 37½, 50, 62½c. per yard.
Tarlatan.— All colors, 12½, 17, 25c. per yard.

TIDY DEPARTMENT.

Antique Lace Tidies.—
8 x 8 inches, 8, 10, 12½, 15, 17, 20, 25c. each.
9 x 9 inches, 12½, 17, 20, 25, 37½c. each.
12 x 12 inches, 17, 20, 25, 37½, 50, 75c. each.
15 x 15 inches, $0.25, .37½, .50, .75, 1.00 each.
18 x 18 inches, $0.37½, .50, .75, 1.00, 1.25 each.

Antique Lace Oblong Tidies.—
8 x 12 inches, 15, 37½, 50c. each.
12 x 18 inches, $0.50, .75, 1.00 each.
18 x 27 inches, $0.75, 1.00, 1.25, 1.50, 2.00 each.
18 x 54 inches, $2.00, 2.50, 3.00, 3.50, 4.00 each.

Russian Lace Tidies.—
8 x 8 inches, 5c. each.
15 x 15 inches, 10c. each.
22 x 22 inches, 25c. each.
30 x 30 inches, 42c. each.
12 x 12 inches, 8c. each.
18 x 18 inches, 20c. each.
24 x 24 inches, 33c. each.

Russian Lace Oblong Tidies.—
8 x 12 inches, 10c. each.
18 x 27 inches, 25c. each.
27 x 42 inches, 62½c. each.
12 x 18 inches, 17c. each.
24 x 36 inches, 42c. each.

Nottingham Lace Pillow Shams.—
$0.25, .50, .75, 1.00, 1.25, 1.50, 2.00 per pair.

Russian Lace Pillow Shams.—
$1.00, 1.25, 1.50 per pair.

Fine Embroidered Toilet Scarfs and Covers.—
18 x 52 inches, $1.50, 2.00, 3.00 each.
8 x 8 inches, 25, 50c. each.
16 x 16 inches, 50, 62½, 75c. each.

Best quality Satin Pin Cushions.—
6 x 6 inches, 25c. each.
9 x 9 inches, 50c. each.
11 x 11 inches, 75c. each.
8 x 8 inches, 38c. each.
10 x 10 inches, 62½c. each.
12 x 12 inches, 87½c. each.

No. 1025. Two Row Vandyke Point Crêpe Lisse, with Loop Centre, Neck Ruche. 25c. yard.

No. 812. Single Row Crêpe Lisse, with Silk Cord Edge. 25c. yard.

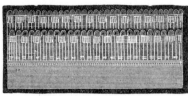

No. 1024. Two Row Crêpe Lisse and Picot Edge Ribbon Ruche. 25c. yard.

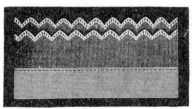

No. 1003. Two Row Embroidered Edge Neck Ruche. 3 yards for 25c.

RIBBON RUFFLING SIDE PLAITED.

No. 697. Plaited All Silk Ribbon Neck Ruche. 25c. yard.

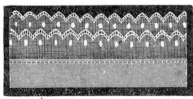

No. 1002. Two Row Embroidered Edge Neck Ruche. 12½c. yard.

SATIN RUFFLING WITH PEARL BEADS.

No. 1412. Two Row Pearl Bead Ruche. 50c. yard.

No. 1347. Two Row Silk Bolton Cloth. 20c. yard.

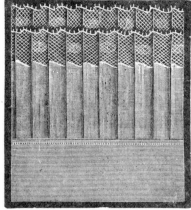

No. 1099. Two Row Lace Edge Skirt Plaiting. 15c. yard.

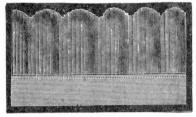

No. 813. Cotton Scrim. 17c. yard.

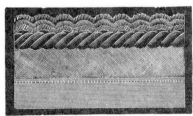

No. 1020. Fancy Braid Edge Neck Ruche. 12½c. yard.

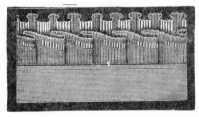

No. 1021. Two Row Plaited Crêpe Lisse Neck Ruche. 25c. yard.

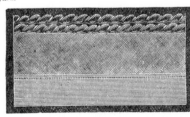

No. 2147. Two Row Silk Bolton Cloth, with Crinkly Cord. 25c. yard.

No. 1004. Silk Cord Edge Neck Ruche on Satin Binding. 3 yards for 25c.

No. 2624. Tinsel and Braid Edge Neck Ruche. 8½c. yard.

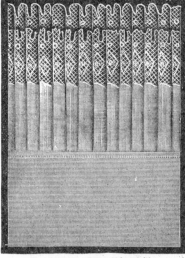

No. 1044. Two Row Lace Edge Skirt Plaiting. 25c. yard.

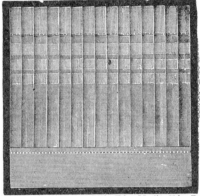

No. 9741. Three Tucked Plain Edge Muslin Skirt Ruche. 37½c. yard.

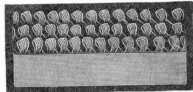

No. 2337. Three Row All Silk Loop Edge Neck Ruche. 25c. yard.

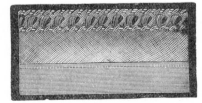

No. 1019. Cord Edge with Loop Centre on Silk Bolton Cloth. 25c. yard.

No. 2334. Two Row All Silk Loop Edge Neck Ruche. 12½c. yard.

No. 1023. Three Row Crêpe Lisse Neck Ruche. 25c. yard.

No. 3487. Silk loop and mull puff neck ruche, 25c. per yd.

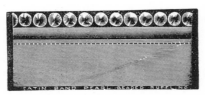

No. 1977. Single row pearl bead neck ruche, 37½ and 50c. yd.

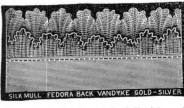

No. 2964. Puff mull and tinsel Vandyke neck ruche, 25c. yd.

No. 3859. All lace Pompadour bonnet ruche, 37½ and 50c. yd.

No. 96. Box-plait, hand-embroidered neck ruche, 25c. yd.

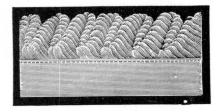

No. X. Full puff mull neck ruche, 25c. per yd.

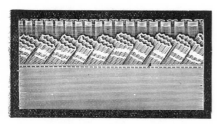

No. 944. Double row fancy crepe lisse neck ruche, 25c. yd.

No. 3119. Single row all lace neck ruche, 37½ and 50c. yd.

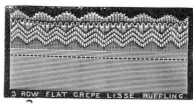

No. 3182. Three row flat crêpe lisse neck ruche, 25c. yd.

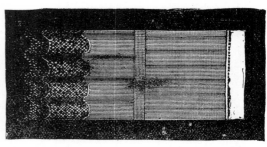

No. XX. Double row lace edge skirt plaiting, 25 and 37½c. per yd.

No. 1013. Gold and Silver Bead, on satin binding. 37½c. per yard.

No. 1014. Gold and Silver Bead, on satin binding. 25c. per yard.

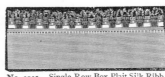

No. 1015. Single Row Box Plait Silk Ribbon Neck Ruche. 25c. per yard.

No. 1016. Crinkly Silk Cord and Embroidered Edge Ribbon. 25c. per yard.

No. 1017. Silk Loop, with gold bead, on satin binding. 37½c. per yard.

No. 1920. Silk Bolton Cloth and Embroidered Ribbon Edge Neck Ruche. 25c. per yard.

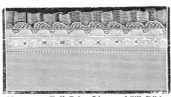

No. 1751. Full Crêpe Lisse and Silk Ribbon Edge Neck Ruche. 25c. per yard.

No. 1871. Silk Cord Edge Neck Ruche. 25c. per box (6 yards).

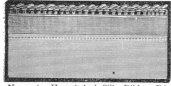

No. 1736. Hemstitched Silk Ribbon Edge Neck Ruche. 25c. per yard.

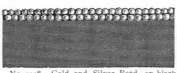

No. 2038. Gold and Silver Bead, on black satin binding. 37½c. per yard.

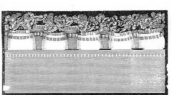

No. 1958. Box Plait Silk Ribbon Neck Ruche. 37½c. per yard.

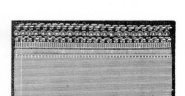

No. 2037. Double Row Crepe Lisse and Gold Bead Centre. 37½c. per yard.

No. 2035. Single Row Gold and Silver Bead Neck Ruche. 25c. per yard.

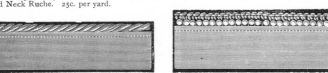

No. 1809. Vandyke Point Duplex Neck Ruche. 25, 37½, and 50c. per box (6 yards).

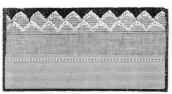

No. 1968. Double Row Vandyke Point Embroidered Wash Neck Ruche. 3 yards for 25c.

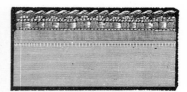

No. 1751. Silk Ribbon and Cord Edge Neck Ruche. 25c. per yard.

No. 1042. Fine Silk Cord, on satin binding. 8½c. per yard.

No. 2051. Silk Ribbon, with gold and silver bead, on satin binding. 37½c. per yard.

THE MERCANTILE HEART OF NEW ENGLAND.

No. 625.   Double Row Silk Bunting Ruche.   25c. yard.

No. 240.   Full Crêpe Lisse Neck Ruche, cream and white.   37½ and 50c. yard.

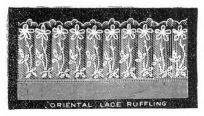

No. 895.   Double Row Oriental Lace Neck Ruche.   37½c. yard.

No. 844.   Two Row Embroidered Neck Ruche.   25c. yard.

No. 1282.   Ribbon and Crêpe Lisse Combination Neck Ruche.   25c. yard.

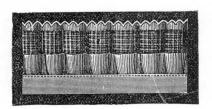

No. 873.   Hemstitched and Embroidered Edge Neck Ruche.   17c. yard.

No. 1574.   Three Row Silk Ribbon.   25c. yard.

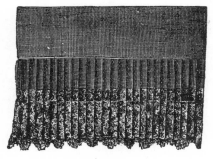

No. 2030.   Black Lace Edge Skirt Plaiting, 6½ inches wide.   37½c. yard.

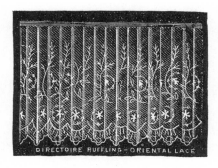

No. 670.   Oriental Lace Directoire Neck Ruche.   62½ and 75c. yard.

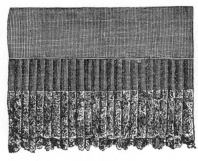

No. 2032.   Black Lace Edge Skirt Plaiting, 7 to 8½ inches wide.   50, 62½, to 87½c. yard.

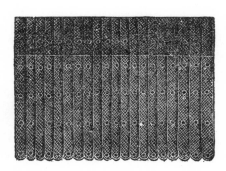

No. 688.   Black All Silk Directoire Neck Ruche.   75 and 87½c. yard.

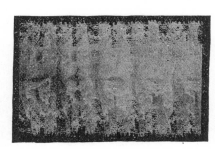

No. 195.   Pompadour Lace Edge Bonnet Ruche.   25c. yard.

No. 884.   Baby Bonnet Ruche.   Cream and White.   50c. yard

No. 175.   Plain Ribbons and Bolton Cloth Combination Ruche.   25c. yard.

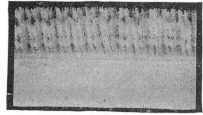

No. 180.   Double Row German Val. Lace Edge on Crêpe Lisse Neck Ruche.   37½c. yard.

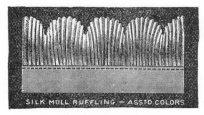

No. 1382.   Single Row Silk Mull Puff Neck Ruche.   25c. yard.

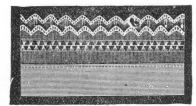

No. 820.   Double Row Hemstitched and Embroidered Edge Neck Ruche.   20c. yard.

No. 1360.   Two Row Crêpe Lisse with Pearl Beads.   37½c. yard.

No. 1312.   Double Row Cotton Bunting Neck Ruche.   17c. yd.

THE MERCANTILE HEART OF NEW ENGLAND.

No. 853.   Double Row Bead Edge Ruche.   75c. yard.

No. 1506.   Plain Cord on Satin Binding.   12½c. yard.

No. 655 b.   Picot Edge Silk Neck Ruche.   25c. yard.

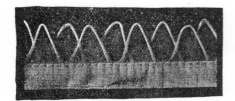

No. 1887.   Double row Vandyke Point Crepe Ruche, Cream, White, and Black.   62½c. per yard.

No. 1838.   Lace Edge Bonnet Facings.   50c. each.

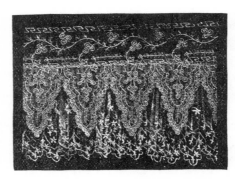

No. 4752.   Combination Imitation Point and Oriental Lace Directoire Ruche, 5 inches wide. $2.00 yard.

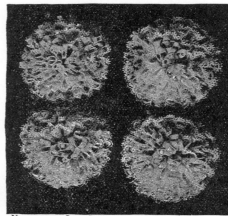

No. 1304 a.   Lace Pompons for Children's Bonnets.   37½ and 50c. each.

No. 1837.   Lace Edge Bonnet Facings.   37½c. each.

No. 2137.   Two row Silk loop edge Ruche.   12½c. per yard.

No. 200.   Two Row Crêpe Lisse Neck Ruche.   25c. yard.

No. 450.   New Style Shell Crêpe Lisse Neck Ruche.   25c. yard.

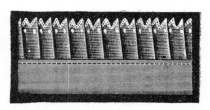

No. 838.   Simple Row Embroidered Edge Neck Ruche.   12½c. yard.

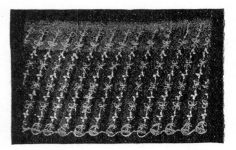

No. 3073.   Oriental Lace Directoire Ruche.   50c. per yard.

No. 2337.   Three row Silk loop edge Ruche.   25c. per yard.

LADIES' AND MISSES' COLLARS AND CUFFS.

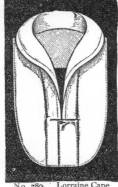

No. 781.   Marie Stuart Cape Collar.   25c. each.

No. 780.   Lorraine Cape Collar.   25c. each.

No. 90.   Boys' Turndown 3-ply Linen Collar.   12½c. each.

No. 120.   Boys' Turndown 3-ply Linen Collar.   Sizes, 11½ to 14, 17c. each.

No. 772.   Ladies' Mourning Cape Collar.   12½, 17, and 20c. each.

No. 312.   Ladies' Mourning Cuffs.   20 and 25c. pair.

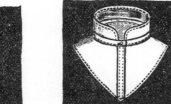

No. 7230.   Ladies' 3-ply Linen Cape Collar, low button.   12½c.

No. 318.   3-ply Misses' Cuffs, 17c. pair.

No. 311.   Ladies' all Black Mourning Cuffs.   25c. pair.

Ladies' New Redfern Cuff.   25c. pair.

THE MERCANTILE HEART OF NEW ENGLAND.

No. 448. 3-ply fine Linen Cape Collar. 17c. each; $1.75 per doz.

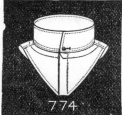

No. 614. Ladies' High Standing Cape Collar. 17c. each.

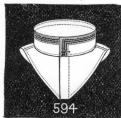

"The Princess" Cape Collar. A perfect fitting cape collar for stout necks. Sizes, 11½ to 17 inch. 12½c. each.

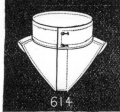

No. 774. Ladies' New Extension Cape Collar. 17c. each.

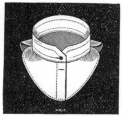

No. 594. Ladies' Mourning Cape Collar. 17c. each. Cuffs to match. 25c. per pair.

No. 449. Ladies' 3-ply Square Corner Double Buttonhole Cape Collar. 17c. each.; $1.75 per doz.

No. 120C. Ladies' Chemisette, Roll Edge Collar. 75c. each.

No. 989. Ladies' Mourning Cuffs. 25c. per pair.

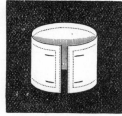

No. 918. Ladies' 3-ply Linen Cuffs, double stitch edge. 17c.

No. 804. Ladies' Solid Linen Cuffs, wide hem. 25c

No. 121C. Ladies' Emb. Edge Roll Collar and Chemisette. 75c. ea.

No. 822. Boys' Sailor Collar. 37½c. each. Hamburg Edge.

No. 693. Boys' Wide Double Stitched Edge Collar, fine quality. 20c. each.

No. 874. Boys' 3-ply Linen Collar. 12½c. each.

No. 824. Boys' Emb. Edge Sailor Collar. 25c. each.

No. 896. Ladies' Turn Point Fine Tuck Front Chemisette. 75c. each.

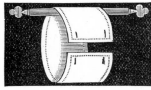

No. 909. Square Corner All Linen Cuff. 25c. per pair.

No. 559. Link Button Cuff. 25c. per pair.

No. 331. 4-ply All Linen Cape Collar. 12½c.

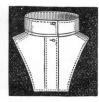

No. 332. Fine Quality All Linen Cape Collar, 17c.

No. 523. All Linen Thin Centre Cuff. 25c. pr.

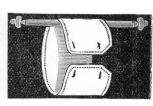

No. 524. Ladies' Linene Reversible Cuffs. 12½c. per pair.

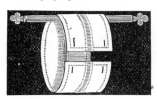

Nos. 456 and 654. 4-ply Thin Centre Cuff. 17c. per pair.

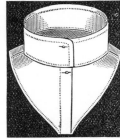

Nos. 1892 and 3640. Fine All Linen Cape Collar. 17c. each.

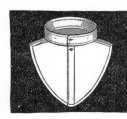

No. 407. Narrow Width Double Buttonhole Linen Cape Collar. 17c.

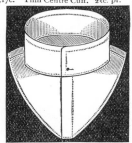

"Bostonian." 4-ply All Linen Cape Collar, double stitch edge. 12½c. each.

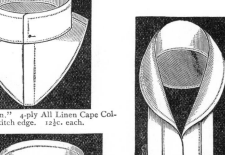

No. 930. Ladies' New Style Bernhardt Cape Collar. 25c. each.

No. 421. Ladies' Byron All Linen Cuff. 25c. per pr.

No. 415. Fine Quality Diamond Cut Front Cape Collar. 17c. each.

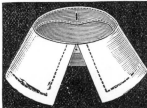

No. 76. Boy's Collar. 20c. each.

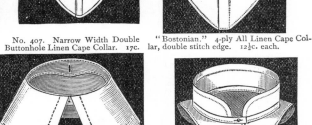

No. 250. Low Cut Cape Collar. 12½c. each.

SMALL WARES.

SEWING SILKS.

Cutter's Spool Silk, 10c. spool, 3 spools for 25c.
  "   Spool Twist, 5c. spool, 6 spools for 25c.
  "   ¼ oz. Silk, 17c. spool.
  "   1 oz. Silk, 68c. spool.
Belding's Spool Silk, 10c. spool, 3 spools for 25c.
  "   Spool Twist, 5c. spool, 6 spools for 25c.
We always have in stock a full and very choice assortment of the staple as well as the novelty shades, representing nearly 1,000 different colors.

SEWING COTTON.

Clark's O. N. T., 4c. spool, 45c. dozen.
  "   Mile End, 4c. spool, 45c. dozen.
Coats's   "   "   "
Brooks's Glace Thread, 4c. spool, 45c. dozen.
Willimantic Thread, 4c. spool, 45c. dozen.
Basting Cotton, 500 yards, 4c. spool, 45c. dozen.
French Cotton, 15c. spool.

SPOOL LINEN.

Barbour's Irish Flax Thread, a full assortment in Black and White; sizes, Nos. 25, 30, 35, 40, 50, 60, 70, 80, 90, 100, 110; 200 yards on each spool; price, 7c. spool or 80c. dozen.
Glasgow Lace Thread, in White and Unbleached, for crocheting, all sizes, at 10c. spool or $1.10c. dozen.
Barbour's Carpet Threads, 3c. skein, or 75c. pound,—36 skeins to the pound.

COTTON AND LINEN TAPES.

Best English Tape, ⅜ in., ½ in., ⅝ in., ¾ in., ⅞ in., 1 in., 1¼ in.
     3c.,   5c.,   7c.,   8c.,   9c.,   10c.,   12½c.
Common Tape, ¼ in., ⅜ in., ½ in., ⅝ in., ¾ in., ⅞ in., 1 in.
     2c.,   3c.,   4c.,   5c.,   6c.,   7c.,   8c.
India Tape, 6 pieces assorted width, in packages. 10c. per package.
Linen Tape, all widths from ⅛ to 1¼ inches wide, 3 to 12½c. piece.
Linen Bobbin, in pieces of 3 yards, 3c. piece, or 2 for 5c.

DRESS SHIELDS.

All Shields bearing this stamp are warranted, and a printed guarantee accompanies each pair of Shields.

THE GEM "REGISTERED" 1

FEATHER WEIGHT "REGISTERED"

NAINSOOK COVERED, RUBBER LINED.

No.	Pair.	Doz.
1	12½c.	$1.25
2	15	1.50
3	17	1.75
4	19	2.10

SILK COVERED.

No	Pair.	Doz.
2	25c.	$2.75
3	30	3.25
4	33	3.62
5	37½	4.00

NAINSOOK COVERED, RUBBER LINED.

No.	Pair.	Doz.
2	15c.	$1.50
3	17	1.75
4	33	2.25
5	30	3.00

MARCELINE SILK.

No.	Pair.	Doz.
2	25	$2.75
3	30	3.25
4	37½	4.00
5	42	4.75

JAPANESE SILK.

No.	Pair.	Doz.
2	30	$3.25
3	37½	4.00
4	42	4.75
5	50	5.25

DOUBLE SILK COVERED.

No.	Pair.	Doz.	No.	Pair.	Doz.
2	25c.	$2.75	4	37½c.	$4.00
3	30	3.25	5	42	4.75

SEAMLESS PURE GUM.

No.	Pair.	Doz.	No.	Pair.	Doz.
1	10c.	$1.05	4	17c.	$1.75
2	12½	1.30	5	20	2.20
3	15	1.50			

GUTTA PERCHA SHIELD.

No.	Pair.	Doz.
2 }		
3 }	10c.	$1.00
4 }		

GUTTA PERCHA SINGLE AND DOUBLE LINED. BEST QUALITY.

No.	Pair.	Doz.	No.	Pair.	Doz.
1	15c.	$1.62	3	25	$2.75
2	20	2.25	4	30	3.25

OUR ADELAIDE.

No.	Pair.	Doz.
3	10c.	$1.00

MEDICATED CHAMOIS.

No.	Pair.	Doz.
3	37½c.	$4.00

SEAMLESS STOCKINET.

No.	Pair.	Doz.
1 }		
2 }	10c.	$1.00
3 }		

DRESS BELTING AND CASINGS.

Fancy Stripes, 12½c. yard, $1.25 piece.
Black and White Watered Silk, 25c. per yard, $2.25 piece.
Extra Quality Silk Serge, 15c. per yard, $1.25 piece.
White and Gray Mixed Cotton, 3c. per yard, 25c. per piece.
Black and White Corded Belting, 12½c. per yard, $1.37 per piece.
Honey-comb in White and Black, 15c. per yard, $1.50 per piece.
Single and Double in White and Black, extra quality, 37½c. piece or $4.00 dozen.
Lion Brand, 25c. piece or $2.75 dozen.
The Bird Brand, 23c. piece or $2.37 dozen, which we highly recommend both in regard to quality and durability.
Taffeta Ribbon in Black and White, 17c. piece or $1.62 dozen.
Silk Prussian Binding, 6 yards in each piece, all silk, for covering dress seams, 15c. piece, in Light Blue, Dark Blue, Seal Brown, Dark Garnet, Cardinal, Scarlet, Slates, and Drabs.
Farmer's Bias Galloon Binding, in all shades, made from Silesia, for Whalebone Casing, 12 yards in a piece, 12½c. piece.

WAIST STEELS.

Ever Ready, assorted sizes, 15c. set, solid length, 20c. dozen.
Taylor's Self-attaching Steels, 20c. per doz.
Horn Bone Strips, all sizes, 10c. per dozen.
Black and White Covered Steels, 3c. per dozen.
Covered Featherbone, in black, gray, and white. Satin Covered, 15c. per yard. Sateen Covered, 12½c. per yard.
Genuine Silver Bone, 37c. dozen.
These Steels are 6, 7, 8, 9, and 10 inches long.

BRAID.

Skirt Braid, in black and all colors, best quality and full measure, 6c. piece.
24-yard Piece Alpaca Braid, 37½c. piece.
36-yard Piece Alpaca Braid, 62c. piece.
85 "Brand" Braid, extra quality and width, $1.25 piece, 36 yards in piece.

HOOK AND EYES.

No. 4, 3c. per card, 12½c. box; No. 8, 3c. per card, 25 per box; No. 10, 5c. per card, 30c. per box.
Patent Hook and Eyes, 5c. dozen or 37½c. gross.
Hook and Eyes on Tape, 10c. per yard.
Extra Quality Hook and Eyes on Tape, 20c. per yard, in black, gray, and white.

DRESS AND CORSET LACINGS.

Silk Dress Laces, 2½ yards, 10c.
Yachting Shirt Laces, 5c.
Black Silk Shirt Laces, 4 yards, 25c.
Linen Corset Laces, round or flat, 2½ yards, 3 and 5c. each.
Cotton Corset Laces, 2½ yards, 3c. each.
Cotton Elastic Corset Lacing, 5c. each.
Silk Elastic Corset Lacing, 25c. each.

PINS.

J., M. & Co.'s White English Pin, in paper, 5c. each.
Ne Plus Ultra, English Pin, in all sizes. BB, 6c.; F3½, 7c.; SC, 8c.; **MC,** 8c. a paper.
Kirby Beard English Pin. BB, 12½c.; F3½, 15c.; SC, 15c.; MC, 17c. a paper.
Fancy Pin Book, assorted, White and Black Pins, 12½c. a paper.
Kirby Black Pins, 15c. a box.
Mourning Pins, 5c. a box.
Book Pins (White), 10c. a paper.

Alcoholic Lamps for heating curling irons. Prices ranging from 25c. to $1.50.

The Clinton Nickel-plated Safety Pins; the sizes Nos. 1 and 2 at 5c. card; size No. 3 at 6c. card; one dozen pins on a card; also in Black.

Cabinet Hair Pins, assorted, at 5c. box.

Hair Pins in boxes, assorted, 3c. box.

Hair Pins in papers, at 3 and 5c. each.

Kirby Beard English Hair Pins in box, assorted, 100 pins, at 12½c. box.

Kirby Beard English Hair Pins in box, assorted, 50 pins, at 10c. a box.

Kirby Beard English Invisible Hair Pins, assorted, in box, at 10c. box.

Assorted Invisible Hair Pins, at 5c. box.

Black Rubber Hair Pins, 12½c. box.

Silk Wound Hair Pins, 20c. box.

HAIR GOODS.

Single and Double Front Hair Nets, 5c.; 50c. dozen.

Mohair Nets, 5c.; 50c. dozen.

Hand-made Silk Nets, 25c.; $2.75 dozen.

We have them in all colors to match the hair.

The White and Gray Hair Nets come a trifle higher in price.

Common Sense Hair Curlers, 2 sizes, 3 and 5c. each.

Kid Covered Hair Curlers, 4 sizes, 9, 10, 12½, and 15c. bunch (1 dozen Curlers in a bunch).

Silk Montague Hair Curlers, at 20c. dozen.

Scott's Electric Curlers, at 38c. each.

All kinds of Curling Irons, at 15, 20, 25, and 37c. each.

Fluffy Fedoras Hair Curlers, at 12½c. box.

HOSE SUPPORTERS.

Ladies' Plain Side Cotton Elastic, at 17c. pair.

Young Ladies' Plain Side Cotton Elastic, at 15c. pair.

Misses' Plain Side Cotton Elastic, at 15c. pair.

Children's Plain Side Cotton Elastic, 12½c. pair.

Babies' Plain Side Cotton Elastic, 12½c. pair.

We have in stock both the Warren and Lindsay Hose Supporters.

Ladies' Side Elastics, with Belt, all sizes, at 25c. pair.

Ladies' Side Elastics, with Shoulder Brace, at 25c. pair.

Children's Side Elastics, with Shoulder Brace, at 25c. pair.

Ladies' Silk Side Elastics and Satin Belt, in all colors, Black, White, Cardinal, Garnet, Pale Blue, and French Blue, at 75c. pair.

Boys' Knee Protectors, 25c.

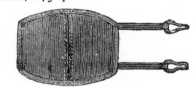

Briar stitch, 15c. a piece of 10 yards.

ELASTICS.

Our importation of Silk Elastics for gartering for this spring and summer is far superior in quality and coloring to any we have ever carried. The prices are 20, 25, 37½, 42, 50, 62½, and 75c. yard. Cotton Elastics in white and black, ⅜ inch, 4c. yard; ½ inch, 6c. yard; ⅝ inch, 8c. yard; ¾ inch, 10c. yard; ⅞ inch, 12½c. yard; 1 inch, 15c. yard. We also have a full line of fancy colored Cotton Elastic at 10, 12½, and 15c.

Non-elastic Webbing, ½ inch, 4c. per yard; ⅝ inch, 6c. per yard; ¾ inch, 8c. per yard; ⅞ inch, 10c. per yard; and 1 inch, 12½c. per yard.

Also a full assortment of choice colorings in Silk Non-elastic, at 15c. per yard.

SUNDRIES.

Woollen Carpet Binding, all colors, 10 yards in piece, 25c. piece.

Cotton Carpet Binding, 3c. yard, or 30c. piece.

Bed-tick Binding, with stripe, 12 yards in piece, 20c.

Bed-tick Binding, with a check, 12 yards in piece, 20c.

Single Skirt Steels in Black, White, and Slate, with or without elastic ends, 3c. each.

Emery Bags, 10c. each.

Glove Hooks, at 3, 5, 10, 15, and 75c. each.

Ladies' Boot Buttoners, 5, 8, 10, and 12½c. each, with wooden handles.

Ladies' Oxidized Silver Boot Buttoners, at 15 and 17c. each.

Celluloid Thimbles, 5c. each.

German Silver Thimbles, 10c. each.

Metal Thimbles, 2c. each.

Tape Measure, printed on both sides, 5c. each.

French Tape Measure, 25c. each.

Spring Tape Measure, full nickel, 17, 20, 25c. each.

Small Dress Weights, 8c. doz.; large, 10c. dozen.

Button Rings, box containing 1 gross, 10c.

Eye-glass Hooks, 8c. each.

Tracing Wheels, 10 and 17c. each.

Beeswax, yellow and white, 5c. a cake.

Vassar Sleeve-holders, 10c. each.

Stocking Darners, with handles, 8c. each.

French Mending Cotton in balls, 3c. a ball.

LADIES' SCISSORS.

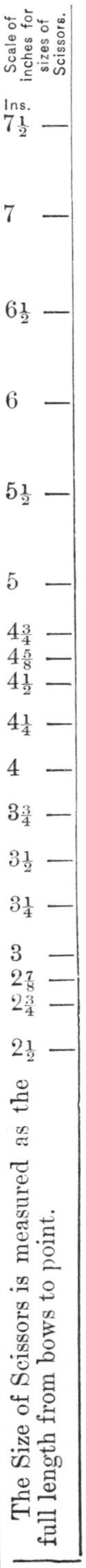

Scale of inches for sizes of Scissors.

The Size of Scissors is measured as the full length from bows to point.

Ins.
7½
7
6½
6
5½
5
4¾
4⅝
4½
4¼
4
3¾
3½
3¼
3
2⅞
2¾
2½
2¼

BUTTONHOLE.

5¼ in. $0.87½
4¼ in. 75

R x 3400.

BEVELLED BOWS.

4 in. . . . . $0.70 pair.
4½ in. . . . . .75 "
5 in. . . . . .87½ "

R x 362.

4 in. . . . . $0.62 pair.
5 in. . . . . .70 "
5½ in. . . . . .75 "
6 in. . . . . .87 "
7 in. . . . . 1.00 "

R x 2307.

4 in. . . $0.70 per pair.
5 in. . . .87½ "
6 in. . . 1.00 "
6½ in. . . 1.25 "

R x 1095.

4½ in. . . $1.00 per pair.
5 in. . . 1.25 "
5½ in. . . 1.37 "
6 in. . . 1.50 "
6½ in. . . 1.62 "

R x 725.

WIRE BOWS.

Extra Fine.

4½ in. . . $1.00 per pair.
5 in. . . 1.25 "
6 in. . . 1.50 "

S x 315.

2⅞ in. Bent . . $0.87½ per pair.
4 " " . . 1.00 "

We always have on hand a full and well-selected stock of Scissors and Knives, ranging in prices from 25c. to $2.50.

MERINO AND WOOLLEN UNDERWEAR.

A COMPLETE and varied stock, including desirable shapes and fabrics, foreign and domestic makes, received direct from the leading manufacturers, gives us important advantages regarding shapes and special values, which benefits we give to our customers. We mention a few reliable numbers.

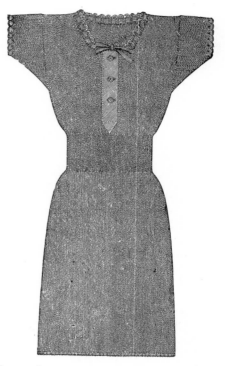

LADIES' UNDERWEAR.

Each

1. Ladies' Gauze Vests, high neck, long and short sleeves, . . $0.25

3. Ladies' Gossamer Vests, next grade heavier than gauze, silk-trimmed, pearl buttons, high neck, long and short sleeves. Drawers to match. The above have the new finished seam, which makes them equal to full regular goods. This number is a leader, ...37½

5. Our standard make Ladies' Gauze Vests, short sleeves and ribbed cuffs : —

Sizes,	26	28	30	32	34	36	38	40
Prices,	60c.	65	70	75	80	85	90	95 cts.

7. Ladies' Gauze Drawers to match : —

Sizes,	28	30	32	34	36	38	40
Prices,	70c.	75	80	85	90	95	1.00

9. Ladies' Spring Weight Merino Vests, perfect shapes, elegantly finished, high neck, long and short sleeves, Drawers to match, .50

11. Ladies' Spring and Summer Full Trimmed Ribbed Vests, low neck, no sleeves, in balbriggan, white, pink, and sky, . . .25

13. Ladies' Fine Egyptian Shape Vests, ½ open front, pearl buttons, finished with tapes, made expressly for us, and the greatest value ever offered in this class of merchandise, in long and short sleeves, with the improved close fitting cuffs, . . .25

15. Ladies' Ribbed Bodices, full trimmed, a trifle heavier than the above, in ecru, white, pink, and sky, ...37½

17. Ladies' Fine Ribbed Balbriggan Vests, manufactured from pure Egyptian cotton, the best and most desirable fabric in this class of goods. High neck, long and short sleeves. These are shaped at the waist by a band of finer texture, thereby giving fulness above and in the skirt.
    Price, short sleeves, ...37½
    "   long   " 50

The following six numbers are manufactured by the well-known and justly popular American Hosiery Co., a make we have used for a great many years, and which has always given universal satisfaction : —

19. Ladies' Gossamer Merino Vests, high neck, long sleeves, Drawers to match : —

Sizes,	26	28	30	32	34	36	38	40
Prices,	75c.	80	85	90	95	1.00	1.10	1.12½

21. Ladies' Vests, same make as the above, short sleeves : —

Sizes,	26	28	30	32	34	36	38	40
Prices,	70c.	75	80	85	90	95	1.00	1.10

23. Ladies' Gossamer Merino Vests, high neck, long sleeves, finished seams, Drawers to match : —

Sizes,	26	28	30	32	34	36	38	40
Prices,	$0.87	1.00	1.12½	1.25	1.37½	1.50	1.62½	1.75

25. Ladies' Gossamer Vests, same make and finish as above, short sleeves : —

Sizes,	26	28	30	32	34	36	38	40
Prices,	$0.75	.87½	1.00	1.12½	1.25	1.37½	1.50	1.62½

26. Ladies' White Summer Cashmere Vests, elegant fabric, silk fronts, finished seams, pearl buttons, high neck, long sleeves, Drawers to match : —

Sizes,	26	28	30	32	34	36	38	40
Prices,	$1.60	1.70	1.80	1.90	2.00	2.10	2.20	2.30

27. Ladies' Cashmere Vests, same make and finish as above, short sleeves :

Sizes,	26	28	30	32	34	36	38	40
Prices,	$1.50	1.60	1.70	1.80	1.90	2.00	2.10	2.20

29. Ladies' Non-shrinking Ribbed Vests, medium weight, Norfolk and New Brunswick make, finished with the anchor stitch elastic seam, high neck, long and short sleeves, $1.00.
    Perfect-fitting shaped Drawers to match, $1.25.

During the past season the above garments have given perfect satisfaction. Very desirable for Spring, and for Mountain and Seaside wear they are unsurpassed.

31. Ladies' Extra Fine 3-Thread Silk Vests, high neck, long sleeves : —

Sizes,	26	28	30	32	34	36	38	40
Prices,	$4.75	5.00	5.25	5.50	5.75	6.00	6.25	6.50

THE MERCANTILE HEART OF NEW ENGLAND.

33. Ladies' 3-Thread Silk Vests, same make as above, high neck, short sleeves :—

Sizes,	26	28	30	32	34	36	38	40
Prices,	$4.50	4.75	5.00	5.25	5.50	5.75	6.00	6.25

35. Ladies 3-Thread Silk Drawers, improved shapes :—

Sizes,	26	28	30	32	34	36	38	40
Prices,	$4.75	5.00	5.25	5 50	5.75	6.00	6.25	6.50

Also, a fine assortment of Novelties in Ladies' Swiss Ribbed Vests, in cotton, silk, etc. :—

37. Ladies' Swiss Ribbed Bodices, good widths, in cotton or soft-finish lisle, ... $0.50
39. Ladies' Lisle Prima Bodices, full-trimmed with silk ribbons,   .   .75
41. Ladies' Swiss Silk Ribbed Bodices, trimmed with silk ribbons,   1.50
43. Ladies' Swiss Silk Ribbed Bodices, elegant shapes and finish, all colors, ...   2.00
45. Also high neck, long sleeves, ...   2.75
47. Ladies' Extra Fine China Silk Ribbed Bodices,   .   .   3.50
49. Ladies' Spun Silk Ribbed Union Suits, in cream :—

Sizes,	Small.	Medium.	Large.	Extra.
	$6.00	6.25	6 50	6.75

CHILDREN'S UNDERWEAR.

  Each

2. Children's Gauze Vests, high neck, long and short sleeves,   . $0.25
4. Children's Gossamer Weight Vests, high neck, long and short sleeves, ...37½
6. Children's Medium or Spring Weight Vests, high neck, long sleeves, ...25
8. Children's Light Weight Vests, nicely trimmed, high neck, long and short sleeves, ...37½
10. Boys' Angola Clouded Shirts and Drawers,   .   .   .37½
12. Children's White Cashmere Vests, high neck, long and short sleeves, pantalets to match :—

Sizes,	16	18	20	22	24	26	28	30	32
Prices,	40	45	50	55	60	65	70	75	80 cts.

14. Our Standard Make Children's White Gossamer Vests, high neck, long and short sleeves :—

Sizes,	16	18	20	22	24	26	28	30	32
Prices,	35	40	45	50	55	60	65	70	75 cts.

16. Pantalets to match the above :—

Sizes,	18	20	22	24	26	28	30	32
Prices,	50	55	60	65	70	75	80	85 cts.

18. Boys' Drawers, same quality as No. 220 :—

Sizes,	22	24	26	28	30	32
Prices,	55	60	65	70	75	80 cts.

20. Boys' Knickerbocker or Knee Drawers, same quality and price as above.
22. Boys' Jean Drawers, Knickerbocker style or knee lengths, 50 cts.

MEN'S UNDERWEAR.

  Each

60. Men's White Gauze Shirts, long and short sleeves,   .   .   . $0.25
62. Men's White Gossamer Shirts, a grade heavier than gauze,   .   .37½
64. Men's 2-thread White Shirts, long and short sleeves,   .   .   .50
66. Men's Medium Weight White Merino Shirts, Drawers to match, finished with pearl buttons,   .   .50
68. Men's Spring Weight Gray Shirts, well made and good finish, Drawers to match, ...37½
70. "Our Special" Men's Medium Weight Blue Clouded Shirts and Drawers, good shapes and nicely finished, ...50
72. Men's White Summer Merino Shirts and Drawers,   .   .   .75
    Sizes : Shirts, 34 to 46 ; Drawers, 30 to 46.
74. Extra sizes, same as above, numbers 48 and 50,   .   .   1.00
76. Men's White Super Weight Lambs' Wool Shirts, made expressly to order, finished with ribbed bottoms. Drawers finished with pearl buttons to match. An elegant and desirable fabric. Customers recommend them as being one of the most comfortable garments ever worn,   .   .   1.25
78. Men's Balbriggan Shirts and Drawers, good shapes, well finished,   .50
80. Men's French Balbriggan Shirts and Drawers,   .   .   .75
82. Men's French Balbriggan Shirts, fine quality and thoroughly made, Drawers well-stayed and finished with pearl buttons to match, ...   1.00
    Sizes : Shirts, 34 to 44 ; Drawers, 28 to 42.
84. Extra sizes made expressly to our order. Particular attention given to the depth of seats in the drawers, affording ample stooping room, ...   1.25
    Sizes : Shirts, 46, 48, 50 ; Drawers, 44, 46, 48, 50.
86. Our standard make Men's White Summer Merino Shirts, short and long sleeves :—

Sizes,	34	36	38	40	42	44	46	48	50
Prices,	$0.75	.80	.85	.90	.95	1.00	1.10	1.15	1.20

88. Drawers to match the above are well made and nicely shaped.

Sizes,	30	32	34	36	38	40	42	44	46	48	50
Prices	$0.75	.80	.85	.90	.95	1.00	1.10	1.15	1.20	1.25	1.30

90. Also, Drawers of the same quality, made expressly for stout men with short legs, of which we always keep a line of sizes, and they are very much appreciated :—

Sizes,	30	32	34	36	38	40	42	44	46	48	50
Prices	$0.75	.80	.85	.90	.95	1.00	1.10	1.15	1.20	1.25	1.30

92. Men's White Gossamer Merino Shirts, finished seams :—

Sizes,	34	36	38	40	42	44	46
Prices,	$0.90	1.00	1.10	1 20	1.30	1.40	1.50

94. Men's Drawers to match the above :—

Sizes,	30	32	34	36	38	40	42	44	46
Prices,	$0.90	1.00	1.10	1.20	1.30	1.40	1.50	1.60	1.70

96. Cartwright & Warner's Celebrated Super or Medium Weight Shirts :—

Sizes,	34	36	38	40	42	44	46
Prices,	$2.12½	2.25	2.37½	2.50	2.62½	2.87½	3.12½

98. Drawers to match, long and short legs :—

Sizes,	30	32	34	36	38	40	42	44	46
Prices,	$2.50	2.62½	2.75	2.87½	3.00	3 12½	3.25	3.37½	3.62½

100. Men's Light Weight or Super Gray Shirts, an elegant fabric, finished seams :—

Sizes,	34	36	38	40	42	44	46
Prices,	$1.50	1.60	1.70	1.80	1.90	2.00	2.10

102. Drawers to match the above :—

Sizes,	30	32	34	36	38	40	42	44
Prices,	$1.50	1.60	1.70	1.80	1.90	2 00	2.10	2.20

104. Men's 4-thread Silk Shirts :—

Sizes,	34	36	38	40	42	44	46	48
Prices,	$5.00	5.25	5.50	5.75	6.00	6.25	6.50	6.75

106. Drawers to match :—

Sizes,	30	32	34	36	38	40	42	44	46	48
Prices,	$5.00	5.25	5.50	5.75	6.00	6.25	6.50	6.75	7.00	7.25

108. Men's 6-thread Silk Shirts :—

Sizes,	34	36	38	40	42	44	46	48
Prices,	$6.00	6 50	7.00	7.50	8.00	8.50	9.00	9.50

110. Drawers to match :—

Sizes,	30	32	34	36	38	40	42	44	46
Prices,	$6.50	7.00	7.50	8.00	8.50	9.00	9.50	10.00	10.50

JEAN DRAWERS.

112. Our "Model" Drawers, manufactured from Pepperell jean, are well known. Once used, always called for. The best value ever offered. 50 cts. per pair.
    N.B.—Lower grades we do not use ; the shapes and quality do not give satisfaction. "A good article is the cheapest."
114. Men's Spiral Seam Jean Drawers. These goods are manufactured from the best Pepperell jean. The shape is perfect. For fit and durability they are unsurpassed. $1.00 per pair.
116. Men's White Linen Drawers, $1.50 per pair.

Ocean Bathing, Sea Foam House, Strawberry Hill, Central Nantasket.

BATHING : OUTFITS : FOR : FAMILIES.

BATHING SUITS.

We shall open the season with a complete stock of Men's and Youths' Bathing Suits, of Foreign and Domestic Manufacture, including Fancy Stripes and Plain Colors. Our own justly popular Indigo Twilled Flannel Suit, manufactured by us especially for medium size and large men, gives better satisfaction than any other one-price suit in the market. We know this from experience, and comments on them from those who have used them; also, our increased sales on this particular style.

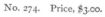

In ordering Bathing Suits, send chest measure and length, according to dotted lines in cut.

150.	Boys' Swimming Trunks, navy and white, cardinal and white, wine and white, ...	$0.25
152.	Men's and Youths' Striped Bathing Suits, ...	.75
154.	Men's and Youths' Wide Striped Bathing Suits, . . .	1.00
156.	Men's Imported Bathing Suits, brighter stripes, . . .	1.25
158.	Men's and Youths' 2-thread Striped Suits, ...	1.50
160.	Also, our own popular Twilled Indigo Flannel Bathing Suits, for medium-sized and large men, ...	2.25
162.	Extra sizes made to order, ...	2.50

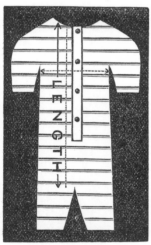

BATHING CAPS,

Muslin, Newport, Oil Silk,

25, 37½, and 50 cts.

Ladies', Misses', and Children's Bathing Suits,

IN STOCK AND MADE TO ORDER.

No. 274.　Price, $3.00.

No. 247.　Price, $2.50.

No. 240.　Price, $3.00.　　　No. 267.　Pirce, $2.50.

BOOKS, STATIONERY, MUSIC, AND ARTISTS' MATERIALS.

BIBLES.

A Rare Chance. The Oxford Bible (Sunday-school teachers' edition). American reprint. Acknowledged by press and pulpit to be the best teacher's Bible made. Minion type. 5½ x 8 inches, and 2 inches thick. 150,000 references. For a short time we can supply these Bibles to teachers or scholars at a price unheard of before. So low, in fact, that all in want of a Bible should avail themselves of this opportunity.

First Offer. French seal, divinity circuit, round corners, gilt edges. Never sold at retail in the United States for less than $4.50. Only $2.50 each.

Second Offer. Persian seal, divinity circuit, silk sewed, leather lined, round corners, gold edges. Never sold less than $6.00. Only $3.50.

Third Offer. Levant, divinity circuit, kid lined, silk sewed, round corners, gold edges. Never sold less than $7.00. Only $4.00. Postage on either, 20c.

AFTER months of preparation, we offer for the careful consideration of the book-loving public a new edition of standard British Authors, entitled the

"WESTMINSTER."

This is a European Edition, and is printed on the finest paper, broad margins, and in the clearest type, and bound in half Russia. The thoroughness and honest make-up of this book entitle it to the attention and respect of all who desire solidity and genuineness in the place of the many meretricious volumes now in such common use. The style and character of the binding will do to place in the library of the most fastidious. As the binding is invariably uniform in style, and will always be kept so, collectors can add to their library from time to time, always maintaining the same high-class standard. We place the price at

75 CENTS PER VOLUME,

and for the first time shall be able to give to the public a series of standard books, which in character vie with the highest-priced European Editions.

SUMMER READING.

The endless variety of reading published in paper covers makes it impossible for us to catalogue it. New and interesting novels are coming every day, and are placed on our counters the morning they are published. We carry all the leading lines, and sell them at prices that demand your attention.

In sending for paper books, state what library they are published in; and, if we do not have it in stock, we will get it for you.

Seaside Library, Ivers Library, Appleton, Riverside, Albatross, Madison Square, Red Letter, Worthington, and many more popular series.

A few new books at low prices.

10 CENTS EACH.

A Daughter's Sacrifice. By F. C. Philips. The First Violin. By Jessie Fothergill. The Burnt Million. By James Payn. The Baffled Conspirators. By W. E. Norris. Plain Tales from the Hills. By Rudyard Kipling. Armorel of Lyonesse. By Walter Besant. Black Beauty. By Anna Sewell. By Order of the Czar. By Joseph Hatton. Cast up by the Sea. By Sir Samuel Baker. Her Last Throw. By The Duchess. Soldiers Three. By Rudyard Kipling. A Fatal Dower. By the Author of "His Wedded Wife." Idle Thoughts of an Idle Fellow. By Jerome K. Jerome. A Woman's Heart. By Mrs. Alexander. The Phantom 'Rickshaw. By Rudyard Kipling. Weaker than a Woman. By Charlotte M. Braeme. Margaret Byng. By F. C. Philips. A Woman's War. By Bertha M. Clay. The Keeper of the Keys. By F. W. Robinson. Three Men in a Boat. By Jerome K. Jerome. Lover or Friend. By Rosa N. Carey. The Picture of Dorian Gray. By Oscar Wilde. Blind Fate. By Mrs. Alexander. Ruffino. By Ouida. A Marriage at Sea. By Clark Russell. The Great Mill Street Mystery. By Adeline Sargeant. Alas. By Rhoda Broughton. Two Masters. By B. M. Croker. The World's Desire. By H. Rider Haggard. Work, while ye have the Light. By Count Lyof Tolstoï. The Demoniac. By Walter Besant. Wormwood. By Mary Corelli. Marcia. By W. E. Norris. Phra, the Phœnician. Retold by Edwin Lester Arnold. The Other Man's Wife. By John Strange Winter. Stand Fast, Craig Royston! By Wm. Black. The Light that Failed. By Rudyard Kipling.

NOTE PAPER.

Good Cream Note Paper, 15c lb. Envelopes, 5c package.
Good Linen Note Paper, 15c lb. Envelopes, 5c package.
Heavy Cream Note Paper, 25c lb. Envelopes, 10c package.
Heavy Linen Note Paper, 25c lb. Envelopes, 10c package.
Heavy White Note Paper, 25c lb. Envelopes, 10c package.
Damask Linen Note Paper, ruled, 35c lb. Envelopes, 10c package.
Damask Linen Note Paper, plain, 35c lb. Envelopes, 10c package.
Cream Plated Note Paper, 40c lb. Envelopes, 15c package.
American Bond Note Paper, 50c lb. Envelopes, 15c package.
Artist's Proof Note Paper, 50c lb. Envelopes, 15c package.
French Quadrille Note Paper, 60c lb. Envelopes, 15c package.
French Overland Note Paper, 50c lb. Envelopes, 10c package.
Marcus Ward's Irish Linen Note Paper, 60c lb. Envelopes, 20c package.
Crane's Grecian Antique Note Paper, 50c lb. Envelopes, 20c package.
Crane's Grecian Antique Note Paper, blue, 50c lb. Envelopes, 20c package.
Linen Cloth Cream Note Paper, 70c lb. Envelopes, 20c package.
Linen Cloth Cream Note Paper, blue, 70c lb. Envelopes, 20c package.
Buckram Note Paper, white, $1.20 lb. Envelopes, 20c package.
Buckram Note Paper, blue, $1.20 lb. Envelopes, 20c package.

ARTISTS' MATERIALS.

Winsor and Newton's Common Tuber	$0.07	Brushes, Red Sable	$2.00 doz.
A First-class Sketch Box, tin	.98	Palette Knives, 4-inch	.20 each
		Palette Knives, 5-inch	.25 each
		Palette Knives, 6-inch	.30 each
American Gold Paint	.25	Academy Board, small	.07
Favorite Gold Paint	.25	Academy Board, medium	.14
Brass Plaques, 8-inch	.17	Academy Board, large	.25
Brass Plaques, 10-inch	.22	Bronzes	.15
Brass Plaques, 12-inch	.27	Canvases, from	.25 upwards.
Poppy Oil	.15	Blenders, small	.20
Linseed Oil	.15	Blenders, medium	.25
Turpentine	.12	Blenders, large	.35
French Retouching Varnish,	.23	Brass Easels, .10, .12, .15, .20, .25	
Siccatiff	.20	Palettes, wood, .15, .20, .25, .30, .35	
Brushes, French Bristle	.50 doz.	Tracing Paper	.08 sheet
Brushes, Fitch	.75 doz.	Impression Paper	.08 sheet

ENGRAVING.

We have lately increased our engraving department, and are doing beautiful work. Our aim is to keep our work up to the highest notch, and yet do it at a low price.

Satisfaction guaranteed in every case.

Card Plate and 50 cards, . . . $1.00 | 50 cards from Plate, ... $0.50

Wedding Invitations engraved in latest style, including inside and outside envelopes.

8 lines, 50 Invitations, . . . $8.00 | 10 lines, 50 Invitations, . . . $9.00
8 " 100 " . . . 9.00 | 10 " 100 " . . . 10.00

SPECIAL.

A Gold Pen is always a beautiful gift for lady or gentleman. We are making a specialty of the ones below, and warrant every one we sell.

SOLID GOLD PENS.

No.		No.	
1. Pearl Holder, gold plated end, $1.00		1. Ivory Holder, gold plated end, $0.85	
2. " " " 1.25		2. " " " 1.00	
3. " " " 1.50		3. " " " 1.25	
4. " " " 1.75		4. " " " 1.50	
5. " " " 2.00		5. " " " 1.75	

Each pen and holder enclosed in a beautiful leather case. We guarantee perfect satisfaction or money refunded. Postage on either, 5c.

A. T. Cross Stylographic pen . $1.75 | Davidson Fountain Pen . . $1.50
A. T. Cross Stylographic Pen, . | Paul E. Wirt Fountain Pen . 2.25
Gold Tip . . . . 2.00 |

JORDAN, MARSH & CO.'S

61 Selections Latest Instrumental Collection.

PRICE, 35 CENTS.

CONTENTS.

Alpine Hunt. La Châtelaine Waltz Fantasie. Ange d'Amour. Leonore Gavotte. Au Moulin. Le Père la Victoire March. Bid Me Good-by and Go. Les Sylphes Impromptu Waltzes. Carter's York Dance. Life's Story Waltz. Centennial Gallopade. Little Annie Rooney Waltz. Clarinet Polka. Little Mischief Galop. Daisy's First Waltz. Love's Dreamland Waltzes. Dancing on the Beach Schottische. Marche de Sacre. Dessauer March. Murmuring Brook. (Op. 113.) Dreams of Home Waltzes. My Greeting to America. Dude's March. New Paris Waltz. Duke of Sparta Polka Caprice. Newport York Dance. El Portico Quadrille. New Vienna Waltzes. Elopement, Galop Brillant. One Heart, One Soul. (Polka Mazurka.) Erminie Airs Medley Duet. On the Ocean. Evening Party Lanciers. Orange Blossoms. (Valse Brillante.) Father of Victory March. Paris Nouvelle Valse. Fifes de la Garde, Polka Militaire. Pearly Dewdrops. (Mazurka de Salon.) Flag of Liberty Grand March. Popular Berlin. Gondolier Waltzes. Princess Waltzes. Happy Thoughts Schottische. Royal Galop, The. Heimath's Träume Waltzes. Schubert's Serenade. In the Mill. (Au Moulin.) Seashore Pleasure Waltz. In the Valley Polka. Serenader's March. Italian Waltzes. Skirt Dance. (From "Faust up to Date.") Jolly Companions Galop. Virginia Rockaway. Jolly Gateman Lanciers. White Clover, Rêverie. Just a Little Sunshine. Woman's Cunning, Gavotte. Kiss Waltzes. World's Fair Waltzes. York Dance. (The Newport York.)

35 CENT NEW MUSIC BOOK.

Published October 1, 1890.

260 Pages of Choice Vocal Music. 68 Charming Selections. Six Dollars worth of Music for only 35 cents.

CONTENTS.

An Old Garden. Love's Old Sweet Song. An Old Sweetheart of Mine. Man the Life Boat. Back Again. Memories. Beautiful Trailing Arbutus. Murmuring Sea. Bring back my Exiled Boy. Must We then Part Forever? Calvary. My Lady's Bower. Come to Me. My Love's Last Smile. Constant. My Only Love. Cottage Light on Shore. My Little Red Umbrella. Cricket on the Hearth. My Old Village Home by the Mill. Cupid Caught Me. O Loving Heart, Hope on. Daily Question. Open thy Lattice. Dear Heart. Queen of my Heart. Dear Robin, Come Back to Me. Sea King. Down on de Camp Ground. Song of the Brook. Dreaming on the Wave. Song of the Sower. Drifting. Songs my Mother Sung. Duschinka, or the Star of the North. So the Story Goes. Felise. Silver Moon. Flower of Calvary (solo and quartet). Sleep, Papa will Come Again. Friends Only. Star of Love. Go and Forget. Star of the North. Golden Dove. Stella. Good-night, but not Good-by. Take Good Care of Mother. Hail dat Gospel Tug. That Lullaby. He has Ploughed his Last Furrow. That is Love. I Dare Thee to Forget Me. Thee I Think of, Margarita. In Old Madrid. They All Love Jack. I Whistle and Wait for Katie. Thine Forever. Just a Little Sunshine. Time and Tide. Killaloe. 'Tis All that I can Say. Life's Story. True Love is Sweet. Listen to Me, Darling. Twilight. Little Annie Rooney. Where has that Sweet Smile Gone?

FRINGES AND DRESS TRIMMINGS.

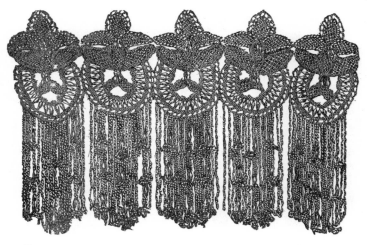

No. 4.　Jet Ornament Fringe, 5 inches deep, 12 ornaments in a yard.　$2.50 per yard.

No. 15.　Solid Jet Gimp, 2 inches wide, 8 sections in a yard.　$1.00 yard.

No. 1.　Jet Ornament Fringe, 7 inches deep, 10 ornaments to a yard.　$3.50 per yard.

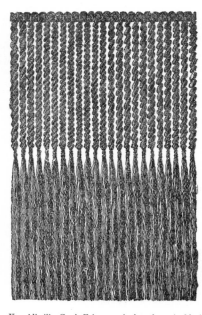

No. 1.　Black Silk Gimp, 4 inches wide, 7 sections in a yard.
$1.25 yard.

No. 4.　Black Silk Gimp, 2½ inches wide, 8 sections in a yard.
$1.00 yard.

No. 5.　Black Silk Gimp, 3 inches wide, 7 sections in a yard.
$1.50 yard.

No. 20.　All Jet Set, 6 pieces: front pieces, back piece, collar and cuffs; best quality.　$5.00 per set.

K.　All-silk Cord Fringe, 9 inches deep, in black. Very handsome.　$1.75 yard.

Jet Galloon, 1½ inches wide.　62c. per yard.

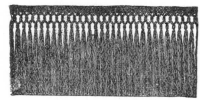

J.　All-silk Cord and Silk Fringe, 4½ inches deep, in black,
$1.00 yard.　Cream and colors, 1.25 per yard.

C.　3-inch All-silk Fringe, 2-knot.　75c. yard.

H.　Braided and Knotted Fringe, 9 in. deep.　$1.50 yard.

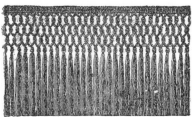

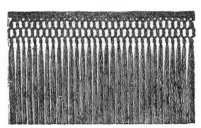

B.　6-inch Silk Fringe, 4-knot.　$1.25 per yard.

A.　4-inch All-silk Fringe, 3-knot.　$1.00 per yard.

I.　Braided and Knotted Fringe, 4½ in. deep.　87½c. yard.

Black Silk Passementerie, 2 inches wide, 8 sections in a yard, $1.25 per yard.

No. 26. Solid Jet Gimp, 3½ inches wide, 8 sections in a yard, $1.25 per yard.

Black Chenille Fringe, 4½ inches deep, 62½c. per yard.

Black Silk Pendant Fringe, 3½ inches deep, 3 dozen in a yard, $2.50 per yard.

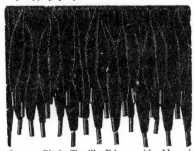

No. 15. Black Chenille Fringe, with oblong jet ends, three rows deep, $1.00 per yard.

No. 14. Black Chenille Marabout Fringe, 4½ inches wide, good quality, 62½c. per yard.

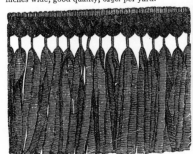

No. 10. Black Tape Mourning Fringe, 4½ inches deep, $1.00 per yard.

Black Silk Gimp, ¾ inch wide, 25c. per yard.

Cut Steel Gimp, 2 inches wide, $1.50 per yard.

Cut Steel Pointed Passementerie, 2 inches wide, $1.25 per yard.

Cut Steel Passementerie, 2 inches wide, $1.25 per yard

Cut Steel Pointed Passementerie, 3 inches wide, $1.50 per yard.

No. 39. Solid Jet Gimp, 3½ inches wide, 8 sections in a yard, $1.50 per yard.

No. 25. Solid Jet Gimp, 3 inches wide, 7 sections in a yard, $1.50 per yard.

Cut Steel Passementerie, 1½ inches wide, $1.00 per yard.

Silk Gimp, ½ inch wide, 25c. per yard. In black and colors.

Cut Steel Passementerie, 2 inches wide, $1.50 per yard.

Cut Steel Pointed Passementerie, 3 inches wide, $1.50 per yard.

Cut Steel Pointed Passementerie, 3 inches wide, $1.50 per yard.

No. 13. Solid Jet Gimp, 3 inches wide, 9 sections in a yard, $1.00 per yard.

No. 54. Black Silk Marabout, 3 inches wide, with braid looped centre, best quality, 75c. per yard.

No. 10. Black Tape Mourning Fringe, 4 inches deep, $1.00 per yard.

No. 2. Jet Ornament Fringe, 9 inches deep, 9 ornaments to a yard, $5.00 per yard.

Black Silk Pendant Fringe, 3 inches deep, 3 dozen in a yard, $2.00 per yard.

No. 16. Black Silk Gimp, 3 inches wide, 8 sections in a yard, $1.25 per yard.

No. 7. Black Silk Gimp, 2½ inches wide, 8 sections in a yard, $2.00 per yard.

No. 18. Black Silk Gimp, 3 inches wide, 8 sections in a yard, $1.25 per yard.

Jet Passementerie, 2½ inches wide, $1.00 per yard. 8 sections in a yard.

E.   All-silk Cord Trimming, 2 inches wide, 37c. yard.

No. 2.   Black Mohair Gimp, 2½ inches wide, 50c. per yard. 10 sections in a yard.

No. 6.   Cut Jet Pendant Fringe, 2¾ inches deep, $2.87 per yard.   3 dozen in a yard.

No. 29.   Cut Jet Pendant Fringe, 3½ inches deep, 3 dozen to a yard, $2.25 per yard.

No. 30.   Jet Pendant Fringe, 2½ inches deep, 2½ dozen to a yard, 87½c. per yard.

No. 8.   Jet Pendant Fringe, 3½ inches deep, 3 dozen to a yard, $1.00 per yard.

No. 11.   Black Silk Pendant Fringe, with heading, 2½ inches deep, $1.00 per yard.

No. 13.   Black Silk Drop Fringe, 2 inches wide, $1.25 per yard.   2½ dozen in a yard.

No. 21.   Jet Pendant Fringe, 3½ inches deep, 3 dozen to a yard, $1.50 per yard.

No. 19.   Black Silk Pendant Fringe, 4 inches deep, $2.00 per yard.   2½ dozen in a yard.

No. 16.   Black Silk Drop Fringe, 2½ inches wide, $1.50 per yard.

No. 12.   Cut Jet Pendant Fringe, 3½ inches deep, 3 dozen to a yard, $2.25 per yard.

No. 20.   Cut Jet Pendant Fringe, ¾ inches deep, $3.87 per yard.   3 dozen in a yard.

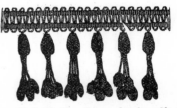

No. 9.   Black Silk Drop Fringe, 3½ inches wide, with heading, $1.25 per yard.

No. 7.   Black Chenille Fringe, with jet head ends, two rows deep, 87½c. per yard.

No. 12.   Black Silk Marabout, 3½ inches, good quality, 50c. per yard.

No. 53.   Black Silk Braid Marabout Trimming, with best quality of cut jet looped in the braid, 4 inches wide, $1.00 per yard.

No. 8.   Black Silk Tape Fringe, 4 inches deep, 87½c. per yard; 4½ inches deep, $1.00 per yard.

No. 50.   Black Silk Braid Fringe, with silk ball ends, 4½ inches deep, $1.75 per yard.

No. 31.   Rat-tail Chenille Fringe, 3 rows deep, $1.25 per yard.

THE MERCANTILE HEART OF NEW ENGLAND.

Colored Rope Fringe, 4½ inches deep. $1.00 yard.

G. All-silk Cord Trimming, 2½ inches wide. 75c. yard.

D. Chenille Fringe, 4½ inches deep, tipped with jet, 87½c. yard.

4-Knot Fringe, in black, $1.00. In colors, $1.25 per yard.

Black Silk Vandyke Gimp. 1½ inches wide, 50c per yard;
2 inches wide, 75c. per yard; 3 inches wide, 87½c. per yard.

Black Silk Vandyke Gimp. 7 inches deep, 12 points to a
yard, $3.50 per yard.

Black Silk Vandyke Gimp. 9 inches deep, 10 points to a
yard, $4.50 per yard.

No. 50. All Silk Girdle, 2 yards long, black and colors, with handsome ball ends, 62½c. each. Same style, smaller balls and drops, 50c.

No. 28. All Silk Girdle, 2½ yards long, with handsome ball and spikes, $1.00 each. Similar styles, in gold and silver, $1.87.

No. 51. All Silk Girdle, 2 yards long, in black and colors, with handsome ball and spike ends, $1.00 each. Same style, smaller ends and narrower braid, 75, 87½c.

Tinsel Gimp. 1½ inches wide in Gold, Silver, Steel, Gold and Silver, Steel and Silver, Gold and Steel, 50 c. per yard.

Tinsel Gimp. 2½ inches wide, same assortment of colors, 62½c. per yard.

Tinsel Gimp. 1 inch wide, same assortment of colors, 25 c. per yard.

Black Silk Vandyke Gimp. 3 inches deep, 24 points to a
yard, $1.75 per yard.

Black Silk Vandyke Gimp. 12 inches deep, 10 points in a
yard, $5.00 per yard.

No. 51123. Cut Steel Bolero, 5 pieces to set, $3 50 per set.

Boleros in all Jet, $7.50 per set; Boleros in all Silk, $4.87½ per set. 5 pieces to a set.

Black Silk Vandyke Gimp. 4½ inches deep, 16 points to
a yard, $1.50 per yard.

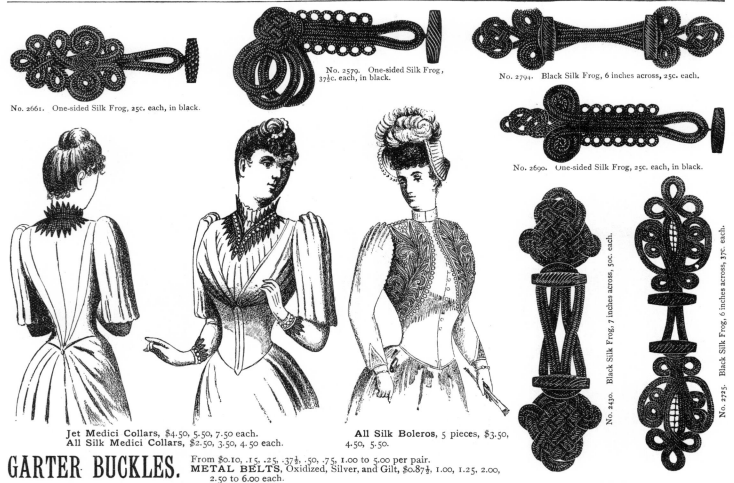

No. 2661.   One-sided Silk Frog, 25c. each, in black.

No. 2579.   One-sided Silk Frog, 37½c. each, in black.

No. 2794.   Black Silk Frog, 6 inches across, 25c. each.

No. 2690.   One-sided Silk Frog, 25c. each, in black.

Jet Medici Collars, $4.50, 5.50, 7.50 each.
All Silk Medici Collars, $2.50, 3.50, 4.50 each.

All Silk Boleros, 5 pieces, $3.50, 4.50, 5.50.

No. 2430.   Black Silk Frog, 7 inches across, 50c. each.

No. 2725.   Black Silk Frog, 6 inches across, 37c. each.

GARTER BUCKLES.

From $0.10, .15, .25, .37½, .50, .75, 1.00 to 5.00 per pair.
METAL BELTS, Oxidized, Silver, and Gilt, $0.87½, 1.00, 1.25, 2.00, 2.50 to 6.00 each.

QUI VIVE.

A solid marble clock of American manufacture, with either Serpentine Green, Pompeii, or Tennessee marble facings. It is in every way a handsome clock, with 8-day movement, striking hours and half-hours on fine cathedral gong. It measures 12¼ inches long, and 10 inches high. Warranted in every way. Price only $11.00, well worth $17.00. Each of the above clocks packed one in a box, ready for shipping.

THE ALERT.

Square nickel alarm, 6½ inches high, has fine distinct dial ; can be seen from great distance. Warranted a good time-keeper. Price only $2.00.

MESSENGER ALARM.

A beautiful carriage alarm clock, with door behind covering winding keys, hand and alarm sets. It is a really good time-keeper, and can be moved without stopping the clock. Only $2.25 each.

THE ULYSSES.

This is a new imitation marble clock, made with either bronze or silver trimmings and pillars ; can be had plain white, plain gilt, or plain silver dial. The movement runs 8 days, striking hours and half-hours on cathedral gong. It stands 10 inches high, and has 5-inch dial. It is a most desirable clock, and exceedingly cheap at $7.50, regular price being $13.50. Warranted in every way. This clock is strongly recommended

THE FORTUNA.

This is our leader in clocks. Imitation marble enamelled iron case, with 8-day best quality movement, striking hours and half-hours on cathedral gong. It measures 15 inches long by 10 inches high. Usual price, $10.00 ; our price, $5.98. Warranted a correct time-keeper.

THE GALATEA.

This is a very pretty enamelled iron clock, with fancy shaped case ; has a first-class movement, and runs 8 days, striking hours and half-hours on cathedral gong. 15 inches long, 10 inches high. Price, $6.75, worth $12.00.

THE MERCANTILE HEART OF NEW ENGLAND.

BRIDAL SETS AND PILLOW SHAMS.

Gowns (neck), size 1, 14 in., size 2, 15 in., size 3, 16 in.
Chemise (band), " 1, 38 " " 2, 40 " " 3, 42 "

Corset Covers, size (bust) 1, 36 in., size 2, 38 in.,
size 3, 40 in.
Drawers, size (length) 1, 25 in., size 2, 27 in., size 3,
29 in.

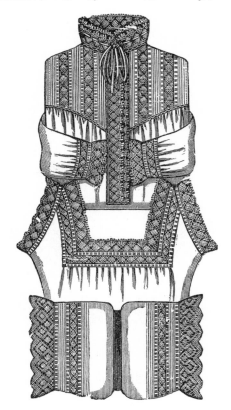

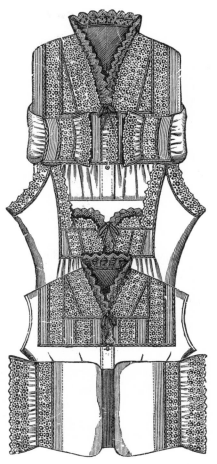

No. 3451. Consists of Night Robe, Chemise, Drawers, trimmed with very fine Torchon insertion between exquisite Hamburg insertion and tucks, edging to match. Price, $9.98.

No. 2202. Consists of Night Robe, Chemise, Corset Cover, and Drawers to match. Exquisitely trimmed with fine embroidery. Finished with lace and ribbon run through. Price, $8.00.

No. 5491. Consists of Night Robe, Corset Cover, and Drawers, trimmed with insertion of Platte lace and fine Hamburg, lace edging to match. Price, $5.98.

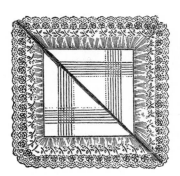

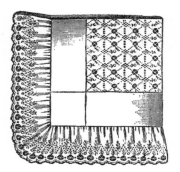

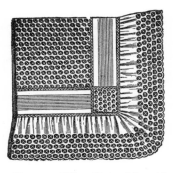

No. 1912. Cambric Sham, with fine tucks, trimmed with wide Hamburg ruffle. Price, $2.00. Same style, with three tucks and a slight difference in embroidery, $1.75.

No. 950. Pillow Sham, all over embroidered centre, finished with Hamburg ruffle. Price, $2.98. Same style, finer embroidery, $4.00.

No. 945. Pillow Sham, elaborately trimmed with choice embroidery, finished with feather stitching. Price, $5.00.

No. 230.   Embroidered Sham, cambric ruffle. Price, $1.00.

No. 952.	Cambric Pillow Sham, 3 tucks, and 3 inch cambric ruffle,	$0.75
No. 954.	Cambric Pillow Sham, 2 clusters of tucks, and cambric ruffle,	1.00
No. 956.	Cambric Sham, with a cambric ruffle edged with neat Hamburg,	1.37
No. 958.	Linen Pillow Sham, with fine Hamburg ruffle, and tucks,	3.50
No. 960.	Linen Pillow Sham, with fine Hamburg insertion and edge,	5.00
No. 962.	Cambric Pillow Sham, with 2 insertions of fine Hamburg between broad tucks, ruffle to match,	3.50

No. 964.	Cambric Pillow Sham, with a broad insertion of Hamburg and ruffle to match,	$5.00
No. 966.	Cambric Pillow Sham, Linen finish, with a 2 inch Hemstitched hem,	1.25
	Same style in all Linen,	1.75
No. 968.	Cambric Pillow Sham, Linen finished, with a row of fagoting and 2 inch hem,	2.50
No. 970.	Swiss Embroidered Pillow Shams, scalloped edge, handsomely embroidered,	2.75, 3.00, 4.50, 6.00, 8.00

NIGHT ROBES AND BLOUSES.

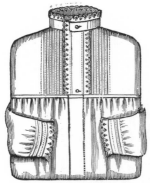

No. 200. Muslin, tucked yoke, edged with Hamburg. Price, 50c.

No. 201. Muslin, Hamburg insertion and edging. Price, 75c.

No. 202. Muslin, Hamburg insertion and edging. Price, $1.00.

No. 203. Cambric, Platte lace insertion and edging. Price, $1.10.

No. 204. Muslin, fine Hamburg insertion and edging, double ruffle in neck. Price, $1.25.

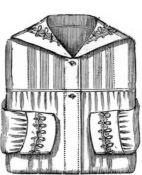

No. 205. Pride Muslin, double ruffle of blind embroidery on neck, sleeves, and down front of yoke. Price, $1.25.

No. 206. Muslin, solid yoke of Hamburg insertion and edging. Price, $1.00.

No. 214. Cambric, fine Hamburg insertion and edging, solid French and fine tuck front. Price, $3.00. Same style, with Platte lace insertion and edging. Price, $2.00.

No. 208. Muslin, embroidered collar and cuff. Price, $1.25.

No. 213. Muslin, Hamburg insertion and edging. Price, $1.00.

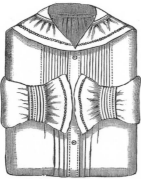
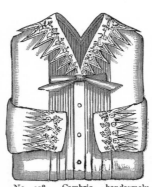

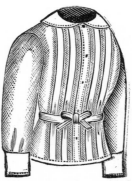

No. 216. Cambric, fine quality, hemstitched collar and cuffs. Price, $1.75.

No. 218. Cambric, handsomely tucked, collar and cuffs of Vandyke point embroidery. Price, $2.50.

No. 611. Ladies' Blouse Waist, made of Percale, white ground, colored stripe. Price, 89c.

No. 544. White Lawn, plaited front and back, plain collar and cuffs. Price, 59c.

No. 599. White Lawn, collar and cuffs feather stitched in colors. Price, 89c.

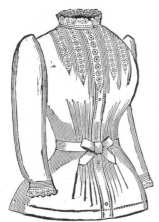
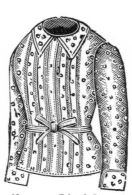

No. 777. Ladies' Blouse Waist of Fine White Lawn, trimmed with choice embroidery. Price, $2.00.

No. 533. Colored Lawn, in both sailor and pointed collar. Price, 89c.

No. 844. Colored Lawn, collar and cuffs trimmed with fine embroidery, very stylish. Price, $2.00.

No. 566. White Lawn, collar and cuffs of hemstitched embroidery. Price, $1.35.

No. 644. Fine Quality White Lawn, yoke, neck, and sleeves handsomely trimmed with Platte lace. Price, $2.50.

LADIES' CHEMISES.

No. 105. Skirt Chemise, colored lawn. trimmed with Platte lace, to match 1009 drawers. Price, $1.75.

No. 101. Cambric, Hamburg insertion and edging. Price, $1.75.

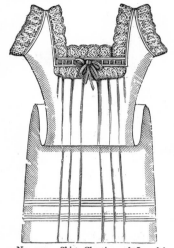

No. 102. Skirt Chemise, of Lonsdale Cambric, trimmed with Platte lace, with ribbon run through. Price, $1.25.

No. 107. Lawn, Platte lace insertion and edging, ribbon run through yoke. Price, $2.75.

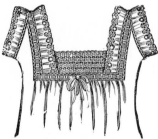

No. 116. Pride Muslin, trimmed with choice Hamburg, finished with herring-stitching, with beading between, ribbon run through. Price, $1.25.

No. 110. Muslin, corded band. Price, 39c.

No. 111. Muslin, corded band, tucks, Hamburg insertion and edging. Price, 50c.

No. 112. Pride of the West Muslin, embroidered yoke and edging, with ribbon run through. Price, 75c.

LADIES' DRAWERS.

No. 1000. Muslin, embroidered ruffle, cluster tucking above. Price, 75c.

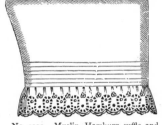

No. 1001. Muslin, Hamburg ruffle and tucks above. Price, 50c.

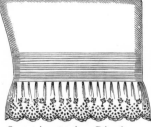

Same style, extra size. Price, $1.00.

No. 1003. Cambric, Platte lace insertion and edging. Price, 85c.

No. 1004. Muslin, fine embroidered ruffle, with 12 fine tucks above. Price, $1.00.

No. 1005. Lawn and Cambric, with two insertions of Platte lace, with beading between, ruffle to match. Price, $1.50.

No. 1006. Muslin Drawers, with tucked cambric ruffle, and tucks above. Price, 50c.

No. 1007. Cambric, Medici lace ruffle, cluster tucking above. Price, $1.25.

No. 1008. Muslin, very choice Hamburg ruffle, 20 fine tucks above. Price, $1.75.

No. 1009. Colored Lawn, deep Platte lace ruffle, tucks above. Price, $1.00.

No. 1010. Muslin, Hamburg insertion and edging. Price, $1.00.

No. 1011. Cambric, Torchon lace insertion between clusters of tucks, ruffle to match. Price, $1.25.

CORSET COVERS

No. 3011. Corset cover, with yoke of solid insertion of fine Hamburg, finished with feather stitching. Price, 59c.

No. 500. Cambric, Hamburg insertion and edging. Price, 75c.

No. 501. Cambric, very fine Hamburg embroidery and beading, with ribbon run through, finished with herring-bone stitching. Price, $1.25.

No. 502. Cambric, Hamburg insertion and edging. Price, 50c.

No. 505. Cambric, Torchon lace. Price, 50c.

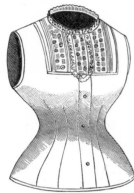

No. 508. Fine durable Cotton, insertions and edge of neat Hamburg. Price, 39c.

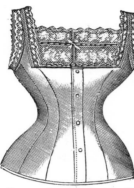

No. 509. Lonsdale Cambric, Torchon lace, with ribbon run through. Also, same style, trimmed with Hamburg. Price, 59c.

No. 2611. V-shaped Corset Cover, of fine Lonsdale, finished with feather stitching. Price, 45c.

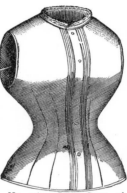

No. 1411. Corset Cover, of heavy cotton, tucked front, neck trimmed with Hamburg. Price, 25c.

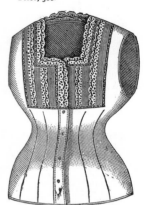

No. 503. Cambric, Hamburg insertion between clusters of cording, finished with double ruffle of embroidery. Price, $1.00.

No. 5011. V-shaped back and front, fine Hamburg, made of Lonsdale cambric. Price, 50c.

No. 504. Cambric, Hamburg insertion and edging. Price, 75c.

No. 506. Cambric, Platte lace insertion and edging, ribbon run through. Price, $1.25.

No. 507. Cambric, Torchon lace, with ribbon run through. Price, 75c.

No. 1471. Corset Cover, V-shaped neck, trimmed with fine Hamburg, in Lonsdale cambric. Price, 39c.

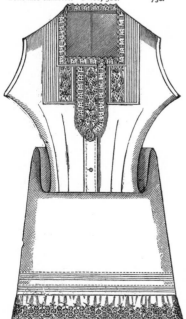

No. 630. Cambric, Hamburg insertion and edging. Price, $2.00.

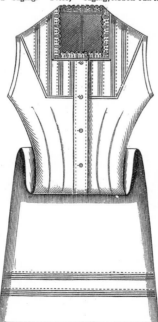

No. 610. Combination Garment, Skirt and Corset Cover, cambric, tucked yoke, edged with Hamburg. Price, $1.25.

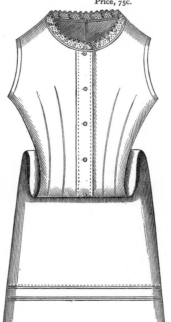

No. 620. Cambric, trimmed with fine Hamburg. Price, $1.00.

No. 12. Combination Garment, comprised of corset cover and skirt combined, of heavy cotton. Price, 75c.

WHITE

AND

COLORED

SKIRTS.

No. 712. Walking Skirt, elaborately trimmed with exquisite embroidery. Price, $6.00.

No. 709. Walking Skirt, ruffle of Platte lace inserting and edge. Price, $2.00. Underskirt to match, 1.25.

No. 711. Walking Skirt, with fine Hamburg insertings between clusters of tucks, edging to match. Price, $5.00. Same style, with one row of inserting and edge. Price, $4.00.

No. 701. Walking Skirt, Platte lace inserting and edge. Price, $3.50.

No. 706. Underskirt, Platte lace ruffle and tucks. Price, $1.00.

No. 710. Walking Skirt, with deep Hamburg ruffle and tucks above. Price, $1.50.

No. 715. Underskirt to match No. 711, fine Hamburg insertion and edge, $2.25.

No. 705. Underskirt to match 701, trimmed with Platte lace inserting and edge. Price, $2.00.

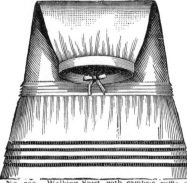

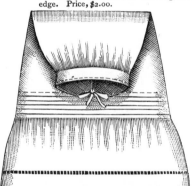

No. 700. Walking Skirt, with cambric ruffle of tucking and hemstitching. Price, $1.25.

No. 704. Walking Skirt, deep Hamburg ruffle and tucks, $1.00.

No. 708. Underskirt, tucked cambric ruffle. Price, 50c. Same style in a Walking Skirt, with tucks above ruffle. Price, 75c.

No. 703. Walking Skirt, hemstitched ruffle and tucks above. Price, 75c.

No. 600. Chambray, fancy piping, 50c. Same style in black lasting, $1.00.

No. 601. Wash Poplin Box pleat, 2 rows of Swiss embroidered inserting, $1.25.

No. 602. Plaid Seersucker, trimmed with braid. Price, $1.75.

No. 603. Seersucker, with Swiss-embroidered ruffle. Price, $1.50.

No. 604. Fancy Plaid Seersucker, three tucks in each flounce, $1.75.

No. 605. Fast Black Lasting, deep knife pleating, $1.50. Same style in alpaca, light and dark shades, $2.75.

No. 606. Fancy Seersucker, deep shirred ruffle. Price, $1.25.

No. 607. Fast Black Lasting, $1.25. Mohair, colors and black $3.50 and 4.50.

No. 608. Black Brilliantine, $3.50. Imported Lasting, $3.50.

No. 609. Wash Poplin, trimmed with braid, $1.00.

THE MERCANTILE HEART OF NEW ENGLAND.

MISSES' AND CHILDREN'S COTTON UNDERWEAR.

No. 405. Cambric, trimmed with Fine Hamburg and Cluster Tucks. Bust measure, 30-32 inches. Price, 50c.

No. 402. Muslin, Fine Hamburg Insertion and Edge. Ages, 6, 8, 10, 12, 14 years. Sizes, 3, 4, 5, 6, 7. Price, $0.90, .95, 1.00, 1.00, 1.10.

No. 403. Muslin, Hamburg Insertion and Edge. Ages, 6, 8, 10, 12, 14 years. Sizes, 3, 4, 5, 6, 7. Price, $0.90, .95, 1.00, 1.00, 1.10.

No. 404. Muslin, Clusters of Tucks and Fine Hamburg Edge. Ages, 2, 4, 6, 8, 10, 12, 14 years. Sizes, 1, 2, 3, 4, 5, 6, 7. Price, 65, 70, 75, 80, 87½, 90, 95c.

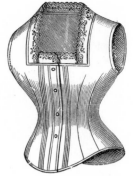

No. 409. Pride Muslin, Square Neck, edged with Hamburg. Bust measure, 30-32. Price, 33c. Also, Round Neck. Bust measure, 30-32. Price, 30c.

No. 400. Plain Hem Skirt, Cluster Tucks. Ages, 2, 4, 6, 8, 10, 12, 14 years. Sizes, 1, 2, 3, 4, 5, 6, 7. Price, 25, 30, 33, 37½, 40, 45, 50c.

No. 406. Muslin, Hamburg Ruffle. Ages, 1, 2, 4, 6, 8, 10, 12, 14, 16 years. Sizes, 0, 1, 2, 3, 4, 5, 6, 7, 8. Price, 25, 35, 40, 45, 50, 55, 60, 62½c.

No. 407. Muslin, Plain Hem and Tucks. Ages, 1, 2, 4, 6, 8, 10, 12, 14, 16 years. Sizes, 0, 1, 2, 3, 4, 5, 6, 7, 8. Price, 20, 25, 25, 30, 33, 37½, 40, 40, 45c.

No. 408. Muslin, Cambric Ruffle and Tucks. Ages, 1, 2, 4, 6, 8, 10, 12, 14, 16 years. Sizes, 0, 1, 2, 3, 4, 5, 6, 7, 8. Price, 25, 25, 30, 33, 33, 40, 40, 45, 45c.

No. 401. Hamburg Ruffle and Cluster Tucks. Ages, 2, 4, 6, 8, 10, 12, 14 years. Sizes, 1, 2, 3, 4, 5, 6, 7. Price, $0.50, .55, .62½, .75, .80, .90, 1.00.

No. 411. Fine India Lawn Apron, trimmed with fine Embroidery, sash ends. Ages, 2 to 12 years. Price, $1.00.

No. 799. Apron, Checked Muslin. Ages, 4 to 10 years. Price, 75c.

No. 778. Apron, Striped Muslin. Ages, 4 to 10 years. 75c.

No. 511. Apron, Checked Muslin. Ages, 2 to 10 yrs. 25c.

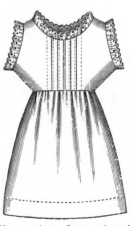

No. 414. Apron, Lawn, waist tucked front and back, trimmed with Hamburg. Ages, 2 to 8 years. Price, 50c.

No. 412. Sweeping Cap, fancy colors, faced with Cambric. Price, 10c.

No. 47. Old Ladies' Black Lace Cap. Price, $1.00.

No. 180. Old Ladies' Black Lace Cap. Price, $1.50.

No. 4. Old Ladies' Black Lace Cap. Price, $1.75.

No. 417. Nurse Apron, in Lawn and Cambric, 3 tucks above deep hem. Price, 37½c.

No. 502. Nurse's Cap. 25c.; per doz., $2.75.

No. 513. Nurse's Cap. 50c.; per doz., $5.50.

No. 804. Waitress's Cap. 17c.; per doz., $2.00.

No. 808. Waitress's Cap. 25c.; per doz., $2.75.

No. 532. Waitress's Cap. 37c.; per doz., $4.25.

No. 415. Nurse Apron, in Lawn and Cambric, 54 inches wide, with 10 inch hem. Price, 50c.

THE MERCANTILE HEART OF NEW ENGLAND.

SHORT DRESSES.

  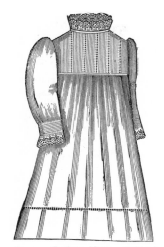 

No. 31. Cambric; baby waist; pointed yoke of fine tucks trimmed with insertion and edging; belt, cuffs, and neck trimmed with insertion and embroidery edge; plain skirt with five-inch hem. $1.50.

No. 32. Nainsook; baby waist; Pompadour yoke of wide insertion and edging, neck trimmed with insertion and narrow edge, cuff of embroidery edge; plain hemstitched skirt. $1.50.

No. 33. Cambric Mother Hubbard; yoke of fine tucks jointed with hemstitching, neck and sleeves trimmed with embroidery edge to match; plain hemstitched skirt. $1.00.

No. 34. Very fine Nainsook; baby waist; yoke formed of very fine tucks and hand feather stitching, fancy puffed and tucked sleeves, hand feather stitched, belt, cuffs, and neck of insertion and embroidery edge; skirt with four-inch hem and tucks, and hand feather stitching above. $3.75.

 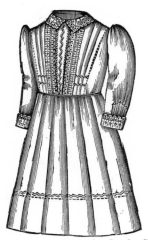  

No. 35. Nainsook; Gretchen waist of revers trimmed with embroidery; yoke of wide insertion, neck and sleeves trimmed to match; plain hemstitched skirt. $1.75.

No. 36. Fine Nainsook; Gretchen V-shaped waist of tucks, embroidery and feather stitching; collar and cuffs of embroidery edge; plain skirt with five-inch hem, and hand feather stitching above. $2.25.

No. 37. Cambric; Gretchen waist of insertion and tucking, with jacket of embroidery edge, neck and sleeves trimmed to match; plain hemstitched skirt. $1.75.

No. 38. Fine French Nainsook; Gretchen waist of fine tucks and fancy feather stitching; collar and cuffs embroidered to match, skirt with five-inch hem and fancy feather stitching above. $2.75.

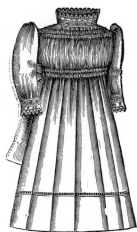   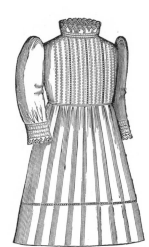

No. 39. Nainsook; baby waist of puffing and shirring, neck and sleeves trimmed with embroidery; five-inch sash, plain hemstitched skirt. $1.25.

No. 40. Fine Nainsook; baby waist of fine tucks, neck and sleeves trimmed with insertion and embroidery edge; skirt with five-inch hem and eight fine tucks above. $2.00.

No. 41. Fine Nainsook; Gretchen waist of fine tucks and feather stitching, jacket trimmed with embroidery edge, embroidered sleeves, neck and cuffs to match; skirt of handsome flouncing. $3.75.

No. 42. Lawn; Gretchen waist of reverse tucks and hemstitching, neck and sleeves trimmed with embroidery edge; plain hemstitched skirt. 98c.

THE MERCANTILE HEART OF NEW ENGLAND.

INFANTS' ROBES AND DRESSES.

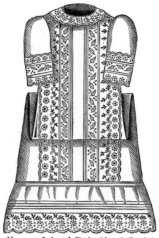

No. 19. Infants' Embroidered Cambric Robe. $2.00.

No. 20. Infants' Robe of Embroidered Muslin. $2.50.

No. 21. Infants' Lonsdale Cambric Robe, insertion front. $2.00.

No. 22. Infants' Lonsdale Cambric Robe. $1.50.

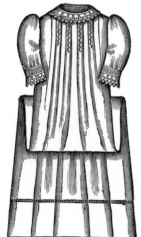

No. 23. Nainsook; yoke formed of five box plaits, and hand feather stitching, front and back alike, neck and sleeves trimmed with edging and insertion; plain hemstitched skirt. $1.25.

No. 24. Cambric; square yoke of tucks, insertion and feather stitching; puffs on shoulders; neck and sleeves trimmed with embroidery edge. $1.25.

No. 25. Cambric; pointed yoke of tucks, feather stitching, and insertion; neck and sleeves trimmed with embroidery edge; skirt with three-inch hem and cluster of seven tucks above. $1.00.

No. 26. Very fine Nainsook; baby waist; yoke formed of fine tucks and hand feather stitching, belt and cuffs of fine narrow insertion, Valenciennes lace on neck; skirt with six-inch hem and eight fine tucks with hand feather stitching between. $3.75.

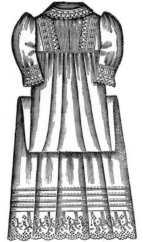

No. 27. Cambric; Gretchen waist of fine tucks, insertion and embroidery edge; neck and sleeves trimmed with insertion and edging; skirt with ruffle of embroidery and space tucking above. $2.00.

No. 28. Nainsook; baby waist, shirred front, neck and sleeves trimmed with embroidery edge; plain skirt, five-inch hem. $1.00.

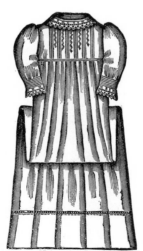

No. 29. Nainsook; Gretchen waist of fancy tucking and feather stitching; neck and sleeves trimmed with embroidery edge; plain hemstitched skirt. $1.25.

No. 30. Very fine French Nainsook; Gretchen waist of tucks, insertion, and shirred embroidery edge; neck and sleeves trimmed to match; skirt of handsome Nainsook flouncing. $4.50.

INFANTS' CLOAKS AND CAPES.

No. 1. Cream Cashmere Hubbard Cloak, silk embroidered. $2.00.

No. 2. Infant's Cream Cashmere Cloak, embroidered on skirt and cape. $2.75.

No. 3. Infant's Cashmere Cloak, cape and skirt neatly embroidered. $3.50.

No. 4. Infant's Hubbard Cloak, of cream-white Cashmere, collar elegantly embroidered, 3 tucks on lower circular. $5.00.

No. 5. Shirred Muslin Cap with full ruching; sizes, 12, 13, 14, 15, 16 inches. $1.25.

No. 6. Infants' Lace Christening caps. $1.50.

No. 7. Infant's Silk Embroidered Cap. $1.50.

No. 8. Infant's Surah Cap, silk embroidered. $1.00.

No. 9. Child's Embroidered Muslin Hat. $1.75.

No. 10. Child's Cashmere "Hubbard" Garment of finest material, neatly finished on skirt with tucks, full shirred cape exquisitely embroidered. Colors, cream-white, tan, and cardinal. $5.00.

No. 11. Child's Cashmere "Hubbard" Garment, handsomely embroidered on skirt and cape; shirred at the waist. Colors, cream-white, tan, and cardinal. $3.50.

No. 12. Child's Shirred Muslin Hat; colors, white, pink, and blue. $1.50.

No. 13. Child's "Hubbard" Garment of cashmere, handsomely embroidered. Colors, cream, tan, and cardinal. $2.75.

No. 14. Child's Walking Coat, in flannel. $2.50.

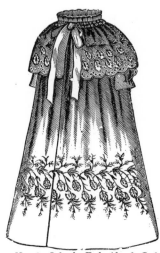

No. 15. Infant's Cashmere Hubbard Cloak, skirt and cape elegantly embroidered. $5.00.

No. 16. Cream Cashmere Cloak, fine quality, silk embroidered. $5.00.

No. 17. Infant's Cream Cashmere Cloak, of the finest quality, elaborately embroidered on both capes. $6.00.

No. 18. Infant's Embroidered Cashmere Hubbard Cloak. $7.50.

INFANTS' WEAR.

INFANT'S TROUSSEAU, consisting of fifteen pieces, for $10.00.

2 Knit Saxony Shirts, 37½	$0.75
2 Knit Saxony Bands, 37½	.75
2 Flannel Pinning Blankets, 75	1.50
2 Flannel Skirts, $1.25	2.50
2 Cambric Night Slips, 37½	.75
2 Cambric Day Slips, 50	1.00
1 Baptismal Robe	2.25
2 Pair Crochet Socks, 25	.50
	$10.00

INFANT'S TROUSSEAU, consisting of twenty pieces, for $12.00.

2 Flannel Bands, 25	$0.50
2 Flannel Pinning Blankets, 50	1.00
2 Flannel Skirts, $1.00	2.00
2 Saxony Shirts, 37½	.75
4 Cambric Night Slips, 25	1.00
1 Cambric Day Dress	1.25
1 Cambric Day Dress	1.00
2 Cambric Day Dresses, 50	1.00
1 Baptismal Robe	2.00
1 Flannel Blanket	1.00
2 Pair Crochet Socks, 25	.50
	$12.00

INFANT'S TROUSSEAU, consisting of seventeen pieces, for $15.00.

2 Knit Saxony Shirts, 37½	$0.75
2 Knit Saxony Bands, 37½	.75
2 Flannel Pinning Blankets, 50	1.00
2 Flannel Skirts, $1.00	2.00
1 Embroidered Shoulder Blanket	1.00
4 Cambric Slips, 50	2.00
1 Baptismal Robe	2.00
1 Basket (pink or blue)	5.00
2 Pair Crochet Socks, 25	.50
	$15.00

INFANT'S TROUSSEAU, consisting of twenty-three pieces, for $18.00.

2 Knit Saxony Bands, 37½	$0.75
2 Knit Saxony Shirts, 50	1.00
2 Flannel Pinning Blankets, 75	1.50
2 Flannel Skirts, $1.25	2.50
1 Embroidered Flannel Blanket	1.00
2 Cambric Night Slips, 50	1.00
2 Day Dresses, 50	1.00
1 Day Dress	1.00
1 Day Dress	.50
2 Day Dresses, $1.25	2.50
1 Day Dress	1.50
2 Bibs, 12½	.25
2 Pair Crochet Socks, 25	.50
1 Baptismal Robe	3.00
	$18.00

INFANT'S TROUSSEAU, consisting of twenty pieces, for $20.00.

2 Knit Saxony Shirts, 37½	$0.75
2 Knit Saxony Bands, 37½	.75
2 Pinning Blankets, 75	1.50
2 Flannel Skirts, $1.25	2.50
1 Flannel Embroidered Skirt	2.50
1 Flannel Embroidered Blanket	1.75
2 Cambric Night Slips, 50	1.00
1 Cambric Day Dress	1.25
1 Cambric Day Dress	1.75
1 Cambric Day Dress	1.00
1 Baptismal Robe	2.75
1 Piece Linen Diaper	1.25
1 Piece Cotton Diaper	.75
2 Pair Crochet Socks, 25	.50
	$20.00

INFANT'S TROUSSEAU, consisting of twenty-one pieces, for $25.00.

2 Knit Saxony Shirts, 50	$1.00
2 Knit Saxony Bands, 37½	.75
2 Flannel Pinning Blankets, 75	1.50
2 Flannel Skirts, $1.25	2.50
1 Embroidered Flannel Skirt	2.25
1 Embroidered Flannel Blanket	2.50
2 Cambric Slips, 50	1.00
1 Cambric Dress with Yoke	1.00
1 Cambric Dress, Robe front	1.00
1 Baptismal Robe	3.00
1 Trimmed Robe Dress	2.00
2 Embroidered Quilted Bibs, 50	1.00
2 Pair Crochet Socks, 25	.50
1 Basket (pink or blue)	5.00
	$25.00

INFANT'S TROUSSEAU, consisting of twenty-six pieces, for $28.00.

2 Flannel Bands, 25	$0.50
2 Flannel Pinning Blankets, 50	1.00
2 Knit Saxony Shirts, 37½	.75
2 Flannel Skirts, $1.00	2.00
1 Embroidered Flannel Shirt	2.00
2 Plain Cambric Skirts, 50	1.00
1 Embroidered Cambric Skirt	1.00
3 Night Slips, 50	1.50
2 Day Dresses, $1.00	2.00
1 Day Dress	1.25
1 Day Dress	1.50
1 Day Dress	1.75
1 Baptismal Robe	2.00
1 Embroidered Flannel Blanket	2.00
1 Flannel Wrapper	2.25
2 Pair Crochet Socks, 25	.50
1 Basket (in pink or blue)	5.00
	$28.00

INFANT'S TROUSSEAU, consisting of forty-one pieces, for $50.00.

6 Linen Shirts, 50	$3.00
2 Cashmere Shirts, 75	1.50
2 Cashmere Bands, 50	1.00
2 Flannel Pinning Blankets, 75	1.50
2 Plain Flannel Skirts, $1.25	2.50
1 Embroidered Flannel Skirt	3.50
1 Trimmed Cambric Skirt	2.00
4 Trimmed Cambric Night Slips, 75	3.00
1 Embroidered Flannel Wrapper	2.25
1 Embroidered Flannel Blanket	2.50
6 Cambric Dresses, $1.00, 1.25, 1.75, 2.50, 3.00, 4.00	13.50
1 Baptismal Robe	4.00
1 Baptismal Lace Cap	1.50
4 Embroidered Quilted Bibs, 25	1.00
1 Embroidered Flannel Sacque	2.00
2 Pair Crochet Socks, 25	.50
2 Pieces Linen Diaper, $1.50	3.00
2 Pieces Cotton Diaper, 87½	1.75
	$50.00

INFANT'S TROUSSEAU, consisting of forty pieces, for $70.00.

2 Cashmere Shirts, 75	$1.50
2 Cashmere Bands, 50	1.00
6 Linen Shirts, 50	3.00
2 French Hand-made Pinning Blankets, $2.00	4.00
2 Hand-made Blankets, $2.00	4.00
1 Embroidered Flannel Skirt	5.50
1 Embroidered French Nainsook Skirt	2.00
1 Plain French Nainsook Skirt	1.50
2 Cambric Night Slips, 75	1.50
1 Flannel Wrapper	2.00
1 Embroidered Flannel Blanket	4.00
6 Fine Cambric Dresses, $1.75, 2.00, 2.50, 2.75, 3.00, 3.50	15.00
1 Baptismal Robe	6.00
1 Baptismal Cap	2.00
2 Pair Crochet Socks, 62½	1.25
6 Embroidered Quilted Bibs, 25c., 37c., 50c., 50c., 63c., 75c.	3.00
1 Piece Linen Diaper	1.25
1 Piece Linen Diaper	1.50
1 Basket	10.00
	$70.00

1. BANDS.

Infants' Imported Shrunk Saxony Bands, in three sizes, 37½c. Finer quality for 50c., 75c. Finer quality, with shoulder straps, in two sizes, 50c., 75c.
Very fine Cashmere Bands, 50c., 62c., 75c.
Infants' Flannel Bands, 25c., 50c.
Ladies' Shrunk Saxony Bands, 87c.

2. SHIRTS.

Infants' Lonsdale Cambric Shirts, trimmed with narrow Hamburg, 25c.
Fine Linen Shirts, trimmed with lace or Hamburg, 37½c., 50c.
French Nainsook Shirts, elegantly trimmed, 75c., $1.00.
Infants' Shrunk Saxony Shirts, in two sizes, 37½c.
Infants' Imported Shrunk Saxony Ribbed Shirts, 50c., in large sizes.
Infants' Fine Cashmere Shirts, silk finish, 75c., $1.00, 1.25.
Fine Cashmere Shirts, buttoned down the entire front, 75c., $1.00, 1.25.
Infants' Silk Shirts, $1.25, 1.50, 1.75, 2.00.

3. SOCKS.

Crochet Socks, in all colors, 25c., 50c., 62c., 75c., 87c.
Silk Socks, $1.25.
Carriage Bootees, 50c.

4. PINNING BLANKETS.

Infants' Flannel Pinning Blankets, waistband of fine Lonsdale Cambric, 50c., 75c., $1.00, 1.25, 1.50.
French Imported Hand-made Pinning Blanket, feather-stitched and bound with silk galloon, flannel waistband, $2.00.

5. INFANTS' SKIRTS.

Infants' Flannel Skirt, with deep hem, waistband of Lonsdale Cambric, $1.00. Finer quality, $1.25.
Flannel Skirt, with silk embroidered scallop, $1.75. With scallop and dot, $2.00. With scallop and spray, $2.25, 2.50, 2.75.
Flannel Skirt, elegantly embroidered, $3.00, 3.50, 3.75, 4.50, 5.00, 7.50, 8.00, 10.00.
Hand-made Flannel Skirts, with hem and tucks, $2.50.
Lonsdale Cambric Skirt, with deep hem and cluster of tucking, 50c., 75c.
Skirts trimmed with Hamburg, 87½c., $1.00, 1.25, 1.50, 1.75, 2.00.
French Nainsook Skirts, elegantly trimmed, $2.50, 3.00, 4.00, 5.00.

6. INFANTS' FLANNEL BLANKETS.

Infants' Silk Embroidered Shoulder Blanket, ¾ square, $1.00.
Blanket with deep hem, feather-stitched with silk, $1.00.
Blanket bound with silk galloon, $1.00.
Infants' Blankets, handsomely embroidered, $1.50, 1.75, 2.00, 2.25, 2.50, 2.75, 3.00, 3.50, 4.00, 5.00, 6.00, to 25.00.

7. INFANTS' SACQUES.

Hand Crochet Sacques of split zephyr, in all colors, 50c., $1.00, 1.50, 1.75.
Sacques Finished with Silk, $2.00, 2.50.
Extra sizes, daintily trimmed with ribbon, $2.25, 2.50.
Fine cream-white Flannel Sacques, prettily embroidered with scallop in white, pink, and blue, $2.00.
Extra large size, $2.25.
Exquisite Flannel Sacques, elegantly embroidered, $4.50.

8. INFANTS' SLIPS.

Infants' Lonsdale Cambric Slips, neatly trimmed on neck and sleeves with Hamburg, 25c.
Six different styles, with yoke, insertion front, tucked robe front, plain and French tucking, for 50c.
Other styles with dainty yokes, 75c., 87c., $1.00
French Nainsook Slips, beautifully trimmed, $1.25, 1.50, 1.75, 2.00, 2.25, 2.50, 2.75, 3.00.
Imported Hand-made French Nainsook Slips, $3.00, 4.00, 4.50, 5.00, 5.50, 6.00, 7.50, 8.00.

9. INFANTS' DRESSES.

Lonsdale Cambric Dresses, trimmed with yokes, and ruffles of Hamburg, in a variety of styles, $1.00, 1.25, 1.50, 1.75, 2.00, 2.50, 2.75, 3.00, 3.50, 4.50.
French Nainsook Dresses, handsomely trimmed with the finest embroideries, $5.00, 6.00, 7.50, 8.00, 8.50, 9.00, 10.00, 12.00, 15.00, 17.00, 18.00, 20.00.
French Imported Hand-made Nainsook Dresses, $10.00, 12.00, 15.00, 16.00, 17.00, 18.00.

10. INFANTS' WRAPPERS.

Fine Flannel Wrappers in cream-white, embroidered with pink, white, or blue silk, exquisitely designed, $2.00, 2.50, 2.75, 3.00, 3.50, 5.00, 8.50.

11. GOWNS.

Infants' Night-gowns, buttoned in front, 75c., 87c., $1.00, 1.25.

12. BIBS.

Infants' Quilted Bib, 12c.
Bib of fleece-lined Pique, 12c.
Imported Hand-embroidered Quilted Bib, 25c., 37c., 50c., 62c., 75c., 87c., $1.00, 1.50, 1.75, 2.00, 2.50, 3.00.
Imported Hand-quilted and Embroidered Bibs, 37½c., 50c., 62c., 75c., 87c.
Table Bibs, 25c., 50c.

13. DIAPERS.

The "Canfield" Diaper, 75c.

14. INFANTS' CLOAKS.

Infants' Cream Cashmere Hubbard Cloaks, elegantly embroidered, $2.00, 2.75, 3.00, 3.50, 5.00, 6.00, 7.50, 8.50, 9.50, 10.00, 12.00, 15.00, 16.00, 18.00, 20.00, 25.00, 27.00, 33.00.

15. BAPTISMAL ROBES.

Infants' Baptismal Robes in Lonsdale Cambric, for $2.00, 2.75, 3.00, 4.00, 4.50, 5.00.
French Nainsook Robes, handsomely trimmed, $8.50, 10.00, 12.00, 15.00.

16. BAPTISMAL CAPS.

Infants' Lace Caps, $1.00, 1.50, 2.00, 2.50, 3.00, 4.50, 5.00, 7.50.
Silk Caps, $1.75, 2.00.
Silk Embroidered Caps, $2.50, 3.50.

17. CHILDREN'S WEAR, FROM 6 MONTHS TO 3 YEARS.

Lonsdale Cambric Skirt, with French waist tucked on skirt, for 50c.
Skirts trimmed with choice Hamburg, 87c., $1.00, 1.25, 1.50, 1.75, 2.00, 2.50, 2.75.
Plain Flannel Skirt, with French waist, $1.00, 1.25, 1.75.
Skirt, with hem and two tucks, stitched with silk, 87c. With silk embroidered scallop, $1.00. With scallop and dot, $1.25. With scallop and spray, $1.50, 1.75, 2.00, 2.50, 2.75, 3.00.

18. DRESSES.

Children's Hubbard Dresses in Lonsdale Cambric, 50c., 75c., $1.00, 1.25, 1.50, 1.75, 2.00, 2.50.
Nainsook Dresses, elegantly trimmed with Hamburg, $3.00, 3.50, 3.75, 4.00, 5.00, 6.00, 6.50, 7.50, 8.50, 10.00.
Children's Gretchen Waist Dresses, 75c., 87c., $1.25, 1.50, 2.50, 3.50, 5.00, 7.50, 8.50.

19. CHILDREN'S CLOAKS.

Cashmere Hubbard Cloaks, handsomely embroidered, $2.00, 2.75, 3.50, 5.00, 7.50, 8.50, 10.00. Color, cream.
Muslin, Lace, and Silk Caps in all styles and prices.
Muslin Caps, 25c., 50c., 75c., $1.00, 1.25, 1.50, 1.75, 2.00, 2.50, 3.00.
Lace Caps, $1.00, 1.50, 1.75, 2.00, 2.50.
Silk Caps, $1.50, 1.75, 2.00, 2.50, 2.75, 3.50, 4.00, 5.00.

THE FLEUR DE LIS CORSETS.

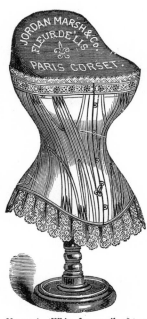

AA. Black Italian cloth, medium length waist, high bust, 18 to 30 inches. Price, $7.00.

No. 202A. White fine coutil, 18 to 26 inches. Price, $5.00.

No. 5. Black Italian cloth, long waist, high bust, 18 to 26 inches. Price, $8.00.

No. 5. Black satin, extra long waist, high bust, 18 to 26 inches. Price, $12.00.

No. 5. Ecru coutil, long waist, high bust, 18 to 26 inches. Price, $8.00.

Fine white coutil, long waist, high bust, 18 to 26 inches. Price, $8.00.

No. 302AA. Fine white coutil, long waist and high bust, 18 to 26 inches. Price, $7.00.

No. 75AB. Fine white coutil, short waist, low bust. For stout figures. 18 to 30 inches. Price, $6.00.

This celebrated Corset is owned and controlled exclusively by ourselves, and is, without exception, the most perfect fitting Corset in the world. Made by the best hands in Paris. Ladies who can purchase these will wear no other.

CORSETS
OF FRENCH, GERMAN, AND DOMESTIC MANUFACTURE.

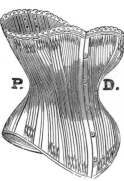

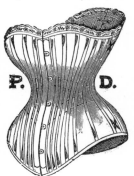

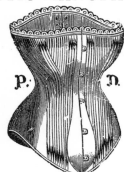

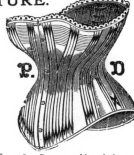

No. 530. P. D. White and drab coutil. Sizes, 18 to 30 inches, $1.75.

No. 397. Satteen, white, blue, black, 18 to 30 inches, $3.25.

No. 152. The Perfect Shape. White and drab coutil, with satteen stripe, 18 to 30 inches, $2.75.

No. 28. Spoon busk, long waist, high bust, white and drab coutil, 18 to 36 inches, $3.00.

No. 248. Satteen, white, drab, medium and short lengths, 18 to 26 inches, $2.50.

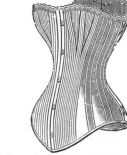

No. 119. Fine imported sewed Corset, medium length, white and drab. Price, $1.50.

No. 172. Fine imported sewed Corset, long waist, beautifully shaped, white and drab, $2.00.

No. 533. French Sewed Corset, finely shaped, white and drab, $2.50; black, 3.00.

THOMSON'S GLOVE FITTING VENTILATING

PRICE, $1.00.

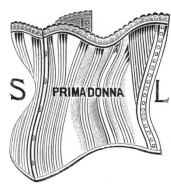

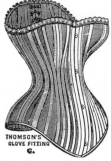

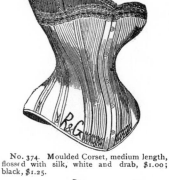

Satteen, medium length, white, pink, and blue, 18 to 26 inches, $2.50.

Very long-waisted, white and drab, 18 to 30 inches, $1.50.

HER MAJESTY'S CORSET.

We are sole agents for this celebrated Corset, and guarantee every pair we sell. It will wear longer, produce a more magnificent figure, and give more comfort to the wearer than any other made.

No. 200. Jean, white and drab. 18 to 30 inches, $2.75. Extra sizes, 25c. additional.

No. 250. Jean, satteen straps, white and drab, 18 to 30 inches, $3 25; 31 to 33, 3.50; 34 to 36, 3.75.

No. 295. Black Italian Cloth, 18 to 30 inches, $4.00; 31 to 33, 4.50; 34 to 36, 5.00.

Nursing Corset, 18 to 30 in. $1.

Coronet. Extra long waist white, and drab, 18 to 30 inches $1.75.

No. 356. Moulded Corset, white and drab Jean, medium length, 75c.

No. 374. Moulded Corset, medium length, flossed with silk, white and drab, $1.00; black, $1.25.

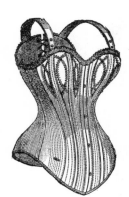

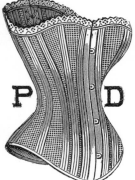

Health Corset, with tampico bust, shoulder straps, white and drab, 18 to 30 inches, $1.25.

White, drab, and écru Jean, finely shaped, 18 to 30 inches. Price, 50c.

No. 314. Summer Net, very durable, white, only $1.75.

Bridal, white, only 18 to 30 in. $1.

Coraline. Best Corset for ordinary use, white and drab, 18 to 30 inches, $1.00; 30 to 36, 1.25.

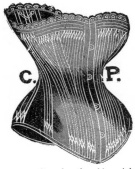

THE MERCANTILE HEART OF NEW ENGLAND.

The Double Ve Waist

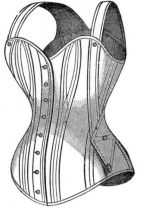

LADIES'.
Style 52, White and Drab. Imperial Jean, $1.00.
Style 62, White and Drab. Satteen, $1.50.

The Double Ve Waist

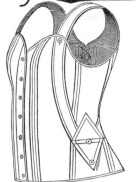

YOUNG LADIES', Style 42.
Age, 13 to 16 years.
Sizes, 18 to 30. Price, 85c.
MISSES', Style 32.
Age, 10 to 13 years.
Sizes, 18 to 30. Price, 75c.

The Double Ve Waist

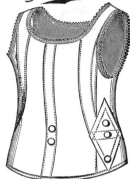

CHILDREN'S.
For Boys and Girls, age 3 to 10 years.
Sizes, 20 to 30.
Buttons in Back. Price, 65c.
INFANTS', age 1 to 3 years.
Sizes, 20 to 26. Buttons in Back. Price, 50c.

GOOD SENSE. Style 218.
Ladies' Medium Form.
Long Waist.
Buttons front. Laced back.
White and Drab.
20 to 30 inches. Price, $1.50.

The Double Ve Waist

BABY'S.
Age, under one year. Sizes, 20 to 26.
Buttons in Back. Price, 50c.

G. M. S. Supporting Safety Belt, 25c.

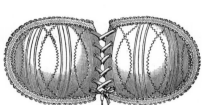

Tampico Pads, very durable, 45c.

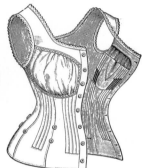

Equipoise Waist, stylish, comfortable, hygienic, genuine whalebone. Pockets allowing the removal of bones without ripping. Colors, white, tan, $2.25; black, $3.00.

MADAME FOY'S

SKIRT SUPPORTING CORSET.

GOOD SENSE. Style 223.
Misses, 12 to 17 years.
Superfine material.
Bust soft as silk.
White and Drab.
Style 223. $1.00.

Pads, with Spiral Springs, muslin covering. 50c.

— IT IS THE —

Most Popular and Satisfactory

AS REGARDS

Elegant Form,

Health, and

Comfort,

IN THE MARKET.

It is particularly adapted to the present style of dress.

FOR SALE BY LEADING DEALERS.

Price by Mail, $1.40.

— MANUFACTURED BY —

THE FOY, HARMON & CHADWICK CO.,

NEW HAVEN, CONN.

60 WHITE STREET,   NEW YORK.

Misses' Corset, corded, white and drab, 50c.

R & G CORSETS ARE THE BEST

ART EMBROIDERY.

Berlin Zephyr, best quality, 2, 4, 8 fld., ... 6c. lap, 12c. oz., $1.90 lb.
Germantown Wool, best-quality, in black, white, and all colors,
         17c. skein, $1.50 lb.
Scotch or German Knitting Yarn (Starlight), . . . 35c. skein, $1.40 lb.
Spanish Yarn, in all colors, ... 25c. skein, $1.60 lb.
Saxony, superfine and very soft, in all colors, . . . 15c. skein, $1.50 lb.
Shetland Wool and Floss, ... 20c. skein, $1.50 lb.
Starlight Manual, handsomely illustrated, and instructions for all kinds of
     worsted work, ... 35c.
J. R. Leeson's Book of Lace Thread-work for Crocheting, . . . 25c.
Glasgo Lace Book, ... 10c.

STAMPED LINENS.

Bureau, Commode, Dressing-case, and Sideboard Scarfs, 25c. to $1.00; Tray
Cloth, 25c. to $4.00; Lunch Cloths, $1.00 to 10.00; Splashers, 25 to 75c.;
Tidies, 20 to 75c.; Stamped Aprons, 25 to 50c.; Pillow Shams (fine cotton), 37c.
per pr.

CANVAS.

Penelope or working, 27 in. wide, ... 25c. yd.

Bolting Sheeting (cotton), 72 in. wide, ... 50c. yd.
   "   "   (linen), ... $1.25 yd.
Bargarran Art Cloth, 72 in. wide, ... $1.50 yd.
Scrim (cream and white), . . . 18 in., 25c. 40 in., 37 and 50c.
Silk Bolton Cloth, ... 75c. to $2.25

EMBROIDERY SILK.

Rope Silk, wash silk, 5c. skein, 50c. doz.; Zephyr Rope Silk, wash silk, 5c.
skein, 50c. doz.; Art Silk, wash silk, 5c. skein, 50c. doz.; Wash Etching, wash
silk, 5c. skein, 50c. doz.; Syrian wash silk, 5c. skein, 50c. doz.; Saddler's, 2c.
skein, 20c. doz.; Embroidery, 5 and 10c. spool; Knitting Silk, 35c. ball.

SUNDRIES.

Bargarran Art Thread, 10c. skein, $1.00 doz.; Wash Linen Floss, 5c. skein,
50c. doz.; Rope Linen, 6c. skein, 60c. doz.; Glasgo Lace Thread, all sizes, for
Knitting and Crocheting, 10c. spool; Crochet Needles, steel and bone, 5 to 12c.
each; Knitting Needles, bone and rubber, 20 to 37c. pr.; Wood Embroidery
Hoops, 6, 8, 10, 12 in., 10c. per pr.; Tinsel in colors, 3c. ball.

Comb and Brush Bag, 15c.

Shoe Bag, 2 Pocket, 25c.; 4 Pocket, 37c.; 8 Pocket, 75c.

Button Bag, 15c.

Laundry bag, 37c., 50c., 62c.

Tray Cloth, 36 inches by 36 inches, $1.00 to 3.25.

Tray Cloth, 18 in. by 24 in., $2.50. Scarfs, 17 in. by 54 in., $5.00; 17 in. by 72 in., 6.00; 36 in. by 36 in., $5.00. Cover, 20 in. by 34 in., $3.50.

Scarfs, 18 in. by 72 in., $6.00; 18 in. by 54 in., 5.00. Cover, 36 in. by 36 in., $7.00.

Bureau Scarfs, 18 x 54, $1.25; 18 x 72, $1.37.

Bureau Scarfs, 18 x 54, 75c.; 18 x 72, $1.00.

Doily, 6 inches by 6 inches, 10c.

LADIES' AND MISSES' SHOES, RUBBERS, ETC.

No. 1. Ladies' French Kid Foxed, Burt Kid tops, hand-sewed, Walking Boots, made by E. C. Burt & Co. of New York. Widths, AA to D. Sizes, 2½ to 8. Price, $6.00.

No. 6. Ladies' Best French Kid Side-laced Boot, medium heel, round toe. Widths, AA to E. Sizes, 1½ to 7. Price, $5.00.

No. 11. Ladies' Fine Bright Dongola Foxed Serge Cl. Top But. Boots, common sense and opera style. Widths, AA to E. Sizes, 2½ to 7. Prices, $3.50, 5.00.

No. 2. Ladies' Best French Kid Button Boots, for dress wear, on common sense and opera lasts, made by E. C. Burt & Co. of New York. Widths, AA to E. Sizes, 2 to 8. Price, $5.50.

No. 7. Ladies' Bright Dongola Front Laced Boots, medium opera toe and heel, patent tips. Very stylish boot for young ladies. Widths, AA to D. Sizes, 2 to 7. Price, $5 00 and $3.50.

No. 12. Ladies' Fine Paris Kid Button Boots, hand-welt, patent calf tips, and patent calf heel foxing, something new and stylish, new English last, new military heels. Sizes, 2 to 7. Widths, AA to D. Price, $5.00.

No. 3. Ladies' Best French Kid Button Boots, in common sense and opera styles, for street wear. Widths, AA to E. Sizes, 2 to 8. Price, $5.00.
Ladies' Fine French Kid Button Boots, same styles and sizes as No. 3. Price, $4.00.

No. 8. Ladies' Fine Paris Kid Hand-welt Button Boots, with patent leather toe caps, opera toe, low heel. Widths, AA to D. Sizes, 2 to 7. Price, $5.00.

No. 13. Ladies' Fine Paris Kid Button Boots, hand-welt, patent calf tips, new common sense last, a style original with us, combining elegance and comfort. Sizes, 2½ to 7. Widths, AA to D. Price, $5.00.

No. 4. Ladies' Finest French Kid Boots, genuine hand-turned, for dancing, dress, and party wear, in styles of common sense, opera plain toe, and opera with patent tip. Widths, AA to D. Sizes, 2½ to 7. Price, $6.00.

No. 9. Ladies' Fine Paris Kid Button Boots, hand-sewed and turned, patent calf tips, new opera last. Sizes, 2 to 7. Widths, AA to D. Worth $6.00. Price, $5.00.

No. 14. J., M. & Co.'s Promenade Boot, for ladies' street wear. Very stylish, bright Dongola, straight foxing, hand-sewed. Widths, AA to E. Sizes, 2 to 7½. Price, $4.35.

No. 5. Ladies' Fine Paris Kid Hand-sewed "Dress Reform" Button Boots, extra wide soles, low, flat heels; correct shape for tender feet. Widths, A to E. Sizes, 2½ to 7½. Price, $5.00.

No. 10. Ladies' Fine Paris Kid Button Boots, hand-welt, with straight foxings, patent calf tips, English last, very stylish for street wear, E. C. Burt & Co.'s make. Sizes, 2½ to 7. Widths, AA to D. Price, $5.00.

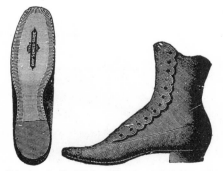

No. 15. Ladies' Button Boots, made by the "Day Sewed Process." Every other way same as No. 17. Price, $3.00.

THE MERCANTILE HEART OF NEW ENGLAND.

No. 16. Ladies' Bright Dongola Button Boots, in common sense and opera style. Widths, A to E. Sizes, 2½ to 8. Prices, $3.00, 2.50, 2.00.

No. 17. Ladies' Front-laced and Button Boots, bright Dongola, straight foxing, with toe caps made on the English walking last. Widths, A to E. Sizes, 2½ to 8. Price, $3.00.

No. 18. Ladies' Fine Paris Kid Button Boots, common sense and opera last, E. C. Burt & Co.'s make. Sizes, 2½ to 7. Widths, AA to E. Price, $4.00.

No. 19. J., M. & Co.'s "Summer Street" Button Boots, for ladies' street wear. Bright Dongola, patent toe caps. Widths, A to E. Sizes, 2 to 8. Price, $2.50.

No. 20. Ladies' Patent Calf Foxed "Florence Ties," French Kid Tops, Hand-sewed and Turned, entirely new and original with us. Sizes, 2½ to 7. Widths, AA to D. Price, $4.00.

No. 20½. Same style, also in fine Paris kid, patent calf tips and lacing stay. Same sizes and widths as No. 20. Price, $3.50.

No. 21. Ladies' Fine French Kid Oxford Ties, in opera and common sense styles. Widths, AA to D. Sizes, 2 to 7. Price, $3.50.

No. 22. Ladies' Fine French Kid Oxford Ties, with patent calf tips, hand-sewed and turned. Sizes, 2 to 7. Widths, AA to D. Price, $4.00.

No. 23. Ladies' Tan-colored Genuine Russia Leather Oxford Ties, with the new Wing tips, "quite English, you know." Sizes, 2½ to 6. Widths, AA to D. Price, $3.00.

No. 24. Ladies' Fine Bright Dongola "Imperial" Shoe, something entirely original and exclusive with us. Sizes, 2½ to 6. Widths, AA to D. Price, $3.00.

No. 25. Ladies Fine Paris Kid Oxford Ties, inlaid with light gray Suède, another exclusive style. Sizes, 2½ to 6. Widths, AA to D. Price, $3.00.

No. 26. Ladies' Fine Paris Kid Oxford Ties, with patent calf quarters and ½ wing tip. Sizes, 2½ to 6. Widths, AA to D. Price, $3.00.

No. 27. Ladies' Fine French Kid Hand-welt Oxford Ties, styles in common sense, plain toe, and opera toe, with tips of the same. Widths, AA to D. Sizes, 2½ to 7. Price, $4.00, 4.50, 5.00.

No. 28. Ladies' Fine Paris Kid Welted Oxford Ties, made on the English walking last, with tips of the same. Widths, AA to E. Sizes, 2 to 8. Price, $3.00.

Ladies Bright Dongola Oxford Ties, same style, sizes, and widths as No. 23, made by the "Day Sewed Process." Price, $2.00.

No. 29. Ladies' Paris Kid Oxfords, hand-sewed, in common sense, plain toe, and opera style, with patent tips. Widths, AA to D. Sizes, 2½ to 7. Price, $2.50.

No. 30. Ladies' Patent Foxed Hand-sewed Oxford Ties, made of the best patent French calf. Widths, AA to D. Sizes, 2½ to 7. Price, $3.00.

No. 31. Ladies' Finest French Goat (color, red russet) Hand-sewed Oxford Ties. Styles in common sense, plain, and opera toe, with tips. Widths, AA to D. Sizes, 2½ to 7. Price, $2.00.

No. 32. Ladies' Oxford Ties, Bright Dongola and Brown Russet Goatskin, in opera and common sense styles. Widths, A to D. Sizes, 2½ to 8. Price, $1.50.

No. 33. The "New Gondolier," for ladies' party and dancing wear, made of Red French Goat and Black Paris Kid. Widths, AA to D. Sizes, 2 to 6. Price, Red Goat, $4.00; Paris Kid, $3.50.

No. 34. Ladies' "Corinne Shoe, new and exclusive, in Gray Suède leather and the new leather, Gray Goat. Sizes, 2½ to 6. Widths, AA to D. Price, $3.50.

No. 35. Ladies' Patti Slipper, Fine Suède Calf, in gray, black, and tan colors. Widths, AA to D. Sizes, 2½ to 6. Price, $3.00.

No. 36. Ladies' Patti Slipper, plain, with patent calf vamp, bright Dongola quarter. Widths, AA to D. Sizes, 2½ to 6. Price, $3.00.

No. 37. Ladies' Pumps, in Patent Calf and Paris Kid, elegant for summer wear at the watering places. Sizes, 2½ to 7. Widths, AA to D. Price, $2.50.

THE MERCANTILE HEART OF NEW ENGLAND.

No. 38. Ladies' Kid Strap Slippers, bead embroidered. Widths, A to D. Sizes, 2½ to 7. Price, $2.00.

Ladies' Kid Beaded Slippers, no strap. Widths, A to D. Sizes, 2½ to 7. Price, $1.50.

No. 39. Ladies' Bright Dongola Slippers, opera last with strap; common sense last, plain. Sizes, 2½ to 7. Widths, AA to D. Price, $1.50.

No. 40. Ladies' French Kid Hand-sewed Pointed Slippers. Widths, A to E. Sizes, 2½ to 8. Price, $2.00.

No. 41. Ladies' Hand-turned Slippers, in common sense and opera styles; French kid. Widths, A to D. Sizes, 2 to 7. Price, $2.50.

Ladies' Bright Dongola Slippers. Widths, A to D. Sizes, 2 to 7. Prices, $1.00 and 1.50.

Ladies' Serge Pointed Hand-sewed Slippers. Price, $1.00.

Ladies' Hand-sewed Serge Buskins. Price, $1.00.

Ladies' Serge Congress Boots, hand-sewed. Prices, $1.00, 1.25, 2.00.

No. 42. Misses' Spring Heel Rubbers. Sizes, 11 to 2. Price, 35c.
Children's Spring Heel Rubbers. Sizes, 4½ to 10½. Price, 30c.

No. 43. Ladies' Rubbers to fit Waukenphast boot. Sizes, 2½ to 8. Prices, 50 and 60c.
Ladies' Rubbers, 25, 40, 50, and 60c.

No. 44. Ladies' Fine Broadcloth Overgaiters, all colors. Sizes, 1, 2, 3, 4, 5. Price, $1.50.

No. 45. J., M. & Co.'s "Old Brick" School Shoe, for girls. Best pebble goat, with common sense heels and sole leather tips. Widths, AA to E. Sizes, 11 to 3½. Price, $2.25.
Same, in sizes 4 and 4½, $3.00.
Same, with spring heels and sole leather tips. Widths, AA to E. Sizes, 11 to 3½. Price, $2.25.
Same, in 4 and 4½, $3.00.
Widths, AA to E, sizes 8½ to 10½. Price, $1.75.
Widths, A to D, sizes 5 to 8, $1.50.

No. 46. J., M. & Co.'s "Old Brick" School Shoe, for girls. Best straight goat, with spring heels. Widths, AA to E. Sizes, 11 to 3½. Price, $2.25.
Same, in sizes 4 and 4½, $3.00.
Same, in sizes 8½ to 10½, $1.75.
Same, in widths A to D, sizes 5 to 8, $1.50.

No. 47. J., M. & Co.'s "Old Brick" School Shoe, for girls. Best bright Dongola, with common sense heels. Widths, AA to E. Sizes, 11 to 3½. Price, $2.25. Same, in 4 and 4½, $3.00. Same, with spring heels, sizes 11 to 3½, $2.25. Same, in 4 and 4½, $3.00. Same, in 8½ to 10½, $1.75. Same, in widths A to D, sizes 5 to 8, $1.50.

No. 48. J., M. & Co.'s "Old Brick" School Shoe, for girls. Dull Dongola, with sole leather tips. Widths, AA to E. Sizes, 8½ to 10½. Price, $1.75.
Same, in widths A to D, sizes 5 to 8, $1.50.

No. 49. E. C. Burt & Co.'s Spring Heel Boots, for girls, straight goat and Troubé kid. Widths, A to D. Sizes, 11 to 2. Price, $2.75.
Widths A to D, sizes 8½ to 10½, $2.00.
Widths A to D, sizes 5 to 8, $1.75.

No. 50. Straight Goat and Bright Dongola Spring Heel Boots, for girls. Widths, B, C, D. Sizes, 11 to 2. Price, $1.75.
Widths, B, C, D; sizes, 8½ to 10½. Price, $1.50.
Widths, B, C, D; sizes, 5 to 8. Price, $1.25.

No. 51. Infants' No-heeled Boots, hand-sewed. Widths, A to E. Sizes, 1 to 7. Best French kid, $1.25. Fine Paris kid, $1.00. Best French goat, 90c.
Bright Dongola. Widths, B to E. Sizes, 1 to 7. Price, 75c.
Infants' French Kid, soft soles, in black, white, bronze, 35c.

No. 52. Misses' and Children's Oxford Ties, in brown russet goat, with tips, and bright Dongola plain toe. Sizes, 11 to 2. Widths, A to D. Price, $1.50.
Sizes, 8½ to 10½; widths, A to D. Price, $1.25.
Sizes, 5 to 8; widths, A to D. Price, $1.00.

No. 53. Ladies' Fawn Colored Suede Leather Tennis Oxfords, with rubber soles and trimmings of the same. Sizes, 2½ to 7. Widths, AA to D. Price, $2.50.

No. 54. Ladies' Light Olive Canvas Tennis Oxfords, with Rubber Soles and Trimmings of Brown Royal Suède. Sizes, 2½ to 7. Widths, AA to D. Price, $2.00.
Also, the same as above, except with felt soles. Sizes and price, same as No. 54.
Also, the same as No. 54, except black canvas, with Dongola trimmings. Sizes and price, the same as No. 54.
Ladies' Drab Canvas Rubber Soled Tennis Oxfords, with ooze leather trimmings. Sizes, $2½ to 7. Widths, AA to D. Price, $1.50.

No. 55. Ladies' Tan Canvas Laced Boots, with Grain Trimmings. Widths, A to D. Sizes, 2½ to D. Price, $2.00.

No. 56. Misses' and Children's Tan Canvas Spring Heeled Laced Boots, with Grain Trimmings. Widths, A to D. Sizes, 11 to 2. Price, $1.75.
Child's widths, A to D. Sizes, 8½ to 10½. Price, $1.50.
Child's widths, A to D. Sizes, 5 to 8. Price, $1.25.

THE MERCANTILE HEART OF NEW ENGLAND.

MEN'S AND BOYS' BOOTS AND SHOES.

No. 57. Men's Fine French Calf Hand-sewed Balmorals, made on the Piccadilly last. Widths, A to D. Sizes, 5 to 10. Prices, $5.00 and 7.00.

No. 58. Men's Best Calf Hand-sewed English Walking Boots, in Congress and Balmorals, with single soles. Widths, A to E. Sizes, 5½ to 11. Price, $7.00.

No. 59. Men's Fine French Patent Calf Balmorals, Piccadilly last. Very stylish for summer wear. Widths, A to D. Sizes, 5 to 10. Prices, $5.00 and $6.50.

No. 60. Men's Patent Leather Foxed, Cloth Top Congress, hand-turned, for evening dress. Widths, M, F, FF. Sizes, 5 to 10. Price, $5.00.

No. 61. Men's Fine Calf Hand-welt Boots, in Congress and Balmorals; Boston Toe. Widths, 2 to 6. Sizes, 5 to 11. Prices, $3.00, 4.00, and 5.00.

No. 62. Men's Genuine Hand-sewed Porpoise Leather Boots, in Congress and Balmorals; made on the Anatomical last. This boot is usually sold for $7.00. Price, $5.65.

No. 63. Jordan, Marsh & Co.'s Avenue Boots for Gentlemen. Fine Calf Hand-welt Boots, in Congress and Balmorals. London last and English Walking Balmorals. Widths, 2 to 6. Sizes, 5 to 11. Price, $3.00.

No. 64. Jordan, Marsh & Co.'s "Old Brick" School Shoes, made light weight, for dress wear. The Boys' are Laced. Sizes, 2½ to 6. Price, $3.50. Youths' Button. Size, 11 to 2. Price, $2.75.

No. 65. Jordan, Marsh & Co.'s "Old Brick" School Shoes for Boys, in Lace and Button, made of the best Calf-skin. Sizes, 2½ to 6. Widths, A to E. Price, $3.50.

No. 66. Boys' Fine Calf Boots, in Lace and Button. Sizes, 2½ to 6. Widths, 2 to 5. Price, $2.50. Youths' of the same. Sizes, 10 to 2. Price, $2.00. Boys' Veal Calf. Sizes, 2½ to 5½. Price, $1.75. Youths' Veal Calf. Sizes, 11 to 2. Price, $1.50.

No. 67. Jordan, Marsh & Co.'s "Old Brick" School Shoes for a Youth, in Lace and Button, made of the best Calf-skin. Sizes, 10 to 2. Widths, A to E. Price, $2.75.

No. 68. Men's Russet Goat Balmorals, medium wide toe. Sizes, 6 to 10. Widths, B, C, D. Prices, $3.00 and 6.00.

No. 69. Men's Kangaroo Strap Low Shoes, hand-sewed. Widths, 2 to 5. Sizes, 5½ to 11. Price, $5.00.
Men's French Kid Strap Low Shoes. Price, $4.00.

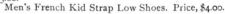

No. 70. Men's Fine Calf Hand-sewed Oxfords, broad toe. Widths, 2 to 5. Sizes, 5½ to 11. Price, $5.00.
Men's Calf Oxfords, Hand-sewed welt. Prices, $3.00 and 3.50.

No. 71. Men's Russet Goat Oxford, Hand-sewed Welt. Prices, $3.50 and 4.50.

No. 72. Boys' Oxford Ties, in Calf and Russet Goat. Sizes, 2½ to 6. Price, $2.75.
No. 73. Youths' Oxford Ties, in Calf and Russet Goat. Sizes, 11 to 2. Price, $2.25.
No. 74. Boys' Russet Goat Balmorals. Sizes, 2½ to 6. Price, $3.50.
No. 75. Youths' Russet Goat Balmorals. Sizes, 11 to 2. Price, $2.75.

THE MERCANTILE HEART OF NEW ENGLAND.

MEN'S, BOYS', AND YOUTHS' TENNIS SHOES.

No. 76. Men's Brown Russia Leather Tennis Balmorals. Price, $3.50.

Men's Dark Brown and White Canvas Tennis Oxfords, with very heavy pure gum soles. Price, $4.00.

Men's Tan Calf Tennis Oxfords, with rubber soles. Price, $3.00.

Men's White Calf Tennis Oxfords. Very stylish. Price, $5.00.

Men's Seal Oxfords, with leather soles. Imported. Price, $6.00.

No. 77. Men's Drab Canvas Russet Calf Trimmed Lawn Tennis Oxfords. Price, $2.50.

Men's Russet-color Canvas Oxfords, with Tournament sole. Price, $2.00.

Men's Brown Canvas Tennis Oxfords, leather trimmed. Price, $1.50.

Youths' Brown Canvas Tennis Oxfords. Price, $1.50.

Youth's Brown Canvas Tennis Oxfords. Price, $1.00.

Men's White Canvas Yachting Shoes, with felt soles. Price, $1.50.

Boys', of the same. Price, $1.25.

No. 78. Men's Dongola Bicycle Balmorals, with rubber soles. Price, $3.00.

Men's Dongola Bicycle Balmorals, with leather soles. Price, $2.75.

Men's Dongola Bicycle Oxfords, with leather soles. Price, $2.50.

Boys' Dark Russet Calf Tennis Oxfords, with heavy rubber soles. Price, $2.50.

Boys' Brown Canvas Tennis Oxfords. Price, $1.75.

Boys' Canvas Tennis Oxfords. Price, $1.25.

EDWIN C. BURT & CO.,
MANUFACTURERS AND EXPORTERS OF
FINE BOOTS, SHOES and SLIPPERS
FOR LADIES AND CHILDREN.
Acknowledged to be the BEST MADE, BEST VALUE and BEST WEARING SHOES manufactured in the World.

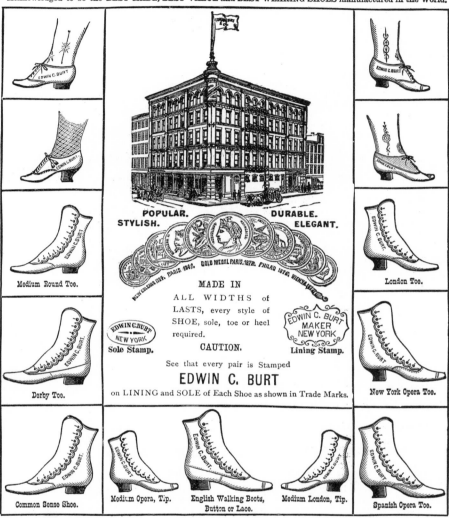

POPULAR. STYLISH. **DURABLE. ELEGANT.**

Medium Round Toe. London Toe.

Derby Toe. New York Opera Toe.

MADE IN
ALL WIDTHS of LASTS, every style of SHOE, sole, toe or heel required.

Sole Stamp. **CAUTION.** Lining Stamp.

See that every pair is Stamped
EDWIN C. BURT
on LINING and SOLE of Each Shoe as shown in Trade Marks.

Common Sense Shoe. Medium Opera, Tip. English Walking Boots, Button or Lace. Medium London, Tip. Spanish Opera Toe.

WE MAKE a complete line of the best grades of Ladies' and Children's BOOTS, SHOES and SLIPPERS, which includes all styles of HIGH and LOW Cut Shoes, Ties, Sandals and Opera Slippers, in Black or Bronze Domestic or French Kid. Also Beaded work of every description.

Particular attention is called to the fact that:
The STOCK is carefully selected.
The PATTERNS are of the most correct and approved models.
The WORKMANSHIP is of the very best.

EDWIN C. BURT & CO., New York, U. S. A.

We are special agents for BURT'S CELEBRATED GOODS in Boston, and shall carry a full assortment of all the desirable styles in stock. Orders by mail will receive careful and prompt attention.

JORDAN, MARSH & CO., BOSTON, MASS.

We have adopted Wheeler & Wilson Machines for use in the manufacturing of our various goods, and take pleasure in recommending them. **JORDAN, MARSH & CO.**

At the Exposition Universelle, Paris, 1889, the highest possible premium, the only Grand Prize for Sewing Machines, was awarded to Wheeler & Wilson Manufacturing Co., and the Cross of the Legion of Honor was conferred upon Nathaniel Wheeler, the President of the Company. The W. & W. "No. 9" has taken First Premium at every State and County Fair at which it has been exhibited.

New High Arm Family Sewing Machine "No. 9."

Factory and Chief Office, 594 Washington St., BOSTON.
BRIDGEPORT, CONN. 833 Broadway, NEW YORK.

THE MERCANTILE HEART OF NEW ENGLAND.

TENNIS RACKETS.

THE ARLINGTON. This racket is strung up in red gut. The frame is selected white ash, all nicely finished. We have this one in all weights. $3.50.

"THE BOSTON." This is a new racket with us this year. It is strung with red and white gut, and has a black throat. We intend to make this our leader for 1891. $3.00.

"NONE SUCH." A large size Racket, strung with real gut. A bargain. $1.00.

TENNIS NETS. 27x2½, 15 thread, $1.00. 33x2½, 15 thread, $1.25. 36x2½, 12 thread, $1.50. 36x2½, 15 thread, $1.75. 36x2½, 21 thread, $2.25. 42x2½, 12 thread, $1.50. 42x2½, 15 thread, $1.75. 42x2½, 21 thread, $2.50.

BACK NETS. 50x7, 12 thread, $3.50. 50x7, 9 thread, $2.50.

TENNIS BALLS. Wright & Ditson Championship Ball for 1891. $4.50. Plain Rubber, for wet weather. $2.00.

TENNIS POLES. No. 100. Polished Maple Poles, unjointed, turned tops, 83c. pair. Casino Poles, with wheel on top. $2.00 pair. No. 10. A Plain Jointed Pole. $1.00 pair. No. 11. White Ash, polished and painted, brass ferrules, 1¼ in. diameter. $2.00.

GUY ROPES. No. 1. Good set. 25c. No. 2. Polished pegs, large cotton rope. 50c. set.

TENNIS SUNDRIES. Galvanized Centre Fork. 75c. The Common Sense Racket Press. 75c. 1891 Rules. 15c.

RACKET CASES. No. 0. Felt Racket Case, 50c. No. 3. Canvas Racket Case, 75c. A Waterproof Case, leather bound, $1.25.

MARKERS AND MARKING TAPES. Dry Markers, $2.00. Double Court Tennis Tapes, $5.00.

TENNIS BELTS. All kinds, sizes, and prices.

CROQUET. No. 1. 8 Ball Set, hardwood, 85c. No. 2. 8 Ball Set, hardwood, $1.00. No. 3. 8 Ball Set, hardwood, $1.50. No. 4. 8 Ball Set, hardwood, $2.00. No. 6. 8 Ball Set, hardwood, 6 in. mallets, $3.00. No. 9. 4 Ball Set, hardwood, $2.00. No. 10. 8 Ball Set, hardwood, 8 in. mallets, $4.00. No. 12. 8 Ball Set, hardwood, 8 in. mallets, $5.00. Better sets, $6.00, 8.00, and 10.00.

HAMMOCKS. Mexican, close woven, and pillow Hammocks, from 50c. to $8.00. Hammock Ropes, 25c. pair. Hammock Spreaders, 25c. pair.

FOOT BALLS. No. 2. Round Rubber, 80c. No. 3. Round Rubber, $1.00. No. 4. Round Rubber, $1.15. No. 5. Round Rubber, $1.25. No. 6. Round Rubber, $1.50.

RUGBY BALLS. No. 5. Regulation size, $3.50. No. 6. Regulation size, $4.00.

Dumb-bells and Indian Clubs, all prices.

FISHING TACKLE.

RODS. A Genuine Split Bamboo Fly Rod, three joints and extra tip, length 9½ to 10½ feet. It has a swelled butt, nickel-plated trimmings, canewound grip, and has metal plugs, all complete in wood form and bag, for $3.00.

We have a bass rod the same in every respect as the above, except that it has standing guides, and the lengths run from 8½ to 10½ ft., for $3.00.

A fine split Bamboo trunk rod, with 5 18 in. joints and extra tip reel below hand, nickel trimmings and zylonite grip, for $3.50.

One same as above in 21 in. joints, reel above hand, for $3.50.

A full line of rods in Split Bamboo, Lancewood, Ash, and Calcutta Bamboo, from 25c. to $25.00.

HOOKS, ETC. Our Fly Hook, in all the best styles. That we sell for 35c. a doz. is hard to beat. Better ones from 60c. to $1.50. per doz.

Our Bass Hook (one on a card), in all the best styles, such as the Montreal, Brown Hackle, Coachman Ferguson Ibis, White Miller, etc., etc. Per doz., $1.20.

We keep a full line of hooks on gut, viz., the Carlisle, Sproat, Aberdeen, etc. Single gut hook, 25c. per doz.; double gut, 50c. doz.

Skinner's fluted trolling spoons. Artificial Bait of all kinds. Bait Boxes, 15 and 25c. each. Spring Balances, 25 and 50c. each. Fly Books, from 25c. to $4.00 each.

SUNDRIES. Leaders, Landing Nets and Staffs, Floats, Creels, or Baskets, Minnow Tackle Cases, Split Shot Sinkers and Swivels, Fish Hook Disgorgers, Buckets, Fish Knives, and Folding Cups, Rod Holders to attach on side of boat.

REELS. A Full Nickel-plated, Multiplying Screwed Reel, with balance handle and sliding click, in three sizes. 40 yds., 50c.; 60 yds., 75c.; 80 yds., 85c. each. Better ones at $1.00, 1.50, 2.00 to 10.00.

Nickel-plated Riveted Click Reels. 25 yds., 30c.; 40 yds., 35c.; 60 yds., 40c. each. Rubber Click Screwed Reels. 25 yds., 45c.; 40 yds., 50c.; 60 yds., 55c. each. We have better Click Reels at all prices.

LINES. Cotton lines, from 5 to 50c. Linen lines, from 10c. to $1.00. Silk lines, from 50c. to $5.00.

BASE BALL. We carry a full line of Base Ball goods, and our prices are as low as the lowest.

Base Ball Bats, from 10c. to $1.00.
Base Balls, from 5c. to $1.25.
Catchers' Masks, from $1.50 to $4.00.

Catchers' Gloves and Mitts, from 25c. to $7.50.
Body Protectors, from $3.00 to $10.00. Base Ball Belts, from 10c. to $1.00.
Shoe Plates, Score Books, Indicators, Base Ball Rules, etc., etc.

PLAYING CARDS AND GAMES.

A good pack cards, 5c.; enamelled cards, 15c.; enamelled cards, gilt edge, 20c.; linen cards, 25c.; linen cards, gilt edge, 30c.; extra fine pack, 60c.; 100 poker chips in box, 25c.; "Tiddledy Winks," $0.25, .50, and 1.00; Halma, 69c.; Parchesi, 85c.; Innocence Abroad, $1.00; Fish Pond, 25, 40, 90c.; checkers and dominoes, blocks of all kinds.

LAMPS AND GLASSWARE.

Decorated Vase Lamps, shades to match, fitted with duplex burners, $2.50, 3.00, 4.00, 5.00.

Banquet Lamps, antique brass finish, central draught burner linen shade, silk fringed, for $3.50. Others, $5.00, 8.00, 10.00, and upward.

Plain Water Tumblers, 36c. per dozen.
Thin Blown Water Tumblers, 50c. per dozen.
Wine Glasses, $0.40 to 6.00 per dozen.
Goblets, $0.50 to 6.00 per dozen.
Belgian Thin Blown Glass Water Tumblers, $1.00 per dozen.
Water Pitchers, half-gallon size, $0.25 to 2.00 each.
Special estimates given on plain and engraved glass orders.

CHINA AND CROCKERY.

Genuine French China Tea Set of 56 pieces, very handsomely decorated. Worth $12.00, for $7.00.

China (Carlsbad) Dinner Set, 130 pcs., nicely decorated, colored flowers, festoon edge plates, gilt edges, knobs, handles, a set worth much more than we ask for it; viz., $25.00.

The **"La Reine" Dinner Pattern** is one of the handsomest we have ever seen, and is extremely popular. The decoration is a lovely colored spray pattern on a good semi-porcelain body, festoon plates, gold edges, knobs and handles. The set contains 130 pieces, combining a dinner and tea set. Matchings can be had at all times. Price, for set complete, $25.00.

English Decorated Dinner Set, 130 pieces, $12.00.

Toilet Sets, 10 pieces, decorated on cream-colored body, pink, blue, or brown, $3.00. Jars to match, $2.65. Better sets from $4.00 to 20.00.

Vases, Fancy Cups and Saucers, Tete-a-Tete Sets, Bread and Milk Sets, etc., etc., at popular prices.

THE MERCANTILE HEART OF NEW ENGLAND.

TOILET ARTICLES.

All the Popular Lines of Perfumes and Soaps at Popular Prices.

Metal Puff Box, 25c. Also other designs, $0.50, .75, 1.00, and 1.50.

Our "Bouquet" Soap, very fine, pure white toilet soap, 10c. cake.

Latour's Toilet Powder. A very fine powder. Violet and Rose Perfumes, recommended for ladies' and infants' use, 15c. package.

Latour's Face Powder. Flesh, cream, white, and pink, 25c.

Latour's Farina Cologne, 4 ounce bottle, 25c.

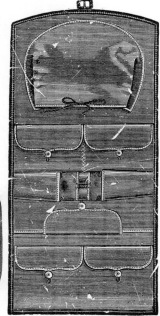

Latour's Extracts, in all the popular odors, in three sizes. Small, $0.25; medium, .50; large, 1.00.

Canvas Backed Toilet Wrappers, rubber lined, $0.50, .75, 1.00, 1.50, 2.00. Leather backed, $1.00, 1.50, 2.00, 3.00, 4.50, 5.00.

Latour's Toilet Waters, Violet, Heliotrope, Lavender, Rose. 4 oz. bottle, 40c.; 8 oz. bottle, 75c.

French Swan's Down Puff, 25c.

Rubber Comb, 10c. Better ones, 25 and 50c.

No. 14. Telescope Set, with hair, tooth, and nail brushes, and comb. Size, 8 x 2 x 1 inch. $2.00.

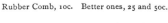

Latour's Violet Soap. A pure soap, sweetly scented. 10c. per cake.

BRASS BEDSTEADS.
For sale by Jordan, Marsh & Company.

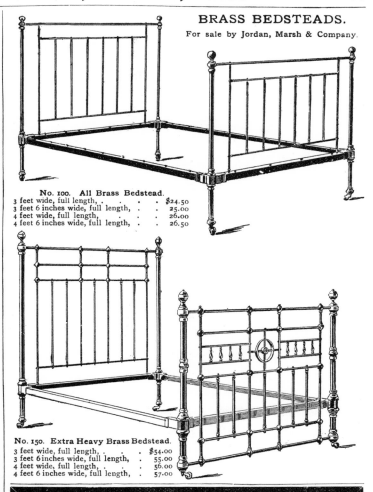

No. 100. All Brass Bedstead.

3 feet wide, full length,	$24.50
3 feet 6 inches wide, full length,	25.00
4 feet wide, full length,	26.00
4 feet 6 inches wide, full length,	26.50

No. 150. Extra Heavy Brass Bedstead.

3 feet wide, full length,	$54.00
3 feet 6 inches wide, full length,	55.00
4 feet wide, full length,	56.00
4 feet 6 inches wide, full length,	57.00

PARASOLS, COACHINGS, SUN, AND RAIN UMBRELLAS.

IN this department we carry the largest, most complete, and best selected stock to be found in the country. All the latest designs in Fancy Black Parasols. We make a specialty of these goods and always keep a large assortment on hand.

Prices, $5.00, 8.00, 10.00 to 25.00.

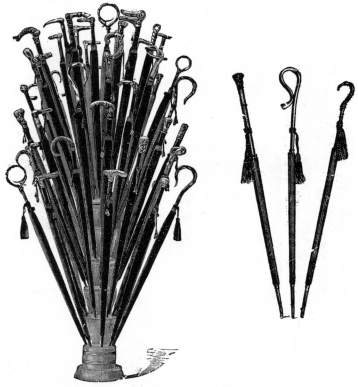

PARASOLS AND SUN UMBRELLAS.

Lace Trimmed Black Parasols, $2.50, 3.00, 3.50 to 5.00.
Mourning Parasols, gloria silks, $1.25, 1.50, 1.75, 2.00.
Mourning Parasols, gros grain and surah silks, lined and unlined union and all silks, $2.50, 3.00, 3.50 to 8.00.
Black Lace Parasols, $5.00 to 25.00.
Small Carriage Shades, in black silk, $1.25, 1.50, 1.75, 2.00, 2.25, 2.50, 3.00.
Black Lace Carriage Shades, $3.00, 3.50, 4.00, 5.00.
Fancy Black Carriage Shades, $3.50, 4.00, 5.00 to 8.00.
Coaching Parasols, all colors, $1.25, 1.50 to 5.00.
Fancy Parasols, in all the latest novelties, $2.50, 3.00, 4.00, 5.00 to 30.00.
Black and White Parasols, we have an endless variety of styles, $2.00, 2.50, 3.00 to 10.00.
22-inch Gloria Silk, paragon frames, natural sticks, or metal handles, $1.00, 1.25, 1.50 to 3.00.
24-inch Gloria Silk Sun Umbrellas, paragon frames, plain and fancy natural sticks, or metal handles, $1.25, 1.50, 2.00 to 3.50.
24-inch Mourning Sun Umbrellas, $1.50, 1.75, 2.00 to 5.00.
24-inch Union Silk Sun Umbrellas, paragon frames, plain and fancy natural sticks, or silver handles, $1.75, 2.00, 2.50 to 5.00.
24-inch Heavy Twilled Silk Sun Umbrellas, paragon frames, plain and fancy natural sticks, or silver handles, $3.00, 3.50 to 10.00.
24-inch Colored Silk Sun Umbrellas, cardinal, navy, etc., cases to match and tassel, paragon frames, with handsome natural and silver-trimmed sticks, $4.00, 5.00 to 10.00.
Ladies' 26-inch Gloria Silk Umbrellas, paragon frames, plain, natural, or metal handles, $1.25, 1.50, 1.75.
Ladies' 26-inch Gloria Silk Umbrellas, cases to match and tassel, paragon frames, handsome natural and silver-trimmed sticks and silver handles, $2.00, 2.50 to 5.00.
Ladies' 26-inch Union Silk Umbrellas, cases to match, paragon frames, handsome natural and silver-trimmed sticks, silver or gold handles, $2.50, 3.00, 3.50 to 5.00.
Ladies' 26-inch Colored Silk Umbrellas, in plain, cardinal, navy, and fancy colors, cases to match, handsome natural or silver-trimmed sticks, $5.00, 6.00, 7.00 to 10.00.
Gents' 28-inch Gloria Silk Umbrellas, paragon frames, plain, natural, or metal handles, $1.50, 1.75, 2.00.
Gents' 28-inch Gloria Silk Umbrellas, cases to match, paragon frames, handsome natural and silver-trimmed sticks, or silver handles, $2.50, 3.00, 3.50, 4.00, 5.00.
Gents' 28-inch Union and Heavy Twilled Silks, cases to match, paragon frames, handsome natural silver-trimmed sticks, or silver handles, $3.00, 3.50, 4.00 to 10.00.

Our umbrellas are made specially to our order by the leading manufacturers, and are the best possible shape and finish, can be used rain or shine.

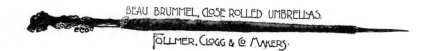

BEAU BRUMMEL, CLOSE ROLLED UMBRELLAS.

FOLLMER, CLOGG & CO. MAKERS.

FOLLMER, CLOGG & CO.

... MANUFACTURERS OF ...

Fine Parasols and Umbrellas

Specially recommend for durability and wear the following brands:

"Henrietta" Silk,

"Century" Guaranteed Silk,

"70 Quality" Selvedge Edge.

New York. **Philadelphia.** **San Francisco.**

THE MERCANTILE HEART OF NEW ENGLAND.

SILK WARPS.

Lansdowne

Dainty, graceful, light and elegant, combining all the soft loveliness of the finest wool with the brilliant sheen of classical silk. The prime favorite in dress goods.

Lansdowne Tennis Stripes

A spring novelty for Outing Shirts, Tennis, Seaside and Boating Waists and Skirts. All that is to be desired by a refined fastidious taste.

Engadine

A novelty for spring of 1891. Designed to fill a want for midsummer use and evening gowns; strong, light and of a fine but open texture, made to allow a circulation of air, and strengthened and beautified by the introduction of satin stripes.

These *trade-marks* are *registered,* and their use on any goods not made by me is unwarranted and illegal.

WM. F. READ,

PHILADELPHIA,

SOLE MANUFACTURER OF

Silk Warp Lansdowne,

Silk Warp Lansdowne Tennis Stripes,

Silk Warp Engadine.

ALSO MAKER OF

Silk Warp Henriettas, etc.

Philadelphia. Office,   **New York Office,**
213 Chestnut Street.   351 Canal Street.

Write to JORDAN, MARSH & CO., Boston, Mass.

Cutter's Dress Silks.

Why are Cutter's PURE DYE SILKS THE BEST?

Because the best stock the world produces is put into them, and nothing else. They are not weighted with dyestuff and dirt.

The aim is to make the best **at a fair price.** Quality is the first consideration. The lowest price is not cheapest.

Width, 25 inches, instead of 19 to 21, have **NO COLORED SELVAGES** (which are needed only to set off poor goods), so cut to much better advantage, therefore cheaper.

Price, $2.50 per yard, and it comes in dress patterns, 16, 17, 18, or 20 yards. Our name on each in gold letters, thus:

WE RECOMMEND

Cutter's Spool Silk.

It is the Strongest Silk Thread Made and the Best for General Use.

Sizes Mathematically Exact.

Strongest and Smoothest Thread.

Uniform and Reliable.

☞ Seams sewed with No. 70, WILL NOT RIP. No. 70 when used for hand sewing, WILL NOT FRAY OUT.

A full line of our goods for sale by JORDAN, MARSH & CO.

Her Majesty's Corset.

EVERY PAIR WARRANTED.

BEST IN THE WORLD.

NEVER CONFORMS to the WEARER'S FIGURE REGARDLESS OF TIME WORN. SUPERIOR TO ALL OTHERS IN DURABILITY, COMFORT, and EXQUISITE SHAPE. WE GUARANTEE that HER MAJESTY'S CORSET will WEAR LONGER, GIVE MORE COMFORT to the WEARER, and produce a MORE MAGNIFICENT Figure than any other CORSET MADE.

INVALUABLE to MISSES, as it KEEPS them ERECT in WALKING, STANDING, or RIDING, and IS ESPECIALLY adapted in these POINTS for ALL LADIES.

WE GUARANTEE every pair of HER MAJESTY'S CORSETS THAT WE SELL, and, IF NOT PERFECTLY SATISFACTORY, MONEY WILL BE REFUNDED.

We, the undersigned, take great pleasure in recommending

HER MAJESTY'S CORSET.

Having sold them to our very best customers, from whom we have received the most flattering reports, we are sure that all who purchase them will be well pleased with their perfect form, fit, and splendid wearing qualities.

We are, yours respectfully,

JORDAN, MARSH & CO.,

SOLE AGENTS FOR BOSTON.

FOR PRICES OF HER MAJESTY'S CORSET, SEE CORSET DEPARTMENT PAGE 84 OF THIS BOOK.

MADAME ROWLEY'S TOILET MASK
(OR FACE GLOVE).

The following are the claims made for Madame Rowley's Toilet Mask, and the grounds on which it is recommended to ladies for Beautifying, Bleaching, and Preserving the Complexion:—

1st. The **Mask** is Soft and Flexible in form, and can be Easily Applied and Worn without Discomfort or Inconvenience.

2d. It is durable, and does not dissolve or come asunder, but holds its original shape.

3d. It has been Analyzed by Eminent Scientists and Chemical Experts, and pronounced Perfectly Pure and Harmless.

4th. With ordinary care the **Mask** will Last for Years, and its *valuable properties* Never Become Impaired.

5th. The **Mask** is protected by letters patent, has been introduced ten years, and is the only **Genuine** article of the kind.

6th. It is Recommended by Eminent Physicians and Scientific Men as a *substitute for injurious cosmetics.*

7th. While it is intended that the **Mask** should be Worn During Sleep, it may be applied, *with equal good results*, At Any Time, to suit the convenience of the wearer.

The Toilet Mask (or Face Glove) in position to the Face.

To be Worn Three Times in the Week.

8th. It is a **Natural Beautifier** for Bleaching and Preserving the Skin, and Removing Complexional Imperfections.

9th. The **Mask** is sold at a moderate price, and is to be *purchased but once.*

10th. Hundreds of dollars uselessly expended for cosmetics, lotions, and like preparations, may be saved by those who possess it.

11th. Ladies in every section of the country are using the **Mask** with gratifying results.

12th. It is safe, simple, cleanly, and effective for beautifying purposes, and never injures the most delicate skin.

13th. The use of the **Mask** cannot be detected by the closest scrutiny, and it may be worn with **Perfect Privacy**, if desired.

14th. The **Mask** has received the testimony of well-known society and professional ladies, who proclaim it to be the greatest discovery for beautifying purposes ever offered to womankind.

COMPLEXION BLEMISHES

May be hidden imperfectly by cosmetics and powders, but can only be removed permanently by the Toilet Mask. By its use every kind of **spots, impurities, roughness,** etc., vanish from the skin, leaving it soft, clear, brilliant, and beautiful. **It is harmless, costs little, and saves its user money. It prevents and REMOVES**

WRINKLES,

And is both a complexion preserver and beautifier. Famous society ladies, actresses, belles, etc., use it. VALUABLE ILLUSTRATED **PAMPHLET,** with proofs and full particulars, mailed free by

THE TOILET MASK COMPANY, 1164 Broadway, New York.

Apply NOW, while you have our address before you, as this advertisement appears only occasionally.
Please mention JORDAN, MARSH & COMPANY CATALOGUE.

B. Wurzburger.
L. Goldsmith.

C. J. Hildesheim.
H. Goldsmith.

Wurzburger, Goldsmith & Co.,

Successors to
GOLDSMITH & PLAUT,
Manufacturers of

Ladies' Cloaks and Mantles,

472 Broadway & 30 to 36 Crosby St.,

NEW YORK.

Write to JORDAN, MARSH & CO., Boston, Mass.

G. KUTNOW,

658 Broadway, cor. Bond St., New York.

SOLE AGENT FOR

B. BIRNBAUM & SON, Limited, London, E. C., England.

MANUFACTURERS OF

LADIES' AND MEN'S
ODORLESS WATERPROOF GARMENTS

OF ALL DESCRIPTIONS.

Every Lady's Garment with Princess of Wales Patent Ventilator.

Every Man's Coat with Patent Ventilators under Arms.

Every Garment guaranteed perfect and flexible for ever.

Our variety of Patterns is simply marvellous.

SOLD BY

JORDAN, MARSH & COMPANY, Boston, Mass.

Coat with Cape.

THE MERCANTILE HEART OF NEW ENGLAND.

TRADE MARK.

BARKER BRAND.

The Celebrated "Barker Brand" of all Linen Collars and Cuffs are the best in materials, workmanship, and style. To be convinced of this fact, gentlemen who once wear "Barker" Collars and Cuffs will have no other.

Barker Collars, all styles, 20c. each; $2.00 per dozen.

Barker Cuffs, all styles, 35c. per pair; $4.00 per dozen.

The "Barker Brand" of all Linen Collars and Cuffs is controlled in Boston by JORDAN, MARSH & Co.

American Cloak and Suit Co.

H. DANZIG & CO.,

Ladies' Suits and Misses' Cloaks,

472 BROADWAY,

30 32, 34, and 36 CROSBY STREET,

New York.

Write to JORDAN, MARSH & Co., Boston, Mass.

BERNARD LEVY.   ISAAC I. LEVY.

Bernard Levy & Co.,

Importers and Manufacturers of

MISSES' and CHILDREN'S

CLOAKS,

NOS. 498 AND 500 BROADWAY,

NEW YORK.

BOSTON OFFICE: No. 10 Temple Place, Room 23.

J. A. MILLS, Eastern Representative.

Write to JORDAN, MARSH & Co., Boston, Mass.

THE MERCANTILE HEART OF NEW ENGLAND.

JULIUS FRIEDLANDER.   JOSEPH BASCH.

Friedlander & Basch,

Manufacturers and Importers of

Ladies' Suits
and Cloaks,

Wraps, Jackets, Tea Gowns,

371 CANAL STREET,

NEW YORK.

Write to JORDAN, MARSH & Co., Boston, Mass.

WILLIAM ROBERTSON,

119 Franklin Street, NEW YORK,

MANUFACTURER OF

| Silk Curtains, |
| Upholstery Goods, |
| Tidies, etc., |

PATERSON, N.J.

SOLE AGENT IN UNITED STATES FOR

JOHN BROWN & SON,	FLERSHEIM & CO.,
GLASGOW, SCOTLAND,	NOTTINGHAM, ENGLAND,
MANUFACTURERS OF	MANUFACTURERS OF
MADRAS CURTAINS,	Lace Curtains, Bed Sets,
ETC., ETC.	ETC., ETC.

Stocks of all Goods carried in New York.

Address all mail to JORDAN, MARSH & Co., Boston, Mass.

FRED'K VIETOR & ACHELIS,

Importers and
Commission Merchants,

66 to 72 Leonard Street,

NEW YORK.

Representing

A. GIRAUD & CO., Silks,
I. L. DeBALL & CO., Velvets.
POIDEBARD MILLS, Domestic Silks.

FULL lines of Hosiery, Shirts and Drawers, Henrietta Cloths, French and Domestic Dress Goods, Domestic and Foreign Woollens, Ladies' Cloth, Blankets, Millinery Goods, Ribbons, etc.

Address all mail to JORDAN, MARSH & Co., Boston, Mass.

ESTABLISHED 1747.

Wm. Ecroyd & Sons,

BRADFORD, ENGLAND,

THE ORIGINAL MAKERS OF

Silk Warp Henriettas,

SILK WARP ALMAS,

SILK WARP VEILINGS,

ALL WOOL HENRIETTAS, ETC.

These goods are put up on SILVER BOARDS, and a full line can always be found at JORDAN, MARSH & CO.'S Black Goods Department.

THE MERCANTILE HEART OF NEW ENGLAND.

JEWELRY AND FANS.

Necklaces. Roman Pearl Beads, gold, pink, blue, and white, ... $0.25
Sterling Silver Necklace, ... 1.58
Best Gold Plated Necklace, ... 2.00

No. 33.

No. 61.
Ladies' and Gents' Shirt Studs, sets of three, 50c.

Extension Fan, with leather-covered sticks, in black, cardinal, and tan, 25c. Same style in Russia leather sticks, 50c.

Japanese Fan, with laced stick, . . . $0.25
Fancy Parchment Fans, ... 10c to 1.50
Satin Fans, plain and painted, . . . 50c to 5.00
Gauze Fans, plain and painted, . . . 50c to 5.00

No. 4888.
Solid Silver Pin, bright and oxidized, 25c.

No. 4795.
Solid Silver clover leaf, 25c.

No. 678.
Solid gold rhinestone Pin, 50c.

No. 1895.
Gold Plate Ball Watch Chain, 50c.

No. 4.
Solid Gold Earrings or Drops, rhinestones, $1.00
Gold Plated Earrings, rhinestone settings, 25, 50c.

No. 633.
French Crapestone Pin, 25c.

No. 097G.
Gold Plate Hair Pin, ball top, 25c.

No. 990.
Gold Plated Whip, with horseshoe set in rhinestones, moonstone centre, 25c.

No. 3161.
Gents' Gold Plate Button, gold stone, agate and pearl setting, 25c.

No. 1.
Roman and Bright Gold Plate Bracelet, 50c. each.

No. 945.
Solid Gold Engraved Band for baby, 25c.

THE
Alaska Refrigerator.

Is the best for ordinary household use. Elegantly finished in Antique Oak.
Furnished with Overlapping Doors, Patent Locks, Syphons, and Solid Metal Shelves.

CHARCOAL FILLED AND ZINC LINED.

SEND FOR PRICE LIST.

Counter Dust Brushes, 25, 45, and 60c. each.

Tampico Scrub Brushes, 10, 20, and 25c. each.

BRASS TAGGED TINWARE.

Every piece warranted. Made of IXX tin. Every culinary article of this high grade of goods always on hand.

Coffee Pots, tin bottoms,   20,   25,   30,   35,   45,   60c. each.
                                1,   1½,   2,   3,   4,   6 qts.
Coffee Pots, copper bottoms, 30,   33,   37,   42,   55,   70c. each.

Maple Chopping Bowls, 10, 15, 20, 25, 30, 40c. each.
Chopping Trays, 25, 35, 45, and 50c. each.

TETLEY'S TEA from INDIA and CEYLON.

Is Fragrant, Delicious, and Absolutely Pure.
Put up in air-tight leaden packages, pounds and half-pounds, in two grades. First grade, 70c. lb.   Second grade, 50c. lb.
Also, INDO KAUDE BRAND mixed with FINEST OOLONG, 3 @ 60c per lb.   2 @ 75c per lb.   1 @ $1.00.

SILVERWARE AND CUTLERY.

Many new and desirable goods have been added since the issue of our last catalogue. We carry full lines of Silverware by such makers as Meriden Britannia Co. (Rogers goods), Reed & Barton, Derby Silver Co., Hartford Silver Plate Co., E. G. Webster & Co., and many other makes.

1847 ROGERS BROS. A 1.

Spoons, Forks, Knives, &c.—Many fictitious stamps of "Rogers" Spoons and Forks have been placed on the market. See that you get the genuine, stamped "1847."

CUTLERY.

We have always in stock a large assortment of Table Knives, Forks, and Carvers, by the best English and American makers, in pearl, ivory, celluloid, rubber, stag, cocobolo, and ebony handles.
Our Great Leader.— English Carvers with stag handles, 50c. per pair.

IDEAL IRON.

WITH DETACHABLE HANDLES.
Patented March 6, 1889.
Improved.

Polished steel finish, $1.35 per set.

Nickel silver finish, $1.50 per set.

THE MERCANTILE HEART OF NEW ENGLAND.

PRINTS.

Prints, Staple and Fancy Ginghams, Printed Satines, Printed Challies, Fancy Shirtings, Printed Chambray, Plain Seersucker Ginghams, Extra Heavy Ginghams, Denims, Table Oil Cloth, Cheviot Shirting, Unbleached Drilling, Bleached Drilling, Roll Cotton Batting, Burlap, Tickings (plain and fancy), Bleached Duck, Unbleached Duck, Furniture Cretonne, and a full line of Fancy Striped Awning Cloth.

Ginghams. New dress styles, 26 inches wide. The Ginghams we are showing for 12½c. per yard are, without question, superior, both in style and finish, to any former years, and compare favorably with the imported article. Price, 12½c. per yard.

Plain Seersucker Gingham, 26 inches wide, in narrow and medium fancy woven stripes, and small and medium checks. This Gingham has for years proved a very popular article for ladies' and children's House Dresses, both for spring and summer wear. Price, 12½c. per yard.

Ginghams, in staple checks, 26 inches wide, small and medium even checks, and medium and small broken checks, in colors, blue and white and brown and white. Price, 10c. per yard.

Dress Ginghams, 26 inches wide. Some extra bargains in large, broken, and medium plaids. Price, 6¼c. per yard.

Printed Satines. "The Persian," 32 inches wide, from the celebrated Arnold Print Works. In calling attention to the "Persian" Satines, we do so with confidence in their merits, as the quality of the cloth, the exquisite printing, the finish (which is something far ahead of any on sale), the beautiful designs and the combination of colors, come very near perfection. Price, 12½c. per yard.

"The Genuine" Challie de Laine, fully half wool, 22 inches wide, of a fine texture, soft and flexible; they drape perfectly, and at the same time the styles, finish, and general effects are not excelled by the more expensive article. Each and every style is of this season's manufacture, and entirely new in design. Price, 20c. per yard.

Armenian Serge, 36 inches wide, double fold. An original and beautifully printed Cotton Dress Fabric. On twilled cloth, by the celebrated Arnold Print Works. The very latest foreign styles. In finish and appearance excelling any previous efforts, and an exact imitation of the All-wool Plaids and novelties. Price, 12½c. per yard.

Choice and New Wrapper Material, "The Zephyr," 27 inches wide. This is a perfect copy (in design and weight) of the fancy French Flannels, in a great variety of fancy colored stripes, particularly adapted for indoor dresses, wrappers, jackets, and children's wear. Price, 12½c. per yard.

Printed India Challies, 22 inches wide, in choice dress effects. A fine cloth and soft finish. A phenomenal bargain. Price, 5c. per yard.

Sea Island Shirtings, 36 inches wide, fast colors, manufactered expressly for J., M. & Co. The styles are printed on a superior cloth, in white grounds only, and, introduced by us last year, have become very popular. Price, 12½c. per yard.

Indigo Blue Ground, Soft Finish Percale, 32 inches wide, small, medium, and large figures. Price, 12½c. per yard.

Printed Chambray, 24 inches wide. We take pleasure in offering again to the public these deservedly popular goods. We show none but the best efforts of the mills, and in their choicest patterns. These goods have extra strength, and are what is called double-faced, being printed by a novel construction of machinery on both sides at once. We unhesitatingly recommend them as a *wash dress* for the million. Price, 10c. per yard.

Printed Century Cloth. An extra heavy cloth, 28 inches wide, and in the latest spring styles. Price, 10c. per yard.

Fancy Colored Dress Prints, latest and choicest patterns, large assortment, 25 inches wide. Price, 8c. per yard.

Mourning Prints a specialty with us, 25 inches wide. Price, 8c. per yard.

Indigo Blue Ground Prints, small and medium figures, 25 inches wide. Price, 8c. per yard.

Dress Prints in an endless variety. Small, medium, and large figures, 25 inches wide. Price, 6¼c. per yard.

White Ground Prints in an immense variety, including a choice selection of small figures, 25 inches wide. Price, 6¼c. per yard.

Crinkled Seersucker, 28 inches wide, in a choice assortment of equal line colored stripes, navy blue, light blue, brown, black, and pink. Price, 12½c. per yard.

Crinkled Seersucker, 24 inches wide, all cream grounds. Price, 5c. per yard.

Crinkled Seersucker, 28 inches wide, all cream grounds. Price, 10c. per yard.

Danish Cloth, half wool, 22 inches wide, plain colors only, in cream, light blue, and medium pink. Price, 12½c. per yard.

Crepe Cloth, 27 inches wide, for evening dresses, light shades. Price, 15c. per yard.

Cheviot Shirting, 27 inches wide, 12½c. per yard; 30 inches wide, 15c. per yard. These are selected styles, and of the best American manufacture.

Extra Heavy Blue and White Check Ginghams. Woven goods. We have a large assortment of these goods in small checks and broken plaids, in the various sizes. They are used extensively for men's jumpers and overalls, kitchen aprons, bundle-handkerchiefs, mattress coverings. We have them in two qualities. 30 inches wide, 10c. per yard; 34 inches wide, 17c. per yard.

Feather Ticking (regular stripe), 32 inches wide. Price, 12½ and 15c. per yard.

Mattress Ticking (regular stripe), 30 inches wide. Price, 8 and 10c. per yard.

Extra Fine Herring-bone Twilled Feather Ticking (regular stripe), 32 inches wide. Price, 28c. per yard.

German Ticking, drab ground, fancy colored stripes, extra fine, used largely for furniture coverings and crumb cloths, skirts, etc., 32 inches wide. Price, 20c. per yard. Samples sent on application.

Table Oil Cloth, a complete line, 45 inches wide, including new designs in wood, mosaic, fancy marble, and black pebble. This line of goods comes from the oldest and most reliable manufacturers of table oil cloth in America, and is sold by us at the popular price of 25c. per yard.

Denims, for Overalls, plain blue or brown, brown and black checks, blue and white and brown and white mixtures. Plain blue or brown, 27 inches wide. Price, 12½, 15, and 18c. per yard. Brown and black checks, and blue and white checks, 27 inches wide. Price, 18c. per yard.

Skirtings. 28-inch, light-weight, black and gray Skirtings, in large variety of stripes. These are the ever popular kind, and only 12½c. per yard.

Kentucky Jeans. 27-inch Jeans, black, gray, brown, and blue mixtures. Price, 37½c. per yard.

DRILLINGS AND DUCK.

Unbleached Drillings, 30 inches wide. Price, 10 and 12½c. per yard; 36 inches wide, 12½c. per yard.

Unbleached Duck, 28 inches wide. Price, 12½c. per yard; 29 inches wide, 14, 18, and 20c. per yard.

Bleached Duck, 27 inches wide. Price, 15c. per yard; 45 inches wide, 20c. per yard.

Bleached Drilling, 36 inches wide. Price, 25c. per yard. These ducks and drillings are especially adapted for hotel and restaurant waiters, cooks, and barbers' coats.

Cretonne, 26 inches wide. Price, 8 and 10c. per yard; 32 inch **Cretonne,** 12½c. per yard.

Gunners' Duck, 28 inches wide. Manufactured expressly for gunners' use, also largely used throughout the country for teamsters' jackets, etc. Having been put through a process, it is made absolutely waterproof, of a dull brown color, and of extra strength. Price, 25c. per yard.

Tan Duck, 27 inches wide. Price, 12½ and 15c. per yard.

Awning Cloth. Ranges in price from 15, 20, 25, 37½ to 50c. per yard, and is quite a feature in our business during the spring and summer months.

Plain Turkey Red Cotton, oil colors, 24 inches wide. Price, 10c. per yard; 34 inches wide, 12½c. per yard; 32 and 36 inches wide, 17c. per yard.

Twilled Turkey Red Cotton, oil colors, 32 inches wide. Price, 25c. per yard.

BURLAP.

Coarse Linen Burlap, for covering, such as used by upholsterers. 40 inches wide. Price, 12½c. per yard; 76 inches wide, 25c. per yard.

Roll Cotton Batting. Price, 12 and 18c. per roll.

MEN'S, BOYS', AND CHILDREN'S HATS AND CAPS.

This department shows the Largest and Finest Selection of Hats and Caps in the United States. Also, all the London and Paris Novelties of our own importation.

OUR DERBY. $1.75

JORDAN, MARSH & CO.

In all the Leading Shapes, and unequalled for its price in the United States.

Our stock of Men's Derby Hats is the largest and most varied of any Hat Store in Boston, comprising the best London makes, as also the best American, ranging in prices from $1.75 to 3.50. Our $2.50 and 3.00 Hats are made to our order, and we guarantee the price to be 20 per cent. under Hat Store prices.

OUR PRIDE $4.50

THE BOSTON HAT.

$1.50 to 4.50. Colors, black, brown, and tan. In ordering by mail, please state size of head, and whether for child, youth, middle age, or old gentleman.

SIZE OF HATS.

Sizes of Men's Hats, 6⅝ to 7⅝
" " Boys' " 6⅜ to 7⅛
" " Child's " 6⅛ to 6⅝

Men's Rubber Hat Covers,	$0.25
Men's Hat Brushes,	.25 to .50
Children's Fez Caps,	.50
Men's Fez Caps,	1.00

MEN'S SOFT FELT HATS.

From $0.75 to 4.50.

THE MASCOTTE.

Felt, $1.50 and 2.50
Silk, 4.00

RUBBER CAP. 50c.

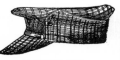

STANLEY. $2.00.

DOUBLE ENDER. $0.25 to 1.00.

G. A. R. $1.00 to 1.75.

THE ETON. $0.25, .50, .75, 1.00.

REGALIA CAPS. Societies furnished at a liberal discount.

THE SAILOR. $1.50, 2.00.

YACHT CAPS. $1.50 to 2.50. Yacht clubs supplied at a discount.

THE CRUSHER. $0.75, 1.00, 1.25. Can be rolled up and put in pocket.

BICYCLE CAPS. $0.50, .75, 1.00, in all colors.

HUNTING CAP. $1.25.

OOZE CAP. $2.00 and 2.50.

1889 CAP. $1.50, 2.00.

BASE BALL CAPS. 25 and 50c. 10 per cent. discount to clubs.

LADIES' RIDING HAT. $4.00 to 4.50.

LADIES' RIDING JOCKEY, in cloth and velvet. $1.50 and 2.00.

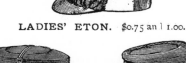

LADIES' ETON. $0.75 and 1.00.

BOYS' POLO CAP. $0.50 to 1.25.

BOYS' CADET CAP. $0.50 to 1.25. Every cap warranted indigo blue.

BOYS' DERBY. $1.50, 2.00, 2.50. Colors, black and brown.

MAN OF WAR. $1.50, 2.00.

BOYS' ALPINE. $1.50, 2.00, 2.50

ENGLISH SAILOR. $1.50, 2.00.

ENGLISH OWL. $0.50, 1.00.

CHILD'S SQUARE CROWN. The latest novelty. $1.50, 2.00, 2.50.

BABY. $1.75.

GIRLS' CADET. $0.75, 1.00.

SCOTCH TAM O'-SHANTER. $0.75, 1.00.

QUEEN. $0.50, .75, 1.00.

THE DAISY. $0.25 to 1.00. In all colors.

PET. 25, 50, and 75c.

HAMMOCKS, from $1.00 to 5.00. Also, Spreaders Ropes, Hooks, and Awnings.

THE MERCANTILE HEART OF NEW ENGLAND.

CARL L. ROSE,

Importer and Manufacturer of

Ladies' · Cloaks,

369 Broadway, New York.

———

A large line of Blazers, Reefers, Stockinet Jackets,
and Stockinet Cheviots.

Write to JORDAN, MARSH & Co., Boston, Mass.

REAL SCOTCH Spool Linen, 3 Cord, 200 yards.
REAL SCOTCH Colored Linen Floss.
REAL SCOTCH Linen Crochet Thread.
REAL SCOTCH Rope Linen Floss.
REAL SCOTCH Mending Linen.
Bargarren Art Thread.
Bargarren Art Fringe.

J. R. LEESON & CO., SOLE IMPORTERS,
BOSTON.

Write to JORDAN, MARSH & Co., Boston, Mass.

FREEDMAN BROTHERS

MANUFACTURERS OF

Cloaks

LADIES' AND
MISSES'

Mantles
AND # Wraps

332 Canal St., 39 and 41 Lispenard St.,

NEW YORK

Write to JORDAN, MARSH & Co., Boston, Mass.

GOLDMAN BROS.,

CORRECT STYLES IN

SPRING COATS,

101 GREENE STREET,

NEW YORK.

FELLOWS AND COMPANY.

FACTORY:
TROY, NEW YORK.
BOSTON OFFICE:
74 AND 76 CHAUNCY STREET.
THESE COLLARS ARE
WARRANTED
PURE IRISH LINEN
BOTH SIDES, AND 2,200 COUNT.
THEY ARE FIVE FOLD.

Write to JORDAN, MARSH & COMPANY, Boston, Mass.

WHEN BUYING

Gentlemen's Neckwear,

ASK TO BE SHOWN THE PRODUCTIONS OF

LOUIS AUERBACH,

NEW YORK.

This make is celebrated for its quiet elegance.

Write to JORDAN, MARSH & CO., Boston, Mass.

C. OBERMEIER & COMPANY,

SUCCESSORS TO

HERRMANN BROTHERS & OBERMEIER,

MANUFACTURERS OF

Children's Dresses and Misses' Suits,

96 GREENE STREET,

New York.

Write to JORDAN, MARSH & CO., Boston, Mass.

THE MERCANTILE HEART OF NEW ENGLAND.

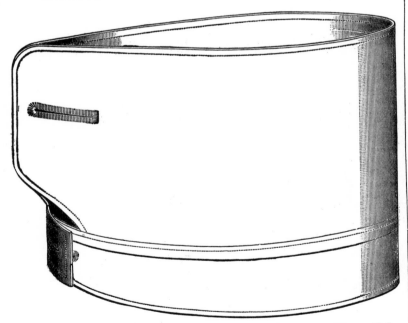

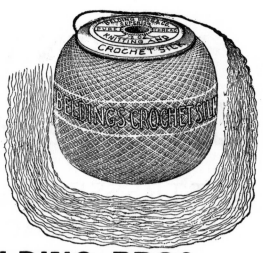

CUNARD LINE.

STEAMERS SAILING DIRECT FROM

BOSTON TO LIVERPOOL EVERY SATURDAY.

CALLING AT

QUEENSTOWN, CORK HARBOR.

CABIN PASSAGE, $60, $80, AND $100,

According to the accommodation desired.

Second Cabin and Steerage Passage at LOW RATES. For further information apply at the Company's office,

99 STATE STREET, BOSTON.

ALEXANDER MARTIN, Agent.

CHAS. E. RYCROFT,

91 FRANKLIN STREET, - - NEW YORK,

AGENT FOR

Richardson, Tee, Rycroft & Co.'s

BARNSLEY LINEN SHEETING

AND

SEAMLESS PILLOW-CASE LINEN

IN ALL WIDTHS.

BARNSLEY LINEN CRASHES, Etc.

A full line of the above are for sale by

JORDAN, MARSH & COMPANY.

VELVET.

There is no question of the universal popularity of Velvet for trimming purposes, and, when you cannot afford to pay for a good quality Silk Velvet, it is wiser to buy a nice "VIOLA" Velvet at half the cost, as it is specially woven for trimming as well as millinery purposes, and comes in all the latest Paris shadings, and in a deep lustrous black.

The blacks have a beautiful orange and the colors a twilled white selvedge, which gives the goods the appearance of a real Lyons all Silk Velvet.

If you want a dress, skirt, mantle, or garment, be sure you buy the Elberon Fine Twilled Velvet. The goods are guaranteed to wear; and they come in all the latest dress goods shades, and a superior black in several qualities.

For the consumer's protection the back of every second yard is stamped "Elberon." Take no other.

Write for these goods to

JORDAN, MARSH & CO.

RICHARDSON'S DAMASK TABLE LINENS.

RICHARDSON'S DOILIES and SHAMS.

RICHARDSON'S PILLOW LINEN and SHEETINGS.

RICHARDSON'S TOWELS, GLASS CLOTHS, and DUSTERS.

RICHARDSON'S CAMBRIC HANDKERCHIEFS.

RICHARDSON'S EMBROIDERED HANDKERCHIEFS.

RICHARDSON'S HOLLANDS and CANVAS.

RICHARDSON'S SPECIAL ANTIQUE GRASS BLEACH,
FOR LADIES' UNDERCLOTHING, ETC.

RICHARDSON'S HEMSTITCHED PILLOW CASES and SHEETS.

RICHARDSON'S FOUNDATION LINENS,
FOR LADIES' DRESSES.

J. N. Richardson, Sons, & Owden, Limited,

84 Franklin Street, New York.

Write to JORDAN, MARSH & CO., Boston, Mass.

COMPLETE HOUSE FURNISHERS.

Time and Money

CARPETS.

Gobelins,

English Wiltons,
Bigelow and
Lowell Wiltons,

English
    Brussels,

Axminsters,

Body Brussels,
Ingrain,

Roxbury
    Tapestries,

Smith's
    Moquettes,

Agra, etc.

Saved.

To those Building a New House, and also to those who Contemplate Refurnishing their Homes.

We can save you days and weeks of worry, and, perhaps, years of after discontent. Bear in mind no other establishment can offer the facilities for quantity, variety, *and comparison.* JORDAN, MARSH & CO., always the *first* to introduce an idea, were the pioneers and original house to show

CARPETS, MATTINGS, RUGS, AND UPHOLSTERY

side by side, thereby permitting that absolute requisite of a well-furnished house,—a perfect match.

We furnish estimates free of cost.

Remember we cordially invite you to at least inspect our great retail establishment before furnishing your homes.

RUGS.

Persians,

Meccas,

Carabaghs,

Ghiordes,

Daghestans,

Cashmeres,

Scotch Brussels,

Smyrna, etc.

———

ART SQUARES

All-wool
Kensington,

Scotch,

Brush Mats,

Oil Cloths and
Linoleums,
all widths,

China Mattings,
direct
importation,

Carpet
Sweepers, etc.

You Can Save Money Now

By Visiting Our Carpet Department.

Hotels, Theatres, Halls, Churches, Steamers, and Yachts Furnished Throughout at Short Notice.

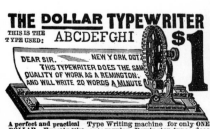

THE MERCANTILE HEART OF NEW ENGLAND.

In the immense volume of business transacted by us during a single day, mistakes are almost unavoidable. But we consider this part of our business of such importance to our patrons and ourselves that we have established a

COMPLAINT BUREAU

under the personal supervision of the firm itself, for the exclusive use of our numerous patrons all over this country; and we shall consider it a favor if our customers will avail themselves of its use and make their complaints known to us through its medium. How else can we do justice to you or ourselves if you do not make your grievance known to us? Do not think anything too small or unimportant for us to know. Remember, little things go to make up our one grand system, and we desire it to be a perfect one, or as nearly so as human ingenuity can make it. Our employees are selected and trained with regard to their deportment as much as their business ability; and, in justice to our thousands of honest, capable, and faithful employees, we desire to know of every single instance wherein their reputation as well as our own is at stake.

All letters addressed to us should be answered by return mail; and, when you fail to receive such an answer, write to us, giving the facts, and address your letter as below.

> JORDAN, MARSH & CO.,
> BOSTON,
> PERSONAL.   MASS.

2 CATALOGUES TO ONE ADDRESS.

SPECIAL NOTICE. Having recently revised our list of *one hundred thousand names* for catalogues, some inaccuracies may occur. You will greatly assist us in making corrections, and confer a favor by notifying us should you receive more than one copy. Should you happen to receive more than one catalogue, will you kindly hand it to some friend who has not received one?

MAIL ORDERS.

Jordan, Marsh & Co. have a fully equipped mail-order department. Prompt service. Utmost care in selection. Errors promptly remedied whenever they occur. Satisfaction guaranteed. **SAMPLES SENT** whenever you write for them. One can often trade with us through our mail-order department much cheaper than by a personal visit, as travelling costs more than a letter, and you have as much choice, since full lines of samples are promptly sent on request.

INDEX

THE MERCANTILE HEART OF NEW ENGLAND.

HOW TO ORDER BY MAIL.

All correspondence should bear the date of writing; also, name, town, county, and State wherein you reside.

Important.— Always state the amount of money you send, and in what shape. Always state how you wish your goods sent. Always send money for postage, if goods are to go by mail. Any surplus will be returned. Do not mix orders with other communications. If you wish to write for samples at the same time you are sending an order, write out the order with complete address, and write your other communication on a separate sheet, with full address also.

Sending for Samples.— When sending for samples, mention the kind of material you wish to see, the color desired, and for what purpose the goods are to be used; also whether light, medium, or heavy-weight goods are wanted. Order-blanks and envelopes, arranged especially for mail orders, will be forwarded free to any address.

Substitution.— It sometimes unavoidably happens that goods ordered are out of stock, and in such cases we take the liberty of substituting what, in our judgment, is equally desirable, both in quality and price. If not satisfactory, please return at once; and we will return cost of goods if money has been paid, and defray all expenses incurred. We would beg our patrons, however, to consider carefully before returning goods, as frequently there are cases where there has been a mistake made in ordering, or that goods are kept unreasonably long, and thus liable to depreciate in value.

Shipping Instructions.— When goods are ordered by one party to be sent to another, distinct and separate instructions should be given.

Exchanges.— We are always willing to exchange goods bought of us, when returned in good condition and a reasonable time after purchase.

Returned Goods.— When returning goods to be exchanged, or for other reasons, mark name and residence on the outside of the package, and address it to the *Mail-order Department, Jordan, Marsh & Co., Boston, Mass.,* also inform us on sending it as to whether it is forwarded by mail or express.

Bills and Change Due.— Whenever a balance is due after filling a cash order, the same is returned the following day, together with an itemized bill. If, after a due lapse of time, no reply has been received to a letter mailed to us, please repeat the same, as it may have been delayed in transmission.

C. O. D.— Goods will be sent by express, cash on delivery, when desired, but cannot be sent in that way by mail.

How Goods are Sent.— Goods are sent either by mail or express. If a package weighs not over four pounds (16 ounces to the pound), it can be sent by mail at a cost of one cent per ounce.

All packages by mail must be securely wrapped and tied (but not sealed), and without writing on the inside, except an address. Any article that would be likely to damage a mail-bag cannot be sent by mail.

If you wish to send a small article by mail, with writing accompanying it, you can do so at the rate of two cents per ounce. (This is called first-class matter.)

Money Rates.— Sums under five dollars can be sent by postal-note, which can be procured at any post-office by paying three cents. Express money orders can be procured at nominal rates in any town or city reached by the American Express Company. Following is a list of the rates charged for domestic money.

For orders not exceeding $5.00, ... 5 cents.
For orders exceeding $5 00, and not exceeding $10.00, 8 cents.
For orders exceeding $10.00, and not exceeding $15.00, 10 cents.
For orders exceeding $15.00, and not exceeding $30.00, 15 cents.
For orders exceeding $30.00, and not exceeding $40.00, 20 cents.
For orders exceeding $40.00, and not exceeding $50 00, 25 cents.
For orders exceeding $50.00, and not exceeding $60.00, 30 cents.
For orders exceeding $60.00, and not exceeding $70.00, 35 cents.
For orders exceeding $70.00, and not exceeding $80.00, 40 cents.
For orders exceeding $80.00, and not exceeding $100, 45 cents.

EXPRESS CO.'S MONEY ORDER.

Any amount not over $5.00 . . . . . 5 cents.
Over $5 to $10 . . . . . 8 cents.
Over $10 to $20 . . . . . 10 cents.
Over $20 to $30 . . . . . 12 cents.
Over $30 to $40 . . . . . 15 cents.
Over $40 to $50 . . . . . 20 cents.
Over $50, Proportionately.

For very small amounts you can send two-cent (U.S.) stamps of the present issue (Canadian stamps cannot be accepted), or you can send *greenbacks;* but you had better *register your letter,* as we do not hold ourselves responsible for unregistered letters sent. Besides the above ways, you can forward your money by express, at but a small expense to you. Certified checks, or checks from responsible persons, on Boston or New York, are, of course, acceptable.

Postage Rates.— Some idea can be formed of the cost of postage from the following approximated rates: they give a general idea of about the cost of having goods sent by mail, in addition to the price of goods ordered. When too much money has been sent to defray postal charges, the difference will be returned.

	POSTAGE.
Bed Spreads,	40c. to 65c.
Boots, ladies',	25c. to 35c.
Boots, children's,	8c. to 15c.
Boys' Suits,	30c. to 55c.
Boys' Shirt Waists,	8c. to 12c.
Children's Dresses,	45c. to 65c.
Ginghams, Cambrics, and Prints,	3c. per yard.
Cottons,	1c. to 3c. "
Flannels,	4c. to 10c. "
Gents' Shirts,	11c. to 18c. each.
Infants' Wear,	5c. to 10c.
Ladies' Cotton Underwear,	14c. to 18c.
Infants' Cloaks,	28c.
Ladies' Dresses,	75c. to $1.25.
Ladies' Woollen Underwear,	7c. to 9c.
Diaper Linen,	35c. per piece.
Table Linen,	13c. per yard.
Towels,	10c. per pair.
Napkins,	40c. per dozen.
Silks,	6c. per yard.
Velvets,	6c. per yard.
Shawls,	35c. to 50c.
Dress Goods,	5c. to 10c. per yard.
Lace Bed Spreads,	30c.
Lace Lambrequins,	10c. per pair.
Lace Pillow Shams,	10c. per pair.
Lace Curtains,	25c. to 50c.
Cloth for men's wear,	20c. to 50c. per yard.
Cloakings,	30c. to 40c. "

Fourth-Class Mail Matter.— Merchandise (glassware and liquids prohibited in the U.S. mail, but the Express Cos. will take them at about postage rates). One cent an ounce or fraction thereof.

Third-Class Mail Matter.— Books, circulars, and papers (called newspapers, but not so recognized by Post-office Department). One cent for two ounces or fraction thereof.

First-Class Mail Matter.— Letters, matter containing writing, matter closed against inspection. Two cents an ounce or fraction thereof.

Second-Class Mail Matter.— Newspapers and periodicals. One cent for four ounces or fraction thereof, when sent by others than the publishers or news-agents. When second-class mail matter is sent by publishers or by the news-agents to regular subscribers, the rate is one cent per pound or fraction thereof. Weight unlimited.

Unregistered Mail.— We cannot hold ourselves responsible for unregistered letters containing money or merchandise packages.

[From the U.S. Official Postal Guide.]

Suggestions to the Public on Postal Subjects.

1. *How to Direct and Mail Letters.*— Mail matter should be addressed legibly, and completely. To secure return to the sender in case of misdirection or insufficient payment of postage, his name should be written or printed upon the upper left-hand corner of all mail matter. The matter will then be returned to the sender, if not called for at its destination, without going to the Dead Letter Office; and, if a letter, it will be returned free.

2. *Avoid Thin Envelopes.*— Thin envelopes, or those made of weak or poor, unsubstantial paper, should not be used, especially for large packages. Being often handled, and in the mail-bags subjected to pressure and friction, such envelopes are frequently torn open or bursted, without fault of those who handle them.

3. *Register Valuable Matter.*— All valuable matter should be registered. Registry fee is ten cents, which, with postage, must be prepaid; and name and address of sender must be given on the outside of the envelope or wrapper. Money should be sent by a money-order or registered letter, otherwise its liability to loss is greater, and a temptation is put before those postal employees through whose hands it passes.

5. *The Use of Mailing Boxes.*— When dropping a packet in a mailing-box or into the receptacle at the post-office, care should be taken that the packet falls into the box, and does not stick in the passage.

6. *Affix Stamps Firmly.* — Postage stamps should be placed on the upper right-hand corner of the address side of all the mail-matter, care being taken that they are *securely affixed.*

8. *General Suggestions.*— A subscriber to a newspaper or a periodical who changes his residence and post-office should at once notify the publisher, and have the publication sent to his new address.

13. All inquiries, whether from postmasters or the public, relative to lost or missing mail-matter of every description, both foreign and domestic, ordinary and registered, should be addressed to the Chief Post-office Inspector, Post-office Department, Washington, D.C., to whom all losses or irregularities should be reported as soon as knowledge is had of their occurrence.

SEND ALL MAIL TO

JORDAN, MARSH & CO., BOSTON, MASS.

.. THE GREAT ..
RETAIL ESTABLISHMENT
.. OF ..

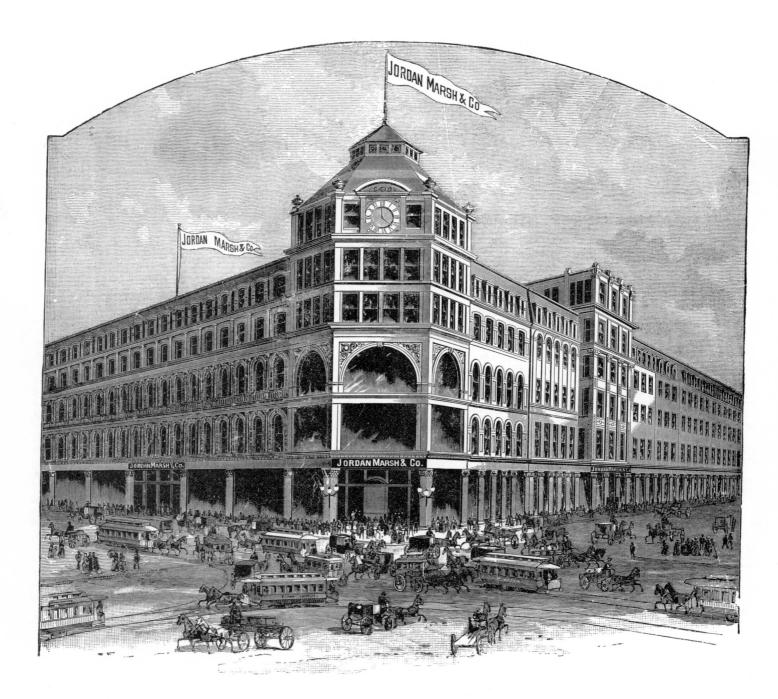

JORDAN, MARSH & CO.
...BOSTON...